The Quality Revolution

To Hilary

The Quality Revolution

Best Practice from the
World's Leading Companies

Steve Smith

2000

First published in 1994 by
Management Books 2000 Ltd
125a, The Broadway, Didcot, Oxon OX11 8AW

British Library Cataloguing in Publication Data is available
ISBN 1-85251-113-3

Printed in Great Britain by BPC Wheatons Ltd, Exeter

Preface

Revolution is a bold word but I have no hesitation about using it in the title of this book. The prime role of a leader in business is to improve that business. To do that well, he or she today has to be revolutionary. Despite that, most of what is happening in business today is far from revolutionary, including many initiatives which go under the name of Quality, Total Quality or TQM. Perhaps this makes the exceptions even more remarkable. Radical change is being created in large global organisations such as Motorola and Xerox and in smaller local ones like L&K: Rexona in Australia and BSS in the UK. The leaders of these organisations are achieving large-scale transformations in the way their businesses work. This is what *The Quality Revolution* refers to. The main theme of the book is that the benefits of such changes are within the reach of any leader of any business or any group. Aspiring leaders have simply to join the Quality movement which unites people from Tokyo to Santiago and from engineering through to health-care. They will discover a rich source of improvement experience freely available. There is a catch, of course. Quality is extremely difficult to do well.

The Quality Revolution draws on those who have done it well. It is not based on theory but on what successful leaders are actually doing. The content is built on observations I have made over a twenty-year period concentrated on how companies achieve lasting improvement. Quality is used in the book as the generic label for planned improvement across whole organisations. This is a broad movement, still developing fast, with a number of schools of thought. This makes it harder for leaders to know what action to take. In the following chapters, I have not sought to make this easy by offering recipes; simplistic approaches are easily beaten by complex organisations with their inert resistance to change. Instead I offer best practices, proven through successful application, and, more importantly, attempt to convey how a leader can weave these practices together to create a powerful result. The approach is applicable to leaders seeking radical change for the first time and those who are well advanced with improvement practice.

To help you through the book, a model is used to convey the

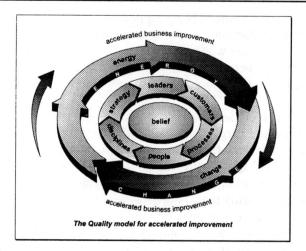

The Quality model for accelerated improvement

multiple activity needed to transform an organisation. The model binds best practices into key disciplines which are introduced a chapter at a time, building up the model into an integrated whole, as the book progresses into how Quality is implemented. Real examples and stories are used throughout to keep the book at a practical level. Chapter 1, 'Believe in Quality', reviews the Quality movement and introduces the model of accelerated improvement. This chapter also concentrates on the core of the model – belief. Successful leaders have a passion for their work and a tangible belief in improvement. The belief might be based on hard-nosed financial evidence or pure missionary zeal but it is observable in all successful business improvers.

The outer ring of the model is about change and energy, two dynamics which feed each other. Most people acknowledge that change is needed for improvement but fewer grasp the need for energy to make the change. This is probably the biggest differentiator between the successful improvement process and the also-ran. For this reason, I deal with improvement energy early in the book with Chapter 2, 'Improvement Energy', describing how some leaders have generated enormous energy for change. Change itself, in the form of a planned change process, is left until Chapter 9. This is because the best change examples are planned to incorporate and integrate *all* the key improvement disciplines. To make sense of this, we need to understand these disciplines first and they are introduced and illustrated in Chapters 3 to 7. I introduce these as the *drivers* of business improvement, six disciplines which make a difference in their own right but are even more powerful when integrated into a full change process. The improvement drivers can also be thought of as prime sources of dissatisfaction and the revolutionary leader seeks out and exploits dissatisfaction with the status quo. These are the areas where there will be gaps between what is currently done and what *could* be done; surfacing the gaps provides the reason, the need, the *drive* for improvement.

The first driver is strategy, which is explored in Chapter 3, 'Strategy Focuses Energy'. Few companies have clear and ambitious strategies and fewer still communicate them well. The Quality company does and strategy presents a major opportunity for business leaders of all types of organisations; improvement must be directed to be effective and Quality must be aligned behind business objectives to be useful. The leader is ultimately responsible for strategy; he or she is also responsible for the style and behaviour of the organisation. The behavioural responsibility of the leader is addressed in Chapter 4, 'Leading Quality'. The clearer the signals a leader sends and the more consistent his or her actions, the greater is the drive for improvement. This is a difficult area for Western managers, but, as the examples in Chapter 4 show, those who do master it can be richly rewarded in the way the organisation responds.

Chapter 5, 'Customers Mean Business', introduces an element of a Quality process which most people would expect to find – the customer. Why not before Chapter 5? Because the belief, the energy, the strategy, the leadership style are all needed before we can have much improvement effect on our customers. That said, the customer is undoubtedly one of the strongest stimulants for change in any organisation and few companies can feel content with their current practice in attracting and satisfying their customers.

In recent years, the concept of process management has triggered some radical changes in the way business is done. Chapter 6, 'Business Needs Lean Processes', shows how many companies today are re-engineering their processes to satisfy the customer better and to gain competitive advantage by doing it quicker and cheaper. Big improvements and lasting changes can be made this way - hence processes are another key driver. The next chapter reminds us that 'People Make Quality' and that most organisations undervalue and underuse the key resource of people. Better organisation, encouragement and deployment of people offers enormous scope for driving improvement and Chapter 7 looks at the progress leading companies are making in the development of their people. To complete the circle of improvement drivers, Chapter 8 looks at how the better companies are always more disciplined than the mediocre ones and 'Disciplined

Improvement' describes the core techniques which make large-scale improvement feasible.

Most organisations, even very prestigious ones, do not make good use of all of these improvement drivers, often concentrating on only one or two. Chapter 9, 'Putting Quality Together', proposes that the sum of these is much greater than the parts and shows how the most successful companies blend the drivers together to accelerate the improvement process. This brings us back to the point made earlier about energy and change; this chapter examines the considerable experience of change processes over the last decade and recommends the core elements which companies have proved to work. Chapter 10, 'Making Quality Pay', presses the point further: if we are going to invest substantial time and money in an improvement process, let's make sure we get a return. A selection of Quality processes which have paid off for their leaders are examined and a core methodology is offered, based on successful practice.

For the last chapter, 'Becoming World-Class', we look at what the leaders of top-class organisations believe in when Quality is well-installed and the systems and behaviours well-aligned. What drives them further? For some, it is the need to be world-class – the best in the world at what they do. We look at the journey to world class, identify the levels of maturity as companies evolve and focus on what makes the winners outstanding. For leaders at any point on the improvement journey, an understanding of what the best are doing can be very stimulating and offers the chance to leapfrog on their learning.

A point of detail: I use the capital Q for Quality throughout the book to distinguish the use of the word from the much narrower area of product quality. Quality is much bigger than a good product. Zero defects is an important goal for a Quality company, but probably no more so than speed of response, ability to innovate, superior service, slick administration or technological mastery. At its best, Quality revitalises an organisation, creating a high-energy, high-achievement culture where improvement is self-generating. This is the revolutionary side of Quality and it continues to attract new believers around the world. As a management consultant, my greatest reward is seeing a company change – sensing the new buzz about the place, feeling the energy, sharing the commitment. Many more companies are achieving this today because of the Quality revolution. I hope that you too will share in the excitement that this brings.

Steve Smith

Acknowledgements

World-class companies give freely of their management philosophies and practices and I am indebted to those great companies in the USA, Japan and Europe who have provided the inspiration and examples for this work. Some are featured as case examples in the book but I have benefited from the wisdom and hospitality of many others – sadly too many to list here.

Of these leading companies around the world who continue to strive for radical improvement, I have been fortunate to work closely with some as clients. Over the years, this experience of helping managers to create change has been priceless in building a model of what practical business improvement is all about. Countless managers deserve credit for this, only a fraction of whom I feature in the text. To those who have worked with me, I thank you for your belief and enthusiasm in implementing new practices. Some clients have given me lasting images of inspired leadership, most notably Sir Michael Perry of Unilever, Dr Heini Lippuner of Ciba, Tony Gilroy of Perkins Engines Group and Dr Tom Little of Colworth Laboratory.

I continue to learn much from my consulting colleagues at Quest Quality who are out with clients every day putting into practice what this book is about. This consulting team has earned a reputation as great implementors in the Quality field and I have plundered their collective wisdom in turning concepts into action. Quest Quality also has a support team of equally high standing, whose members have given great help to this project.

The most telling support has been given by my wife and family who have patiently offered ideas and advice, as well as selflessly allowing me to spend most evenings and weekends glued to the word processor.

Finally, my thanks to all the enthusiasts in the Quality movement around the world, without whom the book would have no meaning.

Other books on Quality available from
Management Books 2000 (see pages 389-400):

The Benchmarking Book (M Spendolini)
But We Are Different (J Macdonald)
The Customer Connection (J Guaspari)
Deming Management at Work (M Walton)
The Deming Management Method (M Walton)
The Deming Route to Quality and Productivity (W Scherkenbach)
Dr Deming (R Aguayo)
The Essentials of Total Quality Management (R Williams)
Extraordinary Guarantees (C Hart)
Global Quality (J Macdonald & J Piggott)
How to Achieve Zero Defect Marketing (A Magrath)
I Know It When I see It (J Guaspari)
The ISO 9000 Book (J Rabbit & P Bergh)
The Keys to Excellence (N Mann)
The QFD Book (L Guinta & N Praizler)
The Quality Makers (R Heller)
The Quality Roadmap (R Svenson, K Wallace & G Wallace)
Quantum Quality (W Miller)
The Theory Why (J Guaspari)
The TQM Trilogy (F Mahoney & C Thor)
Vital Signs (S Hronec)
World Class Quality (K Bhote)

Contents

1
Believe in Quality

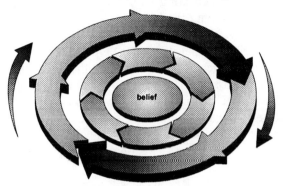

'If we'd done this twenty years ago, today we'd own every market we're in,' says David Luther of Corning Glass. Corning are one of thousands of companies who have rediscovered Quality and used it for competitive advantage. Such companies, big or small, service or manufacturing, local or multinational, have revolutionised the way they work. Their first step was to believe in Quality.

'Quality has become the battlefield of the nineties; only the fittest will survive.' Digital Equipment Corporation

'You either get better or you get worse.' Joe Paterno, coach

A small revolution

Mike Nash believes in Quality. In 1988, Mike became chairman of L&K: Rexona, a business employing 1,100 people to make detergents, shampoos and deodorants in North Rocks, Sydney, Australia. Part of the giant Unilever, by the late eighties L&K: Rexona was a very good business but not performing as well as Mike wanted. He wanted to see market share raised. He wasn't happy that the powerful retail trade complained about too many 'out of stocks' (product lines not available for delivery) despite major efforts to put this right. He didn't like the industrial relations in the factory, where a tangible 'us and them' divide was evident. Management themselves were disunited, stemming from the recent merger of the once-separate

Lever & Kitchen (L&K) and Rexona businesses. Above all, the return on investment to Unilever was not up to his standards. Action was required.

Mike could have taken the tried and tested Unilever approach of 'green-fielding' – stripping the business down to bare essentials and building back only what was necessary. The problem with this approach, Mike felt, was that it was too easy to discard the good parts along with the bad. Instead he chose to adopt the new approach which was becoming popular in Unilever: Total Quality. He was not a Quality beginner – he had used Total Quality in his previous role in another Unilever company, without conspicuous success. The lessons from these previous experiences proved invaluable when he installed a Total Quality process into L&K: Rexona. This time he knew what he wanted to do.

Two years later, L&K: Rexona was a transformed business. The first barrier to go was the L&K/Rexona divide. Mike replaced the sniping over who had taken over whom with a common purpose and a clear direction. The board were in this together and were going to do it together. This took about six months to establish; workshops and practical training under the TQ banner brought them to a common understanding. Next the service was attacked. Why were customers being let down through lines not in stock? Cross-functional teams were set up to find out. Nothing new in this – many projects and task forces had been set up before, to little effect. This time there was a big effect. One reason for this breakthrough was that the problem was now a Board priority, with Board members' involvement in solving it. Another was that customer service was viewed anew as a process which was dependent on and linked to many other internal services. The project team identified the bottlenecks and the Board took responsibility for smoothing them out – wherever in the organisation they occurred.

A small number of key projects, like the out-of-stocks one, was established to have impact on five critical improvement goals. These goals were set to challenge the business to break through the current limits of performance. The goals provided the focus for major improvement and the projects the means of achieving them. Within a year, over a hundred smaller improvement projects were set up – mostly teams of managers trained in Total Quality disciplines. Considerable gains in customer service were achieved (as measured by the customers) and big savings were also made as waste and inefficiency were cut out.

These were very good results – bottom-line results. Unilever's regional management were much happier with L&K: Rexona. But thus far, Mike had not achieved a full Quality revolution – only a management one. The TQ process at L&K: Rexona rolled on. The Board themselves played a key role in training the rest of management. These managers then trained the workforce – in the factories, the offices and out in the field with the salesforce. The outcome was a new work environment. Workteams were given more responsibility – and accountability. They were expected to improve the service to their own internal customers and were measured on it. They had customer/supplier agreements to make the service and the improvements explicit. Improvement projects were monitored publicly on storyboards in the corridors; anyone who paused to look might find a team member come over to talk about them. Hundreds of individual ideas were collected as OFIs (Opportunities For Improvement); these were published widely but implemented locally, involving the originator of the idea.

L&K: Rexona today is a different place. It feels different. There is a buzz about it. 'Us and them' has all but vanished. Management politics have dissipated. Service is sharper. Customers have noticed, suppliers have noticed, Unilever has noticed. Most importantly, management and staff know that they have created these changes themselves. They also know there is a vast amount more to do; they are not going to stop now.

L&K: Rexona's transformation is not uncommon today. Many other organisations around the world have created their own small revolutions using Quality. Some of L&K: Rexona's customers and suppliers have been inspired to join in. Many of L&K: Rexona's peer companies in Unilever are already well underway with Quality revolutions of their own. Thus the revolution spreads.

Quality rediscovered

L&K: Rexona is representative of a movement which has spread all over the world and into all kinds of organisations from local shops to utilities to software houses to research laboratories to shipbuilders to hotels chains. The world has been rediscovering Quality.

Once Quality was a natural fact of everyday trade. Transactions were personal and the supplier took pride in matching the needs of the purchaser. The better suppliers were sought out and their businesses grew. Then, during the thirties, mass thinking began to take over. First mass production – 'get them out of the door'. Mass service followed – 'pile them high...sell them quick'. The principles of the founders which had made companies great were lost in the pursuit of new techniques and the complexities of corporate business. The customer was taken for granted. Volume was the new god.

In the fifties and sixties, the Western world plunged in deeper. Cars went down the assembly lines with clutches or wheels missing – 'we can add them later'. Vacuum cleaners were sold with inherent design faults – 'we've got a field repair team to fix them'. Computer hardware was distributed without instruction manuals – 'we'll get someone to write those later'. Incomprehensible insurance policies were pressed onto unsuspecting consumers – 'don't worry about the details – trust us'.

It couldn't last. The world simply filled up: too much product chasing too few customers. Customers, who were by the 1970s better educated, more affluent and less gullible, began to exercise their choice. They sought value: more features, better reliability, more support for their money. Companies who had maintained high standards – Marks & Spencer in the UK and BMW in Germany, for example – found customers flocking to them. In this environment, it is all the more surprising (with hindsight) that many major companies pursued strategies of systematically reducing value, once the customer was 'hooked' into the product or service. Such companies were blinkered by their strategies and techniques – to be the lowest-cost producer, for example, or to corner a market by taking over the competition.

Today it is clear that companies cannot sustain prosperity without providing increasing value to the customer over a period of time. Those that take short-term advantage of the customer may not be around in the long term. Horizon was one of the top package holiday companies in the UK in the eighties. Its policy of high volume and low price brought short-term prosperity as it packed the resorts with vacationers seeking sun and sand. Unfortunately, Horizon did not listen to the rising complaints and packed more and more people in. Within two years of its peak, Horizon was bust – shunned by the same holiday-makers who were no longer tolerant of overbooked flights, unfinished hotels and crowded resorts.

Those that disdain the customer in times of spiralling standards are simply doomed and many have gone already. But even some of the best are caught out by the accelerating rise in customer expectations. Procter & Gamble saw its market leader in diapers in the USA – Pampers – fall from 80 per cent share to 20 per cent in little over a year, as mothers switched en masse to a new model of Huggies – 'they leaked less'. This happened again to P & G in Japan two years later. P & G learned their lesson quickly and spent more time finding out what their customers wanted (they were already doing more of this than most companies) and acting on what they found. Within two years they had regained market leadership but know well today that they can never afford to become complacent. Like many others today, P & G too has rediscovered Quality.

Competing with Quality

Most companies today are making improvements – everyone knows that standing still is not a viable option. The dilemma for some is that they are not improving fast enough. They are caught in the Quality gap between their rate of improvement and the customers' accelerating expectations. Meanwhile, someone in their sector may be in the enviable position of having the Quality edge...their level of improvement is still ahead of the customer's expectation, giving immeasurable advantage.

The Quality gap from failing to keep up with customer expectations

The Quality edge from accelerating the rate of improvement

An early example of such an edge might be Sony who, having created a new market with the Walkman, maintained their edge by bringing out further derivatives just as customers began to appreciate more features and sophistication. Sony's mastery of this continues well into in the nineties with the Discman and the Mini-disc bringing new concepts to the marketplace. The Quality edge might be technological as with Sony or through design as shown by Apple, who revolutionised computing twice, first with the Macintosh and its user-orientated format and later with its re-packaging for desk-top publishing. The edge might equally be service, such as at Marks & Spencer with their 'no-questions' return policy. Or SAS Hotels in

Norway, with their 'no-excuse' programme – no bill in the morning if anything is faulty. Or it might be speed, as demonstrated by Toyota, where, in Tokyo, the car you specify in detail in your own home can be custom-built and delivered to you four days later. Or L'Oreal, in France, who can put a new shampoo on the market in 16 weeks. Or Kao, in Japan, who can copy a successful new brand and distribute it through five continents faster than the originator. None of these companies have their edge through luck; they have thought hard about what will make them stand out and their whole organisation has been geared up to achieve it.

For those caught in the Quality gap, on the other hand, survival may be questionable. The management practices that allowed them to fall into the gap mean they are ill-equipped to fight their way out of it. Skill with financial budgets does not help to delight the customer. Managers conditioned to moving product out may not readily switch to making only what the customer requires. Conventional improvement techniques do not give the step jump in effectiveness which is demanded. Revolutionary change is needed to pull out of these traps...and that requires a revolutionary management approach.

Motorola in the late 1970s and early 1980s saw their customers in consumer goods, such as televisions, go over en masse to Japanese products, along with the customers of all the other domestic manufacturers in the USA. People wanted the reliability which Hitachi, Matsushita and Sony could provide and which Motorola could not match. Then Motorola's car radios went the same way. Finally, when Motorola had to concede the loss of a critical emerging business, DRAM chips, to the Japanese integrated circuit manufacturers, president Bob Galvin knew something radical was called for. The Quality revolution which he inspired and led enabled Motorola to survive and prosper again. Today, as a result, Motorola's telephone pagers are the market leader in Tokyo.

The only good thing about falling into a big Quality gap is that companies are then all too aware of what has to be done: be radical or perish. Companies like Motorola are the very rare examples who have been 'breathed on by the devil' (in the words of one manager at Houston-based Wallace) and lived to tell the tale.

Many companies do not 'see the devil' until it is too late. Unfortunately, Wallace proved to be one of them. In 1988, Wallace woke up to find their home market, the Houston oil industry, had vanished. Hardly anything they were used to doing was now right. They dug themselves out of this hole using a Quality process to unite and galvanise the whole company. Everybody experienced radical change from the president down – they all learned to work in a flexible, responsive and cooperative way. Within 18 months, they had built new customer relations, raised their productivity enormously and posted a 740 per cent profit improvement. But a massive short-term improvement wasn't enough. They did not have the time to build the longer-term changes needed to sustain new business and continue the huge rate of improvement required merely to compete. Despite the heroic effort, in 1992 Wallace was forced into bankruptcy and a major financial restructuring.

Many companies are blissfully unaware of the Quality gap developing, partly because they are only really looking at themselves (their measures, mostly internal, may show they are still improving satisfactorily) and partly because they don't want to know. Complacency amongst 'good' businesses is widespread and is very hard to overcome. The managers of these businesses see their market share and profitability figures remaining fairly steady and convince themselves they are doing the right things. The point they are missing is that the Quality gap is developing as they sit. They are watching one trend line – their own results – but the line they do not monitor, customer expectations, is rising faster than the numbers they are counting. Their comfortable position has already been eroded by the time it shows on their results, and by then it may be too late. It takes a lot of time to develop an environment that fosters radical change and they may no longer have that time.

Such companies need the vision to look ahead three years and predict what could give them a Quality edge – an edge that will make them distinctive to customers and will attract purchases from them in a future environment inevitably more competitive than today's. In practice, their vision may be only a guide: they are unlikely to anticipate customers' emerging needs with precision but this is not the main aim (tracking and anticipating customers' needs is a continuous and interactive process, where the precision is needed just before delivery). The main point is to make the case for radical improvement in order to achieve distinction – and the revolutionary changes in management practice which will cause the improvements to be made. Federal Express did this with overnight deliveries. To deliver a parcel by 10.00 am next day, a whole new distribution system was needed. Staff *had* to be totally responsible – each package had to be on the right plane. There was no room for error, a mislabelled package simply wouldn't make it. A new information system was also needed to track packages from door to door. All the systems had to be integrated. The resulting edge virtually created a new market in the USA.

A Quality edge gives immense but transitory value. Almost as soon as the edge is created, it is being eroded. The competition will target anything successful and aim to better it; customers become blasé and take it for granted. Domino Pizzas created enormous advantage with their '30-minute delivery or $2.00 back' promotion, which emphasised their speed and reliability, achieved through a radical rethink of the production process. But soon many other Pizza operators copied them and the service is now commonplace. Similarly, Federal Express could not sit on its new market for long. Not only did they need to deliver three million packages by 10.00 am the next day without losing any of them, but to keep one step ahead of the competition they needed continually to improve their delivery reliability and their information service. By 1988 they could state that any parcel would be traced in 30 minutes or no charge – a new Quality edge built from the early one. Many more innovations followed enabling Federal Express to hold a 43 per cent share of a highly competitive market in 1992. This is the essence of Quality. Continuous innovation, continuous improvement...striving always for a better way to do business.

The Q word

Federal Express used a Quality process to bind the systems together and make the whole process work consistently. The 100,000 staff who work the Memphis hub at night feel part of a team – they have to work together to move all those packages each night. Quality is an important word at Federal Express. Fred Smith, as founder and chairman of Federal Express, is not alone in discovering the potency of Quality. Many leaders believe there is no better word to help unite and inspire workpeople than Quality. Few people will argue against it; many become passionate for it. Profitability, productivity, efficiency, excellence, performance, effectiveness, service...these are all complementary words, but on their own tend to be more divisive or threatening than Quality. But Quality is not without its own problems. It is a common word used loosely and variously in everyday language. Some people interpret the word instinctively as up-market, high specification, luxury. To others, it means product reliability and belongs in the world of factories and inspectors. Yet others are wary of using it simply because it is so universal – 'it's too like motherhood'.

It is not only the layman who has difficulty with the Q-word. As a subject or managerial discipline it encompasses several specialist fields from Quality Assurance through Service Quality to Total Quality, although it is now widely accepted that Quality Assurance (QA) and Service Quality (SQ) are subsets of Total Quality. This has evolved in recent years as the disciplines have matured. Looking back over the last two decades, it is intriguing to trace the evolution in the labelling in this movement and see the shifts in emphasis as one label eclipses another. In the 1960s, quality control became very important: this was the era of 'little q', meaning product quality in the days when companies boasted about the size of their inspection teams. This expanded in the West into QA, whilst the Japanese were perfecting TQC (Total Quality Control – a misleading label as Japanese TQC was certainly total but with the emphasis more on improvement than control). This was the era when the Quality gurus emerged, with Edwards Deming, Joseph Juran and Phil Crosby proving the most enduring. By the 1980s, other movements were flourishing in parallel: Excellence, pioneered by Tom Peters, emerged from the management development school; and Service Quality, popularised by Karl Albrecht, grew out of customer-care teachings.

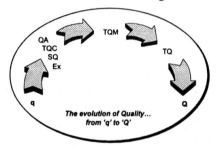

In Europe in the early 1980s, practitioners were searching for a label which emphasised the totality of all these approaches, but also marked the critical nature of management's role. Total Quality Management (TQM) emerged as the most apt generic description. Surprisingly, as it has had widespread use in Europe through the 1980s, TQM only became a very popular label in the USA towards the end of the decade. Meanwhile, those organisations that used TQM early on have, in many cases, dropped the M as the whole workforce became involved – and even the T, as it becomes taken as read that Quality embraces the whole company.

So the 1990s may well see a shift back to using the singular 'Quality' as the expressive label – but 'big Q' now, marking the considerable difference in use that has evolved during 30 years. Of course, many organisations have created their own label to define what they are doing. 'Delighting the Customer' (Unilever Personal

Products), 'Extraordinary Customer Satisfaction' (Perkins Engines), 'Performance Excellence' (Eli Lilly), 'Continuous Improvement' (Du Pont), 'First In Service' (Caradon) are a few examples of a rich variety of expressive themes. The practitioners in these quite advanced applications readily acknowledge their allegiance to the world-wide Quality movement. Quality is the generic that describes the thinking and the practice that unites them in improvement effort and is the heart of many transformations that are being made around the world.

It is helpful to think of Quality as an umbrella concept which integrates a whole spectrum of improvement initiatives such as service enhancement, cost reduction, value analysis and others, which often can be sub-optimal on their own. Used in this fuller sense, Quality is strategic and holistic. But it also embraces smaller-scale local improvement which anyone on any activity can apply. This leads to the positioning of Quality as an *input*, not an output or result, as it is more commonly expressed. Improvement is an action – something one puts in. In this vein, it fits just as well at workteam level, where local continuous improvement is sought, as at the whole business unit, where accelerated overall improvement should be the outcome.

The new thinking	
Old	**New**
quality is about products	Quality is about organisations
quality is technical	Quality is strategic
quality is for inspectors	Quality is for everyone
quality is led by experts	Quality is led by management
good quality is high grade	Quality is the appropriate grade
quality is about control	Quality is about improvement
little q	big Q

There may be many labels for Quality but there are even more definitions. Quality definitions range across a whole spectrum from the dramatic to the prosaic. In practice, no definition can encompass the beliefs and ambitions of all Quality applications. Most organisations create their own form of words to convey the mix of challenge and emotional appeal which is right for them. But for a no-nonsense description of what Quality is about today, think around this: Quality is simply...*accelerated business improvement*.

The revolution spreads

Few movements spread across sectors and national boundaries. Quality does and has. On any one day, for example, Cesar Bautista of the Philippine Refining Company could be reviewing the progress of an action team in Manila...Eduardo Tolosa of Banco Bilbao in Madrid might be meeting with a process team, re-mapping the lending process perhaps...Glen Dalby of the Ramada Renaissance Hotel in Manchester could be learning from a customer circle...David Bonner of Atlas Copco Mining & Construction, Montreal, could be concluding a customer/supplier contract with another business unit...Takashi Saito of Chuba Electric Power in Japan could be in a 'challenge circle' discussion with local community leaders about a recycling project...Linda Lash of Avis Europe might be analysing the weekly customer surveys...Hakon Anderson of OS Denofa in Finland might be leading a group to refine their purpose and goals.... Different countries; different types of businesses. But all have something in common: these organisations and many thousands more are well into their own Quality revolutions. They may not be aware of each other but together they make up a movement which has swept the world.

'If the Japanese can do it, why can't we?'

 The USA today epitomises this revolution. Corporate America in the nineties is an exciting place. Change is normal. Sacred cows are sacrificed. IBM and Apple (chalk and cheese of the computer business and one-time deadly rivals) have set up joint operations. The Baby Bells (once divisions of the national institution AT&T) are forming international alliances for telecom services around the world. General Motors, Ford and Chrysler all have ventures with Japanese or European competitors in their need to staunch the flow of imports.

Corporate America has gone international and along the way has rediscovered Quality. It was a long while before the revolution in the USA really started. In 1980, NBC broadcast a documentary on the success Japanese companies had had with Quality and asked 'if the Japanese can do it, why can't we?' This struck a public chord and it was from 1980 on that the large US corporations really took Quality seriously. By the end of the decade, virtually all major US corporations were in the middle of Quality revolutions, which have continued into the 1990s. Some are dramatic like Motorola who sought a hundredfold statistical improvement in their output; now everything they do has to be 99.9997 per cent correct. Some others are continuations of well-established Quality philosophies which date back to the 1980 movement, such as at IBM, 3M, American Express or Florida Power & Light, all of whom have over a decade of experience with Quality but would still describe their task today as revolutionary.

The Malcolm Baldrige National Quality Award, first awarded in 1988 by President Reagan, has done much to unite the movement in the USA and take it beyond a critical mass. This award has given American business something positive to compete for, after two decades of losing out to the Japanese, and something positive to learn from and unite behind. All Baldrige winners and near-winners have said that the process of understanding and learning was far more significant than winning the award.

Many organisations have used the Baldrige Award to break through complacency and stimulate further action. Digital, for example, were content with their Quality process until IBM Rochester won the 1990 Award. This stung Digital into renewed corporate effort to improve what was already good but no longer good enough; the energy thus generated initiated another wave of improvement across the business. Thousands of others have used the assessment criteria to review and stimulate their own internal progress, with no intention of submitting to the thousands of hours and dollars needed to reach the final stages of the competition (some 200,000 companies requested the Baldrige assessment criteria in 1991, but the number submitting entries was in two figures).

The Baldrige Award with its extensive publicity has accelerated an interesting trend: businesses opening up and sharing what they are doing in Quality. This practice has been building up since the first major US corporations into Quality set up a forum for exchange of information back in 1980. In those days, it was considered bad form to release performance information to anyone inside the company, never mind to other companies. In the nineties, networking (building contacts outside of your immediate organisation) and benchmarking (obtaining data from outside) are practised by managers in virtually all leading US companies and this has also fuelled the revolutionary flame. In the eighties, Tom Peters exhorted people to 'steal shamelessly'. Today the stealing has been replaced by organised trade across different sectors – not in products but in improvement know-how.

Some of the evolution of Quality in the USA can be traced through the transfer of techniques and methodology between the leading practitioners. IBM 'stole' teamwork from FPL; Xerox 'stole' business process management from IBM; Motorola 'stole' benchmarking from Xerox; Milliken 'stole' the six sigma measurement from Motorola; Federal Express 'stole' recognition and stretching goals from Milliken...and on it goes. A revolution simply in information exchange and learning from others.

Europe wakes up

 Europe too has its own Quality revolution – less flamboyant than in the US, perhaps, but developing very strongly. Retailers in the UK and Germany, such as Sainsbury, Marks & Spencer, or Aldi have forced their industry standards up to the highest in the world in terms of stock management and electronic data interchange. Coincidentally, they also enjoy noticeably higher margins than retailers in the US or Japan. European airlines have been competing fiercely to raise service and efficiency standards, during a period in the eighties when US airlines appeared to have abandoned service for a price war. First SAS, then BA, created new products in the early eighties to distinguish their service, such as BA's Club Class, and then used Quality to upgrade these products continually. BA's turnround from a flabby state-owned monolith to a lean innovative competitor has been much admired. By the end of the decade, BA was not only winning many awards for service, it was by far the world's most profitable airline.

However, many service organisations, like BA and SAS, followed the Service Quality sub-discipline, not full organisational Quality. As the airline sector becomes more and more global in competitive terms, like many other industries, the European leaders are finding themselves attacked on all sides: by small niche players such as Virgin Atlantic and Swissair; by the expanding American giants, United and American Airlines; and by the sophisticated Asian carriers such as Singapore Airlines and Cathay Pacific. This continual pressure (and the same is happening in the financial services sector) is forcing the search for accelerated improvement. As a result, the whole service sector in Europe is moving fast along the Quality evolutionary path into Total Quality. The huge insurance sector provides a graphic example. The big insurance societies had little interest in Quality in the seventies and early eighties when the only problem was how to push more policies through the paper factory to back up the phenomenal sales. With the recessionary nineties, all that has changed, forcing a polarisation in the industry between those who are investing in full Quality processes in the belief that this is the only route to survival and those who cannot afford to invest in anything at all.

In Europe, there has been another strand to the rediscovery of Quality. The Quality standard, ISO 9000, has enabled companies, first in engineering then in many other sectors, to demonstrate they are capable of delivering to a prescribed level. Over 25,000 UK companies, ranging from solicitors through to oil giants, had been accredited with BS5750, the British forerunner to ISO 9000, by July 1993. These companies have worked hard for their registration and are proud of what they have achieved. However, most have learned along the way that a standard, even a comprehensive one like ISO 9000, is only a small element of a whole Quality process and a much more radical approach is needed to obtain major competitive advantage. Many of these are prepared to take that radical action; they too have joined the Quality revolution.

The European Foundation for Quality Management (EFQM) was founded in 1989 as a forum for those companies in Europe who have committed to Quality. Many of the founder companies, such as Ciba Geigy, Philips, Electrolux and British Telecom already have many years of serious Quality experience. By 1994, 300 companies had joined them, showing the commitment to the Quality movement in Europe. The European Quality Award, launched in 1991, is helping to gel this movement together and stimulate further interest in Quality, as the Baldrige Award did in the USA. Possibly rather more than in the US at this stage, Quality in Europe has spread across all sectors and down the scale to quite small businesses. Although it took longer to take hold in Europe than the US, the intensity of Quality application today is high right across the continent from North to South and West to East. Perhaps the most resistant European country to the Quality movement was the one which needed it least – West Germany. Here high inherent standards and economic success dulled the need for change and further improvement, but as German unification put unfamiliar pressures on industry, the environment changed. In the tougher economic climate of the nineties, many more German businesses have been joining Volkswagen, Bosch and Siemens in pursuing serious Quality improvement. Even the mighty Mercedes-

Benz has been forced to join the movement, with radical plans to abandon high-priced, over-engineering for Japanese-style lean production.

Survival in Japan

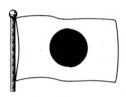 The first and biggest Quality revolution started in the East with the Japanese. The story is now a familiar one but nevertheless instructive. In the fifties, Japanese manufacturers were so far back with the standard of their exported goods that no one would buy them. Stainless-steel knives turned green and plastic toys fell to pieces within hours. For the Japanese communities supplying these goods this was true survival. Their only choice was to raise their standards – of products, of training, of service, of management – to a substantially higher level. Each major company committed to do this and started a process of improvement that began with the company president and carried on through the whole organisation and beyond into suppliers and dealers. It took them 15 to 20 years but from 1970 on they have had the edge in manufacturing and have never looked like losing it again. First with basic technologies – steel, aluminium, shipbuilding – then with increasingly sophisticated products – motorcycles, cameras, cars, hi-fis, televisions, semiconductors, even pianos – Japanese companies invaded world markets. Toyota, Yahama, Canon, Matsushita, NEC and their peers owe their world dominance of many sectors to their disciplined approach to improvement which started in 1950.

The Japanese Quality revolution is far from over. When faced with a major problem, such as the 1973 oil crisis (Japan has no oil of its own), the Japanese companies turned their Quality process to address it. Energy usage was attacked at all points from the mill melting the steel to the power consumption of the product in use. Miniaturisation became popular as a means of focusing power reduction (leading, as so often with improvement processes, to new market opportunities such as the personal stereo). In 1985, Japan faced another crisis – the high value of the Yen was making Japanese goods very expensive and, for the first time for three decades, Japanese manufacturers were facing end-of-year losses. Without drama, these companies turned the Quality process fully onto productivity and cost reduction. Companies like Ricoh and Minolta turned in substantial productivity improvements

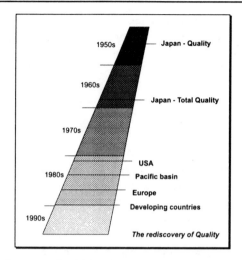

The rediscovery of Quality

and were back to profitability in one year, to the surprise of some pundits who had predicted this as the end of the Japanese miracle.

By the mid-eighties, Japan was becoming a high-wage economy and could no longer compete with Taiwan, Korea and Singapore on price. Instead, Japanese companies went up-market with higher value products and multinational manufacture, locating plants in all the main markets. Again the Quality process has been used to ensure success with these strategies. The Japanese model of improvement remains a compelling one which has been successfully copied by many developing countries. Singapore, an early follower, has also become a high-wage area and accordingly has rapidly shifted from low-cost manufacturing to sophisticated products and services. The role of the lowest-cost operators was taken up by Thailand, India and the Philippines, where everything from chip production to overnight data processing can be obtained. To attract such basic business from customers thousands of miles away, successful companies in these countries have to offer not simply a lower price tag but complete reliability. As a result, they are amongst the most eager followers of the Quality movement. As markets open up throughout the world, more and more enterprising business leaders discover the competitive advantages of using Quality; businesses in Kenya, in Colombia, in the Czech republic are installing Quality processes, often following the examples set by the leading Japanese and Western multinationals.

Meanwhile, in the early 1990s, Japan faced a very unfamiliar problem – recession. Japanese businesses are built for growth and this challenge to their prime driving force prompted many questions in the West. How will they cope with a period of non-growth? Will this finally bring down the much-vaunted advantages of life-time employment and long-term investment? All the evidence of the last 40 years suggests that Japanese manufacturers will cope with this in exactly the same way as with every other hurdle they have faced in this period. They can and will switch to shorter-term profit focus if that is required, as Akio Morita of Sony has been advocating for some time. They will relax the rigidity of their employment system and move people between companies, again, if necessary. But these are not the important factors; they are not at the heart of Japanese management practice. The core of best Japanese practice is company-wide continuous improvement – that is, Quality.

Throughout the 40 years of industrial expansion, Japanese companies have not wavered from the one disciplined overriding approach – Quality. In the same period, Western businesses have yo-yoed from one management fashion to another, discarding both good and bad in the rush for enlightenment. The Japanese too have been vociferous consumers of new management ideas and many of the Japanese practices being exported to the West originally came from Western thinkers. Not only the well-known examples of statistical teaching from Edwards Deming and Joseph Juran, but a whole spectrum of disciplines: management by objectives, market research, product rationalisation, industrial engineering, value analysis, even just-in-time, can be traced back to Western inspiration. The big difference is that the Japanese companies took the best of these disciplines and wove them into their own improvement process. They adapted and integrated them into one overall Quality process which every one in the company could contribute to and benefit from. Over the decades they have used this Quality process to address all problems and opportunities which they have faced in a united way. Despite their phenomenal economic success, Japanese businesses display no signs of complacency. Their Quality process demands persistent development and challenge. Japan will not stop improving.

A world revolution

Continuous improvement is the difference that the West has been much later in understanding and practising. Nevertheless, Western businesses that now have this belief in disciplined improvement, also have other advantages which the Japanese companies are striving to emulate. Japanese companies in the UK admire the flexibility and ingenuity of thinking that they find in the European workforce. Japanese companies worry about their ability to innovate, to make quantum leaps as readily as Europeans, in addition to their natural incremental steps. They are also concerned about the real productivity of individual workers relative to the USA and the inefficiency and bureaucracy of their administration. These are all areas which they continue to work on and learn from the West, whilst we learn from them.

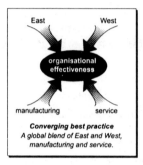

Converging best practice
A global blend of East and West,
manufacturing and service.

Today, best management in the West and East is converging, as the best of both is sought out and applied. The Quality movement has been a major contributor to this mixing and leavening. The way in which the Quality philosophy was installed, East and West, has been different (after all, no one has twenty years to do it now) but the end result is becoming very similar. Leading companies display traits which can be observed in Tokyo, Minneapolis or Paris: clear purpose and direction, customer-focus, continuous challenge, structured improvement and an organisational culture that unites and binds action together. Within these characteristics are many common management disciplines which have been adopted by the companies. The Quality culture that supports these disciplines can be stronger than the national culture. Look at Honda in Ohio or Nissan in Washington, UK – advanced examples of Japanese management practice with a Western workforce performing as well as plants in Japan. Or the remarkable transformation of NUMMI in California, where the once worst-performing General Motors plant became the best, using the same workforce but with an injection of Japanese management. It works the other way too. IBM Japan and Yokogawa Hewlett Packard are more closely aligned to the IBM and HP cultures than to Japan. The Quality movement is creating cultures where people think and act in a compatible and consistent way regardless of location or origin of the organisation.

Quality shock waves

The result of a successful Quality revolution can be transmitted like a shock wave. By 1978, the once-derided Toyota Corolla was arriving in California by tanker-load – perceived as a better product by consumers and selling at $1,200 less than US equivalents. The home producers were stunned into a subordinate position which continues today.

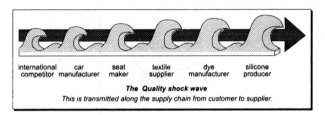

| international competitor | car manufacturer | seat maker | textile supplier | dye manufacturer | silicone producer |

The Quality shock wave
This is transmitted along the supply chain from customer to supplier.

Over a decade later, Toyota, Honda and Nissan still regularly top the customer satisfaction surveys and have not only captured the small car market but have made major inroads into the higher-value bracket. The all-important J D Power Customer Satisfaction Index for 1991 was jointly topped by the Toyota Lexus and the Nissan Infiniti with 170 points each. The highest domestic manufacturer was Cadillac in eighth place with 139 points. The shock of Japanese cars not only entering the luxury car sector, the last preserve of the US and European manufacturers, and going straight to the top, is equivalent to that of the first Corolla a decade before.

The stronger Western companies responded in the late seventies – clumsily at first, with attempts to graft on the Japanese 'miracles', such as Quality Circles or Just-In-Time. These failed – lacking the management philosophy which enables such disciplines to flourish. The lesson was learned earlier by some than others. Ford US reversed a serious financial loss in 1982 through a major Quality drive and saw its market share stay reasonably firm whilst General Motors, with a weaker response, declined alarmingly. In the nineties, all the Western car companies have substantial Total Quality investments – some for many years now – but they still have a way to go to match the rate of improvement of Honda, Toyota or Nissan. In 1991, Ford made another big loss, showing that Quality shock waves don't only strike once. Despite Ford's efforts, their improvement has not been radical enough to avoid another bashing from the Japanese. But because of their conversion to Quality during those intervening years, they were better placed than most to survive this latest shock. Like their

Japanese competitors, they have used the Quality process to become even more competitive in the future.

It's not just the car manufacturers, of course. When the Japanese shock wave hit Xerox, Kodak or Caterpillar they were each seemingly inviolate at the top of their sectors. Such was the devastation caused by Ricoh on Xerox, Fuji on Kodak and Komatsu on Caterpillar, that survival was a real concern. That they have survived and remained strong is down to their own Quality revolutions – taking around five years for recovery in contrast to the twenty of the Japanese.

These large American corporations, like Ford, Xerox and Motorola, have themselves spread the revolution. They have installed Total Quality processes in their subsidiaries worldwide and they have passed the demand on to their suppliers, who in turn have pushed it on further up the supply chain. A typical example: Ford US passed the shock wave onto Milliken, who make their seat covers; Milliken spread it to Swiss-based Ciba Geigy, who make the dyes for the textiles; Ciba Geigy brought in Dow Corning, who make silicones for the dyes.

The Quality shocks are by no means all administered by the Japanese. The Quality wave in the computer hardware sector was, as is frequently the case, started by the market leader. IBM by 1980 had been dominant for so long it was perceived by many as arrogant. Customers were beginning to react. 'No one got fired for buying IBM' was still a strong feeling but it did not mean that the captive buyers were content...a lesson for anyone feeling protected by a large market share. IBM started their Quality process by way of response. For the first few years, it was aimed at products – improving their reliability, their delivery times and their adaptability in use.

By the mid-eighties, despite tremendous progress, IBM realised it was nowhere near enough. The Quality gap was still there and widening. Product reliability was taken for granted by customers and was no longer a differentiating factor. Customers wanted solutions to their needs and buying the latest mainframe was not the only answer. By now, fast moving companies such as Compaq (which was set up from scratch in 1983 with Quality as the managerial philosophy) and Digital were amongst those offering innovative alternatives. IBM needed to shift another gear to bridge the gap. By 1991, there were so many smaller, leaner, sharper outfits taking bites out of IBM's share that chairman John Akers knew he had to do something revolutionary. He told his managers: 'I'm sick of people telling me they are doing this for Quality and then I go to a customer and find problems and complaints.'

In 1991, John Akers started a major restructuring of the business which will continue for many years – if it ends at all – as the mightiest of all corporations adjusts to the realities of pleasing today's customers. Huge product group empires are being broken up into smaller market-responsive units. It is all held together with yet another internal wave of Quality improvement – this time called Market Driven Quality, acknowledging the power of the customer. Everybody at IBM is being trained in Quality again – in a corporation where everyone receives around ten days of training per year already. The training is the easy bit; turning 350,000 people into customer-orientated champions for improvement is something else. IBM may have had serious action on Quality for over ten years but only now is the pace revolutionary. The shock wave which hit IBM reverberated right to the top. John Akers started the revolution at IBM but he was not revolutionary enough, resigning in February 1993 because of the continued deterioration of IBM's market position. Leaders today have to move fast or they too are swamped.

Quality can make a difference

The lesson from Ford, IBM, Xerox and others is that the shock waves keep coming and they are big ones. Each time we have to jump even higher. If we are already moving, we stand a better chance of resurfacing and perhaps clawing our way back in front of the wave...but that big leap will still be needed. Will we be capable of making it? It depends on many things. Better products may help but won't take us very far. Slicker marketing may attract attention but not necessarily more customers. Cost reduction won't do it, neither will new technology, courteous service or electronic data interchange. Some or all of these may be critical but they won't make enough difference on their own. We have to go beyond good practice and challenge the very nature of our organisation: how managers manage and how people work; how things get done. We need a transformation in what people do at work, if we are serious about prospering in business. We need nothing less than a culture of improvement. And we will need a Quality revolution to get it.

In one sense, there is nothing new about Quality. Many (if not all) of the tools of improvement have been around for years and the principles which guide Quality are not especially novel or original. Indeed, when Marks & Spencer began a new Quality programme in

1986, they searched around for some lively video input to reinforce the messages they wanted to convey to their rapidly expanding base of staff and suppliers. To their surprise, they found exactly what they wanted in a British Productivity film they had contributed to called 'Right First Time'...made twenty years earlier. But tools and simplistic statements of principles are not what the Quality revolution is about. Quality is about making substantial improvement everywhere in an organisation, using tools and principles as and where appropriate. In this sense, *everything* is new about Quality, for what is sought is continual renewal of every aspect of our business.

So what's new about Quality?

A good Quality process changes the way things are done, by:

- *Driving the business from customer needs*
- *Setting a clear vision which is deployed down into coordinated action*
- *Using the contribution of every person to the full*
- *Managing well beyond company boundaries*
- *Managing processes to their optimal capability*
- *Partnering with customers and suppliers, both internal and external*
- *Developing workers to manage and managers to lead*
- *Breaking down hierarchy and functional divisions*
- *Becoming faster, leaner and more responsive to market opportunities*
- *Integrating all the above for competitive advantage.*

Quality can make the vital difference by looking at business afresh from a new perspective and using the insight as the stimulus for radical improvement. At the focal point of this new perspective is people. Business is about people working with other people...customers, managers, staff, suppliers. A Quality process makes us look again at the way all these people work together with the challenge that it can and must be done better than before. Do we know our customers? Do we understand their needs? Do we know the processes which pull together our work for customers? Do we know how to create more value and less waste in those processes? Can they be made faster, more robust, more flexible? Are we giving our people the power to do their best? Are we giving them the guidance, support and inspiration to want to do better? A Quality process concentrates on these issues, focusing on people. All the above questions are independent of technical and functional expertise, applying equally to marketing and to operations, to manufacturing and to service, to Western business and to Eastern. Every individual can improve what they are doing. The Quality process gives people the inspiration and impetus to do just that. But Quality can then do much more. It binds these improvements together throughout the whole organisation to make a big difference. This is the revolutionary bit...changing the way things are done.

Anyway, who wants to run a non-Quality business?

If you were the manager of a company or department that did not have Quality you would recognise these symptoms:

- Complaints: you spend a lot of time dealing with (or avoiding) irate customers
- Wasted time: up to two days of your week goes on unnecessary work
- Frustration: you never have enough time for the necessary and important work (because of the time wasted)
- Hassle: there are always fires to put out
- Confusion: no one seems to know whats going on, least of all you
- Overload: you always have too much to do ...
- Underload: ... but your staff still dump their problems on your desk
- Neglect: no one wants to hear your views or problems.

If you have experienced any of these problems, you will appreciate why managers are keen to promote Total Quality as a way of doing business.

Unnatural improvement

Revolutions do not happen naturally, especially Quality ones. Most teams and most systems settle into a natural pattern of working which is steady, reasonably reliable and very ordinary. Whole organisations also follow this pattern; most companies provide a service which is not bad but not startlingly good. This is the natural state and it takes a lot to disturb it. Leaders such as Mike Nash have to be prepared to do a lot of stirring up if they are to dislodge the heavy weight of 'business as usual'.

Revolutions are also dangerous. The natural state may be slow and dull but it is working; change destabilises and customers and staff may be alarmed at the disruption. The Quality leader has little choice, of course. To accept the status quo is to sink slowly into the sand until a shock wave comes along and buries him totally. Instead, he must make his leap now and power through to a new level of performance. But before he makes the big jump, he needs to know how he is going to sustain such a major effort.

At the heart of it all is belief. The Quality leader needs to believe that it is possible, in order for him to stick his neck out and go for it. He needs the belief that people will perform to a much higher level if given the right opportunity; that anything can be improved; that customers prefer a Quality service; that organised improvement leads

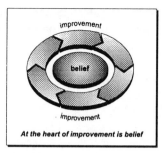

At the heart of improvement is belief

to better results. The Quality leader believes these things implicitly. The challenge is to convert the belief into reality.

The Quality leader may have unlimited potential for making accelerated improvement in his organisation. But, as this potential is not realised naturally, he has to line up and mobilise all his forces for improvement. There may be many of these...and equally many counter-forces capable of negating any gain. To ensure the positive forces are not dissipated away, the leader needs to concentrate his effort on those that will generate a major shift in the way the organisation behaves. These are the forces he can mobilise to drive Quality – the Quality drivers – which interlink to build momentum for improvement and power the big jump in performance which is sought. These Quality drivers will not be new; they have been well-known for decades, but are mostly underexploited. The Quality leader begins his quest for substantial improvement by seeking to exploit each of them to the full. But to make a difference, he then needs to set his ambition even higher by aiming to integrate them; they all have an essential role to play and their integration multiplies the impact.

The Quality drivers for business improvement

There are six main drivers for improvement in organisations: strategy, leadership, customers, processes, people and disciplines. All quite general management issues but ones which many managers tend not to manage explicitly, either because they are too busy with the task at hand or perhaps they see these as soft or abstract. There are other drivers, but these are the primary and universal ones. The first is strategy: we need to be clear about what we are and where we are going. A business without strategic direction is going nowhere; conversely a business on a clear road can be driven hard. Major improvement is unlikely without a forward vision and business strategy to pull everything together: a strategic focus harnesses and channels our energies and activities.

The second driver is leadership: little changes, little improves without it. The leader makes it happen. He or she provides the inspiration for improvement. The effectiveness of the leadership role, in terms of setting the right strategic direction and inspiring people to go for it, is a major source of improvement potential.

Whatever our business, it must always revolve around customers. Everyone knows that without customers the business dies, but most organisations continue to assume a 'we know best' stance, focusing on the little world inside the company walls more than the big one outside. Therein lies much improvement opportunity; customers are the third big improvement driver. Organisations are complicated and we cannot deliver to customers unless we have processes to make up the order, produce the service and receive payment. Partly because of our emphasis on functions and hierarchy, processes are often taken for granted in day-to-day practice, to the extent that some are quite invisible and many are left to manage themselves. The scope for radical improvement of business processes is very high. Managing processes effectively is the fourth driver.

Customers are served by people; processes are run by people. Only people can ever do the work – not systems, not machines, not computers. Every business leader knows this, but not so many make people a major focus in their own right. For lasting improvement there is no choice – only people will make that improvement. A better understanding and practice of how people work effectively in organisations is a fundamental need. As more than one successful leader has noted: 'Quality starts with people and ends with people.' Releasing the talents and capabilities of all of our people is a core improvement driver.

As business units evolve, different ways of doing things naturally develop around the business, miscommunications arise, inefficiencies creep in. The counter to this is discipline, little coveted in many Western organisations but another vital way of ensuring lasting improvement. Disciplines give method, consistency, repeatability and control. Applying disciplines to drive improvement covers a wide spectrum of structured approaches – from the way projects are set up and run, to how the competitive factors of time and cost are measured. Disciplines, as an improvement driver, bring us full circle back to strategy: the most powerful discipline of all is creating strategic clarity.

All of these Quality drivers are interdependent and reinforce each other. This mutual dependence is what lifts the organisation onto a higher plane of performance. Any weak area constrains the whole endeavour to a lower achievement. Thus organisations with a strong emphasis on customer service may find outstanding efforts in front of customers negated by weakly-managed processes a long way back from the counter. Or enthusiastic, motivated teams are frustrated in their efforts to improve by indecisive managers or through unstructured activity. The Quality leader must orchestrate overall improvement through the management of *all* these improvement drivers.

Quality accelerators

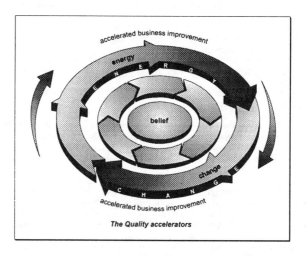

The Quality accelerators

Understanding the role of these drivers in making organisational improvement is the key ingredient for success. But it still doesn't make for a Quality revolution. The Quality leader needs to do yet more to achieve a result in five years rather than 20. He needs to manage two more vital ingredients: the accelerators of organisational improvement. One accelerator is the process of change. Change is both a *result* of improvement as people do things differently to before and a *means* of getting there. Change can and must be managed.

L&K:REXONA

Belief... The Quality process started because of Mike Nash's belief in Quality. Gradually others shared it and then it spread across and down the company. Quality became an important word at L&K: Rexona.

Improvement Energy... The programme was planned and managed to be intensive, involving and challenging and continues to be so. Training workshops are active, participative experiences, always followed by real improvement action. Communications keep people informed continuously; reporting and display of improvement keeps a sense of importance and urgency. The feeling that it is a one-off, just a fad, has been left behind; there is always something new to be involved in or to learn.

Strategy...The L&K: Rexona strategy was thrashed out over many workshops, involving many levels of management. Once it became firm in practice, the vision and mission were communicated to the whole team. Five stretching improvement goals ensured that the strategy was not an academic one but one which had to be achieved. Every year performance against these goals is rigorously assessed and the strategy refined for a further year of improvement.

Leadership ... Mike Nash started it and set the strategy with his Board, but, by the end of 1992, only two of the original directors were left in the company; the others had moved on in the Unilever group, including Mike himself. The Quality process has helped mould a common style which is much less dependent on individual style than before. New chairman, Ross Peterson, had no difficulty fitting in to this style and adding his own experience to the pot. Enthusiasm today is higher than ever and the business and improvement strategy clearer than ever.

Customers... Customer satisfaction has become the objective of every section and the ultimate aim of every improvement project, whether in sales, manufacturing or administration. Consumer preferences are the trigger for decisions on brand development, on product formulations, on packaging design, on advertising. Retail customer needs are the trigger for manufacturing re-layout, for distribution developments, for invoice re-design, for supplier management. Internal customers are the trigger for efficiencies between departments.

Processes... Ross Peterson is pushing systematic process improvement hard, looking for targeted and identified multi-million dollar gains by delivering customer needs more efficiently and responsively. This is possible because it builds on an environment where people are now aware that they are major components in processes and look to improve the whole as well as the parts.

People... Everybody has been trained in Quality; everyone has an opportunity to contribute to improvement. Most do, becoming involved in improvement teams, ranging from major cross-functional projects to small local workteams, with hundreds of individual suggestions put forward. All contributions are recognised; achievements are on display.

Disciplines... Processes are mapped and analysed in a methodical way; projects are managed; problem symptoms are traced to root causes; data is collected before decisions are taken; trends in customer preferences are detected and fed back; improvement activity of any kind is reported and coordinated; improvement action is measured. Just about everything that is done is done to a discipline ... the ad hoc is not encouraged.

Change... L&K: Rexona is a more united, disciplined, vital organisation than it was. Managers manage in a different way; they support and guide more and instruct less. People take more responsibility for themselves. Suppliers and agencies are bound up too. Everyone has a better idea of where the company is going; they talk to each other about it. There is an expectation of more change - the company is moving, going forward, taking on more. Change is embraced, managed. It is only the start of a long revolution.

Accelerated improvement at L&K: Rexona

There is so much in-built resistance to change and so many forces pulling back towards the status quo, that a designed, planned and resourced change process is necessary to cut through the barriers and allow the improvement drivers to work. This is no simple A to B process, for organisational dynamics are tricky and many approaches tend to raise resistance rather than lower it.

The second accelerator is energy – improvement energy. Absolutely no one has succeeded in making change at a leisurely pace or as a low priority. Anything less than wholehearted dedication, even obsession, is simply ignored by the organisation. A great deal of energy must be put into an improvement process, before the changes, during and after. This energy needs to be harnessed and focused for effective use or it can be easily dissipated. Improvement energy, like change, can and should be managed. It is needed to make impact on a complacent organisation; it is needed to divert activity from one direction to a new one; it is needed to sustain enthusiasm after setbacks; it is needed to power through blockages; it is needed to keep the pace up when it is natural to ease off. A high-energy organisation tends to embrace change and use it. Energy and change feed off each other...providing the acceleration in the improvement process.

Learning with Quality

Quality is deceptively simple. One of its great values is that anyone in an organisation will fairly readily understand it and relate to it. On the other hand, it is a sophisticated approach to managing substantial change in a complex dynamic organisation. Many managers have pursued too narrow an application of Quality and been disappointed with their return from a lot of effort. Some have been cavalier with the subtleties of Quality and have attempted to force through a cultural change rather than inspire it. They rarely win...organisation cultures are formidable opponents. Nevertheless, such managers may learn much from such setbacks and those with stamina may go on to achieve success later. This is another great value of Quality – there is nearly always something positive to be had from it. It is hard not to gain something from a Quality process, even if a hash is made of a first or a second implementation.

For example, many companies moved on from fruitless attempts to sustain Quality Circles in an unsympathetic managerial environment in the seventies, by realising that their focus should have been on management in the first place. Many others have found the evangelical approaches which inspired wonders in the USA can feel quite alien in, say, Germany or Holland. Undaunted, they have learned, amended and progressed. Others may receive a raspberry from the staff in, say, an advertising agency, to training or tools originally designed for a manufacturing workforce. As long as the leader is sufficiently responsive and resilient, then the only lasting loss from such setbacks is time.

But time too is a competitive factor. Those Western companies that started Quality processes in 1980 expected to take eight to ten years to create their new way of working. They freely admit they took wrong turns, blind alleys and a few U-turns. Looking back on the Hewlett Packard process, as one example, one can detect sweeping shifts in emphasis as a product reliability drive was supplanted by a business-process emphasis and later still with a market-driven thrust. Over the years, HP evolved its own worldwide process, later gaining much from networking and benchmarking other Quality implementations. Today no one has ten years to spare to evolve a Quality process; the next shock wave may be on its way now. A Quality process today has to be more efficient, more direct, more revolutionary...from the start. It has to make a visible difference; one that can be seen in the things people do, in the market place and in the bottom line.

Quality is not magic. It cannot ...

- *pull new customers out of a hat*
- *vanish away regretted decisions*
- *trick customers that our service is better than it really is*
- *spirit away persistent competitors*
- *provide a crystal ball into the future*
- *solve all our problems overnight*
- *expand time to suit*
- *transform difficult people into angels*
- *manage the business for us.*

In the nineties, there has been something of a backlash against Quality, especially TQM as applied in the USA. A number of management reporters have questioned whether companies obtain a good return from a Quality process, citing examples of extravagant claims not being realised and companies becoming disenchanted. Much of this stems from misunderstanding. Quality is far from being free...it has to be paid for like anything else. The price of Quality is hard managerial graft and the leader pays most. There is also no magic which can run our business for us. We still need expertise: a Quality process cannot do the marketing and selling or devise the strategy for us. If a company is going out of business because its customers have deserted it, not even Quality can turn the clock back to have another try.

None of this is likely to daunt the Quality leader too much, although he would be wise to listen and learn from the criticism which has been levied. For here lies more opportunity. Not everybody will make a huge success of Quality. Many will make only modest gains. Only some will achieve and sustain revolutionary change. The Quality leader naturally will want to be one of these successes and not make the mistakes of the many who may jeopardise their future competitiveness through a weak process. Each company which fails to create its Quality revolution may be one less to compete seriously against in the future.

There is another great value to Quality; there is always something more to learn and something more to do. As companies become more experienced with Quality, they move up to another plane of understanding which reveals how much more they need to do and how much they need to understand. As Bob Cahalan of Xerox said in 1987 after three years of intense Quality application: 'We're only now starting.' David Kearns, as CEO, said much the same at the time of Xerox winning the Baldrige award two years later. The art of Quality is knowing how to improve further regardless of the progress already made. Quality can be rediscovered on a regular basis. Quality is as relevant to managers at Xerox and Hewlett Packard after many years of application as it is to the manager of the small printing business or the private hospital who has just heard about it.

The first step is belief

Quality leaders like John Young at HP, David Kearns at Xerox or Mike Nash at L&K: Rexona have all been through this learning process and none would say they ever reached the zenith. Their successors started higher up the learning curve thanks to their pioneering, but still do not expect to get there. Quality is forever...there is always something new to learn and to do. The Xerox revolution did not pause when Paul Allaire took over the reins from David Kearns. Far from it, he gave it a renewed intensity and vitality for the nineties, believing that Xerox will have to change more in the

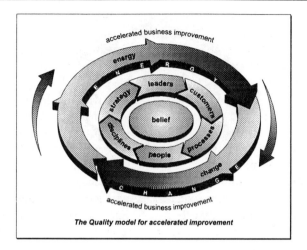

The Quality model for accelerated improvement

next five years than they have in the past ten. His aim is 'to get the benefits of a small company of quickness in time to market, decision-making and the elimination of bureaucratic activities without losing any of the advantages of the big organisation'.[1]

Similarly, the revolution at L&K: Rexona also continues apace under new chairman, Ross Peterson. Every year an objective review of the Quality process and its results is conducted. For 1993, two main thrusts were identified: more advanced work on business process improvement to realise major competitive benefits; and a sharper focus on leadership behaviours to achieve a more consistent and effective style from the whole management team. At giant Xerox or small L&K: Rexona, there is no relaxation of energy and no let-up on the change. Accelerated improvement cannot stop.

However far these leaders reach on the upward spiral of improvement, each step is based firmly on belief. For every leader of any size or type of organisation who is seeking to accelerate the rate of organisational improvement, the first step is the same. Believe in Quality.

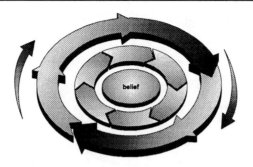

SUMMARY

Ten reasons to believe in Quality

1. Quality is profitable

Would you like to improve your long-term profitability?

Think about Yokogawa Hewlett Packard's 244 per cent increase in profitability through a five-year Quality process. Or the $700 million Motorola put on the bottom line as cost savings as a direct result of Quality. Or the 100 per cent profit improvement small wholesalers BSS made from their Quality drive.

By and large, the ultimate test of a Quality process is the bottom line. For some companies, the end result is survival; for others prosperity in the form of enhanced market share or margin. But there is no magic and there are no short cuts; it takes hard work, a lot of skill and some time to see bottom-line benefits. The very best Quality processes will show a bottom-line result; the indifferent ones will never get there.

2. Poor Quality is penalised

Would you like to eliminate those nasty incidents which cause the customer not to come back but tell his friends (other customers) what happened instead?

Think about the cost of losing one customer (the price of the service multiplied by the number of occasions that customer might purchase over a buying lifetime). Then think about the Washington survey that showed that customers tell at least ten others when dissatisfied; multiply your first cost by, say, three, to cover the lost custom *from damaged reputation. Add the selling cost of replacing your customer with a new one (usually five times as much). Your large figure is the penalty for poor Quality. Can you afford not to have a Quality process?*

3. Quality distinguishes

Would you like your service to stand out from the rest?

Think about Marks & Spencer who achieve premium prices on mass products such as foods...or Van Leer with steel drums...or Perdue with chickens. These are distinctive to customers because of the high standard of their products and the personal nature of their service. In a crowded market, commonplace service – that which doesn't stand out – is simply ignored. Even tougher, in a fast moving climate, today's exceptional service is tomorrow's norm; distinction is a continuous need.

A Quality process helps maintain an edge with a sharper focus on those factors which distinguish tomorrow's service and continual improvement to ensure the reality matches the image. If Frank Perdue can differentiate a dead chicken, then anything can be made distinctive...provided you have the Quality process to back it up.

4. Quality is expected

Your customers want it; your competitors may already be doing it...wouldn't you be better being ahead of the game?

Think about Motorola which tells its suppliers today that merely improving the supplied product and the ensuing service is not enough: a full Total Quality process is required, including applying for the Baldrige Award. Think about why Ford, 3M and Westinghouse are similarly uncompromising with their demands on their suppliers...it is because their own customers are equally demanding on them. Think about the way Quality shock waves are sent reverberating along the supply chains, crossing borders and sectors. One may hit you soon, if it has not done already. Think about your competitors and others who may enter your market: might they be better equipped to respond to the new demands? Your customers will want Quality; be ready to give it to them.

5. Quality renews

Would you like a sharper, leaner, more flexible organisation?
Think about revitalised Xerox and Motorola...or even Rover and Unipart, once riddled with restrictive practices as part of British Leyland, both now operating with a flexibility learned from their mutual partner, Honda. Think about the transformations at British Steel, from Britain's biggest loss-maker to productivity levels as high as anywhere in the world. Think about the waste in your own organisation and how it can clog things up and slow you down. Think about IBM and Westinghouse who, over the years, got rid of billions of dollars worth of unnecessary activities as a by-product of their Quality processes – helping them adapt quicker to new competitive threats.

Think also about Tesco, who have deliberately and successfully moved out of the low-price retailing to compete head on with up-market Sainsbury and Marks & Spencer. Or Allen-Bradley who saw the writing on the wall with high-volume electromechanical switchgear and made a huge step up into bespoke computer-integrated manufacture (CIM). A good Quality process energises the organisation, permitting much greater change. If change is needed, use Quality to make the change telling and lasting.

6. Quality unites and inspires

When you have set a clear business strategy, would you like the organisation to follow it, quickly and decisively?
Think about your organisation...is it fragmented with units, departments and levels operating in a divisive, sub-optimal manner? Then think about Nissan, who achieve consistent practice of management and workforce in Tokyo, Sunderland and Ohio, all working to the same mission. Think about turf battles and empire-building in conventional businesses and think how process management can convert this negative energy into competitive power.

Think also about The Body Shop, whose 1,500 staff are united behind Anita Roddick's ideals and apply them with enthusiasm; think how this spread to customers, enabling The Body Shop to grow phenomenally in a few years. What about Komatsu and NEC, whose annual policy objectives are translated into improvement tasks for every workteam...and all add back-up at the end of the year to achieve the target set? Or the stretch goals of Milliken and Hewlett Packard, with tenfold improvement targets for the whole business to strive for and achieve?

Think about how many ideas you get from your workforce. Then think about Milliken's 200,000 or Toyota's two million suggestions for improvement from their people every year. A hundred documented ideas per year is the minimum target for companies like Ricoh or Minolta. A united, energised workforce allows opportunities to be taken fast. It also gives service distinction just by the way people behave.

7. Quality delivers

Would you like a better return from your projects and restructuring endeavours?

Think about Hewlett Packard who have numerous major Quality projects with major results, such as $540 million from one inventory reduction as a consequence of introducing 'just-in-time'; another $200 million from the space released from the same initiative; or $150 million from an accounts receivable process improvement. Think about the very many companies who are achieving a regular six to one, or better, return on their Quality projects. As American Express says: 'It is easy to justify further investment in Total Quality because the return is so high.' A Quality process brings discipline, direction and energy to projects and can transform the end result. A good Quality process can bring in well over 10 per cent of sales revenue per year in cost savings simply from removing the waste. But this is only one dimension of the multiple benefits which a strong improvement process should deliver.

8. Pride

Would you like your organisation to be one which everyone is proud to work for?

Think about Merck who topped Fortune's *most admired businesses for five years. Merck always recruit the best and the best want to work for them; it is no coincidence that they also deliver the best results (an average of over 30 per cent return to investors). The US executives polled for this survey cited quality of management as the most significant factor making up a corporate reputation (82 per cent), with quality of products and services next (63 per cent). A Quality process should have direct impact on these factors.*

Think about Marks & Spencer whose reputation as a Quality business has grown a small store offering value for money into Europe's biggest retailer with profit increases despite recession. Marks & Spencer managers still take pride in providing value for money even though the company is now very large; their staff share this pride in the service and the company. Staff in a Quality business enjoy continual recognition from pleased customers and this spurs them on to perform even better. They are allowed to take pride in their work. Who wants to work for a non-Quality company anyway?

9. Self-interest

Would you like to better yourself...be a better manager, achieve more, have greater prospects?

First, think about the planned humility of Japanese companies such as Ricoh or Fuji. Their Quality process, driven from the customer back, doesn't allow them to become complacent and arrogant; there is always something better that can be done for the customer. This gives their managers unlimited scope for development. Think about the personal growth from experiencing a transformation such as Jan Carlzon led at SAS or Colin Marshall at BA. Think about the concentrated learning from being at the centre of a massive shift in the way an organisation works such as at General Electric or Rank Xerox. And think about results...what we, as managers, are paid to achieve. Lasting results come from managing the whole in a significantly better way.

Believing in Quality did not do the presidents of Toyota or Matsushita any harm in their struggles to build their businesses in the 1950s. Neither did it harm the careers of Heini Lippuner, who introduced Total Quality to a division of Ciba Geigy and is now chairman of the whole company, or Mike Perry who did likewise in a Unilever division and went on to become chairman of Unilever plc. Quality leaders tend to do well for themselves as well as for the business.

10. Quality is accelerated improvement

Would you like to create a better way of doing business, to adapt, to innovate, to improve continuously...and do it faster than others?

Think about many of the world's leading organisations today.

Toyota, Marks & Spencer, Hewlett Packard, British Airways, Sony, Komatsu, Motorola and perhaps 30 others. How have they sustained their success? Through continual improvement, through adaptation to changing environments and through reinvention of their services and processes. A Quality process is the means to institutionalise this rare ability for continuous positive change. It is not something that is exclusively available to the very best; any organisation of any size and any nature can learn from and emulate these world-class companies. Accelerated improvement is available to all businesses and all units...provided their leaders are prepared for revolution and believe in Quality.

2
Improvement Energy

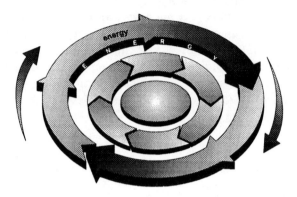

Some companies achieve remarkable transformations with Quality; others find their organisation has changed hardly at all after a lot of effort installing a Quality process. The biggest difference is energy: those companies who generate a large amount of improvement energy and harness it well, break through the organisational inertia and achieve change. The Quality revolution starts with belief but will only progress with improvement energy.

'Most improvement efforts have as much impact on company performance as a rain dance has on the weather.' Robert Schaffer and Harvey Thomson

'Cut through the organisational arthritis.' Leo Fisher, Boeing

No energy, no change

Historically, most revolutions fail. Quality revolutions are no exception. Many leaders start a Quality process with the expectation of achieving miraculous results, as others have done at YHP, Xerox and Motorola. Later on, they are disappointed; despite their good intentions, the organisation behaves much as before and there is little tangible benefit to show for the heroic efforts made. A 1992 UK survey of 100 companies who had embarked on Total Quality programmes showed that only 20 per cent had achieved significant improvement in performance over 12 months (30 per cent did not report any improvement, and 50 per cent did not respond to the question on performance). A US survey of 500 companies in 1992 showed a similar spread with only one third believing their Total Quality programmes were having a significant effect on their competitiveness. Yet another survey of 300 electronics companies in 1991 showed 63 per cent of the companies with Total Quality programmes (73 per cent of the 300) had failed to improve product defects by 10 per cent or more, an important characteristic in this sector.

The conclusion is clear: some can do it, the majority cannot. The analysis is more complicated. Researchers and observers of the implementation of Quality programmes report a wide variation in approach and emphasis. Few companies make good use of all the improvement drivers introduced in the last chapter – strategy, leadership, customers, processes, people and disciplines. Most concentrate only on one or two – customers and people, perhaps, by focusing on service attitudes, or people and disciplines, by teaching improvement tools to staff. Fewer still learn to orchestrate these crucial drivers to optimal effect. But most of all, the companies with weak results seem to miss altogether the improvement accelerators – energy and change. These are the keys to unlocking organisations and releasing the enormous potential. Energy and change are completely intertwined. Without energy, it is hard to change. Without successful change, it is hard to sustain the energy.

The early Quality processes in the West illustrate this. In the early eighties, Quality programmes tended to begin with awareness and education – definitions and principles of Quality, for example – and followed on with tools and techniques. This was fine for people already converted to the Quality cause but ill-suited to capturing the attention of indifferent or too-busy people. Hence the committed minority had an engaging time for a year or two putting in such steps, but the energy was limited to themselves; meanwhile the remainder carried on their business as they always had. Bit by bit, the indifferent majority sapped the will of the enthusiasts and the process withered away to die or be replaced by a new approach.

Mike Nash at L&K:Rexona found many supporters for Quality within his management team. His directors found similar enthusiasm within their own teams. This provided a platform for their revolution. Quality became the rallying-call, providing a language of improvement and a set of beliefs for these enthusiasts to share. But as every manager knows, for every enthusiastic follower there will be a determined objector and for everyone who has a view, positive or negative, there will be two or three who are totally apathetic.

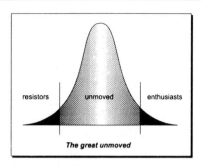

The great unmoved

Revolutions have to be active, involving, exciting. For the revolution to take hold, the non-believers – the great unmoved – have to be converted. To engage the interest of the unmoved, we have to grab their attention. For this, real work issues have to be addressed, not the abstract concepts of the early Quality programmes...and in an inspiring, challenging, even shocking way. We have to restate the purpose of the business – what we are all there to do. And the direction – what our customers are going to buy from us in the years ahead. Why our current service is not going to be good enough tomorrow. Why our current improvement initiatives are not going to close the gaps that will occur. Why we need to set goals far in advance of our current targets – further than we know how to do at the moment. How we are going to pull together to achieve these goals. And how we can use Quality to help us do all of it.

All the above should be obvious points...what management is paid to do anyway, the cynic might say. Quite right. Unfortunately we do not do it well enough or consistently enough, especially as the size and complexity of an organisation grows. Every manager knows this if he or she ever has the time to think about it. To the 'ordinary' worker, it is even more obvious – he or she may see little in the way of direction and purpose of the business but will see an awful lot of panic, waste, miscommunication, confusion and ambiguity. Few people think this is the way the organisation should really be working and most would prefer to work in an ordered, purposeful environment in a business that knows where it is going.

So the leader who makes his case well and displays a determination to address these issues may find more believers in Quality than he thought. But the majority will still remain unmoved. They won't do anything differently than before. This is because they are trapped by current practice – the systems they work within, the habits they have acquired over the years, their low expectation of change for the better. The leader must build the energy to break through these barriers before others in the organisation are able to join in and create a groundswell for change.

The early Quality approaches did not penetrate the thick skin of the organisation to address these underlying needs. They did not make enough impact, either at the start or later on in the process. They did not have enough energy behind them. Some companies are still enthusiastically embarking on similar programmes today and can expect to go through the same learning process. What may seem a logical step-by-step approach fails because organisations are not logical. Much more is known today about organisational behaviour and change processes. A planned change process will play a major factor in achieving results from a Quality process and this is discussed more fully in Chapters 9 and 10. But energy remains the crucial ingredient. It is improvement energy which transforms a Quality programme into a Quality revolution. No energy, no change. No change, no gain.

Generating the energy

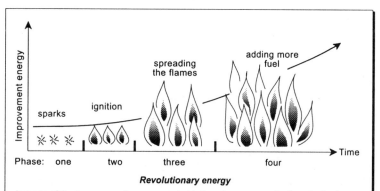

Revolutionary energy

In terms of the improvement energy needed to transform an organisation, the leader at this early stage is akin to an electrical charge. He is setting off sparks around the place. In some revolutions, this is enough to cause spontaneous combustion. With Quality, this is unlikely; there is usually not enough passion for improvement around. The Quality leader will almost certainly have to create the conditions for ignition. He not only has to make the sparks but ensure they catch light. Once alight, he has to keep pouring in the fuel until it has spread everywhere - across the whole organisation. He must then fan the flames continually, otherwise it can die out as quickly as it started. At a critical point , the intensity is such that a fire storm can develop where the fire feeds itself. This is what the Quality leader is striving for...when Quality engulfs everyone and transforms from a process into a revolution .

Revolutions need leaders; the leader generates the energy. Behind every example of a transformed business there is a dominant figure who has strong ideas on what the business is about and how it should be run. These leaders may be founders or owners such as Anita Roddick of The Body Shop or Akio Morita of Sony, but more often they are business managers, like Mike Nash of L&K: Rexona, hired to do the job. Mike is a Unilever-trained manager with experience gained from running Unilever businesses around the world. Unilever did not tell Mike to start his revolution – in fact, at the time, much of management above him were highly sceptical – he did it from his own conviction. The origins of a successful Quality revolution – whether it is in a small workshop, across a hotel chain or throughout a massive multinational – can usually be traced to the conviction and inspiration of one person.

The revolutionary leader is convinced that Quality is what his business needs. He may have a lot of evidence through having experienced it elsewhere or his conviction may be pure faith. But he believes it and he is prepared to take the lead. The leader does not succeed alone, of course. An individual pursuing a solitary route is merely a crank. To create change, others in the group have to be receptive to the new thinking. The leader provides the inspiration but he speaks and acts what others think is right too. He becomes the champion for a shared cause. Champions inspire other champions.

Tony Gilroy is such a champion. He is the managing director of the Perkins Engines group of companies headquartered in Peterborough. Perkins Engines are a world leader in small to medium diesel engines with a fine reputation with customers around the world, who are themselves highly reputable companies such as JCB or Komatsu. Perkins already had an enviable quality assurance process and advanced marketing and manufacturing systems. But Tony Gilroy wanted further improvement. Before he embarked on a major Quality process, he had re-shaped the four semi-autonomous business units into limited companies in order to stimulate change and to move closer to customers in different applications of Perkins' technologies. This allowed sharper strategic focus. Building on this, the Quality process was aimed to vitalise what was a high-standard but fairly traditional business coping with a deep recession.

Tony was no beginner with Quality; previously, he had successfully transformed the fortunes of Land Rover, as managing director. He knew enough about organisational change to understand the enormous resistance and the need to build up the forces for change, steadily but irresistibly. Tony was very clear about what he wanted at Perkins. He did not believe the order of competitiveness needed in the 1990s and beyond could be achieved by techniques alone. He didn't want just short-term one-off hits on the organisation that maybe reduced some cycle times and lowered some returns from customers or internal product defects. He wanted to change the way everything was done, so that all of these objectives and more were realised on a continual basis. In other words he wanted a Quality revolution that reached all management and all staff. He knew that to do this he would have to engage the interest and direct participation of the 5,000 people working in the business.

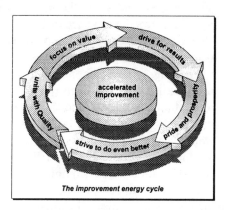

The improvement energy cycle

To do this, Tony carefully built up the energy and kept it high over the next two years. His build-up was planned; he was seeking to reach not only all the people but in a way which would unleash that 'firestorm' of improvement throughout the business. He followed a model which integrates the main improvement drivers into a cycle of accelerated improvement. This improvement energy cycle applies to small units or workteams on short cycles or large complex organisations like Perkins on longer timeframes.

Unite behind Quality

The first energy-building step is to involve people in making the case for Quality. Change requires dissatisfaction and if people are comfortable and complacent, then the leader has to stir things up. It is not too difficult to make the case: the Quality gaps will be all too evident if one bothers to find out. Many companies have no time for this; their preference is for action, so they go straight into training and projects. This is a critical omission; they miss not only good data for guiding improvement but, crucially, the best opportunity to prepare people for change. A person whose view has been sought, who has heard what the customers are saying, who has seen how his work compares to the competition, who can see how it will affect his job, is more likely to be in tune with the changes needed than one who is just told to report for a project meeting tomorrow.

At Perkins, Tony Gilroy spent many months building this foundation for change. Surveys were commissioned inside and outside the company to pinpoint the gaps and show the need for improvement. Discussion groups were formed to air views and provoke debate. Workshops to thrash out direction and draw people in. Communications to inform everyone about what was going on. All of this was before any training or any technique was introduced. Tony was priming the pump, building up the energy level ready for action. The feeling he built up at manager level (and then again with staff at a later stage) was something like this: 'this affects me'...'we need to improve in a big way'...'I am expected to improve'...'I am going to have the freedom to improve what I do'...'I will be given help and support to do it properly.' Such an environment is far from easy to create and certainly takes time to achieve but, if carefully handled, a point will be reached when the energy level rises, frustration with current systems boils up, calls for action are made. The organisation has begun to unite behind Quality.

At this point at Perkins, Tony and his team were ready with a plan – an implementation process, well-prepared and ready to roll. Workshops brought senior management together to set improvement goals. Training followed, not in Quality principles but in the practice of making improvement. Managers in these training sessions literally practised making improvements in a disciplined way, then went back to do it for real. Some broad measurements were fixed to give guidance. Key managers made themselves visible, seeking out opportunities to champion the cause. The pace was high to keep the energy level up. The emphasis at this stage was involvement and direction – bringing people, managers first, into the Quality process. The workshops involved managers in setting the direction and the targets; the training (which had been customised in advance using examples drawn from the earlier surveys and analyses) let them share the ways of making improvement. The process rolled on – it was now down to managers to start both improvement in their area and the involvement of their own people.

Turning the power on

Although this uniting stage is aimed to bind people into the Quality process, it would be wrong to see it as a passive or soft phase. Throughout, the leader will have to balance demands for more progress from the enthusiasts (and probably his own boss, who may be worrying about the investment return) with the need to capture the unmoved. As the leader senses that people are coming along, he will need to turn the power on and keep it on. At Perkins, Tony Gilroy was implementing a top-down process, in order to ensure that the commitment to improvement could be sustained. He wanted ownership of the process to be with local management and he wanted his managers to be ready to support the staff when it was their turn. This is a great strength of a top-down process; the disadvantage is that it can take an eternity to work through difficult managers to reach the staff. Tony's plan to build ownership started with workshops for the group executive committee and then went onto the business unit management teams. He wanted to see some pace in this and the plan called for 11 days of committed time from each executive before Christmas 1990. It was already October and they understandably requested more time – they had full diaries and it was a busy time of year. Tension built up immediately but Tony was unrelenting and 11 days were found and achieved.

At the end of this stage, the executive committee were elated – through the Quality process, they had new common goals, a new language to share improvement technology and stronger relationships. They had lost no business by forcing in the 11 days – everything still got done. Their energy to take the process down into their own businesses was very high. If Tony as their leader had bowed to the pressure, they would not have felt so strongly about their achievement. In addition, as Quality role model, he displayed a style to his team which they were expected to replicate in their units. Tony sensed when to step up the energy level and power through.

Energy barriers

Not everyone wants to unite...behind Quality or anything else which implies change. Many people will feel they have a vested interest in the status quo, misguided though that may be. As one energy-sapping hurdle is surmounted, another looms just ahead. In the early days of a top-down process, the most common hurdles are attitudinal and emanate from senior management. Managers in established businesses play games and Quality quickly comes into the games arena. Political points are scored as managers manoeuvre for position in this new match. But this should not trouble the leader unduly; he not only has the best cards but can set the rules too. The only danger is diversion. Even at senior levels, the normal distribution of enthusiasts, opposers and unmoved will apply. The leader uses his enthusiasts to help persuade as many unmoved as possible but sidesteps the outright opponents rather than be diverted by them. The aim is to reach the critical area: the middle level of the organisation.

In larger companies with plenty of historical evolution, a whole layer has been created of managers whose existence is based on the inefficiencies and imprecisions of the business. A high degree of management muddle operates here with much fixing, chasing and correcting.

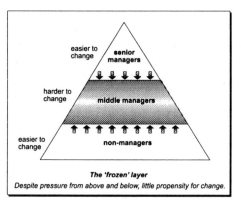

The 'frozen' layer
Despite pressure from above and below, little propensity for change.

In contrast to non-management levels, where Quality is a very natural concept, fitting well with the work people do, middle managers can find Quality quite alien and sometimes very threatening. Their roles can be so ambiguous and reactive that it is hard to pin down any processes and harder still for them to work out what to improve. The threat is real enough, for as we will see in later chapters, much of the work done by middle managers is not required in a Quality organisation and can be eliminated or absorbed into the jobs of people doing the real work. In a Quality process, everybody has to change, but perhaps middle managers have to change more than others.

Middle and junior managers make up the bulk of the great unmoved and the Quality leader will have to move them his way. It is a mistake to bypass this level because of the influence, positive or negative, which they exert on non-management levels. They are individuals too and should be treated as such. Persuasion is by far the most successful approach. Persuasion is itself a personal issue and the leader will need to appeal to a range of interests in overcoming apathy and concern at this level.

Persuasive messages for the unmoved manager:

- *Self-interest: 'Quality can reduce the hassle in my job and help me deliver my short-term targets'*
- *Progression: 'Getting involved with Quality is the way to get on'*
- *Development: 'This could be an opportunity for me'*
- *Interest: 'We've never done anything like this before'*
- *Peer-pressure: 'The team is keen to do this'*
- *Competition: 'We've got to do better than they do'*
- *Concern: 'I'd better get into this before I'm left behind'*
- *Example: 'If the boss is doing it, then so shall I'*
- *Ownership: 'I can do this my way'*
- *Inevitability: 'It's going to happen anyway, so I might as well join in'.*

Natural opposition to change is only one of many other energy sappers...the capability of a mature organisation to soak up improvement energy and frustrate progress at times can seem limitless. The Quality leader should be constantly on the look-out for these enemies of a Quality process which can very effectively choke up the improvement activity even with committed people. Potential energy sappers should be attacked as soon as they are identified; if they are allowed to remain they may prevent the Quality process from delivering results and deflate the energy of the whole improvement mission.

The big energy sappers

Bureaucracy ... is a dead weight on any improvement process. All organisations seem to have redundant and cumbersome procedures around the place, which grow like weeds unless they are cut out.

Waste ... is anything the customer isn't going to be interested in. It is everywhere, often hidden, often disguised as work. Waste clutters and clings; slowing, confusing and demotivating people.

False customers ... create waste in big piles by wrongly directing effort to activities which the customer does not value. Managers are the main culprits.

Ambiguity ... the middle management muddle enveloping organisational layers, encouraging fire-fighting, duplication, chasing and miscommunication.

False boundaries ... the valueless artificial boxes built for ego defences which confine creativity and limit cooperative action.

Fear ... of questioning, of speaking-out, of stepping out of line. Such fear inhibits initiative, stifles innovation and buries problems.

Focus on Value

 Value is an important concept in Quality. Value is the customer's judgement of the worth of our service. If the customer, external or internal, values what we have done, then our work has been worthwhile and, ultimately, we will be rewarded for it. As the Quality leader senses a good response to the need for and understanding of large-scale improvement, then he needs to focus this response. Are all of us giving value? This question is as strong a focus – and challenge – as there is. It applies to every individual and every team, every process and every department...and the whole organisation too.

After about nine months of Perkins' Quality implementation, it was becoming evident that this was something different. Many managers were now actively involved – in workshops, training or taking their own improvement action. For the managers at Perkins, it was clear the company was moving down an irreversible direction led by Tony Gilroy. Some of the unmoved were beginning to move. For them, Quality was already something not only for the company but for themselves too. But many were still locked into the systems and behaviours they had grown up with. The pressure to change was less than the pressure to conform to well-learned patterns. Mike Nash, at L&K: Rexona used to say at every opportunity: 'this train is going North.' His message was unequivocal: a direct challenge for his remaining unmoved to get on board. The train was going one way only; this was not a loose alliance of independent minds, but a coordinated directed movement and only paying passengers were wanted. At Perkins, a much larger organisation with more tradition, the train was pointing in the right direction but moving very slowly. Tony had created a base for change, using a key improvement driver, leadership, to mobilise and unite the organisation, ready for the major changes ahead. The improvement energy was building up; he was now ready to use it...and turn the power up further. The objectives now were to avoid dissipating the energy on fruitless activity, whilst stirring up the remainder of the unmoved. Both aims were addressed by focusing on value. Using two of the major Quality drivers, customers and processes, Tony brought this focus home to all managers, regardless of position.

Managing for customers

One of the strongest drivers for improvement is the customer – neglected over previous decades, now reinstated with authority. The customer can be a powerful arbiter. For instance, I should always have a customer for every work activity I do. My customer may not want to pay for what I am doing now – if he or she only knew – or might prefer me to use my time on something else. But I do not know that because I have not asked. To know I am giving value, I need to find out directly from the customer, for if I am not giving value, I am creating waste. This is the challenge the Quality leader seeks to put to everyone in the organisation. The customer becomes the focus forcing us to question our service continually – is this what the customer wants? – not in a vague way, but precisely, for every transaction and every activity.

Paradoxically, the strength of customer attention really focuses on activities well away from the sharp end where money changes hands. For instance, if I work deep in the data processing section of a bank, I may never have personal contact with the account holder but if I make an error on a transaction on his account, he might be very upset indeed. So the external customer, the consumer of the service or the user of the product, must become a reality to me. I must understand his requirements and adapt my work accordingly; in that way I am focusing on providing value for that customer.

Customer-focus can be taken much further. Continuing the example of the back-room of the bank, I will have customers inside the bank too – the branch staff for instance – who are the users of the service I provide. Kodak were one of the pioneers of this internal customer concept in the early eighties. At this time, they were suffering from the onslaught of Fuji breaking into the US market and they knew they had to be radical to compete. Like all large businesses, service functions at Kodak had grown to feed and support the main business; relative to those at Fuji, they had grown too large. Kodak's solution was to demand that these service departments prove they were competitive with external suppliers of services. The result, after a year of transition, was precise customer/supplier agreements, satisfied internal customers, more efficient departments and, to everyone's surprise, highly motivated service staff. No one had foreseen that the staff in these remote departments would respond to the challenge and, in particular, appreciate their work being directly challenged – in this way it was valued, not taken for granted or ignored.

The customer concept is a most powerful way of breaking out of organisational boxes. There are no exceptions – we all have customers. For every activity, we should identify the customer – a real person who we are working for. The customers of a workteam are the next receivers of the product or service, who in turn have their customers and so on through to the external customer. With practice and persistence, the environment of even a large company can be transformed into an internal market of customers and suppliers. Most significantly the manager's role is turned 180°. The primary customers of a manager become his team. At Toyota today, the departmental manager has little say in what his assembly teams do – they do not need him for instructions. Instead they summon him from time to time with requests to talk to a supplier about a component or to check out an idea with another section, whilst they carry on working. He is their representative, as well as their coach and mentor.

The first application of an internal customer focus at Perkins was much less radical than this. Quite early on, it became evident that the split into business units was working a little too well – the units were becoming less attentive to their internal commitments because of their concentration on building business. External customers complained in the survey that they sometimes had to bring the different parties in Perkins together and act as mediator in order to get what they wanted. This was addressed head on with customer/supplier agreement workshops facilitated using a 'fishbowl' technique. This allowed each business unit head to say what he wanted from the others and hear what they wanted from him. The structure of the workshop forced each person to listen to the others and systematically flushed out the important needs. The end result was unambiguous commitment to deliver to each other – contracts between business partners – which Tony made clear he expected to be upheld. They were, and the business units gained enormously in confidence from not having to worry about whether their colleagues might let them down. As a result, service between them improved noticeably to the satisfaction of external customers as well as themselves.

Managing processes

There is one major problem with an out-and-out customer-service environment. There is no counterbalance to prevent oversupply. Supplying a customer with more than is expected can give an important competitive advantage, provided this is the strategic intent and can be replicated consistently and profitably. If not, it is merely excess, waste and a possible irritation to the customer. Multiply this oversupply across the internal market of an organisation and we can have serious inefficiency. The counter to this is the next major Quality driver: the concept of process and the management and improvement of business processes.

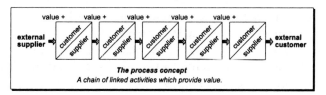

The process concept
A chain of linked activities which provide value.

A process is the stream of activities which are linked together to supply a service. A car assembly line is a process; invoicing or billing is a process; product development is a process; advertising is a process; bank lending is a process. Business is made up of processes from large ones to small local ones. Indeed everything we do is part of a process; no one works in total isolation, and our local process will link in with others to make up a major business process.

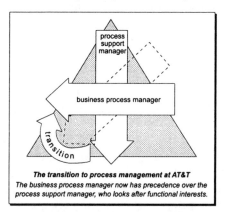

The transition to process management at AT&T
The business process manager now has precedence over the process support manager, who looks after functional interests.

Of course, there is nothing new in this concept, as in most of the Quality disciplines; it is the application which makes the big difference. With Quality, business processes are made much more visible and tangible – people at all levels are made aware of their interdependence with others in their process – and responsibilities for improving the processes are laid down. Thus today within many divisions of AT&T, IBM or Unilever, process responsibility is becoming superior to function responsibility in the eyes of senior managers. AT&T have two categories of manager: process manager and process support manager, where the process support manager looks after the functional expertise – purchasing, marketing, development – but only to ensure a first-class service for the process managers.

The process concept forces people to think beyond their immediate activities. Some companies, NCR, for example, have process maps on every corridor wall, displaying that the distribution department, say, has much wider involvement than its label suggests. But the power of process really comes with the improvement challenge. Why do we send this product from section A through B, C, D then back to A? Why not A to E directly? Why does this form need five signatures from dispersed departments? Processes which have evolved over time are full of duplications, redundant steps, long and tortuous routes, unnecessary checks, long pauses, ambiguous decisions. They were never designed that way...they just grew. Looking at them anew with the challenge of process can offer enormous benefits. IBM Japan applied process improvement to their software release procedure and brought the time to release down by 80 per cent with better reliability, by cutting out steps and reassigning responsibilities. Hewlett Packard released $150 million tied up in the accounts-receivable process and a staggering $450 million tied up in work-in-progress in their manufacturing process. Honda has reduced its product development cycle from seven years to three. All this was achieved from applying a process focus towards providing value more directly and eliminating all the wasted time and cost.

Above all these results, though, it is the way in which process and customer focus can winkle people out of their departmental boundaries to exist in a real and demanding environment that continues the Quality transformation. Eventually the biggest and toughest boundary of all is broken through – the company itself. Processes do not end at the company walls but go right back to the suppliers' supplier and forward all the way to the consumer or end-user. Quality companies find it much easier to set up single sourcing lines; to have partnership relationships with suppliers, dealers and agents; to establish joint ventures; to have work teams permanently at customer premises; to share new product concepts and transfer information, technology and people. They can do this because their focus on customers and processes shows them the value which will come from it.

Breaking out of the boxes

 Organisations like the status quo. They prefer things as they are and where they are. The bigger the organisation, the more the tendency to lock things into place. People build boxes around themselves – 'my department', 'my job', 'my customer' – and defend their patch vigorously. Breaking out of this mode requires enormous energy. A determined leader can achieve much through force of personality – acting as a missionary to inspire change. But the attraction of 'business as usual' is very often stronger than the most zealous missionary. To break people out of their boxes, the leader needs the combined power of these two main improvement drivers – customers and processes. The concept of a prescribed customer for everything and a defined process for everything demands new thinking and ultimately new practice. These drivers are potent on their own but used in tandem, they can be very confronting. The challenge of having to supply to your customer's needs rather than your own is a strong one. It immediately demands 'outside of the box' thinking and managing. The extra challenge of then having to make the process of supplying the customer as effective as possible is doubly so. To achieve an efficient, low-waste, flexible process means managing upstream as well as down.

The two drivers together also protect against excess; good process analysis, for example, shows up excessive service to the customer, which is wasteful. Conversely, overoptimisation of a process might squeeze out value to the customer and this will show up through sharp focus on the customer. But above all, the challenge to the status quo, to the box-mentality and to business as usual can be direct and unequivocal. Managerial misbehaviours, such as empire building or political in-fighting, can lose much of their appeal when there is more direct benefit to gain from lean and cooperative resourcing.

One UK bank which successfully applied this dual focus on value is the Co-operative Bank. There, managing director Terry Thomas and his senior management team changed track in the middle of installing a Quality process as a result of this strong focus on value. Terry had already begun to unite the 5,000-strong organisation with Quality and had undertaken a comprehensive survey of Quality inside and outside. The findings showed that Bank customers rated the counter service at branches highly in comparison to competitors. But Terry knew that some of his financial ratios were being beaten by others, particularly the new entrants to the market – the best of the building societies. The internal survey gave another pointer to where attention was needed: many staff felt they were not receiving the best service from other departments inside the bank. An analysis of waste confirmed that much inefficiency was built in to the back-room processes. This data, pulled together, convinced Terry and his team that the original plan to concentrate Quality attention at the front-end first, with service enhancement at the branches as most of the banks were doing at the time, would not lead to competitive advantage. Rather the focus shifted to the huge data processing areas and a phased programme of Quality action was introduced starting in the processing centres and working down the process chains to the branches. All of this was supported by a major top-down Quality process for all managers, regardless of location.

The resulting changes in attitude and behaviour over a three-year period, enabled Terry to follow through with structural changes: branches became customer contact points, not administrative areas; regional hierarchies were abandoned. The focus on value along each process right through to the external customer led to a leaner more responsive operation. Terry's team were able to adapt more rapidly than many rivals to market changes, creating three successive Quality edges: telephone banking (quickly becoming UK leader); a Gold card for life; and ethical banking. Without the focus on value and without the changes brought about through the Quality process, they may not have been able to take these leads.

Drive for results

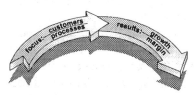

A strong customer focus helps us to give customers what they want and thus retain our existing customers and attract new ones (provided we do this better than the competition). A strong process focus should ensure we do this at an attractive margin, by eliminating low-value or wasteful activities. Thus Quality at its best can deliver growth and profit. But the interdependence of customer and process orientation is critical for this. We can identify a Quality edge from better customer focus but to deliver it we will need better processes. We can aim for a higher margin as a result of process efficiencies but will only realise it when we have correctly identified the customer value. As with all other steps in building improvement energy, growth and margin improvement will not happen naturally and easily. The link between the focus on value and these results has to be managed explicitly. The Quality leader has to drive for results.

Perkins' managers used these two Quality drivers more and more as their confidence in the Quality process developed. Evaluating external and internal customers' requirements became a regular part of the job, as did seeking feedback from customers on performance against those requirements. Processes were analysed and many improvements implemented simply as a result of seeing what actually happened. In one example, an overhead conveyor holding 300 engines was eliminated, reducing the engine transfer time from one hour to two minutes and saving £650,000 per year in inventory and maintenance costs. Overall, engine lead time was reduced from 14 weeks to four, generating enormous benefits for the company and for customers. Underscoring this big achievement were many smaller local gains, linked together by the process thinking and the Quality process overall.

These improvement successes were in themselves a vital ingredient in the change process at Perkins. We all know that success breeds success and as people of all levels were introduced to the Quality process they could quickly be involved in successful improvement themselves. This encouraged more people to join in. The training input was maintained at a high energy level to keep up the enthusiasm as hundreds of people were taken through it. The trainers were drawn from all levels of the company including the office and the shop floor. By this time, the Quality process had been spread throughout all levels and all functions. As a result, shop floor Quality facilitators quite often trained managers – very successfully. Every person in the company went through the training led by these facilitators.

The concept of value works well at the small team level where people can learn what is giving value and what is merely wasted energy. As soon as non-management teams were trained at Perkins, they were off making value improvements. One team discovered that the swarf (very small waste cuttings from machining) level on cylinder blocks exceeded the specification. No one had thought to measure it before. Having traced the cause back to the block supplier, the team worked directly with the operators there to reduce the level from 1248 mg to 118 mg, well within specification. The value of this?...prevention of a possible engine failure in the field, an event which not only costs £2,500 for a refit but is very damaging to reputation. Another team listened to customers who specified an engine which was sourced from Japan and which was taking too long to deliver. They devised a new ordering and supply process with the supplier and took one month out of the process.

In another example, a shop floor team analysed a customer problem and pinned down a less than robust component. This component was specially designed for Perkins. The team found a stronger substitute off-the-shelf thus winning a double gain of better reliability and saving £17,000 per year. Previously no one had either the inclination to dig out the problem nor the empowerment to do something about it.

Within months of the training events, everything that might not be giving value was being challenged. The procedure for design changes, for instance, had grown with the company and, when one team decided to analyse it, they found a change could take 15 months and required ten signatures. This elaborate and ponderous process (one manager had signed one design change request three times through moving jobs faster than the document's progress!) was simplified and speeded up without losing any of the discipline of good documentation. Only two signatures proved necessary and value-adding.

This disciplined, enthusiastic attack on the old and accepted way of doing things emerged from the inspiration created by the training events coupled with the different environment that management was beginning to create as a result of their own prior exposure to Quality practice and behaviours. The workteams responded to the enthusiasm and energy of the key managers who were spearheading the process, following Tony Gilroy's example. Once they had made real improvements by working together and applying the disciplines they had learned, they were elated. Their own energy level shot up and this, in turn, encouraged others. The value element plays a crucial role here, not only in benefits to the company but in the positive feeling which providing value encourages.

Spreading out

 It is at this stage that the Quality leader is seeking to amplify the energy level by expanding the improvement activity across the whole organisation. By this time, management is prepared and ready to sustain the response from the workforce in a positive manner. The aim is not to light the Quality fire and let it

burn wherever it catches hold, but to harness the energy towards an intense firestorm of improvements. This means a lot of guiding, coaching and encouraging, but also a lot of discipline and organisation too. Discipline is one of the key Quality drivers which is often underutilised. Quality disciplines provide people with sound and effective ways of making improvement. It is very common to see teams make breakthroughs in old problems that could not be resolved before, simply through the combination of two Quality drivers – energy and discipline. The energy gives the motivation; discipline provides the route. Discipline also helps direct improvement towards the main business goals. Teams and individuals at all levels can be very arbitrary about what to focus their energy on, if left to their own devices. The Quality process should channel improvement activity to what matters most for the business.

To this end, the improvement activity, which should be intensive by this stage, should be operating on different but interrelated levels. For instance, at Perkins, whilst all the team activity was under way (some 200 Quality projects by the end of 1991), a small number of people concentrated on the major processes – particularly the manufacturing supply chain. In this way, much of the improvement activity has contributed to what would make a big difference to customers and the business. The 70 per cent compression of lead time achieved for most of the product lines allows much more precise and early delivery to customers, huge savings of inventory and a much more flexible and robust production process. This is the overall business value which can be accumulated from intensive improvement activity which is well coordinated and managed.

Pride and prosperity

 There is much evidence today to demonstrate the link between Quality, value, growth and profitability. The PIMS database demonstrates a strong link between relative perceived quality and relative market share. That is, those companies who display Quality grow faster than others; they also have higher profitability, as the same PIMS data shows. A recent study on Baldrige finalists confirms this; despite a recessionary period in 1988/9, the finalists of those years achieved measured improvements in market share, profitability, reliability, customer satisfaction and many other parameters.

Market share, possibly the best test of value in the long run and the hardest to influence, went up by an average of 13.7 per cent in these companies. Quality has paid off for them.

In Japan, studies on Deming Prize winners have shown similar patterns. No Deming Prize winner has had a serious financial problem in the 30-year history of the award. Contrast this with a few of the companies reported in *In Search of Excellence* or the British equivalent, *The Winning Streak,* whose performance has diminished. In general, the 'excellent' performers who have not sustained top performances – STC, Saatchi & Saatchi and MFI, for example – have not had a Quality philosophy to guide them, unlike those such as Marks & Spencer, 3M or Hewlett Packard, who have and have gone from strength to strength. These perennially successful businesses have achieved a threshold of performance which itself inspires them to do more. They have generated both prosperity and pride.

Prosperity for the whole business is the long-term goal of most organisations and is the prospect which keeps up the determination of many Quality leaders through difficult times. Higher revenues means more funds for development, for newer technologies, for a better working environment, for more training – all helping fuel further improvement and continued success. There may even be occasion to enjoy the fruits of success through higher personal reward. But for most, the factor which spurs people on to ever greater improvement is pride.

Pride was one of those ingredients discarded in the mass production era. Most people want to work for a good company – one they can take pride in. Staff at Marks & Spencer are proud to say 'I work for Marks & Spencer' rather than 'I am a shop assistant'. Pride can apply at all levels and is dynamic, not static. During a factory visit of businessmen to Elida Gibbs in Leeds, UK, one lady operator exclaimed 'I love this line', referring with emotion to the toothpaste-filling line which she and her colleagues had improved through a Quality process.

Pride, like prosperity, is directly linked to value. Unless we know someone else values our work, it is very hard to feel proud of it. So as the contact with internal customers increases, as we try harder to give these customers precisely what they want, as the feedback tells us we are getting it right...then we begin to take pride in what we are doing. Quality at this point becomes a personal thing – no longer a programme or a crusade from above, but something for *me*.

Releasing the pride

Vera Stewart tells this story about her conversion to the Quality movement at Pacific Bell in San Francisco:

'I've been with PacBell for sixteen years and through the years I've been through many processes and many programmes. So when TQ came along I thought another one of those, huh! At the time I was working in cash management and responsible for writing out all the cash statements. I'd just been given responsibility for North and South Carolina – which doubled my work load. It was taking me three hours to write the statements and I thought if only I had a typewriter I could do it in one hour. So I asked my supervisor...he said "I'll look into it"...nothing happened. Then I got a new supervisor. I asked the same...again nothing happened. So they asked me to go to this Total Quality meeting. I waited for questions and then said: "Does this mean you're gonna listen to me this time and give me a typewriter?" Within a week I got a typewriter. It helps me and therefore the customer, the reps and the engineering office. TQ is like having a door opened. I decided if they're gonna listen to me, I've got some real neat ideas...and that's why I've joined a TQ team.'

Seven thousand miles away at a Legal & General office in Brighton, a team manning the help-line to give information and support to thousands of financial advisers, found out by asking their customers that a source of irritation was the time they were kept on hold when calling in. The team measured the times and found calls held during a day were indeed high. Their solution was very simple: put a light on each desk which showed a caller was waiting. Management, true to form, was very dubious about this gimmicky idea, but had learned enough to make them bite their tongues and let the team carry on. Within a day of installing the system (at very low cost) the number of calls held dropped from 500 to three.

A Quality revolution in an organisation should lead to numerous such examples of empowerment every day. Teams and individuals should have the freedom to make improvements without fuss; to put something right when they see it is wrong and to probe opportunities to do better, there and then as they carry out their work. But empowerment does not mean democracy. The workteams still have their basic work to do – probably even more of it as their value is better recognised. As well, they must use the improvement disciplines which they will have been taught. As a Renault manager said after much experimentation with different team approaches: 'You cannot afford too much democracy.' Hasty, unverified, overstated, uncoordinated, unreported improvements can be worse than none at all because they may disrupt a stable process (in a non-Quality business most managers spend their lives fiddling with and disrupting processes, thinking they are fixing things).

Empowerment and discipline fit together under Quality. As workteams become more self-managed, they need more data from their customers and suppliers, they need to set measurements and standards to guide their actions and they need rigour in the way they conduct improvement. The fitters supporting the toothpaste line at Elida Gibbs did not wait to be asked to start a project which reduced changeover time from five days to three-and-a-half hours (they knew it fitted one of the company's published improvement goals to reduce cycle time by 50 per cent). But they did need to register the project, record the formal PDCA (plan, do, check, act) steps and report progress. This discipline also allows recognition, another vital ingredient for empowerment (and improvement in general) to be brought in play. Recognition helps the link between value and pride and is a managerial practice greatly used in a Quality company. Peer recognition is also a strong reinforcement, so visibility becomes very important. The toothpaste changeover project is displayed on a corridor storyboard at Leeds for all to see, with the pictures, names and accomplishments of the team members.

Pride and prosperity are the end product of managing the energy in a Quality process effectively. The result is that a person within the organisation feels part of something different, something which he is contributing to and which he feels part of. It can be startlingly different to before. One good example of this is at NUMMI in California, where Toyota and General Motors established a joint venture in 1982. The NUMMI operation was an existing GM plant at Freemont, where GM opened a factory in 1962 as the world state-of-the-art; 6,500 people were employed there, at a time when domestic car manufacturers accounted for 95 per cent of the market. Twenty years later GM closed the plant. By that time, Freemont was troubled with labour-management wars, wildcat strikes and frequent stoppages. The state-of-the-art had gone badly wrong. Absenteeism was 25 per cent plus, thousands of grievances were lodged, productivity was low, product quality poor. By 1982, Japanese and European imports had also made a big dent in the market. No wonder GM closed it down – it was their worst plant. It opened up again because Toyota wanted to build in the USA and GM wanted to learn from them. The deal was that Toyota would take over the management of the place. Everyone was re-hired, including the union organisers. The only difference was 30 Toyota managers from Nagoya bringing the Toyota way of managing. Rick Holdsworth, once a union organiser, now a team member at NUMMI, gives his perspective of the change that then occurred:

'The big difference between NUMMI and the General Motors system – the old American system – is four key words...what do you think? Those words involve the individual...they recognise the fact that the grunt on the line is the expert, he's the pro, he's the guy who knows the job. In the old system he was told what to do, when to do it and how to do it...he was a non-thinking piece of machinery. NUMMI recognises the fact that we need each other...we need upper management and we need the grunts on the line, so the grunts are involved. Everything we do is done together. The old system was "it wasn't my fault it was his"...but now we sit down together and solve the problem as a team. Here they recognised us as intelligent human beings, our knowledge of the job is appreciated and we are treated with respect and trust...so we reciprocate. Honesty is important...if I say we're equal, we're the same, but you can't park next to me, you can't eat in the same cafeteria as me and we're not going to the same bathroom, then we've already set up a difference and that's a problem.

'Communication and honesty works. We all want a certain form of recognition and a certain form of power. The power we all have is the ability not only to pull the line, but the ability to do our job the best way possible.

'And it is going to continue to improve. We have one Japanese word here, *kaizen*, which means continual improvement and we continually improve by education and knowledge. At this plant they will teach you, send you to class...they have classes for everything...you are taught about a new model even before they run it. There are classes for team leaders, group leaders' classes...it's a continual teaching process. Whether you're a team leader or a group leader, you are still a teacher. To teach you have to know your subject, so you are continually learning and studying at home or wherever. The difference is that we're friends and that's amazing...we respect each other.

'Before when I saw someone in a Chevrolet, I thought you deserve that damn thing. Now, when I see a Nova, I take out my business card – yes, grunts with business cards – and I tuck it behind the windshield wiper with a note saying "I helped build this car". That's what I feel about what we do here and how we do it.'

Within two years, the NUMMI plant was outperforming all other GM plants. A short while later, productivity and quality levels were comparable with Toyota City in Nagoya. The plant enjoyed prosperity, which continues today. The workforce enjoyed pride. The transformation was truly revolutionary.

Keeping the power on

Such transformations are not without pain. Organisations do not roll over and allow the new order in – they fight back. At Perkins, everything did not go as smoothly and effortlessly as it sounds. Energy-sapping resistances and barriers lurk all over an organisation and it is at this point, when the process is being taken seriously, that more begin to show. At Perkins, just when everything seemed to be building up well, there was a strike. The strike, which involved blue- and white-collar unions, was a test of management's resolve to achieve changes in day to day practices.

At such difficult times, the Quality leader needs to do one major thing: carry on, with even more determination. He needs to think whether all the key Quality drivers are being used fully to counter the resistances and energy sappers. Leadership...are we visible enough? Are we being consistent? Strategy...is it clear what we expect people to do? Are we getting the messages through? Customers...is the voice of the customer being heard? Are internal customers feeding back to their suppliers? People...have we got enough people involved...are they sufficiently empowered? Disciplines...are Quality disciplines being applied? Are appropriate tools and techniques being deployed? With these drivers properly orchestrated, with no let-up on the energy, the Quality leader can overcome these barriers. But he cannot relax. This stage of intensive improvement activity is not the time to ease off: rather the accelerator pedal should stay flat on the floor.

At Perkins, the dispute was handled sensitively but firmly. It was allowed to have little impact on the Quality process. At the time, it seemed that the seriousness of the impasse would destroy all the good uniting work which had been achieved. People talked about it taking decades to recover. Six months later, it was forgotten: people, operators, managers, office staff, were too busy improving the business. The energy of improvement generated by Tony Gilroy and his team had overwhelmed the barriers.

Striving for more

At Perkins Engines in June 1992, the first feelings of pride and prosperity were beginning to form. Many people were involved in Quality projects; many more were involved in improvement activity of one form or another. More value was being generated inside the business to internal customers. Inventory turned over at up to 25 times per year on some lines which previously managed four. Millions of pounds worth of savings flowed as a result of process enhancements. Above all, greater value to external customers enabled Perkins to increase its customer base by 25 per cent despite a deep recession. A huge new contract for Caterpillar will bring in $1 billion of business over ten years...won through the renewed Perkins Quality edge.

Tony Gilroy could feel very satisfied with all this – but he didn't, of course. Far from it. Like many other Quality leaders, Tony knows that the more you improve, the more improvement you can see is needed. To find out what more he needed to do, Tony commissioned a Quality maturity review to draw out weaknesses and areas for further development. He already has a world-leading business; his sights are set at nothing less than world-class in all Perkins activities. The energy for improvement at Perkins remains very high. The challenge likewise. There is no likelihood that Tony and his colleagues will ever feel content. Their Quality revolution is forever.

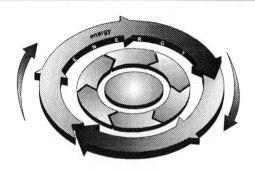

SUMMARY

Have you got enough energy for Quality?

1. **Are you using and balancing all the Quality drivers** – *strategy, leadership, customers, processes, people and disciplines – not just one or two?*
2. **Are you managing change explicitly and positively, rather than reacting to changes as they occur?**
3. **Has your Quality process got pace?**
4. **Are your training sessions active, practical and fun?** *Bored people won't join you.*
5. **Are you ready to power through the resistance and inertia?**
6. **Are you removing the organisational boxes, false customers, bureaucracy, ambiguity and other waste that will slow you down?**
7. **Are your communications about real things** – *customers, people, improvements – or more like rhetoric, theory, dreams or exhortation?*
8. **Are you focusing hard on value from everything and everyone?**
9. **Are you really committed?** *Is this number one priority? Are you prepared to see it through five years or more? Are you giving it time? Are you sticking your neck out?*
10. **Are you setting a high-energy example?** *Are you active, visible, involved? Are you serious about it?*

3
Strategy Focuses Energy

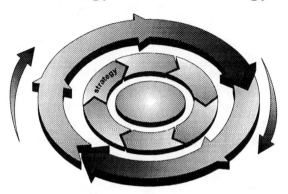

Quality can revitalise and unite an organisation...but only if it is aligned totally behind business objectives. A Quality process divorced from real business will lose its energy; the same process fully integrated into strategic business aims can help ambitions become reality. Only the very best companies master this integration of Quality and business. From the start, the Quality leader must put Quality behind business...and use business needs to stimulate Quality. Directed, measured, effective improvement will follow.

'Quality has become the way of life for most of us and will be for all of us.' Robert Galvin, chairman, Motorola

'In God we trust, otherwise please bring facts.' Roger Milliken

Quality and business integrated

Selsdon Park is a 16th-century English mansion with much history, converted in modern times into a hotel and conference centre. It was the scene of further historic moment as the venue for a Quality conference for Unilever Personal Products. Anglo-Dutch Unilever is sometimes described as a hard-nosed no-nonsense company; even holding a three-day conference on Quality was viewed as very unusual. But this was no ordinary conference. Mike Perry, main board director responsible for the Personal Products group, had brought together 150 executives from the boards of about 20 Personal

Products businesses throughout Europe and the USA (including businesses like Elida Gibbs, Chesebrough-Pond's, Pierre Robert, Calvin Klein and Elizabeth Arden). There were no speeches or presentations: for the whole of the three days, the delegates worked in groups on set tasks. They had been given papers to discuss in their own boards before the conference and they were there to thrash out and agree common practice across the group.

The companies were not beginners with Quality; most had already installed their own Total Quality programmes, some with four years of experience. A lot of effort had already been made towards compatibility and transfer of their improvement processes, without undermining the strong Unilever culture of independence for the local businesses. The conference was aimed at maximising the commonality of approach whilst leaving each company the freedom and responsibility of action.

That this was achieved was a surprise to some of the delegates, who arrived with mixed expectations about spending three days in a 'talking shop' or 'jamboree'. On the contrary, they started immediately on arrival, working through a very disciplined agenda covering half a dozen major topics. The executives discussed each topic in groups of ten, focusing on set questions in one-and-a-half hour sessions. Each group session generated output which was consolidated by the group leaders into a common statement on the selected topic. This was then desk-top-published and fed back into the groups. In this way, the conference built on its own work and a tremendous energy developed.

Over two years later, the output of the Selsdon Park conference was still seen as a major highlight and stimulus for all the companies with respect to their own improvement processes. A common purpose was agreed – what the businesses were in business to do and what they should focus on. Five stretching improvement goals were set which have been used subsequently across the whole group to drive the local improvement plans. Embryo measures were assigned to the goals with responsibility given to the companies to establish their own measures in sympathy with them. Business processes were identified, mapped and analysed. Relationships and interdependencies were thrashed out and customer/supplier agreements struck between the companies and the centre. Thorny issues of performance-related pay and appraisal were brought into line with the improvement thrust.

This outcome was not down to good fortune. The three days of activity were preceded by six months of careful preparation to ensure that common practice across the businesses could be defined and agreed. This provided a framework which guided discussion and encouraged alignment.

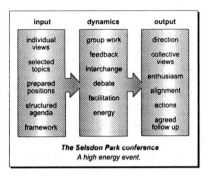

The Selsdon Park conference
A high energy event.

The Selsdon Park conference was a very significant step in building a common approach across a complex group. The participants were involved and energy was high – it was *their* conference and the outputs were theirs. Quality was clearly aligned behind business objectives: purpose and direction were set for accelerated improvement. At the same time, follow-up action was all down to the companies, as the owners of the improvement process. This they pursued with enthusiasm, having convinced themselves of the advantages of a common understanding and approach. Improvement activity moved on to a higher plane. Mike Perry had put Quality behind the Personal Products business.

Positioning Quality in business

One of the hardest tasks of the Quality leader is to position and direct Quality so that the maximum improvement gain is achieved. Most leaders know that Quality as a 'bolt-on' to the business does not work. As Robert Persig says in *Zen and the Art of Motorcycle Maintenance*: 'Quality isn't something you lay on top of subjects and objects like tinsel on a Christmas tree. Real quality must be the source of the subjects and objects, the cone from which the tree must start.' To avoid the Quality process becoming an end in itself, the leader must make business itself a key driver. This seems an obvious point but most organisations ignore it until one day they realise that Quality and business have diverged. Symptoms are a proliferation of Quality committees, burgeoning head office Quality staff, Quality bureaucracy (additional documents, procedures and controls) and non-business measures of progress such as the number of teams or the amount of people trained. Champions of the Quality process find it hard to see the excess in all this because it is all in the cause, but objectively it is as wasteful as any other unnecessary work activity and just as damaging. The main antidote to Quality proliferation is business itself; the needs of the business should dictate Quality action. Every Quality initiative must relate to the business and its improvement.

A most public (and extreme) example of the very common divergence between a Quality process and business needs is Florida Power & Light's campaign to win the Deming Prize. FPL are one of the leaders of the Quality movement in the USA and well respected for pioneering Quality in the non-manufacturing sector. After six years of a successful Quality progress, they felt that undertaking the rigorous preparation for the Deming would provide renewed impetus and not inconsiderable kudos as the first winners outside of Japan. Over the next four years, it is no exaggeration to say that the Deming Prize dominated FPL. The harsh no-compromising counselling from Japanese advisers filtered down from management and changed the atmosphere. The heavy administrative load to feed the data to the assessors began to conflict with time for customers. The Baldrige Award has been criticised for the man-hours required for the submission; the Deming Prize takes man *years*. Even some Japanese companies balk at this loading: Minolta, for example, have always refused to apply for the Deming Prize because the heavy procedures are contrary to their lean style. Their verdict is 'we would rather win customer prizes'.

FPL did win the first international Deming Prize in 1989. It was a monumental effort but the overall price was very high. Many observers view the gains as very small: 'While customers saw some improvements in the quality of its services, these were insignificant when set against the sheer scale of the firm's quality effort.' Or 'many employees seem as interested in the appearance of quality as in quality itself.' FPL were diverted from their main driving force of becoming the country's best utility. They had allowed Quality and business to separate. In the years since, they have learned this lesson. Much of the Deming Prize infrastructure has been dismantled; the central Quality staff of 85 has been cut back to six; the Quality process has become 'a lot less rigid'. After losing their way, FPL have reunited Quality with buiness.[2]

Containing Quality

The Quality leader has another dilemma with respect to positioning Quality: just how far to let it go? The leader wants the energy and enthusiasm for improvement which Quality can give but does not want expectations hyped up to a level where Quality is seen as the solution for everything. Where does business stop and Quality begin? Will the Quality thrust supersede the business strategy? When is it better just to concentrate on business and not Quality? Just what are the limits to Quality?

There are no simple answers to these questions and the leader has to make his own mind up how far to emphasise the Quality process and how much to put in it. One way of looking at it is to say that the perfect business would not need a Quality process: Quality is needed only when we fall short of perfection. Of course, any organisation is less than perfect on any number of attributes and therefore there will always be a role for an improvement process. Quality offers the philosophy which confronts any illusions about perfection and the disciplines for doing something about the shortfall. But the Quality process should not and cannot run the business – it can only improve it.

This leads into another line of argument for positioning Quality. Quality at its best is not about problem-solving or gap-filling, even though much of its early history was. Quality will not provide the best solution to a marketing weakness or a technological barrier. The solution must come from best practice within marketing or technical expertise. Quality, as the accelerator of improvement, enables that expertise to be deployed more effectively and ensures that the particular process continues to be developed for business advantage.

This distinction is particularly significant when it comes to business strategy. Mike Perry does not expect his Quality process to define Unilever's strategic intentions – he expects his business leaders to do that. But Mike very much sees Quality being a key ingredient in delivering those strategies and in testing whether a strategy has been sufficiently well-defined and well-articulated for the organisation to gear up to achieving it. Mike's counterpart at Procter & Gamble, President Edwin Artzt, has a similar perspective. He says: 'Total Quality does not guarantee that companies will produce winning strategies; winning strategies have to come from the minds of the leaders.' He goes on to say that 'Total Quality ensures the success of a winning strategy and sustains that success.'[3] In other words, use Quality to help achieve competitive advantage but don't expect it to do your thinking for you.

Quality is thus best viewed as a delivery strategy – the way to obtain the maximum contribution from the organisation, once we have set the competitive direction. This, as we shall explore in the rest of this chapter, is about practice – the way things are done. For many organisations, though, that winning strategy, the company's Quality edge, is far from clear. Equally vague in many businesses is the way the company must act in order to achieve advantage and capitalise on it. Thus Quality and business needs should be complimentary but also in dynamic tension. The Quality process should test and challenge business strategies and business expertise; business needs should control and direct the Quality process.

Common sense to common practice

Some two years before Selsdon Park, Mike Perry was discussing such issues with his number two, Mike Johnson. Mike Perry wanted to inject into the Personal Products group some of the spirit and practice of the Japanese companies he had learned from during his time running Nippon Lever, the Japanese subsidiary of Unilever. This was an old debate between them and Mike Johnson took up the corner of many pragmatic managers: 'The philosophy is all very well, but what do I do tomorrow?'

Quality is sometimes described as organised common sense. This is a fine concept until one has to extract a common view of what is sensible from even a small number of people: a whole spectrum of viewpoints will be offered, putting a lot of reliance on 'organised'. Common *practice* presents more scope, inviting further development of Mike Johnson's rhetorical question – what will we *actually* do tomorrow and what *should* we do tomorrow?

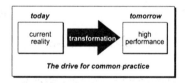

The answers to these questions are not obvious and certainly cannot be left to common sense. There is vast energy loss in many organisations because people are heading in different directions or are doing things in different ways – or even don't know where they are going or what they are doing. Assumptions are rife; clarity is rare. To guide the business successfully through an improvement revolution, the leader needs a detailed understanding of common practice today as his starting point. He then needs to formulate a picture of his end point – the common practice which he would like to see predominate in the business. As we will see, there is no point setting his sights on ordinary performance; to achieve a transformation, his future practice will need to be to the highest standards – common practice but uncommon performance.

Current reality

Leaders are not always in touch with reality. In a sense, perhaps they shouldn't be; the leader's role is to inspire and guide, not do the work for people. However, actual business is done minute to minute and that is what we must improve. At the start of a Quality process, immersion in the real practice can be very salutary; as the Arkansas politician used to say: 'Let me hit you with some reality.'

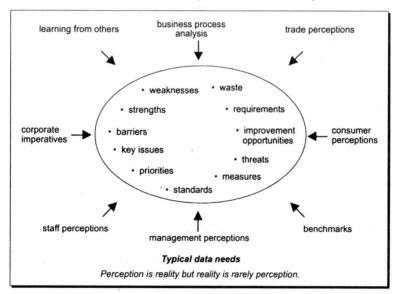

learning from others — business process analysis — trade perceptions

corporate imperatives → — consumer perceptions

- weaknesses • waste
- strengths • requirements
- barriers • improvement opportunities
- key issues
- priorities • threats
- standards • measures

staff perceptions — management perceptions — benchmarks

Typical data needs
Perception is reality but reality is rarely perception.

The Quality leader can go on a personal mission to unearth his reality – talking to customers, watching what they do, visiting his own units unannounced, buying his own services and so on. There is nothing like seeing for yourself. But this won't be enough to build a robust Quality process; to determine what we commonly do day to day – the current reality – requires thorough and subtle investigation. By and large, we will not have the data which tells us how we really work; how we treat our customers; what our customers really think of us; what they think of our competitors; what our staff think of the company, the service, the management, the work they are asked to do; whether management are pulling together or competing; how much time and energy is lost between the organisational boxes; how much activity is waste...and many more aspects of daily working life.

For Mike Johnson, the answer to his question about what to do tomorrow which most satisfied him was: find out the current reality. He encouraged each company in the Personal Products group to set up an objective survey to give them this information. These surveys revealed rich sources of data to help the board of each company understand its strengths, its weaknesses and its inconsistencies, in preparation for a Quality process. For we can only improve from our current base, and if we are unsure about that we will be unsure about the improvement process.

The Fat Busters Club

On BBC television there once was a Fat Busters Club dedicated to helping viewers slim. The programme researched slimming and found what everyone knows: that slimming is very difficult and most people end up back where they started or perhaps a little worse. But some succeed, not with single-dimension solutions but with disciplined holistic regimes based on diet and exercise. The key is replacing current habits with an improvement process which is measured, has goals and attacks day-to-day habits. The Fat Busters Club also had a computer which shows the slimmer what he or she would look like when slim - they found that such a vision is motivationally very important for maintaining the discipline.

A Quality process in business is very much like slimming: miracle techniques, like diets, don't last; improvement activities, like exercise regimes, need guidance and motivation to be beneficial; business as usual, like old eating habits, will drag us back. Like slimmers, many companies will fail. Like slimmers, to succeed we have to be determined and we have to have a vision, like the computerised leaner image, to inspire us. Perhaps businesses should have a Fat Busters Club too ... until then, it is all down to leadership.

Mediocre performance

We can expect to be disappointed with what we find. Organisational reality, even in good companies, is full of ambiguity, inefficiencies, wasted energies and frustrated people. IBM in 1980 was probably the most admired business in the world for the way it was managed. When IBM executives started their first Quality drive, they undertook a technical analysis called 'Cost of Quality' which looks at the way resources are used – people and materials – and assigns costs according to whether the work done is directly valuable, i.e. it contributes to customer purchases, or is one of the activities which have grown parasitically around the real work. IBM were astonished to find the cost of these activities was as much as 35 per cent of turnover. About half of this cost was pure waste or failure. This applied to every plant around the world and was even higher in the marketing divisions. IBM, through their Quality process, eliminated much of this excess quite early on, reducing the Cost of Quality to less than 10 per cent in many cases, saving an amazing $4 billion. But the main point is that they were unaware of the existence of this waste until they looked at the business in a fresh way.

Motorola discovered another angle to this. When they researched performance in organisations, they found that many stabilised at a performance level described statistically as 3σ. This equates to 0.27 per cent of errors continually and is pretty mediocre performance. 99.73 per cent sounds good but it is a lot of mistakes by the end of the day. Surprisingly, even those organisations which had procedures to maintain a consistent performance level and those where one would assume very high standards (such as doctor's prescriptions or payroll processing), managed only about 4σ (0.05 per cent of errors). Armed with this research, Motorola looked at themselves. They found that their organisational performance tended between 3σ and 4σ. This may seem adequate but such is the complexity of Motorola's business that the 0.05 per cent errors at different steps were being multiplied to the extent that it was very likely that a product would have a defect at the end of the line. In other words, an average error of 0.05 per cent per operation would be 100 times 0.05, or 5 per cent, after 100 operations.

IBM and other reputable businesses who copied the Motorola approach found they were not much above 3σ either...even after they had eliminated much of the waste found through the Cost of Quality studies. So businesses who thought they were pretty slick were only mediocre in true practice. Meanwhile, Motorola found that the very best (which included their Japanese competition) had raised their performance level consistently up to 5σ and even 6σ. There was nothing natural about this result: it certainly wasn't the Japanese culture that was achieving such levels, it was the end result of thirty years of disciplined and planned improvement. The competitive advantage was stark. At 6σ (three errors per million), a defective product was extremely unlikely to ever reach a customer. For customers of Sharp or Toshiba, reliability was no longer an issue, they

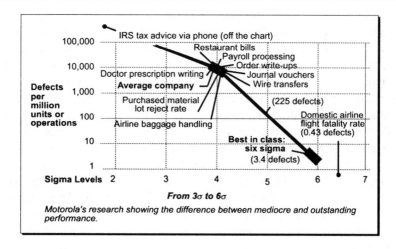

Motorola's research showing the difference between mediocre and outstanding performance.

could forget about it. This was the spur that led Motorola to their 6σ programme – the inspiration for their own spectacular Quality revolution. Motorola put facts behind their Quality belief. Today every section of the company has to show progress, factually, towards the 6σ performance.

Uncommon performance

The Quality leader does not dwell on the present shortcomings for too long. Robert Galvin at Motorola used the image of mediocre performance to shock his colleagues. Having caught their attention, he then shocked them more by setting the target. The move from 3σ to 6σ is a hundredfold statistical improvement. His ambition was to go from the mediocre to the spectacular. He outlined this challenge in 1987 and stated that he expected to be there by 1992. Most people thought this was lunacy. Astonishingly, many parts of the Motorola business achieved 6σ consistently within a few years. A Motorola telephone pager can now work for 150 years without fault – which means customers of Motorola, like those of Sharp, can also forget about reliability. Motorola constructed a major Quality process around 6σ to make the transformation, but a crucial element of its success in a short timeframe was Roger Galvin's challenge. This gave the focus and the impetus to what could otherwise have been an abstract and theoretical programme.

So while the survey work on current practice is being done, the

Quality leader has another vital task – to define how we *should* be working tomorrow, the *desired* common practice. This is very difficult and many sidestep it, but the leader who can paint a picture of where the business is heading will find many more followers than without it. There will be more boarders of the 'train going North' if people have some idea of what it is like up North. This applies not only to management and staff within the business but also to customers, suppliers, other business units, shareholders – all those with an interest in the organisation will appreciate clear direction and clear guidelines.

Pinning this down takes a lot of debate and a lot of time and the Quality leader should expect to have to spend more effort on this than could be imagined. What to define is the first problem. The conventional way is to analyse the market, review the systems and devise a new structure. Large organisations spend fortunes and many months on such set-piece reviews and reorganisations. Senior and middle management are often paralysed during the review whilst they wait for their roles to be redefined. After the review, a period of structural change ensues when units are rationalised or derationalised. After sometimes years of disruption, what do we find? – often the same 3σ performance yet again.

The Quality leader needs to look beyond structure and find a better way of guiding action than organisational boxes and job descriptions can do. This becomes even more important as the Quality process develops. Quality generates high-energy teams and a high-energy team which is not directed can be more disruptive than a low-energy team which is content with its role. We still need to put a frame around the team's activities but, instead of a rigid box, one which channels teams towards business aims whilst allowing them the freedom and responsibility to act.

A practice-based focus does not replace roles, responsibilities and structures; it is an overlay which goes beyond their restrictions. As such, roles and responsibilities will certainly need to be modified as new common practice is established – but as a result of the new ways of working, rather than as a means for change. John Towers, MD of Rover Group, subscribes to this view after living through decades of structural change. The rate of change at Rover today is almost certainly more intense than at any previous time, but the organisational structure is not a major issue. As John says after introducing radical work practices at Rover: 'The structure will broadly establish itself.' John isn't concerned whether one unit looks the same as another, with a similar spread of people and reporting arrangements; he is concerned about what people *do*.

Framing future practice

 Designing future practice is exciting but can be frustrating. We are looking for the new way – something unique for us but which applies at every level and to every person. How can we begin to describe it? One way is to think in terms of a frame which encapsulates the practices we wish to encourage and support. Rather like viewing through a SLR camera, we can home in on a particular role in the organisation. With the focus sharply on this role, the picture describes the kind of practices we wish to achieve consistently with the frame defining the boundaries. Anything outside of the frame we may wish to discourage. In Rover's case, as an example, the frame focusing on a line operator would specify flexibility, teamwork, continuous local improvement, responsibility for product quality, process monitoring, local decision-making, planning and scheduling. This is a dramatically different picture from the simple volume and speed criteria of previous regimes, and one which John Towers and his colleagues know is vital for survival.

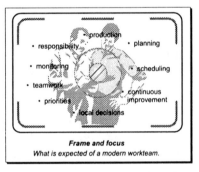

Frame and focus
What is expected of a modern workteam.

To achieve this as day-to-day practice, the focus on management would show equally radical departures from the old style practice. The new frame around a manager at Rover would capture images of the manager supporting workteams, creating an improvement environment, coaching and training, encouraging personal growth, measuring and recognising achievement, challenging processes, reducing barriers, setting and meeting stretching goals, meeting customer needs. Moving the focus above manager level, Rover executives are expected to spend their time testing what will make the company's products distinctive and planning what improvements in services and processes are needed to achieve competitive advantage, rather than second-guessing decisions made by the fact-holders lower down the organisation.

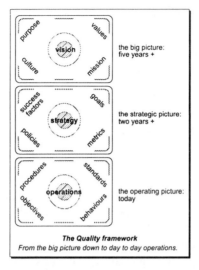

The Quality framework
From the big picture down to day to day operations.

The Rover example illustrates practices which many large organisations are seeking to create today, using a Quality process to accelerate the changes. Each frame provides guidelines to people in the organisation on the practices which will ensure Quality work in their roles. It should help each person to know what is required of him and how he is required to do it. The frames do not have to be drawn around organisational levels as described; indeed, Rover, as with most modern companies, is seeking to compress levels and blur their boundaries. Many practices in a Quality company can be made common to everyone and this is one of the objectives which the Quality leader is seeking to achieve. Thus one big picture may capture how the company and everyone in it should be working – 'The way things get done here'. On the other hand, in any organisation, practice ranges from the tactical through the strategic to the visionary (or at least it should: too many companies tend to be light on strategy and non-existent on vision). These can require quite different perspectives, with improvement horizons ranging from day to day up to ten years or more ahead.

The strategic picture

The most useful of these perspectives is the strategic one. Jack Walsh of GE says: 'If you haven't got competitive edge, you shouldn't compete.' But many people in an organisation do not know what constitutes their edge and therefore do not have the opportunity to help make a difference. To guide people at all levels in our organisation we need to draw a strategic picture which shows what we need to do, together, to make a competitive difference. With this as overall guidance, the improvement process can help focus the energy on what matters.

Most US and some European organisations have mission statements. Many, unfortunately, are bland and uninformative. They may state that the company seeks to be the best in its chosen field but not what will make them the best. As everyone else's mission is also to be the best, it does little to distinguish or inspire. To be useful, a mission should provide further focus and guidance – the things we have to do to create our Quality edge. In practice, many companies are content to have one mission statement which gives overall direction, but provide the tight focus with a subset of more specific strategic factors: together they provide distinction. In the West, these factors are often termed critical success factors; in Japan they are called *hoshins*. They say what we have to do to be competitive and achieve and maintain an edge.

 An example of this disciplined strategic planning is at Hewlett Packard, where the *hoshin* approach was adopted worldwide in the mid-eighties, after it was perfected in their Japanese subsidiary. One *hoshin* example from the UK company was to achieve a number one rating on customer satisfaction in the prestigious Datapro survey of computer users. The achievement of this status would provide a Quality edge over the competition and was seen as a breakthrough target in that much would have to be improved in order to get there. In fact, the quest for number one status led to major rethinking within HP in Europe, involving amongst many changes the creation of a network of customer response centres to focus much more closely on customer issues. The result was success at topping the Datapro survey, with the recognition this gave of satisfied customers. The *hoshin* goal was then re-targeted at putting more distance between HP and the number two in the survey, to keep the improvement energy flowing.

Strategic improvement goals

 Missions and critical success factors can describe the business distinctions we must create. To help us realise them, we must define how they can be achieved and what changes are needed to do it.

Improvement goals are by far the best device to give this additional focus. In fact, a *hoshin* or critical success factor is of limited practical value without a corresponding goal to aim for. Indeed, if the Quality leader used no other means of defining future practice, well-crafted stretching goals would provide a good enough platform to inspire and direct the big improvements.

One year after Selsdon Park, John Rothenberg (who took over from Mike Johnson when Mike moved to another Unilever role) was reflecting on the impact and significance of the conference. 'The best output of all,' he felt, 'was the improvement goals.' The improvement goals that the Personal Products executives set themselves at the conference captured the big business issues and turned them into something tangible to go for. Innovation was one hot issue – it always is in organisations like Unilever. This time the debate on bigger and better brands was harnessed into a challenging goal – a minimum percentage of turnover was to be from new products and proven new brands were to be introduced into markets around the world much more rapidly. This, and another four goals, defined performances not achievable at that time. To launch a new brand around the world quickly in an organisation where local national companies had full autonomy, required cooperation and mutual trust to an unprecedented degree. There would be little time for not-invented-here.

In a half-page, these goals gave the business focus: distinction was to come from sharper brand development, closer customer service, reduction in process time and wasted cost and trained empowered staff. They forced everyone to look outside of their boxes to learn how to achieve the targets set. These were not goals imposed on the companies by the centre – these were goals created by the business leaders together with their peers. When they returned home from the conference, they were not put on the shelf with the conference papers: all of the company Boards have subsequently used and refined the goals to add stimulus to their own Quality process.

Well-constructed goals have great improvement power. They say what is important and set the direction. As a result they can give guidance across the organisation on where improvement should be concentrated. This reduces the likelihood of well-meaning teams spending man-years of effort improving a little-used system. All improvement effort can be aligned behind the improvement goals – provided they are good. To be sound, an improvement goal must directly address a factor that will make a difference and lead (with the others) to a Quality edge. An example of such a goal is at 3M: to have 25 per cent of annual revenues from products which did not exist five years ago. 3M's edge comes from innovation and this much-admired goal has now been stretched to 30 per cent and four years. So improvement goals have to be stretching. Milliken's 10/4 goals are classic examples of stretch goals. Set in 1989, performance against the target of these six goals has been plotted and displayed on main corridors. The target is a tenfold (1000 per cent) improvement in four years. Such is the focus achieved and such is the effectiveness of Milliken's Quality process that by 1992 they were well on schedule to meet such astonishing targets. Milliken's goals well demonstrate another essential for a good improvement goal – it has to be measurable.

Measurement

Critical success factors and goals go hand in hand to give sharp strategic focus. But what gives them real bite is measurement. 'What gets measured gets done' is a familiar but apt expression. John Sharpe, Chairman of Elida Gibbs UK has a variation on the same theme: 'WYMIWYI...what you measure is what you improve' (adapted from the computer-world's 'WYSIWYG...what you see is what you get'). Roger Milliken has yet another angle: 'In God we trust, otherwise please bring facts.' Tony Burgmans, who took over at Unilever Personal Products from Mike Perry (now Chairman of Unilever plc) has a similarly forthright view: 'If you can't measure it, forget it.' Whilst Tony's view is a little severe in practice (if you can't measure something that is important, keep trying till you can), all these leaders are stressing the vital point that measurement fuels improvement. Without measurement, improvement fades away.

A measure is a quantification of progress towards a goal. 'Metrics' is a term used to denote the means of using measures. In business, we have tended to operate mostly with result-type measures such as volume, market share, profitability or return on investment. Any input metrics tend not to stray far from a cost base – the easy common denominator. Budgets, for instance, are mostly historically-derived costs and often heavily manipulated. All this is fine if we are a 3σ company and content with it. But if we want Quality, we need metrics for all factors and every level.

To keep improving, 'people need to read the meters', as Davies Richardson of Shell US puts it, and the meters need to be relevant ones. Try driving a car well without its dials and gauges; you would probably still get there but not so efficiently and you would feel uneasy. In business generally we tend to manage with too few meters – cost against budget and direct/indirect ratios for example. They do not tell us enough. The aim with Quality is to find the appropriate measures which guide improvement action at all levels and point us towards competitive advantage.

The ultimate example of a strong metric is Motorola's 6σ – now heavily copied by others. 6σ means delivering whatever you have to do to a standard of 99.9997 per cent – or three defects per million actions. This standard originated from Motorola's aim for consistent product reliability but, once established, spread out of manufacturing into all business areas, including support functions. Needless to say, if you are in Personnel or Legal or Accounts Receivable, proving that you are creating no more errors than three per million is challenging. 6σ is an example of universal metrics which can apply everywhere in an organisation. Other companies have a range of individual metrics which they use as indicators and then aggregate them to give an overall picture. Thus Federal Express has a Service Quality Indicator which itemises twelve critical parameters which all units worldwide track. These are monitored continuously and Fred Smith, President, uses them to debate the performance everyday with all his unit managers worldwide by video conference. He is looking for exceptions: why any indicator is below standard and what is being done immediately to improve it. A Federal Express target is to improve the SQI performance by a multiple of ten in five years.

Du Pont has created a matrix of key metrics to bring attention back to a strategic picture. They discovered, as most Western businesses

Employees Satisfaction index	Society Favourability index

• TRC/LWC
• Diversity demographics
• Job satisfaction index
• Leadership/development
	• Community opinion
	• Emissions
	  - total
	  - hazardous incidents

Shareholders Return: P/E	Customers Satisfaction index
• NPC(CROI) • ATOI • Cash flow • Sales growth • Profit margin • NWC cycle time • PI Productivity	• Satisfaction index • Market share index

Corporate metrics at Du Pont

do, that their only metrics at company-level were financial results, despite the extensive improvement efforts in other areas, including a crucial new area, the environment. The measurement matrix puts financial emphasis in the right balance for them – no more or less than the emphasis on customers, employees or the community. At first, there were few metrics to put under these other categories, but now indices have been developed for all of them. The hierarchy of metrics cascades down through all the businesses including relatively unmeasured areas such as research. AMP Inc. have a similarly detailed framework, but in their case they have left out the financial measures in order to put more emphasis on what they believe are the *enablers* of financial success. At Du Pont and AMP, what gets done gets measured.

	Customers	AMP	Suppliers	
	Elimination of defects			QUALITY INDEX
Q	credits & complaints as % of shipments previous year = current year estimate = goal =	defects per unit of work previous year = current year estimate = goal =	% lot acceptance previous year = current year estimate = goal =	
	Cycle time reduction			DELIVERY INDEX
D	% of shipments to customer request-date previous year = current year estimate = goal =	delivery to customer request-date previous year = current year estimate = goal =	% of shipments to AMP request-date previous year = current year estimate = goal =	
	Elimination of waste			VALUE INDEX
V	inventory turns previous year = current year estimate = goal =	cost reduction previous year = current year estimate = goal =	total acquisition cost reduction previous year = current year estimate = goal =	
	Responsiveness			SERVICE INDEX
S	turnaround time proposals complaints catalogs & samples previous year = current year estimate = goal =	turnaround time previous year = current year estimate = goal =	turnaround time quotes complaints, returned materials previous year = current year estimate = goal =	
	customer feedback index	AMP profile index	supplier performance index	Total corp. Excellence Index

Corporate metrics at AMP

'Live' policies and plans

 For accelerated improvement, the strategic frame must give a sharp and clear future picture. Clarity on all the elements is required to guide management and workforce action. Policies are really the core principles of an organisation. Many companies have a few policies; they can appear dated, arbitrary, inconsistent and often irrelevant. Policies should clearly translate strategic guidelines into management principles. They should be active and regularly reviewed and updated. So should business plans. Most organisations have business plans to link business activities together. Few have, at least until recently, put much rigour into aligning business units or departments with a common direction and consistent practices. In the main, Western business plans are about financial results; the plan provides the assurance merely of how the results are accumulated. Once the budgets are established, the plan is often filed and forgotten till next year's round. A major opportunity to provide continual strategic guidance is missed through the limitations of this practice.

The Japanese have a different view of business policies and plans: they should be active, consulted regularly to guide actions and amended as circumstances change or new knowledge is acquired; they should be accessible to everyone in the business and open to challenge. A good business plan is inspirational in style with a statement of belief or philosophy that is enduring. The main aim is to convey lasting purpose and rise above short-term action. To this end, the plan may project forward many years (hundred-year plans have been created).

But the plan should not stay up in the sky for long. It comes right back to today and focuses on improvement – what is needed in the current environment to maintain the philosophy and progress towards long-term goals. This then becomes an annual improvement plan which is used to stimulate and coordinate action at all levels. The planning itself is an interactive dynamic process involving ultimately every team and thus every person in the organisation.

In Japan, sanitary-ware producers Toto provided a classic example of putting Quality behind business through the planning process. Since 1959, they have had five-year rolling plans along the lines described above. By 1984, well into the last year of the fourth plan, they saw a problem. With a dominant market share and high profitability, they had been slow to see a big downturn in their market as new housing starts plateaued. They needed both a new business focus and a leaner, sharper way of working. This is when Toto adopted TQC, much later than many Japanese companies, for they had not felt the need until then. From 1984 on, TQC was used to achieve the new business objectives and create the new business practice to go along-side it. At Toto, Quality and business are now synonymous; the policies and plans are active 'living' documents.

Hoshin kanri

When a senior Western executive heard Hisaei Kikuchi of Tohoku NEC describe NEC's *hoshin kanri* (which translates as policy deployment but is more accurately described as structured strategic planning), his response was: 'the clearest explanation of strategic planning I've ever heard'. Hisaei Kikuchi explained NEC's approach very simply...because it is simple. He first sets his long-term policy, which naturally fits with the aims, philosophy and requirements of parent NEC. He creates this through a long, extended dialogue with his senior team, passing a document round and round until consensus is achieved, and with head office. Out of this, *hoshins* are created to describe the key strategic aims – the very few factors that will give the company an edge in the marketplace. The long-term plan is then divided down into medium and short-term objectives. This is handed down the line and debated always with three levels involved, thus overlapping discussions. This means that bottom-up responses are heard and reported up. This will go up and down and across the lines until the plan has a shape which everyone understands and can agree to. The *hoshins* usually remain intact – the debate is mostly about how they can be achieved and who is going to do what.

Obviously this planning process takes time but it is done with discipline and in advance of the coming year, so at the beginning of the year NEC Tohoku goes straight into action. The *kanri* element ensures that progress to goals is tightly monitored, and once or twice a year Mr Kikuchi conducts a presidential audit to see for himself that the plan is on schedule. Naturally, other levels of management have checked progress themselves before the president's review. Changes are made wherever necessary – problems are investigated from the standpoint of *what* is holding things up, not *who*. If there is any doubt, the presidential review will take place more often. In this way, the plan is always achieved and the next year further targets are debated well in advance, taking performance to a new level.

The reasons for this seemingly inevitable success are a mix of the very tight focus on what is important (three or four priorities only at any time), the openness and involvement built into the planning, the clarity of the data and the regular reviewing and adjustments. The plan is the live document which helps keep the drive for improvement together.

All the big Japanese companies use *hoshin kanri* in a similar way to NEC but with some variation in application. Komatsu, for instance, has a novel flag system to ensure the crucial data, the *hoshins*, the measures and the progress are very visibly displayed. Each flag at every level is visible to anyone else, giving both peer pressure and support.

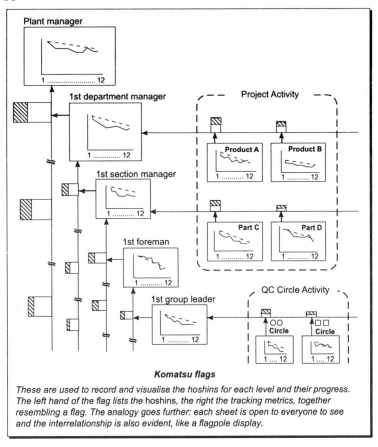

Komatsu flags

These are used to record and visualise the hoshins for each level and their progress. The left hand of the flag lists the hoshins, *the right the tracking metrics, together resembling a flag. The analogy goes further: each sheet is open to everyone to see and the interrelationship is also evident, like a flagpole display.*

The Komatsu *hoshins* are down-to-earth and unequivocal. They will state what must be done by when, with a linked cascade from an overall goal at the plant manager's level, e.g. to reduce the cost of an engine by 20 per cent to maintain competitiveness down to, say, removing 30 per cent of non-value time for a workteam on a particular part of the production process.

Some Western companies have adopted *hoshin kanri*, notably Hewlett Packard and Florida Power & Light. HP rate it as one of their most significant developments in management practice. Pioneered at Yokogawa Hewlett Packard, the methodology is credited as a major factor of YHP's survival in the seventies. HP, meanwhile, already had a powerful MBO process which pushed responsibility down the line, encouraging creativity and initiative in field and factory operations. As the competitive screws were turned on in the eighties, though, this simply wasn't enough. HP needed that creativity and energy channelled into a few key competitive thrusts, not dissipated across disparate objectives. *Hoshin* management (or 'turbo MBO' as HP first called it to show it was a development, not a replacement, for MBO; this title was soon dropped in favour of *hoshin*) added this dimension, enabling breakthrough goals to be seen alongside day-to-day management goals. Corporate distinction could be translated into local objectives without losing other important tasks; in other words, breakthrough improvement for the future and customer satisfaction for the present were married together with minimal conflict. At least that was the objective. In practice, the *hoshin* planning tables used to cascade goals down from division to region to area to district worked very well at senior levels, with Quality performance measures set at each level and monitored by the level above. The problem came at junior levels, where HP's matrix structure combined with the planning cascade to give too many goals across too wide a spread of activities. With further practice and a more disciplined sequence, limiting top-level *hoshins* to two or three and a maximum accumulation at lower levels of ten, this was finally overcome. *Hoshin* management is now second nature to many HP managers. Indeed many feel John Young's ground-breaking goal of ten times improvement for hardware reliability (which was achieved in five years) could not have been done without this process.

Unilever Personal Products has a very advanced planning process which has a similar cascade to *hoshin kanri*. The main criticism prior to the Selsdon Park conference was that it was too much of a once-a-year process – not a live plan in other words. Following the conference work on this, John Rothenberg introduced a new section to the annual plan – schedule one – which describes progress against the improvement goals. This has brought many more dimensions and real-time action into the process. Crucially, the financial results now

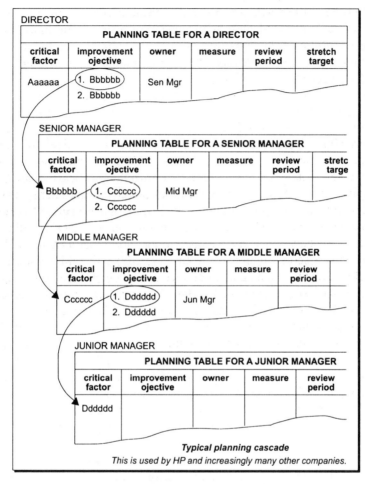

DIRECTOR

PLANNING TABLE FOR A DIRECTOR

critical factor	improvement ojective	owner	measure	review period	stretch target
Aaaaaa	1. Bbbbbb 2. Bbbbbb	Sen Mgr			

SENIOR MANAGER

PLANNING TABLE FOR A SENIOR MANAGER

critical factor	improvement ojective	owner	measure	review period	stretc targe
Bbbbbb	1. Ccccc 2. Ccccc	Mid Mgr			

MIDDLE MANAGER

PLANNING TABLE FOR A MIDDLE MANAGER

critical factor	improvement ojective	owner	measure	review period	
Cccccc	1. Dddddd 2. Dddddd	Jun Mgr			

JUNIOR MANAGER

PLANNING TABLE FOR A JUNIOR MANAGER

critical factor	improvement ojective	owner	measure	review period	
Dddddd					

Typical planning cascade

This is used by HP and increasingly many other companies.

follow on from schedule one. Thus the emphasis has switched from a results-dominated document, about which a bargaining ritual can build up between the centre and the companies, to the *means* of producing those results. The discussions before, during and after the planning process are now much richer: the business plan has gone live.

'Policy deployment', whether Japanese style or Western style, is a key way of locking the Quality process into the management process. It becomes a managerial discipline, probably the most crucial one for the Quality leader. It takes a defined business focus and converts it into action. It makes the linkages from a five or ten-year vision down to daily practice, from the CEO in one continent down to a workteam in another. It sets the priorities. It says what to do and what not to do. It directs what needs to be improved. Without a dynamic framework like this, the Quality leader has no way of channelling energy into improvement that matters. Without it, he will not influence common practice – it will remain forever mediocre. With it, he can do something special.

The bigger picture

 We can drive the improvement process from a strategic picture alone and this is more than enough for most leaders to grapple with, especially in the first few years of Quality implementation. But, at some stage, the revolutionary leader will want to go further and paint a bigger picture for the business and the way it acts. He will want to establish a vision of the new Quality business: what it should be like way down the Quality journey. He will need to answer some questions to set the frame for this picture. What are we in business to do? What do we stand for? What is important to us? What will characterise our image and reputation? What would make us more distinctive and more effective? Where is the edge? These are the type of questions worth asking so that we know what we are trying to create and what we will need to improve and change.

 Let's start with the core purpose of the business. Do we exist to make cars, to sell transportation or to make money? The tighter we can focus this the better (making money, for example, is such a broad purpose it allows any activity as long as it is profitable and thus does encourage a core expertise or unique distinction). A good challenge is to focus ten years out (or further if the development time is long) and define the business purpose for that anticipated market. We need good vision for this and we clearly have to read the trends and make good judgements – very difficult, but that is what the leader is paid to do.

Allen-Bradley is a market leader in switchgear. Prior to their Quality process at the end of the seventies, they had the leading reputation in electromechanical switches. But they anticipated the move over to solid-state electronics (a quite different technology) and put their Quality process behind that. The result, a decade later, was a doubling of market share. If they had stayed with the current expertise too long, Quality process or not, they could have been out of business.

This is an example of redrafting the big picture and redefining the purpose of the business.

Thus the purpose component of the Quality framework is set as far out as the market can be assessed but may well need amendments as market and technological changes move the emphasis. For instance, Ricoh has moved successfully in recent years from a core business in cameras to one in printers and copiers. Their purpose statement reflects this in the description of office automation – a term they created to describe and define their new area of focus. Toto, Japanese makers of sanitary-ware, is another example. During the rebuilding of Japan after the Second World War, Toto had a seemingly unlimited market for toilets. Recognising the limits to this in the eighties, Toto very deliberately changed its focus to 'water technology' – embracing new markets from a derivative technology.

Another example is Tohoku NEC, the NEC plant in Japan described already. In 1985, it was very successfully supplying NTT (Japan's national telephone company) with electromechanical components. This service was also reaching maturity, so the local NEC management established a new focus on printers and keyboards. Western attempts at such diversification are littered with failures and disappointments, but NEC made the transition successfully in a few years by clearly defining the new framework and deploying focused action down the whole organisation through *hoshin kanri*.

Throughout these major shifts of business direction, neither Ricoh, Toto nor NEC changed their overall philosophy, their core beliefs or their style of managing, although the application has clearly altered considerably. This leads us to explore elements of our vision way beyond our current trading: is there an ultimate reason for our business existence that transcends the market and technological parameters with which we are currently familiar? For some companies, this is relatively easy for they have developed over the years a clear understanding of what they are about. Kelloggs, for example, is quite clear it is in breakfast cereal and that's it. The marketing and technical changes over the years will reflect new trends, e.g. healthy eating for adults, but the focus on these is at a strategic rather than visionary level. Their core purpose is to remain as producers of the finest breakfast cereal. Disney gives another example – their stated primary focus is entertainment software. This guides Disney in creating relatively enduring characters and building experiences around them (from films to theme parks to soft toys), which they can service to the highest standards; at the same time it keeps them deliberately out of film distribution, for instance, with its rapid changes in technology.

What do you really value?

Which of the following are the most important contributors to the long-term success of your business? It might help to think both of those factors which we value now and those we should put more value to ensure future prosperity...

Values	Now	Future
• customer loyalty • long-term return • short-term return • market share • beating the competition • profitability • information • external image • technology • productivity • innovation • synergy between units • being the best • balancing the budget • return on shareholder investment • improving society • protecting the environment • helping the local community • speed • cost reduction • flexibility • managing suppliers • our products • our people • the management team • trust • integrity • value for money • distinctive products • superior products • others...		

What do we really value?

What we are – our purpose – is one dimension of the big picture. Another is what we stand for or what we value. Value statements have been quite popular in the West, especially in the eighties. These say what the company (i.e. the leaders) fundamentally believe in and are often constructed around 'promises' to the company's stakeholders – customers, employees, shareholders, suppliers and the local community. If backed by action, they can be powerful. BP has a comprehensive value set to guide a vast and

diverse empire. Grapevine law has it that a manager would be fired for releasing toxic waste into the River Mersey but not for poor financial returns: managers at BP now know the environment is a serious business issue.

The senior management of the Co-operative Bank thrashed out a core set of values before embarking on a Quality process. These stated beliefs were woven into the Quality process, being debated in the training sessions, for example. This led naturally to the Bank being able to adopt a bold stance later on ethical banking, which proved to be popular with young people and brought in half the Bank's new business in 1992.

The C(O)PERATIVE BANK

We, The Co-operative Bank Group, will continue to develop a successful and innovative financial institution by providing our customers with high quality financial and related services whilst promoting the underlying principles of co-operation which are:

Quality and Excellence to offer all our customers consistent high quality and good value services and strive for excellence in all that we do.

Participation to introduce and promote the concept of full participation to all our customers and staff.

Retentions to manage the business effectively and efficiently, attracting investment and maintaining sufficient surplus funds within the business to ensure continued development of the Group.

Education and Training to act as a caring and responsible employer encouraging the development and training of all our staff and encourage commitment and pride in each other and the Group.

Co-operation to develop a close affinity with organisations which promote fellowship between workers, customers, members and employers.

Quality of Life to be a responsible member of society by promoting an environment where the needs of local communities can be met now and in the future.

Freedom of Association to be non-partisan in all social, political, racial and religious matters.

Integrity to act at all times with honesty and integrity and within legislative and regulatory requirements.

Statement of Values at the Co-operative Bank

British Airways is another good example of using values to guide practice in the company. From continuous research over many years, BA has found out what customers value and how BA service rates against these values. As BA has refined and consolidated this long-term data, it has been able to turn it inside into its own values. Thus

BA's values are built around key words such as 'trustworthy', 'professional', 'caring', 'knowledgeable', 'value for money', 'enjoyment'. These are turned into statements of appropriate behaviour and are a key part of BA's current Quality focus.

Value statements in isolation can appear bland and woolly, failing the 'so what' test. However, there is no reason why they should not be sharp and precise – provided we genuinely believe they are our prime concerns. It is counterproductive to state we value personal relations with our customers, for example, when we really want fast transactions and minimal contact. To ensure we state only what we really value, we should draw up a list, such as the one in the table on page 102, and select our top half a dozen. If profitability, or return on assets, is high on the list, there is absolutely no reason why we should not say so.

The way we do things

 Yet another dimension to the big picture is worth the leader's attention. This is how we do things, or the culture of the organisation. Many pragmatic leaders are uncomfortable with terms like organisational culture. But organisational culture is real and the wise Quality leader will understand it and shape it towards his vision. There already is a culture in the organisation, whether it is articulated or not. It is the way we tend to respond and react – the way we do things. But it is probably not consistent and may be far from our ideal. In which case, what is our ideal way of operating?

Defining a cultural vision not only gives direction but also early pointers to the barriers to be overcome. For instance, if we know our vision is for self-managed workteams, then what do we do about the current layers of supervision and how will local managers relate to the newly-franchised teams? Or, if we intend to move over to process management and make our top executives process-responsible, how do we maintain centres of excellence such as buying, accounting, planning? What about the grading and appraisal systems – how will they need to change? These issues can be thought through and the inevitable changes planned in advance.

A well-defined culture can help shape the personality or character of the business – the unique identity which will reinforce unity and team spirit. After Akio Morita had opened his first UK Sony plant at

Bridgend in Wales in 1973, the tiny management team sat around a table and defined the culture for Sony Bridgend. 'We decided at the beginning that we weren't going to be British, Japanese or Welsh; we were going to be something new called Sony Bridgend,' says John Bevan, one of the early Sony managers. The uncompromising belief in this vision and the consistency with which management acted it out in day-to-day situations brought early loyalty from the workforce in a community then notorious for poor labour relations. Sony Bridgend is a popular employer – a recent announcement of a new factory brought 5,000 job applications in a week.

A Quality culture

Imagine your business after a successful Quality process - i.e. after the revolution. How would it run? Which of these Quality practices would you expect to see more of?

	more	much more	very much more
• *self-managed teams* • *continuous improvement of processes* • *customer-driven behaviours (service mentality)* • *partnership relationships (with customers, suppliers and third parties)* • *waste reduction (excessive or misaligned time and cost removed)* • *minimal hierarchy (towards just professionals and leaders)* • *one status only* • *performance-related rewards* • *data driven (relevant information at the right place and time)* • *internal market (with customer/ supplier contracts)* • *internal networks and temporary issue-focused teams* • *empowered workforce* • *high energy* • *learning, developing environment* • *innovative, challenging environment* • *feedback* • *disciplined focused action* • *positive communication flow* • *measured benchmarked activity* • *pride with humility* • *others...*			

Mission

 The final image to be added to the big picture has been introduced already: mission. A mission is the link between the vision and the strategy. A mission is a long-term overarching goal – something we continue to strive for, something aimed further out than the strategic improvement goals but still embracing them. A mission statement is usually descriptive and is often used to communicate the essence of the vision to a wider audience.

Examples of Mission Statements

WRc Mission Statement

To be a leading independent European research and consultancy organisation in the fields of water, waste water and environmental management with a worldwide reputation for high quality, good service and value for money.

Perkins Group mission statement

To make the Perkins Group the most successful diesel engine business in the world, in the eyes of our customers, our employees and our shareholders.

BT mission statement

To provide world-class telecommunications and information products and services.

To develop and exploit our networks, at home and overseas, so that we can:

* *meet the requirements of our customers*
* *sustain growth in the earnings of the group on behalf of our shareholders*
* *make a fitting contribution to the community in which we conduct our business.*

Caradon mission statement

We will delight our customers by delivering superior quality in product and service. We will achieve this through the development of our people and the continuous improvement of our processes and facilities, thereby sustaining superior long-term financial performance.

Royal Mail Business mission

As Royal Mail our mission is to be recognised as the best organisation in the world distributing text and packages

We shall achieve this by:

* *Excelling in our collection, Processing, Distribution and Delivery arrangements*
* *Establishing a partnership with our customers to understand, agree and meet their changing requirements*
* *Operating profitably by efficient services which our customers consider to be value for money*
* *Creating a work environment which recognises and rewards the commitment of all employees to customer satisfaction*
* *Recognising our responsibilities as part of the social, industrial and commercial life of the country*
* *Being forward-looking and innovative*

Thus key elements of culture, values and purpose are sometimes rolled into the one mission statement for publication. However, a long mission statement will be counterproductive in terms of inspiration and clarity; anything over half a dozen pithy lines loses impact. This argues for having a separate mission statement.

The Quality framework

Does it all stack up? Having thought through the strategic picture and the big visionary picture, do they fit together? Could we go further and frame a picture at operations level, focusing on the shop floor or the sales force? Here our elements would be the procedures and standards which guide day-to-day behaviours. This, indeed, is worthwhile but takes us outside strategy and into people as an improvement driver, so these aspects are discussed fully in Chapter 7.

The full Quality framework
From vision through strategy to operational practice.

At some point, the new practice framework will need a reality test – a way of ensuring it comes back to earth and fits the notion of organised common sense. In devising the unique new practice for his business, the Quality leader may well have brushed with an unfamiliar and probably unwelcome world of behavioural science. Most leaders bridle at the jargon and find the distinctions between missions, visions and the like, unnecessarily semantic. However, the leader will also be aware that his picture of future practice probably does contain a mix of aspirations which are different – some values, some standards, some goals perhaps. Does this matter? Most experience suggests it does not; precision and elegance are less important than relevance of the content. So the reality check could be along the lines of: is it meaningful?...does it inspire?...does it give clear direction?...does it help discriminate between constructive and non-constructive action?...does it guide people in what to do in marginal situations?...does it make sense?...who will use it? Finally, it is always useful to apply that most salutary test – so what?

	hierarchy of terms	meaning	related terms
vision	• purpose • values • culture • mission	- the reason we exist - what we believe in - the way things get done - what we strive to achieve	• philosophy • credo • charter • principles
strategy	• policies • success factors • goals • metrics	- the core principles - what will make a difference - the big improvement aims - how we track progress	• guidelines • hoshins • targets • measures
operations	• objectives • procedures • standards • behaviours	- tasks to be achieved - standardised practice - minimum acceptable achievement - how we act	• key result areas • methods • performance level • actions

Hierarchy for designing a future practice
Use only those terms which have most meaning and relevance for what you want to achieve.

Communicating common practice

Let us remember why we are going to all the trouble of defining common practice. It is to promote revolutionary activity and direct it towards business advantage. If this becomes an academic or esoteric exercise, it becomes self-defeating. So we want people to use our statements of defined common practice – our Quality framework. Who will use it depends to a large extent on who has been involved in creating it. Quality is something that is put into a business by the people who work in it. The idea of a Quality framework is to guide what is put in at all levels and to achieve consistency and linkage between them. To do this the elements of the Quality framework should be readily accessible. They cannot travel far if they remain locked inside the leader's head, however inspirational he may be. He will need, like all missionaries, to spread the word.

This will mean converting the concepts into written statements but in formats which are still live and relevant. The best way of doing this and ensuring the framework is used is by involving people directly in their application. Indeed, this will be one of the major activities of the

Quality process. The aim is to work the framework into documentation which is used in the business process. Thus management at all levels can look at their work and their decisions and check mentally or physically against the statements. If they are involved in, or could become involved in, a business activity that is not consistent, they should question it closely. Energy spent on non-focused or non-aligned activity is vital energy lost and they should know this and act accordingly. With time, the understanding will be second nature and lower levels of management can be fully empowered to interpret them as Quality guidelines in day-to-day situations.

Clerical Medical is a typical illustration of a company that had implemented a thorough Quality process leading to new ways of working. They reinforced this with a well-publicised corporate statement (see overleaf).

One potential blockage to this is the terminology. Senior managers may become used to the terms over the many months that it takes to craft and agree good statements. But as the work is then revealed to other levels, headings like values and missions may impede acceptance. A successful way round this is to cut out all the outside language and create an 'own brand' couched in everyday words. Hence ' The ICL Way', 'Rover tomorrow', 'AD2000' (Allied Dunbar) – these corporate statements are company-branded with subheadings, if appropriate, explaining 'what we believe in', 'what we are here to do', 'what our aims are', 'what will ensure our competitiveness', etc.

To keep the Quality framework visible, companies can do many things. Noticeboard displays, alongside the measurement and reporting data which makes them real, can be very effective. Set on their own, in the visitor's reception, is perhaps the least effective presentation. Some companies print credit-card-sized cards as reminders of the Quality statements and issue them to all staff and often suppliers and customers. The main benefit of such visibility is one that was probably not originally intended. Making the statements public means that managers become more aware that their actions are under continuous scrutiny...against a check-list. Clarke American have devised a neat folded card to stand on a desk with 'the Clarke American Way' on one side and 'Company Values' on the other (see page 111). This is no wish list – these statements accurately reflect a management style and whole-company ethos which has operated for some years, but which always needs reinforcement. The immediacy of these simple but very visible cards placed before each person in a meeting room or on a training session helps to do this.

Clerical Medical
INVESTMENT GROUP

Our Mission
To make Clerical Medical the most professional and profitable UK based international Investment Group.

Our principal objective
To develop the business in the best long-term interests of our with-profit policyholders.

Our Vision
We are a professional organisation unified and motivated by the desire to provide for the needs of our customers through quality products and services.

We are committed to creating an environment based on mutual respect, honesty, fairness and responsibility in which every one of us can contribute to our success and have that contribution recognised.

Our Values
Our common aim is to:
• Conduct our business with uncompromising professionalism.
• Continually test and update our understanding of customer needs.
• Seek achievement through team work.
• Establish clear performance objectives and provide regular, constructive and timely feedback on performance.
• Recognise and reward those who take the initiative to improve the way we work.
• Encourage innovation, and actions which forestall problems.
• Avoid waste and seek ways to eradicate it.
• Communicate openly and honestly, including sharing both successes and mistakes.
• Trust and have respect for each other.

Our Measure of Success
The achievement of a faster increase in the value of the Group than that of leading competitors, while maintaining financial strength.

The Mission and the Principal Objective will be achieved by implementing six key strategies:
Market Strategy
By adopting a focused approach to each of our markets.

Quality Strategy
By providing a standard of service which consistently satisfies the changing needs of our customers.

Employment Strategy
By employing staff appropriate to the needs of the organisation, by enabling them to develop and by recognising the contribution of each of them to the success of the Group.

Business Development Strategy
By seeking a spread of development opportunities that offer good rates of return.

Distribution Strategy
By developing additional sources of business while maintaining commitment to the independent sector.

Accountability Strategy
By ensuring that financial accountabilities are understood and achieved throughout the Group.

WE WILL BE JUDGED BY OUR DEEDS, NOT OUR WORDS

Example of a Corporate statement

The Clarke American Way

Our objective is superior performance, ultimately defined in profit dollar terms.

Our business foundation will be built upon outstanding quality and service together with low-cost production, and value-added selling vs low price.

To accomplish this we need superior performance from all employees - we need the most talented and energetic people we can find at all levels.

In order to attract, maintain and encourage such people, we shall provide a working environment that is stimulating and rewarding, both in terms of career development and remuneration.

We welcome vigorous debate and encourage constructive disagreement in order to continually improve the process and our company.

In return, we want each employee's commitment and loyalty as together we move this company forward.

This is how Clarke American intents to go about its business - providing superior performance for our customers, our employees and our shareholders, to become the First In Service check printer.

Company values

Integrity - It is every employee's responsibility to approach all business situations, both internal and external, with the utmost integrity.

Esteem - It is the responsibility of all employees to respect and enhance the self-esteem of every other employee.

Trust - It is our responsibility to select the right people and trust in their ability to support and accomplish the objective of the company.

Autonomy - It is our responsibility to give every employee as much autonomy as possible within the realm of his or her position. We must try to solve all problems at the appropriate level.

Teamwork - It is our responsibility to work together to insure the company's future. The mission that Clarke American has set for itself cannot be accomplished unless there is complete teamwork.

Profitability - One important measurement of a superior performing company is superior profitability. It is our responsibility to generate above average return on our shareholders investment.

Clarke American

Communicating common practice

Every one of these statements describes an element of the way Clarke American works. Led by Jim Coln for twenty years from his San Antonio headquarters, the Clarke American business has grown and prospered because of Jim's clear and unequivocal beliefs. When Jim took over as managing director from the founder, the small cheque printing business had stagnated. Jim talked to customers, the local banks, and found that what they valued was reliability coupled with low price. He set out to do that, specifying the standards to be achieved outside and inside the business. He talked to his people and found them to be subdued and underachieving. Development of people became the bedrock of Jim's improvement process. Standards were set for recruitment, for training and for involvement. They were never compromised; a vacancy would be left unfilled for two years rather than lower the requirements. Jim reasoned that they could never provide the best service if they did not have the best people and if those people were not fully supported. To provide the best service at the lowest cost, all processes were measured and a battery of metrics was constructed so that local team efforts contributed into an effective overall achievement. People of all levels found they had to account for what they were doing through these metrics - a shock to those coming from other cultures, but something soon valued as recognition followed.

Jim applied these simple beliefs - aiming for the best service, hiring the best people, measuring all activity and continually improving - with such single-minded dedication that other managers caught on quickly. Customers also caught on to the difference and opportunities for business came from across the USA. By the end of the 1980s, all Clarke American's 42 printing plants operated to this practical philosophy - the Clarke American Way. Of course, like other outstanding leaders, this was not enough for Jim. In the early 1990s, Jim and his successor, Charles Korbell, have been implementing a Total Quality process over and above their established best practice. Called First in Service®, Clarke American are using this process to ensure they are a strong survivor in a consolidating marketplace.

The drawback of visibility is when the difference between the statements and the reality is too much for people to accept. It is like the infamous British Rail advertising campaign in the eighties, which boasted 'we're getting there' when the public's perception was that they were not. No one is persuaded by written words alone and the difference between lofty statements and everyday behaviour is obvious to most people. The key to this is timing. The Quality framework can be integrated into business documentation quietly and relevantly. It should only become something which is marketed – internally or externally – when there is enough new common practice to support it.

Again the communication should be relevant. The person on an assembly line or a bank counter has little expectation of influencing the future direction of the business and therefore finds 'big picture' statements difficult to relate to. The normal reaction is indifference. But linked with statements of local practice, they begin to make sense to people. So if the workteam has created its own procedures and standards and has its own norms about what is good and bad behaviour, there will be interest in the business goals and how the team's efforts fits in with them. Like common practice itself (indeed the whole Quality process), the communication must always be dynamic and continuous not static.

From concept to practice

The Royal Mail (the big part of the UK Post Office) may not seem like a business going through a transformation, but it is. The business is enormous (£5 billion turnover and 170,000 staff) and used to be run on civil service, almost militaristic lines. The Post Office in the eighties was not adjusting happily to modern life; the monopoly was under real threat, share was declining although the market was growing, industrial relations were abysmal with 228 disputes in one year (nearly one in six of the whole of the UK). The official response was to prepare 'a strategy for decline'!

Bill Cockburn, as managing director of the letters business (The Royal Mail), had other ideas. Supported by the new Post Office chairman, Bill Nicholson, who was previously with Xerox, he set about transforming his business. He recruited a Quality Director to help him, Ian Raisbeck, who, coincidentally, had also learned his skills at Xerox. Together with the other directors, they thrashed out what sort of business they were and what they wanted to be. The mission and values took them 16 months to get right, with Bill Cockburn talking endlessly to managers across the business about the need to change and about what to change to. They talked to customers and found that, whilst the official performance of next-day delivery was 90 per cent, the actual was nearer 70 per cent. They talked to staff and found the postmen were sympathetic to customers but were ignorant of the business. For example, Ian Raisbeck tells the story of doing a round with a postman in Luton one Saturday morning. They had been talking about customer service and the postman remarked that delivering a telephone bill on Saturday morning was not what Mrs Brown wanted. True, but it was what BT wanted – a major customer of Royal Mail. The typical postal worker had no concept of business customers and their particular needs.

After pinning down the current reality and defining the future practice, Bill Cockburn and his team began a major process of change, starting with management and working down. Key managers were taken on study tours to the USA to open their eyes and see what other business had done; 13,000 managers experienced five days of Quality training – many of them twice, as follower and then leader. Gradually, the mission and values were brought to the fore, but not for nearly two years after they were first created: the gap between the aspiration and the current reality just after the national strike was too great. Improvement programmes were set up, managed locally...'What you improve is up to you provided it is consistent with our mission and values.'

As the Quality process took hold and non-management were being trained and empowered locally, Bill turned to the organisation structure. Doing the rounds of managers again, he talked about the need to go further and build on the stronger environment being formed. After 16 months of talking, a broad structure was developed. District boards were removed and 120 post code centres established to give smaller unit, customer-centred businesses. Head office manning was cut from 2,000 to 162; three layers of management were removed. Along the way, management focus groups were created to design the changes. These brought together people from different disciplines and ultimately involved 1,000 managers. They were so successful and natural that they became a new way of managing and are now an integral part of the new operations. The management transition was not a reshuffle. Every manager, from managing director down, was individually assessed for the new way of working and appointed accordingly, often in a radically different role.

The bottom line of the transition? Over four years, next-day delivery was improved from 74.5 per cent to the goal of 90 per cent...a true 90 per cent, now measured independently from end to end. Internationally, this is one of the highest service achievements in the world at a cost (25p) considerably lower than most. The tight linkage between the Quality process and the business direction is felt to have been a crucial ingredient in this success. In a 1992 survey, 90 per cent of staff felt that the mission was driving the business. As the Quality process continues to empower people down the line with the message 'improve what it is you do', the Royal Mail board continue to refine their forward vision, spending no less than nine full days on the strategic direction. For Bill Cockburn and Ian Raisbeck achieving their first big goal is only the start of a massive transformation at Royal Mail. As Bill says, 'Our aim is to be a world-class benchmark, not just to be the best Post Office – we're already that – but to have people come and visit us because, whatever we do, whether it's PR or transport systems or finance, we're perceived as amongst the best there is.'

Meanwhile at Unilever Personal Products, the integration of Quality and business continued. At Selsdon Park, Mike Perry's team had constructed the skeleton framework of new practice across a huge and complex multinational business – unique practice for a unique business. It did not happen naturally; much experimentation had been done beforehand; much more follow-up activity was done afterwards. But the energy of the multi-meeting conference permitted a huge leap forward. The outputs from the group work defined the new order. Seemingly outrageous goals now had to be achieved. These would require new methodologies, new disciplines and new relationships. The executives were not left up in the air without the means of achieving the challenges – this was a planned step in a comprehensive Quality process. They already had the common language of Quality and the disciplines were there to help them.

Post-Selsdon Park, the Personal Products business has continued its transformation. The new Quality framework has led to new behaviours. Information flow across boundaries is noticeably easier; networks are stronger. Inter-company teams were created to address areas of mutual interest such as the European supply chain or harmonisation of materials or information technology. The energy level remains high as companies from Turkey to Sweden to Canada learn from each other and continue to drive hard. Quality has become their way of doing business.

Process management, partnership relationships, customer/supplier

agreements, benchmarking...these disciplines were already understood by the companies; post-Selsdon, they were applied and used for
competitive advantage. Tony Burgmans, on taking over from Mike
Perry in 1991, could see the potential from the carefully planned
investment in Quality across the group. He saw his job as capitalising
on that. Building on the new environment and exploiting the new
disciplines, Tony has focused the improvement energy on two
breakthrough areas. One is to pull together the extended supply chain
– the whole process from supplier's supplier to the end consumer –
and radically upgrade the end result. This means integrating previously separate disciplines and previously separate units, often in
different countries, towards this one objective. Without the foundation
of Quality, it is difficult to conceive this concept working. The second
macro-task is partly dependent on the first – greatly enhancing the
rate of innovation in the business. As Tony says: 'To be a great inno-
vator, you must be a great operator.' By putting Quality behind business, Unilever Personal Products aims to be both.

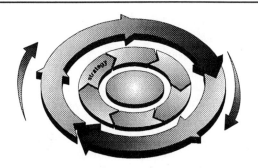

SUMMARY

Put Quality behind your business. *Ensure your Quality process maintains its energy and your business obtains most benefit from the investment in Quality by aligning Quality and business together:*

1. **Do you understand the current reality?***...How the business actually works?*
2. **Have you designed the future practice?***...How the business could work?*
3. **Have you set a clear business direction?**
4. **Do you use stretching goals that point towards the direction and the future practice?**
5. **Have you determined the transition steps between today's practice and tomorrow's?**
6. **Have you deployed the goals down the organisation as objectives for people to attain?**
7. **Do you measure performance against these objectives?**
8. **Do you review progress towards the goals and realign activities accordingly?**
9. **Do you question any activities that are not aligned to the direction or contributing to the goal?**
10. **Have you established a Quality framework?***...Is it used and understood?*

4
Leading Quality

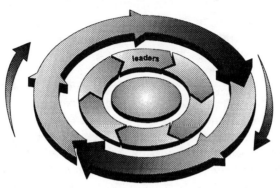

To many people, Quality is a great thing for others to do... 'I do my bit well, it's the others that let the side down.' Quite often, a leader accentuates this attitude by imposing a major Quality process on the rest of the organisation, whilst ignoring his own role. He may wish to delegate the responsibility for the process and he may wish not to change his own habits. But if he wants results, he has to participate fully: improvement applies to everyone and no one is more important in a Quality process than the leader. People make Quality but the leader makes it happen.

'Quality starts with me.' Jan Timmer, president, Philips

'Unless behaviour changes, nothing changes.' Pat Donovan, Managing Director, BSS

The revolutionary leader

Virgilio Gallo is the TQM Director of Digital Europe. On taking up his new appointment in early 1992, after many years as a senior line manager at Digital, he decided he would spend time seeing what had been done with Quality around the corporation. On one of his rounds, he met up with the head of the Digital US payroll department in Maynard. Leo Haug's team pay some 60,000 Digital staff, on a weekly basis, spread over 320 locations. All of his customers expect nothing other than zero defects in their pay packets. Virgilio, anticipating a large and complex organisation, was somewhat bemused by Leo's small office and friendly and informal manner. He was even more surprised when Leo described his organisation by showing on a computer screen a job plan for each person on his team, explaining that each plan was visible to everyone else and was coherent with the overall strategic vision. As Leo talked, Virgilio began to think about the number of staff they must have in Maynard to set up such a strategic plan for the payroll.

Leo continued, explaining that each person could modify his plan on the computer system whenever conditions changed without having to ask permission of his boss. Virgilio became even more intrigued as Leo talked with familiarity about all the people whose plans appeared on the screen. How could he possibly know them all? Reluctantly, for Leo was passionately expanding on the planning process, Virgilio interrupted and asked how Leo managed to visit all his operations and get to know people so well. Leo laughed and explained they were all in one place – just outside the office – and there were only 26 in total. Virgilio was now downright sceptical. Did he use an outside bureau? Was the work locally distributed? No, it was all done week in week out, with no mistakes, by the one small team.

Leo took over the payroll eight years before, when it was already a good operation. He immediately set about changing it, starting with a review of the needs of his customers – Digital operations throughout the US. From this data, he created three customer-orientated goals, which have been used to drive the operation ever since: one, support the US operation; two, increase the service level; three, reduce the payroll cost per employee. Involving his team, he constructed a long-range plan around these goals, cascaded down into the detailed job plans. With this clear direction, he implemented a Quality process to deliver the radical improvement he thought necessary, graduating to advanced applications such as 'six sigma' (reducing the defects in a process to less than three per million) and QFD (actively and continually probing customer preferences and desires). His team receive ten days of training each year and are well used to meeting spontaneously to solve problems and probe opportunities.

When Leo started in 1985 there were 80 people in the unit and the payroll staff to paid staff ratio was 14.0 to every 1,000 people paid. Leo brought this ratio down each year: 11.8, 10.0, 8.0, 6.3, 6.3, to 6.2 in 1992. The cost of each payment came down in proportion in 1992. When a management consultancy ran a benchmarking survey on payroll services in March 1991, Digital came out 'best in class' with just one third the average cost per employee of the others, which included Xerox, General Electric, Honda, Shell, Matsushita, AT&T, Du Pont and many other leading companies.

Leo could be a model Quality revolutionary. He refused to accept that good was good enough. He set stretching goals which were customer-orientated. He created a vision and he translated it into day-to-day practice for his team. He used a Quality process and Quality disciplines to achieve quantified results. And he carried his people with him; despite the much higher throughput as a result of the better ratios, employee satisfaction went up each year from 6.2 out of ten in 1989 (when it was first measured) through 7.3, 7.4 to 8.2 in 1992.

To be evolutionary, a leader has to be radical; to be revolutionary, the leader must become fanatical. A leader who sets out to achieve evolutionary change may achieve no change at all, such is the inertia and lassitude in most organisations. Radical actions at the top of an organisation become diffuse by the time they emerge lower down; sharp focus at the top is just a blur at the middle. Great leaders are not shy of being extreme. Roger Milliken thought he knew all about management, having been involved in the family business all his life. But he was prepared to admit his style was totally wrong for modern business needs and publicly shifted through 180 degrees as a result. This symbolic change was a critical catalyst for the management team at Milliken and provided the foundation for their successful Quality process. Roger was able to convey more about the Quality process by what he did day to day and how he did it, than any speeches, rallies, or training sessions could do (which he did very thoroughly too). His group president, Tom Malone, was equally positive, both leaders spending up to 70 per cent of their time on the Quality process – not so much in the structured activities, such as projects or training sessions, but in talking to people about their improvement activities. This style was quickly picked up by the divisional presidents and led to a positive and unambiguous environment: at Milliken, the Quality process became the one and only way of doing business. Jack Welsh of General Electric is another extreme Quality role model, continually stirring up the massive GE organisation, challenging convention, creating new insights and opportunities for people at all levels.

The Quality leader's role is not at all easy to master and has risks. Bob Horton's reign at BP was viewed as radical. In a few years he created new focused business strategies for the giant corporation, cut out much of the old imperialism and orchestrated a new management style built around core values. In the space of two years, BP severed much of the hierarchy and committees and attacked the old culture of 'bureaucracy, stuffiness, lack of delegation, rampant mistrust and second-guessing'. His senior colleagues accepted, probably reluctantly, the new practice. Russell Seal, head of BP Oil, reportedly made a 'radical change in the way he managed people' away from 'the classic commander-controller'. As BP number two, David Simon was quoted: 'I stand four-square with Bob Horton on triggering this change throughout BP; we senior managers at BP want a nimble new culture for our company. New cultures – new behaviours and motivations – are taking over the business world fast these days.'[4] Unfortunately, Bob Horton omitted to do the equivalent of Roger Milliken's 180-degree turn. He didn't practise what he preached and adopt a new leadership style; instead, his own abrasive style appeared more and more at odds with this new vision. He resigned in June 1992 after a boardroom rebellion. A Quality leader must learn to be a missionary as well as a visionary.

The ultimate role model

The leader is a very powerful role model. People are much more aware of what he or she does than the leader appreciates. He is watched and studied and talked about. And his actions count far more than his words, especially negative ones. This means it is far from easy to be a successful leader, especially a Quality one. Adding a Quality dimension to everything raises the whole game. Catching the boss out becomes a new interest; actions which would have passed without comment before will now be labelled 'not Quality'.

So each leader must prepare in order to lead. As a leader, I must think through my words, my actions and my time. All must reinforce my image as a Quality leader. I will need help to make this change, because I am unlikely to hold an accurate self-perception. I may already think I am good because I am operating within my own self-assessed framework; but like the organisation as a whole, in practice my impact is probably pretty mediocre.

One reason for my modest impression on the organisation is that I may simply not know how to act as a Quality leader. I may not know what behaviours are valued and respected and thus how I can best influence people around me. Another reason is that even if I know, my good intentions may be misinterpreted; I may believe I am listening and consulting, for example, but the perceptions of others is that I am telling and instructing.

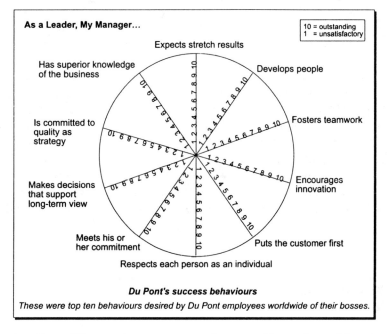

As a Leader, My Manager...

10 = outstanding
1 = unsatisfactory

Expects stretch results

Has superior knowledge of the business

Develops people

Is committed to quality as strategy

Fosters teamwork

Makes decisions that support long-term view

Encourages innovation

Meets his or her commitment

Puts the customer first

Respects each person as an individual

Du Pont's success behaviours

These were top ten behaviours desired by Du Pont employees worldwide of their bosses.

Du Pont Electronics overcame these problems by asking in a worldwide survey what behaviours they expected from successful leaders. This data was then converted into an evaluation form for Du Pont people to assess their leaders on the top ten desired 'success behaviours' which could then be plotted and displayed as a wheel. The aim was not for appraisal but for feedback; what the manager did with it was up to him. Dr Gordon Jenkins, VP of Du Pont Electronics, found the feedback to be immensely valuable. As a hard-driving successful manager, he was pleased to see his team score him 9.6 out of ten for 'expects stretch results' but was taken aback to receive only a 4.5 for 'develops people' and a 6.0 for 'committed to Quality'. Gordon makes his ratings public and encourages discussion amongst his team about them. In this way he has seen his weaker scores improve over the three years this has been operating.

So an early step for the leader and his senior colleagues on the Quality journey is not only to reveal the current reality of their business but also the current reality of their own behaviours. They would benefit from using a third party to do this objectively and anonymously. They will find that the people they work with and the staff they employ do have a starkly clear picture about them. It is this picture that they will want to change, moving the image towards a new role – that of the leader in a Quality environment.

Self-image

Our self-image as leaders may be quite different from how others see us, as this chart from John Nicholson shows. Feedback helps develop a more realistic picture and a more effective style.

How I see myself	How they see me
confident	arrogant
enterprising	opportunistic
humorous	frivolous
ambitious	ruthless
helpful	controlling
forceful	bullying
competitive	combative
open to change	wishy-washy
thorough	obsessive
tolerant	uncaring
caring	nosy
prudent	indecisive
focused	tunnel-visioned
supportive	interfering
generous	irresponsible

The new leader

Being in the exposed position of Quality role model is not all downside. Many people will be ready to follow your lead and adopt new behaviours. Many will do this quite naturally and almost unconsciously; others will need a lot of training, counselling and support (which will become a key element of the leader's role anyway). But no one will change until the leader has taken the first step and shown the way.

Notwithstanding Roger Milliken's conversion, a dramatic overnight shift is neither required nor desirable. Colleagues and staff would be astonished if the uncaring results-orientated boss came in one day and asked how everyone's family was. They might be impressed in the short term but not if the effort faded away after a couple of days as the real priorities re-emerged. A progressive change over a period of time, together with colleagues, is much more sustainable. This is one of the many reasons why a successful Quality transition must start at the top and progress down in a controlled way. With respect to leadership behaviours, each level can support the next level down.

The Quality leader does not have to create a new personality. Far from it, he or she must be sincere in behaviour or the effect is more negative than positive. Contrary to expectation, he will not have to turn into a showman, an extrovert or a totally people-person, entertaining the troops. The real benefits come from behaviours which are much more prosaic. The aim is simple – better focus on what is important and more energy going into what is being done. For the new style of leader, enthusiasm, involvement, interest, consistency and discipline are what count. In this way, the new leader is able to transfer his improvement energy to others.

John Craddock became a new leader in more ways than one. John was appointed as managing director of Legal & General some months after a full Total Quality process had begun. As sales director previously, he was certainly well aware of the Quality process and supportive of it, but it had not really engaged him in any real way. Taking on the MD's role at a time when a decade of continued growth in the insurance industry had just come to an abrupt halt, John had more than enough to do without the additional demands of a Quality programme in its infant and vulnerable stages. John's first instinct was to kill it and concentrate on shaping up the business. But, on reflection, he saw the longer-term value in an industry where Quality could soon be a competitive necessity. Having made this decision, he knew he had no choice but to be even stronger in his demonstrated commitment to Quality than his predecessor.

Over the next few months, John became a new leader for the second time: this time as a Quality champion. He started by learning about Total Quality the same as everyone else, attending four days of training as a participant. He then made sure he was involved in all the other training events, dropping in for lunch or joining in the sessions. He worked exhaustively with his senior colleagues to draft a comprehensive framework of mission, values and Quality policy, which were then debated around the company. John involved as many people as he could in this aim to define 'the world we want to create, not the world we have today'. To involve more people and for a better feel of what people wanted, John stepped up his walkabouts, becoming very disciplined about listening as well as talking about improvement and customer needs.

Having taken the lead, he made sure his colleagues kept up with him. All the directors manage the Quality process explicitly in their area and continually review progress. Each director takes the role of project leader on an improvement project to learn more about the practice of Quality and to encourage more interaction. To make sure the Quality leader's role is truly being played, each manager, including John, has a self-assessment form which checks behaviours against the Legal & General mission and values. In case the leader is not learning from this, another form goes to direct reports, who point

Legal and General Behaviours Self-Assessment Questionnaire

People   Score
- *I delegate authority and trust others to do their job*   ☐
- *I empower my managers to make decisions and fully support their decisions* ☐
- *I encourage my managers to be honest about their mistakes*   ☐
- *I do say 'No' and explain why*   ☐
- *I am accessible, staff can see me when they need to*   ☐
- *I make myself visible to staff*   ☐
- *I maintain good relationships and informal contact*   ☐
- *I coach my managers to adopt Quality behaviours*   ☐
                                                                Total   ☐

Performance   Score
- *I encourage feedback on my actions and behaviours*   ☐
- *I regularly talk to my customers to find out what they think*   ☐
- *I regularly talk to staff*   ☐
- *I censure anyone who deliberately compromises Quality*   ☐
- *The need for Quality is an integral part of how I make decisions*   ☐
- *I make decisions by seeking available facts, not purely on supposition*   ☐
- *I promote tough standards for myself*   ☐
- *I continually challenge the status quo as a way to stimulate improvement* ☐
                                                                Total   ☐

Integrity   Score
- *I always do what I promise*   ☐
- *I am honest about my own mistakes*   ☐
- *I accept responsibility for my actions*   ☐
- *My actions reflect what I say*   ☐
- *People see me as a champion of Quality*   ☐
- *I criticise constructively - not destructively*   ☐
- *I act honestly at all times*   ☐
- *I do not promote rumours*   ☐
                                                                Total   ☐

Professionalism   Score
- *I am always punctual and prepared*   ☐
- *I deliver on time, meet my deadlines*   ☐
- *I insist on punctuality in others*   ☐
- *I am honest in criticising an individual's poor performance*   ☐
- *I fully recognise good performance*   ☐
- *I always make my requirements clear*   ☐
- *My meetings always have a clear purpose, start and finish on time*   ☐
- *I spend time planning the personal development of my staff*   ☐
                                                                Total   ☐

Teamwork   Score
- *I seek all views and give everyone their say*   ☐
- *People feel free to express their views to me*   ☐
- *My direct reports work, together with me, as a team*   ☐
- *I have respect for and work together with my peers*   ☐
- *I encourage new ideas from others*   ☐
- *I am perceived as decisive but not as autocratic*   ☐
- *I do not obstruct collective decisions once made*   ☐
- *I show a willingness to listen generously with an open mind*   ☐
                                                                Total   ☐

Determination   Score
- *I fight hard for what I believe in*   ☐
- *I see things through to the end*   ☐
- *I set clear priorities and maintain consistent direction*   ☐
- *I do not allow departmentalism/blinkered attitudes to colour decisions*   ☐
- *I treat errors as opportunities for improvement*   ☐
- *I work to prevent errors, not react to them*   ☐
- *I insist that output matches customer requirements*   ☐
- *I talk about Life and Pensions mission, values, guiding principles and culture* ☐
                                                                Total   ☐

out where the leader is erring. From his and his team's assessment, the leader must identify three behaviours to improve and report on progress to his team. Thus continuous improvement has been built into the management process.

The new style has been readily noticed and appreciated by L & G people. It is not seen as 'soft'; neither is it seen as distinct from the business. Far from it: the other leadership dimension which John has successfully carried through is that the improvement process is directly about business. Exceptional customer service is the goal of most improvement projects at L & G; waste reduction and/or process improvement is the aim of the rest. Within six months, nearly £1 million of waste had been saved. Much more significantly, the service and process improvements have led to the achievement of a keen Quality edge with the publishing of 'A Commitment to Customer Service' – 'the most significant thing we've done for customers ever' according to one manager surveyed. John has continually demanded results from the Quality process. By setting the right environment and the right example, he's getting them.

Of managers and leaders

Workers manage; managers lead. This is one of the major transformations that can be expected from a Quality process. The people doing the work can also do the managing of it, leaving little apparent role for 'professional' management. There should be no need to instruct people to do work they know better themselves. The fix-it, process-chasing, paper-moving type roles should be weaned out as waste, along with the political, turf-defending ones. What is left is pure leadership.

The transformation at workforce level is considerable, but easily absorbed by 'ordinary' people who have the capacity to operate at a sophistication and complexity many times higher than we may currently expect. The transformation at manager level can be traumatic. A manager who has spent twenty years carefully collecting and nurturing status, control of information and instructional authority has to give it all away. In its place, he will be expected to be a teacher, a coach, a strategist, a supplier...a servant even. He is certainly going to resist and look for excuses not to change. Is my boss going to do this too?...Will he be my supplier?...If not, why should I? There is no alternative in a Quality process to leading from the top and setting the example first.

Jamie Houghton provides a classic example of Quality leadership. He comes from the family which founded and built Corning into a world-renowned business. He was expected to inherit the leadership of Corning. What was not expected was that he would bring a completely different style to the organisation. Jamie was one of the early believers in Quality in the USA. He campaigned vigorously for national Quality and helped lead what became known in the mid-eighties as the renaissance of American Quality. Inside the company, he was even more outspoken about the need for improvement, for customer satisfaction, for partnerships and for training. People at first thought that this was just the new chairman sounding off. They gave him a year or two to settle down but Jamie confounded the sceptics. Nearly a decade after first embracing and expounding Quality principles, Jamie is as passionate as ever. Some overseas units may only see the worldwide chairman every two years or so but at every visit, without exception, Quality remains the dominant topic. Quality leaders, such as Jamie Houghton, demonstrate such consistency that belief in their conviction is total. With such tenacity, many more people follow their example and become leaders themselves.

Pat Donovan is another living example of Quality leadership. He is not from a global corporation like Jamie Houghton, but the transition in the small UK heating and ventilation wholesaler known as BSS is no less impressive. Pat had worked his way up from a branch manager in this down-to-earth business which supplies the mechanical services industry from many small depots across the UK. Although business had been good, by 1986 the senior management team felt there ought to be a way of managing the business which did not rely so heavily on their managers' abilities to firefight. Total Quality was discovered and Pat homed in on this. He believes there is no substitute for single-minded and passionate leadership if one's aim is to sustain enthusiasm and set about communicating this passion early. He was quoted as saying at the time: 'You don't have to work in a Quality way, but you do if you want to work for BSS.'

Pat went through a number of phases of improvement which led to a complete reshaping of the way business was done. In 1987, BSS (UK) had no clear competitive edge. By 1991, on the 18 most important aspects of service that customers identified, BSS was the best supplier in every area, with an average lead of 8 per cent. Meanwhile, market share had increased by 30 per cent, revenue by 90 per cent, profits by 100 per cent. Pat puts a lot of this success down to the new leadership style, which is not only about clear direction and passion for Quality, but also about trust in people. He says: 'The key to success is to create an environment in which people feel able to try and fail. People perform well when they feel comfortable.'

At BSS, the people in the branches are allowed to manage their own work. This is no false empowerment. 'Acting on facts' is a requirement, and measurement and accountability is strong. Competency profiles are used to complement recruitment, role alloca- tion, objective setting and appraisal. Single status applies throughout. At Quality evenings, which Pat and his senior manager hold with staff around the country, attendance is voluntary, but 96 per cent turn up. Staff turnover has dropped by 40 per cent since the Quality process began. Pat's four imperatives of 'clear leadership', 'trust in people', 'customer first' and 'acting on facts' have paid off handsomely for everyone at BSS.

Bias

The bias control is an important tool for the leader to start the conver- sion to Quality behaviour within management. Instead of attempting to behave in an entirely new way from day one, and risking a highly visible failure, he can start by biasing his existing actions towards the new culture he is seeking to create. Thus, he can look at his forward schedule and bias his time more towards customers, as one example. When a retired director from a multinational with a strong Quality process joined the Board of another major company, he asked each of the other directors: 'When did you last spend time personally with a customer?' There was silence around the table. Those directors had not biased their time to ensure they visited customers and stayed close to them. It wasn't that they didn't think it was important – hence the embarrassed silence – but they had not forced time into their full agendas.

Bias can be transmitted in many forms, of which allocation of time is the most powerful and successful. Many leaders make Quality the first item on the agenda at meetings. This gives it immediate status and shows that everything else is subordinate. It also ensures that enough time is given to it – the other items are the ones that are squeezed. Robert Galvin went even further at Motorola. He not only made Quality the first item at Board meetings, he only stayed for that item. Everything else he felt could be left to others to review...but not Quality. Such bias is quickly picked up by others and copied.

The bias to Quality can be transmitted in simple ways. Pat

Donovan started to ask 'How's Quality?' before 'How's sales?' and found this sent a strong signal through the business.

Bias can be both personal and subtle. Don Peterson, who transformed Ford through Quality as chief executive for ten years, used to act massively unmoved when managers told him how many improvement projects were running or how many people were being trained in Quality techniques. The message was: tell me how the real measures are doing – reduction in variation on the lines, improvement in the customer satisfaction index, cuts in the development time. Colin Marshall, during BA's major transformation in the early eighties, simply wouldn't respond to any request for funds or action that did not impact on customer service. His management team quickly got the message; customer service moved to the top of every agenda and every memo.

Visibility

The Quality leader may not have to be an entertainer, but he or she does have to be visible. Once the leader has determined his vision and strategy, the next most important thing to do is to demonstrate what it means through example. He cannot influence people without contact. Apart from thinking time, his own office is about the least appropriate place to spend his time. He should be out and about with customers, with managers in different units, with salesmen, with operators, with all those whom he would like to influence. This should not be aimless wandering. It should be planned and it should be purposeful. He should listen to people and understand their practice. He should give his view and he should help people to see the strategic direction. He should invite feedback and comment. He should talk about work, not football or the weather. Above all, he should be positive. He should bias his talking towards opportunities, not problems; the future not past difficulties; successes not failures. He should be seeking to praise not censure; unite not divide. This does not mean he should be suppressing problems and difficulties – far from it, he is always seeking out the reality as opposed to opinion, this is a vital listening and probing role. But his response should be turned into the positive. These are the leader's moments of truth. He should have mentally rehearsed some of the situations and issues he will find himself in. The positive response, the Quality example, the uncompromised action...these will quickly spread his reputation.

One leader breaking the mould in accessibility is Richard Branson, who founded and built up the Virgin group into a billion pound business before selling a major chunk to Thorn EMI. Until recently, he ran this empire from a houseboat, where he also lived, only going onshore reluctantly as the meetings and his children outgrew the narrow space. Richard believes in informality and empowerment. He doesn't care for hierarchy: 'I believe in "small is beautiful" and that companies should be run from the bottom up not the top down.' The Virgin companies are run in small units of 50 or 60 people each spread around Notting Hill in London, where he is now based. 'We've got around 30 different switchboards in the area – it might be more expensive, but it's much more personal.'[5]

Team playing

Richard Branson is an example of a leader who sees himself as part of a big team, but many managers tend not to think of themselves as team members. Their self-image is more about being an individual at the top of a pyramid as opposed to being one of an interdependent team. Much coherence is lost this way. Indeed, the floors managers build between hierarchy levels are as great a barrier to improvement as walls between functions. Any hierarchical barrier (such as status differences, withholding of information, deferment to rank) will inhibit smooth transfer of policy and strategy into practice.

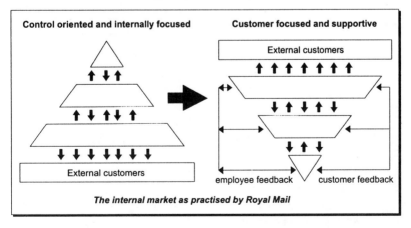

The internal market as practised by Royal Mail

The internal market concept inverts the pyramids and the manager becomes the supplier to the people in his area instead of the dominating force he may have been before. When faced with this prospect, the manager tends to see more value in being a team player. He now needs to cooperate with others to ensure smooth service to his customers so that they can deliver to theirs in turn. Empowering an organisation puts much more reliance on teamwork at all levels – but this tends to be on much looser membership criteria. In a conventional functional organisation, the team is defined by the functional structure – the boxes. The Quality process rapidly places emphasis outside of those boxes onto the processes which link them together and the interfaces between them. Managers become used to working in cross-functional and process teams. As a further evolution, the manager feels much less need for the security of the home box and feels comfortable operating way outside it, provided the whole team identity is strong. At this stage, managers have become team players in the big game and will move easily in and out of an array of temporary groupings to get things done.

Crosfield Chemicals is an example of this management transition. Crosfield is a medium-sized company with a diverse customer base and operations on several continents. It needs to move fast to compete with both multinationals and local nationals. Peter Joslin, personnel director, sees their management team operating in overlapping circles of interest in order to do business successfully in this environment and chairman, Richard Duggan, is vigorously leading a Quality-led transition of management style to suit.

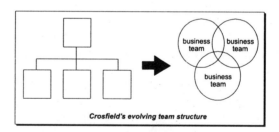

Crosfield's evolving team structure

Digital has taken the team concept of organisation a stage further. Digital's culture has always been to minimise structure and rules and to encourage entrepreneurship. There is no denying the success of this approach with Digital becoming number two in the computer world through the ability to respond flexibly to customer needs without concern for internal constraints. Despite this, Digital grew to be a 100,000 strong global organisation with countries, divisions, areas, etc. Founder Ken Olsen was never comfortable with too much structure and was always looking for ways back to the original pioneering spirit.

Digital has thus always been in a state of flux, with a permanent search for a non-obtrusive structure. Nonetheless, Digital too found itself caught out by shift in computer buying brought on by the recession. Suddenly, the biggest and best technology was not the preferred solution. Customers wanted a practical application at a good price; who made it mattered less.

In response to this, the latest organisational format re-emphasises the need for entrepreneurs. The concept creates and empowers a network of customer-orientated entrepreneurs. Each entrepreneur is responsible first and foremost for satisfying his or her group of customers and second for profit. The entrepreneur can sell non-Digital products (some even sell IBM equipment – Digital's biggest rival) and can buy non-Digital services, if that is the most effective solution for the customer. He can hire whoever is most appropriate and set up whatever structure fits his business.

This network of entrepreneurs is based firmly on the inverted triangle concept. If two entrepreneur triangles are working in overlapping space, they will bargain with each other and form contracts. To smooth out the road blocks, Digital has a second key role – the coach. A coach at Digital is a senior executive, who is not profit-responsible, but there to support and encourage his entrepreneurs. Between the European president and the entrepreneur (who might be quite young and junior in experience) there can be no more than three levels. The business is therefore managed more as a series of Boards (some 40 or 50 in Digital Europe) than a hierarchy. As a foundation for the entrepreneurial teams, three dimensions of support are on hand – geography (the country or location), skills (technical or functional expertise) and industry (sectoral knowledge). The result has been a closer focus on customer needs, a considerable flattening of structure, the checking of a tendency towards baronies and real empowerment for the entrepreneurial teams. Naturally, Digital has a strong Quality process to bind it all together and, as a consequence of market pressure, Digital Europe is intensively revamping its own Quality process to extract more out of the organisation.

Empowerment

Edwin Artzt, chief executive of P & G, believes there are two key steps to empowerment. One is to equip people to be successful, through training and coaching. The second is delegation: letting them do it. Great leaders delegate well. Empowerment means achieving good delegation throughout the whole organisation. It is not something we do to our staff, it's more a case of removing the impediments preventing them doing their work to the full. As Clem Smyth of Amdahl Ireland says: 'You don't get people to do things; you create an environment where they enjoy what they are doing.' Amdahl is a good example of practical empowerment. The computer manufacturer has created semi-autonomous workteams. They are not fully self-managed; they do not decide what to build and when. But they do control their time, the local layout, their level of skill (they can be trained to do as many operations as they wish) and they have complete responsibility for the Quality of their work.

To create an environment where this succeeds, Smyth has shaped a new managerial environment over the last five years. Teamwork is pervasive at Amdahl (managers are spending up to 60 per cent of their time in cross-functional teams) and training is the fuel that keeps the energy high. The role of the first-line supervisor has shifted from being the centre of control and decision making to 'being a leader, a provider of resources and a facilitator'. Supervisors are spending half their time in cross-functional teams on issues which may not relate directly to their area. They have developed a company-wide perspective and have grown into the roles of more senior managers.

Similarly, the workteams have absorbed the supervisor's old role as well as amalgamating many divided jobs back into build and test teams who make complete customer-ready products. Workteam emphasis has progressed from self-correction of errors through to prevention techniques to achieve defect levels in the low parts per million. They have adopted just-in-time service from team to team, reducing the time to build a mainframe from 135 days in 1985 to 59 in 1990. Associated paperwork has dropped too – the work orders recording internal transfers of parts and assemblies dropped from 800 to 14.

Many other parameters came down too, including some surprising ones. Overtime, which is decided by the workteams themselves, has dropped from 7 per cent of time worked to just 0.4 per cent. 'People here take responsibility,' says Clem Smyth. 'To fall behind schedule is something they are not proud of. It is an embarrassment not to function properly. Overtime is not seen as an opportunity to earn more.'[6]

Ultimately empowerment means letting go; letting people do the work we have employed them for and not second guessing them. Empowering a whole organisation is a major undertaking and is a net result of a successful Quality process. It requires a whole supporting environment in which management behaviour is consistent and the management process is efficient. This will take a lot of time and effort to create, but the Quality leader should start it off early by beginning to empower his or her own team.

Team coaching

The Quality leader does not seek unlimited and unconstrained empowerment; he very much wants to keep the released energy concentrated towards his strategic focus. He is also continually seeking to keep the energy high; an empowered team needs fuel and direction. The leadership style of coach is admirably suited to this. The coach knows the game and the competition; he sets the strategy; he trains the players; he rehearses tactics; he leaves the playing to the players.

One test of Quality leadership in an organisation is when the chief coach is changed. Philips were one of the first European multinationals to believe in Quality and as they dug deeper into it they believed even more: 'In the past, we have had every type of managerial programme and every kind of consultancy advice in Philips but they have not improved our overall profitability; we believe Quality will,' as one top executive has said. Alas, the Quality process wasn't strong enough to prevent Philips taking a beating from Japanese competition in the late 1980s. When the recession of the 1990s was added on top, Philips found themselves in deep trouble. Major surgery was demanded and a new chairman, Jan Timmer, chosen for his tough reputation, was brought in to do it. Big and painful cuts were indeed made and can be expected to continue, but, to the surprise of many, the Quality process was not cut out too. Far from it, Jan Timmer made it central to recovery. 'Philips Quality starts with me' was his proclamation, meaning not only that he recognised that he had to be the first to live up to Quality standards but that everyone else in management had to be prepared to as well. His coaching role was to help everyone to be able to make a similar statement and act as coaches for others to adopt rigorous standards. His own position with Quality was made abundantly clear: 'I consider it my personal task to accelerate the movement for change in Philips and the movement for Quality as part of that.'

A critical role of the coach is to communicate. Poor communications leads to energy loss and all organisations seem to suffer from communication difficulties. Internal surveys invariably rate 'communications' as weak, seemingly irrespective of size of organisation and, ironically, often after much effort has been made to enhance the communications process. Guy Peerboom, chairman of Elida Gibbs in Belgium, a marketing company with no manufacturing base, reveals a very typical problem. After two years of a very successful Total Quality initiative, with everyone involved and teams delivering major benefits, Guy was feeling quite pleased. He had himself spent many days attending all the training programmes as a participant and felt he had worked hard mixing with everyone and encouraging them. So he was somewhat disheartened to hear from a review of progress that people felt they did not know what was going on and what others were doing. Guy's company (at that time) numbered 32 staff. If Guy has this trouble how can anyone successfully communicate with 1,000 or 20,000?

The role of communications in the effective implementation of a Quality process will be looked at in more depth in Chapter 9, but, in a nutshell, the use of the widest variety of media as is practical, and plenty of them, is how this problem is managed. For this chapter, the focus is on the style of a Quality leader, of which being an effective communicator is a crucial aspect. Guy discovered for himself one of the side-effects of a successful Quality process, particularly with empowered teams: the demand for information expands geometrically and seems to be insatiable. There appears to be no real substitute for direct contact between the leader and his team, reinforcing the need for visibility. Team briefing, which is widely practised as a means of structuring communications in a complex organisation, can only real- istically provide the background. Once a message has gone through more than two levels, it becomes diffuse and distorted, losing its vitality and essence. One survey showed that 80 per cent of managers thought they were carrying out team briefings, but that only 30 per cent of their staff thought they were receiving them.

In even a moderately sized company, the leader simply cannot meet everyone face to face on a regular basis. But he can develop other leaders around his organisation and meet *them* – coaching, listening, informing and inspiring. In turn, these leaders can meet their teams, not passing on lifeless messages, but coaching, listening, informing and inspiring too. As this develops and people feel more empowered, the team leaders talk directly with one another and pass information around first-hand. In this way another important practice can be developed – networking. Networking becomes essential in flatter, faster organisations. Partly the need for people to network can be facilitated through technology. Digital, for example, has a world- wide system called 'notes' which literally allows any one of 100,000 Digital people to talk to anyone else and obtain information on any topic. The screen-based system has a few rules to keep some order but it is very easy to start a communication. One person may request help with a problem and half a dozen others might respond, all seeing the others comments. A round-table discussion builds up with others offering comments or suggestions – except there is no table and the participants might be thousands of miles apart, on different time zones, and may never meet face to face.

But technology is not really what networking is about. Networking is for people to have access to others for exchange of knowledge and information – really ad hoc and fluid team-forming with no boundaries. A network meeting might be two people and last five minutes or 20 people for a day. There is no formal setting of agendas or even choice of participants; it happens because there is a need. Apple, in Cupertino, California, has worked this way from the start. Today, as a large corporation, they see little reason to change. Often wearing T-shirts and sneakers, Apple people will wander into a meeting if it looks interesting and join in if they have something to contribute. The individual seeks out his or her own information and own learning. But the organisation makes this very easy to do, with no barriers, no restrictions and much support.

Again, the Quality leader can set the style for establishing networking. He can bring people together, show common interests, make the first linkages. As part of his coaching style, he can then encourage further development of informal interchange. Effort spent this way may go some way to alleviate all the pressure coming back up the line for answers to what is really going on.

False customers

One related barrier to organisational improvement is the phenomenon of 'false customers'. A false customer is anyone who interposes their needs between the supplier and the true customer. In the absence of a close relationship (and good data) between customer and supplier, the influence of false customers can be very strong. The forward links in the supply chain (dealers, advisers, agents, etc.) can distort customer data and become false customers. In fact, these are rarely the major source of false customer influence. By far the major influence will be inside the organisation.

As organisations grow, work is subdivided, eventually leading to specialists being developed for key needs. The specialist or expert is usually not doing the work but advising or instructing on it. When the

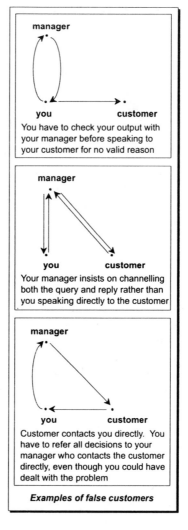

manager

you   **customer**

You have to check your output with
your manager before speaking to
your customer for no valid reason

manager

you   **customer**

Your manager insists on channelling
both the query and reply rather than
you speaking directly to the customer

manager

you   **customer**

Customer contacts you directly. You
have to refer all decisions to your
manager who contacts the customer
directly, even though you could have
dealt with the problem

Examples of false customers

running of the business is looked at afresh from a process viewpoint,
it can be seen that these specialists may be distorting or disrupting the
meeting of customer needs because of their different perspective. The
Quality leader will need to be aware of this issue, which will create
conflict and tension as the organisation transforms into a customer-
driven business. In the pre-Quality mode, the specialist may be more
powerful than the direct suppliers to the customer and thus the false
customer pull is strong. This aspect is dealt with further in Chapter 6
on process improvement; however, this type of false customer is still
not the most disruptive.

The category of false customer which can be most damaging is the leader himself in the role of 'professional' manager. Most workteams of any kind from sales to factory will have a fund of examples of management interference and its bad effects. The workteam have a job to do and they know how to do it. When instructions come down from high, without explanation, to do it some other way or to do something else, then the team feel confused and demotivated. This happens regularly in most organisations as managers attempt to control the dynamics of a complex system without appropriate data and with too little thought. It is management interference and is highly wasteful. A classic example is the New South Wales state rail-road general manager who took decisive action if a train was more than three minutes late. Station managers up the line were severely berated; corrective action down the line was triggered in order to speed things up. Unfortunately, the normal statistical variation for the line was plus or minus five minutes, as was found later by analysis. Thus the three-minute train was still in control...until the general manager took action. Every one of his reactions moved the system more out of control and his subordinates' responses even more so.

The Quality leader should think hard about his interaction with his team and beyond into the processes of the business. Am I acting in an informed and constructive way or is my intervention more of a knee-jerk? Is there purpose behind what I am asking people to do, or is it more of a whim or a hobby-horse? Does my request fit in with our improvement strategies and is it consistent with Quality disciplines? If the answer is no to these types of questions, I should keep my nose out of things.

The leader is the most powerful person by definition and his requests may well be met first regardless of customer needs or agreed priorities. He should proactively try to eliminate anything he does that might be seen as a false or unnecessary intervention. Once teams have been successfully empowered, they will have the confidence and the data to stand up to false customers. Until then, it is the responsibility of the leader to resist any tendency to act in that way.

Changing the game

One of the Quality leader's biggest problems (and thus conversely a big opportunity) is that much of what people do at work in the West has little to do with prescribed roles and responsibilities. Many people at work are simply playing games – sometimes sophisticated games, especially at management levels. Managers compete with each other; they try and outsmart their internal rivals; they withhold information to gain a little advantage; they defend their own and lay blame on others; they manipulate budgets, tucking away little amounts here and there. At senior levels, political jockeying can be very intense with resources tied up in making a case which may be purely territorial. A vast amount of energy is diverted into these political games, with many false customers demanding as much or more attention than real customers. That such wastage of talent and capability is allowed would be astonishing to an outsider, but inside the game is real and played by most – after all this is one of the ways the big players get to the top.

What are the rules of the new game?

It might be easier to think through what you would put people in the sin bin for if this were basketball or attract yellow or red cards if football. Which of the following behaviours are the greatest sins in your eyes?

	ticking off	yellow card	red card
• rubbishing an employee			
• rubbishing a customer			
• rubbishing the company			
• rubbishing a supplier			
• being rude to a customer			
• letting a customer down			
• keeping a customer waiting			
• letting errors out of the door			
• selling a substandard product			
• deceiving a colleague			
• not doing what you say			
• not saying what you mean			
• playing not-invented-here			
• playing overt politics			
• playing covert politics			
• being invisible			
• being unapproachable			
• taking a safety risk			
• taking an environmental risk			
• avoiding business risks			
• taking an unauthorised financial risk			
• covering up a mistake			
• walking past a problem			
• saying it's not my problem			
• short-term expediency			
• being self-serving			
• not being a team player			
• 'shooting the messenger'			
• intellectual bullying			
• battling over territory			
• others ...			

Take the most important ones and turn them into positive statements, e.g.: 'In this company, we pride ourselves on never inconveniencing a customer' or 'We will always treat our people with individual respect' or 'I, as a team member, will attend to any problem I detect, regardless of its origin.' Many companies thrash out in workshops lists of desired behaviours; these are displayed prominently to encourage feedback and reinforce the new practices.

Such games occur at all levels – at the extreme, they may have become more engaging than proper work. The games are often most intense and most destructive between the organisation boundaries – night shift/day shift, workteam/supervisor, sales/marketing, ground staff/air staff, head office/field...and even spread outside of the organisation – buyer/supplier, distribution/dealers.

The Quality leader should have a clear intent about this. All the energy, cunning, inventiveness should go into the one big game: becoming more successful as a whole team. Playing games is OK as long as it is this game. The Quality leader can be well prepared for this. By defining future practice in the form of a vision and strategic picture, he can say what the game is and what the new rules are. How the game is played comes with the Quality process, together with training, coaching, challenge and competition needed for an exciting game. Quality, the new game, has the potential to attract as much participation as all the old ones. The Quality leader ensures that playing it is not voluntary.

Shadows

Richard Paine of South West Electricity uses the term 'shadows' as a lucid description of a kind of behaviour that is one of the toughest tests for the Quality leader. Shadows are those people who definitely do not want to go North, to use another metaphor. The Quality process inevitably spawns a number of shadows and they need to be dealt with. The Quality leader knows that for any revolutionary change, there will be outright opponents. He can choose to take them on early to demonstrate his determination or by-pass them to return to later when he has built up the head of steam and the process is rolling. He most definitely should not be diverted by them. Adjusting the direction by a few degrees either side of North is acceptable, but aiming North-East or North-West means he is being pushed too far out. Outright opponents, the very black shadows, have to go. They do not want to be on this train and they should be helped off.

The greyer shadows are more difficult. These are people who profess support, even enthusiasm, for a course of action, but back in their own stronghold do nothing towards it or even subtly undermine it. The leader needs antennae sensitised for this type of behaviour, which is very prevalent and energy-sapping. It can happen at all levels, from the board member who continues to defend his territory, to the sales manager who books a trip abroad rather than attend Quality training, to the technical director who dismissively rejects a project team's findings, to a supervisor who ignores an improvement suggestion from a worker. If the expected Quality behaviours have been discussed, debated and published, then the shadow is going to become more visible over time. If the appraisal system has been aligned to the Quality process, then evidence will become apparent compared to role model behaviour.

Being neutral is not enough. At Xerox, any manager not positively displaying behaviours consistent with the Quality role model (all Xerox managers are assessed by their subordinates) has no chance of promotion. A persistent shadow should be counselled to modify his actions. If this is not successful, then more severe action, as for any serious misdemeanour, should be taken. Ultimately, the organisation will not have room for such people. Fewer leader roles are required in a Quality organisation anyway, so the inference should be clear: all those who stay on the train going North should be prepared to pay for the trip and make a positive contribution to the journey.

Recognition

Recognition makes the energy flow – probably better than anything else. As Tom Malone, chief executive of Milliken has said: 'Recognition is the fuel that keeps it happening.' Like most things in Quality its effect applies at all levels and the most important influencer is the person at the top – the Quality leader. As Motorola state in their key beliefs: 'To get people to care about Quality, you have to care about them.' Constant respect for people is Motorola's first and most important belief.

Recognition from the leader counts. There is a seemingly unlimited range of ways to recognise contributions and the leader needs to develop as wide a range as he can handle well – this whole area is discussed in more depth in Chapter 7, People Make Quality; here, the emphasis is on the behaviour which the Quality leader should develop and learn to practise. He should start with his own team and begin to apply some key practices. The first is that recognition means what it says – recognising a person. Organisations can become impersonal and people do not like being treated as cogs or numbers. Everyone responds to being noticed as an individual. A further Motorola key belief states: 'There's only one way to care about people and that's one at a time.'

People like to get thank you's. Indeed research on teams of all levels shows that this is what people mostly want by way of reward, even for exceptional effort. On the other hand, in practice a thank you needs to be more thoughtful than just saying the words. As with all the factors of Quality leadership, words are very empty compared to behaviours. One effective form of thank you is simply to acknowledge positively work that has been done. Many people feel that the boss does not know what they are doing and is unaware of the efforts they are making. This can be rectified by devising a response mechanism: a short note, perhaps, that shows that you have registered what has been discussed (perhaps from a walkabout meeting or a report sent in) with some comments, just as you would respond to a letter or meeting with a customer (we hope!).

Another significant recognition factor links strongly with empowerment. The second reward people tend to covet after a thank you is to become more involved. Thus an improvement team who have recommended an improvement path, or an individual who has made an improvement suggestion, will nearly always ask to be involved in the implementation. The Quality leader can anticipate this and be ready to reward people with further involvement. With thought and planning, this can become a natural progression into team empowerment.

Aligning the infrastructure

'People watch your feet and your wallet, not your lips.' This old adage is pointing out that people pick up on many signals to guide the way they work and only if we have most of them aligned our way will the majority be inclined to move. Some seriously mixed signalling can occur when we move strongly down the road towards new practice. For instance, we may have established new focus and direction, and be setting the example as leader, but still continue to appraise, promote and reward people in the old way. The infrastructure is saying the old way is still the most important when it comes down to it.

In time, virtually every procedure needs to be changed to support the new practices, but not all at once. Some can wait and are best left until the Quality process has energised and empowered people; they will then take out many of the barriers themselves, replacing them with something more suitable. But some need tackling earlier because they are complex and influential processes in their own right and could prevent the energy rising. Laurie Stark, as TQ Director for BP Chemicals, has been centrally involved in BPC's Quality process since it began on a company-wide basis in 1987. Reviewing the substantial progress three years later he was surprised to find that the one system which had not changed significantly was reward. As he said: 'After all the training and communications about prevention and planning, we still pay managers to be heroes and firefighters.' This was clearly inhibiting further progress.

The appraisal and reward systems need to be reviewed quite early in the Quality process to prevent barriers arising. Many appraisal systems have evolved into one more elaborate internal game and can add little to the purpose and direction of the business. Some leaders simply take the whole thing out. Others turn it around to support and reinforce their messages. Thus, for example, teamwork might be high-lighted. At Amdahl Ireland, Clem Smyth believes that all their major changes are being achieved through teamwork outside of the functions and has aligned the appraisal and reward system accordingly. 'The more thoughtful managers learn that the way to get on is to be on a well-functioning team, not through empire-building. The criterion for moving up has changed. Where individual stardom was rewarded, it led to people not sharing information. Teamwork makes that sort of behaviour redundant. If they are rewarded on the basis of motivating and leading teams then that's what they engage in. Departmentalism and territorialism are seen as delinquent. Achievement through collaboration is what's rewarded here.'[7]

The appraisal mechanism will certainly need an overhaul if not an outright replacement. Coupled with the Quality framework (see Chapter 3), this may be all that is needed to define a manager's role. He will have the strategic missions and improvement goals for the business which he will understand and believe in, having been heavily involved in their construction. It is his responsibility to translate those into local priorities and objectives for his area and to involve his people in that translation. His colleagues from other areas will be involved too, for they acknowledge a strong interdependence.

When the manager's performance is reviewed, the criteria are clear, having been unambiguously stated as objectives towards the overall goals. These will be tougher and more meaningful than looking at budget variances for they are forcing the manager to show and deliver significant improvement. Many companies have recog-nised the power of this type of appraisal and many large US corpora-tions – Ford, for example – have switched from paying bonuses on quarterly financial returns to demonstrated improvements which will sustain those returns. But the appraisal system in the Quality business goes further than this. It not only requires the manager to demonstrate improvement in prescribed performance but in behaviour too – also prescribed. For this, the Quality leader's role should be expressed as a model to relate to – an image of what the ambitious manager should aspire towards. ICL, Europe's largest computer maker, has a ten-point Quality leader role model. Xerox' questionnaire for subordinates is a 28-point check list to fill out about their boss. If he is not playing the Quality role, this shows it.

Making Quality personal

In practice, the toughest test for the Quality leader is to do it himself. Believing in Quality is one thing; doing it is another. For some reason, most leaders feel that the practice, the disciplines, the tools – the everyday stuff of Quality – are not appropriate for what they do. This is a cop-out. Senior management teams can make very poor decisions, which may not become apparent until years later, but are still poor. Bankers can make lending decisions which can burden the bank for decades. Industrialists can make acquisitions which are never going to fit with the main business. Of course, even senior managers must be allowed to make mistakes and they will continue to do so, but there is little defence for those who make their decisions solely on judgement and intuition. Important though these are, the disciplines and practices of Quality can enhance the result.

Very few top executives, outside of Japan where the exact opposite applies, can be bothered with the improvement methodologies which a Quality process offers. The Quality leader should consider this and ask why. The leader who tries to apply some of the learning himself will find he is well rewarded. Not only will he see that it is relevant to him too but he will understand it so much more and feel more in tune with the difficulties many of his people will have in turning the concepts into daily reality.

It is not just the big issues. Improving some of the basic routines of the leader's daily life can be fruitful. Leaders are as prone to ineffective habits as anyone else, but their effect can be much greater. Quality disciplines offer a good route to changing some of these and there is no better time than when you are expecting everyone else to do it too. How you organise your day or your paperwork, how you run meetings or decide which ones you run, where you spend your time...

Twenty ways to become obsessive about Quality
(... and influence people)

Most successful business leaders have developed their own ways for conveying what is important to them to others. Here are some ways of demonstrating by action that Quality is important to you.

1 Be visible on Quality

Walk about in the office; talk about Quality to everyone; put your nose into all Quality issues and be seen to spend time on them.

2 Make Quality item one on the agenda

For your regular management meeting, put Quality first on the agenda as the standing item for every meeting.

3 Book time to spend with customers

Block off a significant amount of time to visit customers, talk with the people using your products or services, watch what they are doing, listen to their views; let your staff know you are doing this ... and ask them how many customers they've talked to recently.

4 Bias decisions using Quality

At any meeting or discussion where a decision is made, make Quality the determining factor (eg is this requisition going to improve our service to our customers?); bias your actions heavily towards the Quality way wherever a choice is presented; never be seen to make a decision on cost factors alone.

5 Tell stories about Quality

Develop a fund of anecdotes about good and bad Quality that you have experienced; tell them to everybody at any opportunity (you won't become too boring ... Quality stories are just as interesting as football, share prices or the weather - try it).

6 Be scathing about memos which are not about Quality or improvement

Return any self-serving, political memo covered with red ink (how will this improve our service to customers?... what value does this add?) and copy others.

7 Watch the details

Quality in the eyes of the customer often comes down to small details and you should be the guardian of these; be finicky (where it counts), point out little inconsistencies or lack of care; your staff may not like it but they will soon learn that they are important to you.

8 Reveal errors

We can only improve if we know the errors; talk about your own mistakes and how you learned from them; make error-identification and correction a visible and legitimate part of daily work through problem boards, meetings, informal discussions.

9 Make Quality live

Quality should be real and lively: feedback from customers, recovery from errors, ideas for improvement and performance against standards should be displayed and discussed ... in imaginative and dynamic ways.

10 Celebrate positive Quality results

A good new idea, an encouraging letter from a customer, hitting a higher performance level ... is enough of an excuse for a small spontaneous celebration, with credit and praise going to everyone remotely connected with it.

Twenty ways to become obsessive about Quality
(continued from previous page)

11 Censure anyone who deliberately compromises Quality

Find the appropriate penalty and use it publicly ... but first be very sure it is deliberate and not the fault of the system the person is operating in.

12 Be generous on Quality

If someone has an idea which will improve the service to your customers but requires some funding, pay for it immediately and worry about where to put it in the budget afterwards (better still, create a budget solely for such incidents).

13 Build models

Where a section, team or location has done something interesting on Quality, set them up as a model for others to look at and think about, not necessarily to copy them but to learn from and be encouraged by their experience (note: avoid making heroes of the people involved; this can have the opposite effect).

14 Expose yourself!

Set your own improvement goals (for your own work, not your team's) and display your progress; avoid being too ambitious, you have to succeed!

15 Do what you say you will do and do it very well

Ruthlessly limit what you become involved in to a very few (no more than five) key priorities and stick with them to 100 per cent completion; discourage all from the opposite approach: taking on too many initiatives and leaving them 80 per cent complete or worse.

16 Encourage training

Pertinent training has a strong influence on Quality; ignore pleas of being too busy to go on a training programme; go yourself too.

17 Make your customers real

Circulate letters, stories, articles from or about customers; invite them in to mingle with the staff; let the staff show what you are doing for them.

18 Challenge/prod/dispute the existing order

Why do we do it this way? is there a better way?

19 Rehearse situations

To have maximum impact, think through and prepare the Quality decisions, the celebrations, the customer visits, the talks on Quality and deliver them with enthusiasm.

20 Respect your customers and your staff

Displaying an interest in the people you are dealing with and being ready to respond to them is the foundation on which all Quality activities are built; without individual respect, all these activities are built on shaky ground.

there is great scope for challenging these and asking whether they are consistent with the Quality message and Quality behaviours. Prioritise those which can have an impact, set some goals and measures – and start improving. This is your personal improvement plan. Make sure you have a good feedback system (your secretary is a good starting point) and plot the improvement against the plan. It may be personal but you can be sure everyone else will notice.

Commitment

Quality gurus, management consultants and academics do not readily agree with each other – yet all will say that the number one necessity for successful business improvement is commitment from the leader. Commitment means determination, courage, passion, even ruthlessness in the pursuit of the vision. Revolutionary leaders need all of these to make an impact on an organisation. They also need subtlety, patience and humility to succeed in coaxing people to follow into new and unfamiliar territory. This is also commitment. This combination of driving strength and organisational sensitivity marks out the Quality leader and his commitment.

No one at Dun & Bradstreet in Europe doubts Richard Archer's commitment. Richard is President of Dun & Bradstreet International and responsible for developing the famous Dun & Bradstreet information service in Europe, the Middle East and Africa. Richard did not embark on a Quality process because it was fashionable or because he had seen it somewhere else; indeed it was only after a couple of years of intensive improvement that he realised that what he was championing was very similar to what others were doing under a Total Quality banner. Richard's need was simply to improve the performance of the business. Dun & Bradstreet International had grown from 10 per cent of the whole business to 45 per cent by 1989, but had stagnated. Margins were low, market share was declining, technology was outdated despite major investments, and internal structures and attitudes had deteriorated (separate cultures in the two main businesses had evolved and 'country fiefdoms' dominated). Things had to change and Richard was committed to changing them.

Richard set up a senior management workshop with an open agenda on 'what do we need to change?' The outcome was five critical change factors covering how the business obtained information, how it was sold, how customer needs were met and how products were created; but the big one was to change the 'cultural heritage', which Richard put into sharper focus as 'changing ourselves'. Excited by this outcome, the senior team went off to change things. Good progress was made but after nine months or so, Richard realised that the big issue of cultural change was being skirted around.

His response to this was to bring together a bigger group of managers – over 100 from across Europe to make sure that all the key players were there. This was the first ever all-management meeting and it had a big impact. Richard demonstrated his flexibility by accepting the meeting's rejection of the mission statement he had carefully crafted. He said 'if it is right, we must feel it in the gut' and his managers said they didn't; another was drafted there and then. Richard followed up this unique event in Malaga with another work-shop six months later in Cologne for the same group. To demonstrate his commitment to the process, he had undertaken some wide-ranging changes to the organisation structure to address points raised at the first meeting. To ensure everyone felt bound-in to the decisions, an electronic voting pad was used and the new structure was endorsed in this way. In addition, project teams with cross-border, cross-function membership were created to address the key business issues raised. But the key output of the second meeting was the emergence of Quality as the vehicle for the change in culture that the management team now fully understood was needed.

Meanwhile, Richard had two big worries: most of his 3,500 staff were not involved in this revolutionary process and his financial results were no better than when he had started. He tackled the first problem with a major emphasis on communications and involvement, launched with a company-wide attitude survey. From this point on, internal marketing was given a high priority and was matched to external communications, geared to inform and attract customers. The second problem was a tough one. By now many of the early recom-mendations of the change team had been implemented: for example, the whole selling process had been improved and the entire sales team retrained. But no hard results were coming through. Richard was under mounting pressure from corporate to concentrate more on the bottom line and curb the experiments. This is when the Quality leader has to have determination, belief and guts. Richard did the opposite to what was expected. His reading of the position was that he was not being revolutionary enough. He called for a third conference and put to the 'organisation engine', as the big meeting had been christened, a series of radical proposals. Rather than cut costs further he proposed a dramatic investment increase in marketing, in training and in data systems, some $9.4 million worth. He suggested establishing a guarantee for customers, common performance standards based on customer needs, a whole range of new customer-orientated products and European-wide product branding. Revolutionary indeed for a company that had been doing more or less the same things for 120 years.

At the third conference, Richard asked the 'organisation engine' for commitment to change. 'You have it' he was told but they did not agree to everything. They did not want a universal branding and they were very nervous about a customer guarantee. 'OK,' Richard conceded for the moment, 'but go away now and improve your own standards from a customer perspective.' This proved to be a break-through: by handing ownership over to his management teams, Richard had removed an impediment to progress. Up until this point, they felt this was 'Richard's programme'. Now they were empowered to act and required to act. Soon countries and functions competed to show improvement gain. The improvement energy exploded and results started coming in. But Richard was relentless; he was not going to drop the idea of a guarantee which he believed would be a clear differentiator. He started by installing an internal guarantee between units. This focused attention smartly and gave good learning experience. Standards rose higher still. To support the units, Richard provided extensive training to underpin the guaranteed service elements with best practice. Tony Glasborough, Director of Human Resource Development, consulted with managers in the units to find out their needs and created a programme called 'Service Quality in Action' to meet these needs. Thus, the Quality training was seen to be relevant and appropriate and was well received across Europe and beyond.

Eventually, Richard felt the time was right to launch his 'three-point promise', a guarantee covering the three things that customers cared about: Quality (of information), Speed (of delivery) and Service (interaction). The lawyers said you cannot do it; his staff said it would cost too much in credits; his managers said they could not live up to it. Nonetheless, in July 1992, after much preparation, the three-point promise was launched across Europe. It has been a great success, appreciated but not abused by customers, and providing tremendous focus on customer needs.

By late 1992, Dun & Bradstreet International's financial results were above target for the first time for many years. Many new products were out in the marketplace (with a much reduced time to market) and comparative surveys showed Dun & Bradstreet back in the lead position. Corporate Dun & Bradstreet began investigating Richard's improvement process for application across the whole group. Richard's commitment to Quality leadership had cut through decades of convention to turn around a company and delivered hard results. Richard did not set out on a Quality revolution...but ended up leading one.

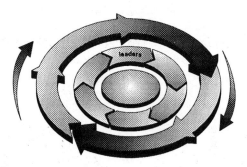

SUMMARY

Are you a Quality leader?

1. Can you paint the big picture (the vision) for people to work within?
2. Can you describe what will give your business a Quality edge and can you convert this into stretching goals for your people to aim for?
3. Do you see change as one of your fundamental aims?
4. Deep down, do you need the trappings of the old style (status, authority, control...)?
5. Are you prepared to let go and give people the freedom to deliver?
6. Do you know how to coach?
7. Are you ready to give and receive feedback on behaviour...including your own?
8. Are you prepared to change your own style?
9. Do you have improvement goals for yourself?
10. Are you committed?

The best revolutionaries are both visionaries and missionaries. They show which way to go...and are first down the road. But much of this can be learned by the business leader, like any management practice (even by old dogs!).

If you have any doubts about your answers to these questions, try working on a personal development plan now; the pressure and intensity of the Quality process will expose any weak areas.

5

Customers Mean Business

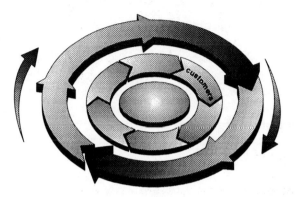

It is obvious that businesses cannot survive without satisfied customers; yet, in many companies, only a small proportion of managerial effort is spent on customers. Those who have prospered by aligning the business around customer needs, plan to spend even more time this way. For attracting customers today is very tough; losing them is disastrous. Even satisfying our customers may not be enough...the competitive edge may only come from customer delight.

'We do not need financial pundits to tell us how to run our business. We have customers who tell us.' Sir Richard Greenbury, chairman, Marks & Spencer

'The customers' prizes are the ones that count.' Yoshiro Okishima, general manager, Minolta

Rediscover your customers

Mr Smith runs a family nursery business in Surrey, a part of England where there seem to be as many nurseries as there are gardens to put the plants in. Mr Smith's nursery is always packed, with queues of cars way down the road. His prices are much the same as the others; his plants are quite a bit superior. But what brings people back is Mr Smith himself. Mr Smith gives service. He is always there, answering questions all day long ('Mr Smith, would these grow well on a south wall?'), helping carry bags of peat to cars (laying out newspaper in the boot to put them on), even guiding the traffic. Mr Smith has plenty of other staff but he wants to be out there with his customers, listening to them, giving and receiving advice. Mr Smith's business is his customers.

Many businesses start out like Mr Smith's but lose something as they grow. They become detached, decoupled from the customers who created them. The personal contact is lost, replaced by 'modern professional management'. One of the first actions a Quality leader can take is to reverse this trend. Under a Quality process, customers have the answers to improving the business. To profit from this, the leader must first rediscover his customers.

Customers are people

Without customers we have no business. Customers define the purpose of our business and provide the revenue which funds it. But customers are people and people need constant attention. This conflicts with a growing organisation's needs to regularise and standardise. The common jest 'this would be a good business, if weren't for the customers' reflects a real issue. Do we drive the business by the vagaries and unpredictabilities of customers, or by the more predictable disciplines of financial accounting?

Or to use a real example: when a woman takes a badly stained dress to the dry-cleaners ten minutes before closing and wants it back the next day, which of the following is the better response at the counter? A large UK chain said a minimum of 24 hours is needed and removal of the bad stain cannot be guaranteed. Small Spot Cleaners' franchise-holder John Mitchell says 'I'll see if I can do it now.' The former response is one derived from volume-thinking and is correct from an accounting viewpoint because the price will not cover the extra work and disruption involved. John, however, has no doubts. 'If I help the lady sort out her problem, she will come back to my shop.' He cleaned the dress there and then, while the customer did some more shopping, and when she returned 20 minutes after closing time, the dress was ready. He did not charge for the service because it hadn't gone through the dry-cleaning process. His payment for half-an-hour's work: an impressed customer who may well remain loyal for years and even bring in other customers. The cost to the large company that didn't respond? A lost customer with a story to tell others about the poor service. This cost will not show up in the management information system. Management will only know when sufficient customers have voted with their feet and the revenue is down. Then it is often too late. Turning around a poor service reputation is tough and no one has done it quickly.

What organisations need are more staff like John Mitchell who win customers and then keep them. That many businesses appear to have a shortage of such people is not that they are very special and rare; rather it is because organisations suppress and discourage such behaviour. Although management would indignantly deny it, business can be anti-customer in practice. The Quality revolution reverses this, but not by starting at the shop counter or the sales office. Being customer-driven starts at the top with the Quality leader and the policies and practices which he or she adopts.

Value for money

Marks & Spencer are at the other end of the retailing scale to Mr Smith and Spot Cleaners, but they have much in common. M & S started out much like Mr Smith by focusing hard on giving value for money. They have never lost that vision and are proud that the £6 billion business is 'run by retailers not accountants'. To M & S leaders, giving value starts with the customer. Every sale is monitored, every return analysed, every complaint followed up. M & S wants to know everything about its customers. They strive to give their customers exactly what they want and have constructed their supply chains to deliver precisely that. As Alan Walter, Technical Director states: 'We used to sell what we bought; now we buy what we sell.' This very significant distinction means all the responsibility is down to M & S at the front end of the chain. As a result they are obsessive about detail and very much hands-on.

Alan has never forgotten the lesson from his first M & S store in Yeovil, where the manager threw out the whole of the day's bread because it didn't seem fresh enough. There was nothing wrong with the bread and the customer almost certainly wouldn't have noticed but it was not up to the manager's standards and that was that. The fact that the shelf was now empty was something he could defend to a customer; accepting a lower standard was indefensible (Mr Smith's nursery has exactly the same attitude: Mr Smith is very reluctant to sell a plant that is less than top class, even if the customer wants it; he would much rather withdraw it from the shelves). In the quest for managing the detail, the deputy chairman at M & S does not think his time is being wasted spending an afternoon in a meeting about loose buttons on blouses. The chairman, himself, will walk the stores as often as he can: 'I have to buy and sell each day – I love it.' He checks the products, the service, the environment; if anything is not up to the highest standard – a peach is not a full rich colour for example – word goes all the way down the supply chain, in this case right to the grower in Spain.

M&S

Company Principles (UK)

Selling clothing for the family, fashion for the home, and a range of fine foods - all representing high standards of quality and value.

Creating an attractive, efficient shopping environment for customers.

Providing a friendly, helpful service from well-trained staff.

Sharing mutually beneficial, long-term partnerships with suppliers, encouraging them to use modern and efficient production techniques.

Supporting British industry and buying abroad only when new ideas, technology, quality and value are not available in the UK.

Ensuring staff and shareholders share in the success of the Company.

Constantly seeking to improve quality standards in all areas of the Company's operations.

Fostering good human relations with customers, staff, suppliers and the community.

Acting responsibly towards the environment in all our operations and also, with our suppliers, in the manufacture of the goods we sell.

Marks & Spencer company principles

Over the years, this uncompromising but straightforward approach has become second nature to people working at M&S. In 1991, the company set out its principles on the back of a little booklet – not because people were beginning to lose the instinctive understanding of the M&S way of doing things, but because expansion into mainland Europe had brought a lot of new people into the group.

The clarity of this operating practice is very evident; the M&S image for service and product quality is unsurpassed. If people in the UK are asked to name a company renowned for service (or simply a Quality company) invariably the majority will suggest Marks & Spencer. In both 1991 and 1992, difficult retailing years, M&S made over £600 million profit (around 12 per cent), boosted to £736 million in 1993. Sales per square foot in 1991 were a well-above-average £517 and over the two years 1991/92 more than a million square feet of new retailing space was added. Perhaps even more telling, M&S is the only retailer in the world with a AAA credit rating. Having a simple value-for-money focus is not such a bad way to run a business.

Who is the customer?

For an organisation seeking major improvement, the customer is the primary driving force. Obviously, the external customer who pays for the service is important for the reasons outlined above in winning and losing customers. But who is he or she? Which one? Do we respond to the needs of the big customer or the small one?...the demanding one or the passive one?...the immediate purchaser or the consumer? The reality is we will be dealing with many customers on a continuous basis and they are all important. In a Quality organisation, the customer is a generic word for the receiver of a service. For every transaction, we must have a customer – a person to tell us whether we have got it right or not. Without an identified customer, we should question why we are doing this activity. With an identified customer, we can find out what is needed. If everyone is thinking 'customer' in this way, a strong movement for improvement is created.

At the beginning of a Quality process, many companies define categories of customer to help people understand the need for customer-orientation. Distinctions are made between internal customers and external and sometimes between customers and consumers if both are supplied, e.g. a PC manufacturer who sells to the public as well as through dealers. Ultimately though, the same generic concept applies throughout – *my* customer is the person receiving *this* service which I am providing *now*. Ian Vallance, Chairman of BT, thinks of his customers as 'constituents' including the government, the public (he receives 20,000 letters a month), industrial users and the people reporting to him. They are all his customers and he ruthlessly manages his time to devote appropriate attention to all of them.

In fact, most managers and also staff have complex constituents like Ian Vallance. We will find that we can categorise them as we understand their needs better. For example, until the Quality movement hit the airlines, passengers were just passengers; now there are many

From product-out to market-in as seen by Ricoh

The 'market-in' reverse of 'product-out' thinking provides tremendous challenges. Much of the improvement drive in Japanese manufacturing has its origins in tighter and tighter customer focus. From Henry Ford's 'any colour you like as long as its black', Toyota, Nissan, Honda and Mazda can offer any permutation from literally thousands of options and produce these to order on the same production line. No two cars on the line will be the same and yet the stocks of parts are very small to keep costs down. Further back in the supply chain, component manufacturers will produce a batch of just one component if that is what their customer wants. This in turn has required machine tool manufacturers to make highly flexible manufacturing systems to achieve fast and accurate changeovers - all driven by the market-in need to satisfy customer needs more precisely.

subdivisions such as business travellers, vacationers, family visitors, children travelling without parents. Such categorisation provides crucial focus on the differing needs and enabled British Airways, early on in their Quality process, to provide directly for each group, with, for example, the Young Fliers programme.

Identifying market segments from which distinct customer requirements can be characterised moves the supplier further away from 'product-out' thinking, where it is up to the customer to adjust his needs around our offering. Each customer category is still a compromise though and the smaller and more sharply defined the grouping, the closer we are able to match each customer's need. The customer concept can be used to challenge each business unit, each work team and each person in a Quality organisation to make the focus tighter and tighter until, ultimately, it is one person – the person being served now.

As such, the customer concept, as with Quality itself, is both strategic and tactical. We need strategic customer focus in order to design the products to attract customer interest and also to create the processes to deliver to their needs. But to really satisfy customers we have to be able to adjust tactically too. When it comes down to winning or losing customers, service is personal – one to one. The customer has no interest at all in our other customers. John Mitchell's customer felt as if there was no one more important to him than her and the stained dress. However big our company is, that is the feeling we should be giving each customer.

Winning customers

We do not sell to customers today; they buy. That is, they call the tune; they have the choice and will only buy from us if we make it easy for them or special for them. This applies whether they are existing customers or new ones. Customers buy on the value to them. The value is a perceived balance of features against cost. The customer is buying for a need, which might be to fulfil the requirements of another customer, to make life easier or more interesting, to counter a concern. The need is what determines the judgement of value and hence the attractiveness of particular features. The need may well be as much emotional as physical. Thus the judgement of value is a complex one going way beyond point-in-time product or service attributes. The cost element of value is not simply the price tag either. The customer may well be weighing up the cost of use as well as purchase and the cost of doing business with us as opposed to someone else.

Value is an individual judgement. What is important to one customer may be less so to another. Velcro USA President, Theodor Krantz, discovered this from Velcro's better understanding of their customers' needs as their Quality process took hold: 'Quality is not absolute, it depends on the customer's perception and requirements. For textile customers, appearances are important, whereas in the medical business the concern is cleanliness. The auto makers want durability, reliability and capability. With government, the specifications are all-important.'[8]

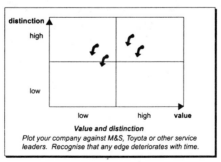

Value and distinction
Plot your company against M&S, Toyota or other service leaders. Recognise that any edge deteriorates with time.

Value is also a relative judgement. 'In the shoe industry, the hook and loop on a pair of kids sneakers is not especially important since the goods are barely used for three months. But with a $600 knee brace, the quality of the hook and loop closure is very important.' Relative value is equally influenced by competitive offerings and novelty. For this reason alone, we have to continually upgrade our products and services. For many years, reliability has been a top factor in car buying. Today, most cars (not all) are very reliable and this factor is beginning to be taken for granted, like safety in airline travel. Car makers have to retain reliability because to lose it would be disastrous, but have to provide many more new features as well. Ford US discovered this a few years ago. They had spent many years of an intense Quality programme concentrating on the vital need to raise reliability. Somewhat to their surprise, when they launched their highly successful Taurus, customers rated them pretty average on reliability but very good on extra thoughtful features. In fact, Ford had

M&S plus

For Marks & Spencer managers, achieving distinction is a way of life. If they cannot define a Quality edge, they simply do not do it...whether it is a product, a service or a whole business venture. They call this M & S plus - any new product or venture has to have an added distinction over the best previously on offer. Thus, for own label canned food, one target was certain Heinz brands, which the M&S products had to exceed in some way. Other examples are:

- washing powders: the first introduction of concentrated formulae to cut down the bulk and weight for the customer

- men's clothes: suit trousers sold separately to jackets; other shops only sold jacket and trousers together forcing a size compromise on to many customers

- recipe dishes: must contain over 50% meat, eg Chicken Kiev packaged as convenience food but visibly recognised as breast of chicken

- coordinated bedroom: duvets, curtains, sheets and wallpaper in fully coordinated packages, previously only sold in separate shops

- cut flowers: freshness and garden smell, created by growing for fragrance through sacrificing yield

- full flavour fruit and vegetables: new varieties of tomatoes, for example, grown for taste not yield and seasonal apples to move away from bland varieties

- furniture: delivered on time on the appointed day and arranged where the customer wants it

Through these and countless other applications of M & S plus, M & S have provided a recognisable Quality edge which the customer notices. As a result of adopting the separate trousers concept and other innovations, for instance, M & S has become the UK's biggest seller of men's clothes. In making flowers smell nicer and plants look healthier, M & S has become the biggest horticultural outlet in the UK, from a standing start five years before.

M&S plus

put a lot more effort into listening to what customers wanted and had built in some 1,200 items from a customer-wish list. These were quite mundane things like cup holders or quiet door-closing but they made a noticeable difference. Ford describe this success as focusing on 'the things that go right' as well as 'the things that go wrong'. Value is perishable and has to be renewed.

When it comes to attracting new customers as opposed to retaining existing ones, the supplier has to work even harder. Customers have the power to switch and may do so without compunction when persuaded, but they are also lazy. They are not going to seek you out; you have to attract them. This requires a distinctive offering in the market place to stand out from all the others. Again this factor is perishable; what is distinctive one year is ordinary the next unless it is continually upgraded.

Losing customers

The loss of a customer can be devastating although we may be bliss-fully unaware of it. Each customer who walks away takes away future years of repeat revenue. It has been calculated in the US that, for an automobile manufacturer, the average customer is worth $140,000 of revenue. For an appliance manufacturer, each customer generates $2,800 of revenue in a 20-year period and, in the service sector where there are many more customers, each one is worth $4,400 to a local supermarket and $80 profit to a bank. A lost customer goes from the bottom line not once but year after year.

The accumulated loss from upset customers

Number of customers, say	10,000
Percentage upset	5%
Number of upset customers	5% x 10,000 = 500
Average annual profit per purchase	£100
Number of purchases over five year period	10
Loss per upset customer	10 x £100 = £1,000
Lost profit over five years	500 x £1,000 = £500,000
Number of other customers influenced by each upset customer	10
Number not purchasing now	20% x 10 x 500 = 1,000
Additional lost profit	1,000 x 500 x £1000 = £1,000,000
Total profit loss over five years from one year's upset customers	£1,500,000

Estimate the equivalent figures from your own business and see the scale of loss, which is straight off the bottom line. This approach, pioneered by TARP, has led to quite sophisticated models being used to predict, and hence reduce, loss to business.

When they go, so too go living advertisements who may take our service to other potential customers. What goes too is one more source of intelligence for our business and a major stimulation for improvement. We cannot as easily find out what a customer wants and needs if the contact is broken.

An everyday upset

The integrated information system in the head office of a major company was due for a planned maintenance and everyone was informed that the system would go down at five o'clock. Instead it went down at four. The secretary of one executive lost sixteen pages of a report as it went off-line. It was an important report. Her boss happened to be responsible for commissioning the system from an outside supplier. This supplier now has a penalty clause in the contract which penalises them for any downtime. The secretary's frustration, the boss's rage, the reaction leading to a penalty on the supplier, could all have been avoided if everyone had been informed that the system might go down at four o'clock.

If the customer has walked away because someone has offered a better solution, then the loss is considerable but potentially recoverable. It may well cost us five times more to bring in a new customer than keep the old one, as Hewlett Packard found in their research. But if the customer has gone away because we have upset him or her, then we are into serious penalties. That customer will not want to return to buy from us again: HP found that 91 per cent of 'wronged' customers never bought from them again. Further, they may well have a story to tell to friends about us. Bad news travels further than good news. British Airways' research shows that a happy customer will tell four people about their experience; an unhappy one will tell 11. HP found their upset customers told up to 16 others.

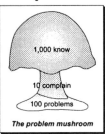

The problem mushroom

The ratios vary according to the type of encounter between supplier and customer and the value of the transaction, according to studies across different sectors. But a good rule of thumb would be that the disenchanted customer will tell about ten others of a bad experience. On the other hand, probably less than 10 per cent (survey findings range from 4 per cent to 50 per cent) bother to tell the supplier about it. This creates the problem mushroom effect – if we have 100 problems with customers over a period, we may hear about ten of them but 1,000 other people will also know. This problem mushroom is how companies develop a bad reputation. In the current climate of rising customer expectations and global competition to satisfy those expectations, a bad reputation could be terminal.

Service mentality

All companies are *service* businesses; some merely have more tangible products. The financial difference between winning and losing customers is enormous, yet the critical role of service is under-played in most organisations. Many companies will go so far with service but do not pursue it to the degree needed. Some manufac-turing companies, for example, will develop technological advantage and incorporate this into new products but then neutralise this edge by being a difficult company to do business with. A service mentality is required in order for all offerings, however technically advanced, to be seen through the eyes of the customer. Customers want support, comfort, information, interaction, response, recognition...as well as a good product. If they do quit buying, it will mostly be through a service inadequacy rather than a product factor.

Customer service in Japan

In Tokyo, 24-hour delivery is the normal standard. The complex distribution system works well despite the appalling round-the-clock traffic jams and the many links in the chain; the middle man is rarely cut out or by-passed in Japan. Instead everyone in the chain delivers exactly what is required when required and nearly always within 24 hours. OTDT (order today, deliver tomorrow) is expected.

Sanyo Shokai is a fashion clothing company with many thousands of lines. They will deliver anywhere in Japan in 24 hours and within four hours in Tokyo. They employ 4000 saleswomen to work in the big Tokyo stores, directly with the customers. Everyone reports in person to the local Sanyo Shokai office, not to give sales figures - that could be done by computer - but to feedback customer impressions about the products.

Yamato are Tokyo's equivalent of Federal Express but focused more on home delivery in direct competition with the Japanese Post Office. To Yamato's president "customer service is the first pillar of competitive advan-tage". Yamato practise what they believe: a delivery driver will try three times to deliver to an address in one day. It is not the customer's fault if they are out, Yamato believe, and they will carry on trying the next day, probably well outside of normal hours, until the customer is found at home.

Kirin have almost 50 per cent of Japan's share in beer. Despite this domi-nance, they continue to invest in state-of-the-art distribution centres closer to the customer, so that the local retailer always has fresh supplies. Although all the beer is canned or bottled, Kirin operate a FIT system (Fresh In Time) from 'brew to you' in 24 hours; out of stock is almost unheard of.

In Tokyo, you order your latest Toyota from your home. The salesman comes to see you and takes your precise requirements from an infinite permutation of models and options. Your car can be built and delivered to your home in four days.

Japanese manufacturers are often thought of in the West as being super-efficient at production but less efficient at service. Superficially this is so, for Japanese companies have shown less interest in automating their sales or administration teams, which are often vast. But this view misses a vital point: these companies do not want to cut them back, despite apparent excesses, because this might limit their ability to understand and stay close to the customer. In fact, some Japanese companies routinely move people into sales from manufacturing lines when they are displaced through automation. Their view is that you cannot have too much information on customers or too much contact. Western businesses tend to allocate much less of the total resource to market research or direct customer contact.

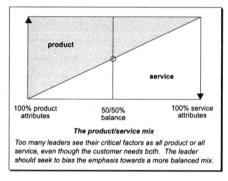

The product/service mix
Too many leaders see their critical factors as all product or all service, even though the customer needs both. The leader should seek to bias the emphasis towards a more balanced mix.

Whilst manufacturing companies underplay the service factors, many service companies rely too much on the interpersonal elements. This also can make it hard for a customer to do business with them; the customer wants to sum up the offering quickly and easily and this is hard to define if the elements are built solely around staff skills or professional competencies. When such service companies package their offerings up as products, they are often as user-unfriendly as those from manufacturing companies. Thus the insurance policy that is totally unintelligible or the instruction book which is gobbledygook.

Managing satisfaction

Reputations are built or lost through satisfying or dissatisfying customers. What does it take to satisfy a customer today? The customer will have a need which we are trying to fulfil. This may be well-articulated or very vague; either way it is our responsibility to identify the need as precisely as possible and meet it. If we do, then the customer will be satisfied. In a service environment, such as a shop, it is apparent that customer satisfaction is immediate and spontaneous, although much care may have been taken to standardise the experience and maintain a consistent interaction between the store and the customer. In business-to-business supply, it is much less so.

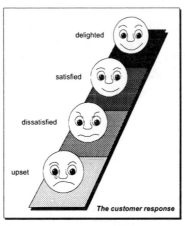

delighted

satisfied

dissatisfied

upset

The customer response

Most organisations assume that because they have a specification, if they deliver to that the customer will be satisfied. In the store the customer's response may be obvious. Pleased, disappointed, upset, annoyed...the shop assistant can sense this and respond. In the situation where the customer is more remote we cannot see the reaction and yet the customer's response could equally be disappointed, upset, annoyed. This response could be for an infinite number of causes: we might simply have got it wrong this time; the customer might have an internal problem; the customer's customer may have changed the requirements. Whatever the cause, if we want to ensure our customer is satisfied, we should be monitoring the response continually, exactly as a good shop assistant does.

In practice, we need to do more than monitor: we should manage the response. Every transaction with the customer creates a response, even if it is neutral and passive. Indeed, customers who have hardly noticed our service can be satisfied customers. They have more important things to deal with and if we have met the need and have taken the minimum amount of their time then we have done a good job. But then again there may be other related parts of the service that the customer is affected by which we may not be aware of. The service provided by an airline is often thought of as flying someone from A to B. But the service really starts some time before the journey with the airline schedules and arranging a ticket. The journey begins as the passenger leaves home and can involve considerable anxiety before real contact with airline staff is made. Similarly, at the end of the journey, the passenger is dumped in, probably, a strange land and left to himself to reach his real destination. For the passenger, the experience is from door to door, not just the relatively straightforward bit cocooned in the airliner. The customer's response will be to the whole experience, not the cabin service. We will know this if we have built the feedback mechanisms and from these we can make whatever adjustments are needed to keep the customer happy. The management of customer satisfaction is the responsibility of the supplier.

Providing value and distinction

So managing for customer satisfaction is no simple task. It is providing continual value in the eyes of the customer, knowing the perception of value is transient. It is being attentive to *today*'s customer's demands, right now, as well as preparing for *tomorrow*'s customer's needs. It is giving personal service – and efficient back room preparation. It is managing this moment's transaction – and the whole experience for the customer. It is providing value – and maintaining a distinction.

To achieve all of this dynamically, the Quality leader needs data and the mechanisms to provide it. He needs a minimum of four channels of information. One to keep him in touch with the customer's changing requirements; a second to monitor his output against those requirements; and a third to feedback his performance in matching the two. But these are all reactive, so he needs a fourth channel to anticipate his customer's needs and help keep him one step ahead. This data applies at the macro level of the whole company and at all levels down to one individual supplying another. Many suppliers, whether whole companies or internal departments, rely on a single channel – output – and build everything around that. The most outstanding product will fail to sustain perceived value with this alone and the most persuasive salesperson or the most charming representative will fail to recover it when it is lost.

The General Chemicals division of BP Chemicals has many industrial customers and lots of environmental pressures. For managing director, Mike Buzzacott, staying close to customers is about survival, for no individual, not even the legislators, has all the answers to the environmental issues. Only by working together can the answers be found. To Mike, environmental problems are a big threat...and a terrific opportunity. Basic chemicals are commodities whichever way you look at them. Product differentiation is unlikely, competing company products are interchangeable. As Mike sees it, differentiating on price is self-defeating. So what is left?...service. Mike is using the established Quality process at BP Chemicals to attract customers on 'true value' in a way which could be hard for smaller traders to follow.

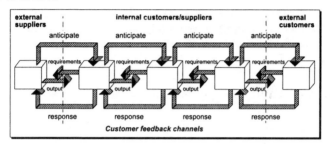

Mike anticipated this being in the area of scientific advice and support around the environmental concerns. A sound idea but what does the customer actually want? Having built the feedback channels and talked to customers in great detail, General Chemicals did their analysis. Top requirement was product consistency – no surprise. Next was cleanliness control in transportation – a big surprise but not a difficult one to achieve; the process was well under control although obviously customers were not fully aware of this. But what about technical support, SPC data, innovation, more frequent visits from the sales team? All ranked much lower than General Chemicals expected and a great disappointment after a lot of work providing extra service. They dug in deeper and eventually developed what they call a 'hierarchy of customer requirements'.

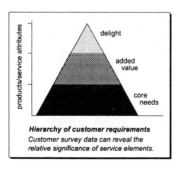

Hierarchy of customer requirements
Customer survey data can reveal the
relative significance of service elements.

This illustrates that their customers have core needs – product consistency, on-time delivery, for example – which have to be met first to give satisfaction. Above them are added value features such as technical support and sales office access which offer scope for 'true value'. Higher still are the delight factors, SPC, product innovation, research findings, which their customer is simply not interested in until the lower levels are satisfied. Only 10 per cent of their customer base sees the value in SPC data, for example, yet Fuji in Holland, their most advanced customer, demands specific SPC information. Armed with this enhanced knowledge of their customer base, General Chemicals have no illusions about today's customer needs, but, at the same time, by anticipating how these might develop, they are ready with their 'true value' service as each customer's needs rise.

Really knowing your customers

Two separate surveys showed that 47 per cent of UK and 40 per cent of US business executives could not define their customers. Furthermore, another survey showed that 90 per cent of researchers had no real idea what their customers wanted. What are these key people doing? How do they make decisions? What data do they use to say we'll make this or that? Understanding customers should be as natural to the Quality leader as understanding the balance sheet or understanding the technology of the business. But it is not as easy. Customers are people and therefore much more complex.

The Quality leader should always try to put himself in the customer's shoes. The perspective can be very different. The customer may see a spectrum of suppliers, not just us or our immediate competitors. Solutions to his needs may come from outside of our industry as it currently operates. This could well mean studying the customer's customers and the customer's competitors to gain intelligence. We should also look to the end of the supply chain we are in – to the final consumer – and tease out the trend. If, through the customer intelligence we have created, we can anticipate what the customer is going to need and have it available just as the need emerges, then we are definitely going to enjoy a competitive advantage. At this point, we focus very hard on delivering to our Quality edge.

Revolutionary banking

Revolutionising banking may sound like a contradiction in terms but it has happened in the UK. 'Project rain cloud' was conceived from customer data. Research for Midland Bank showed that one in five people had not visited a branch in the last month and one in ten in the last six months. Over half said they would prefer not to visit at all if possible. Of those who had visited a branch, one in three left without speaking to any branch staff. From such data a revolutionary concept was born, which became First Direct. Why have branches at all?

The idea was not original but making it happen was. Digging deeper into the research, the planning team found that 76% would rather deal with a person than a computer and that only 27% wished they could do more business by phone. So First Direct had to construct a new service which was very personal, very easy to deal with and which had none of the other things that some people disliked about branches, such as lack of privacy for discussions, inconvenient opening times, waiting to be served. First Direct was aptly named offering the first direct service to banking customers 24 hours a day. Some feel it represents the start of a new era in banking.

The Cooperative Bank was quick off the mark in following First Direct. They had the advantage of a well-established Quality process to assist. This had already sharpened up the key processes on which remote services depend - linking the telephone and the internal information system - and developing the staff to respond to customers in a different way. Telephone banking has become a major business initiative for both First Direct and The Cooperative Bank. This type of service will not suit every bank customer but for those for whom it has appeal these two organisations have a clear Quality edge to exploit. Some two years after First Direct was launched, all the major clearing banks are developing direct telephone banking services.

Tracking

There are many sources of customer data, direct and indirect, and a variety of media is often needed to build up a useful picture. Surveys (questionnaires and interviews) can provide a repeatable means of data collection. Xerox mails some 70,000 customers a month in the USA with a request for very specific feedback points. Komatsu takes it further and pays customers to complete detailed questionnaires. For each new Komatsu product, a sample of customers is selected and requested to complete the paid survey every six months for the life of the product. This provides Komatsu with a fuller understanding of how their products are used and maintains close tabs on whether the customer remains satisfied.

The easier it is to reach us with a complaint or comment, the more information we receive. Van den Bergh Foods' complaint ratio must be at a world-class low level of less than one per million on their Flora line, for example. Yet they still seek to find out more. They learned for instance that the lid on one of their pack designs was a little awkward for some people – but they only learned this when they installed their 'Careline' (a freephone number). Their previous listening mechanisms did not surface this tiny percentage of problems. Van den Bergh Foods know a lot about consumers. They know, for instance, from following up their complaints that at least a third are problems caused by the customer and are nothing to do with the company. This is possibly universally so. Avis find about the same ratio of complaints, which stem from customer misuse or ignorance. Far from being annoyed about this, Van den Bergh Foods, Avis and other sophisticated customer-listeners welcome the data. There may just be a trend or pattern of behaviour within that third that would allow them to minimise the potential problems further or even an opportunity for a new variant to suit better the people involved.

Improving the complaints process

Some companies have a complaints process, some have none; few think about improving it. Elida Gibbs-Faberge, in France, some two years into their Total Quality process, decided that improving their complaints process would be a good project for an improvement team. They received 4000 complaints annually from their trade customers (supermarkets and local retailers), with about 1600 outstanding at the start of the project. This was far from satisfactory, affecting the relationship with some key customers and tying up the time of four people in the commercial department, not to mention the salesmen's time explaining the problems to customers. On top of this, payment on 15 per cent of invoices was being held up as customers sat on them as they waited for their problem to be sorted out. The project team looked at the data. They found that 45 per cent of the complaints were disputes over the amount of rebate (a negotiated arrangement which varies with volume) and the rest mostly about inaccurate orders and deliveries. Only 4 per cent were about defective products. The team worked through a disciplined improvement methodology, digging into root causes and analysing the process. The resulting improvements cut the elapsed time for resolving a rebate issue from 167 days to 35 (16 of which are in the customer's hands) and from 49 down to 13 for resolving delivery queries. By reorganising the routine in the sales office, some 40/50 days came down to near zero.

Usually a company will build up an array of data sources. Toto uses four main feedback systems. They have questionnaires direct from purchasing customers; surveys by market research teams; information cards submitted monthly by their own sales teams; and reports from 'fixed observation points' – 4,500 wholesalers who monitor consumer purchasers. In addition, Toto frequently commissions analyses of social trends (political, economic and cultural) to understand other influences on their customers.

Feedback times provide more than a complaint channel: they can open up a dialogue with a customer. Van den Bergh Foods' small

Careline teams are used to receiving questions on health and nutrition, way beyond the product itself. Unusual or complex queries are passed on to the relevant expert. A small proportion are business opportunities, where the caller did not know who to approach. For example, one request was for the cost of transporting a 20-foot container of vegetable oil from the UK to Nigeria!

Focus groups are another powerful way of understanding customers. Essentially they are customer discussion groups where a facilitator will lead the discussion and an observer will record the discussion and responses. Although this technique is frequently used to test responses to the company's ideas, often the best information comes from permitting the discussion to freewheel and allowing people to fantasise around a topic.

Toto's routine use of salespeople for information highlights yet another way we tend to underuse our staff. The people in direct and regular contact with customers can provide a rich source of regular data on customers and indications of shifting trends. Hewlett Packard found they had to de-programme their salespeople before they could use them to obtain data on customers. They developed a 'shut-up and listen programme' to remind them to capture the customer's complaints, problems or needs and channel them back for analysis, rather than jumping straight into a sales pitch.

Customer returns as a data source

Sanyo Shokai have 35 per cent of their fashion clothes returned unsold. It does not worry them; they want to run with the fashion and this is one way of finding out what sells well. Having extracted this vital information, this does not mean they write off the returns as a loss. Far from it, they use their speed and flexibility to distribute the returns to other outlets, selling 92 per cent of them.

Marks & Spencer probably gain even more from their world-renowned returns policy. Only a few stores in the world have followed M & S's lead in actively encouraging customers to bring back anything which is not wanted for whatever reason; other stores are fearful of being inundated with a continual turnover of goods being sold and brought back. But M & S have no regrets at all: their gains are multiple. For customers, the returns policy is a major attraction, lowering the sense of pressure to make the right decision. This in turn means customers may buy more and will probably not spend so long on the sales floor making up their minds. Rather less changing space is needed; rather more goods can be on display.

But there's more to gain than sales per square foot, important though that is. Through this policy, M & S are the first to learn about any problems. Customers do not tell all their friends about a poorly stitched seam on a blouse; they bring it back to get another and tell the M & S staff instead. M & S learn first-hand about the colours and the styles which people are not happy with when they return clothes bought for them. For M & S, the undisputed customer returns policy is not only a major Quality edge, it is also a rich source of customer data.

Information technology is providing many new opportunities to understand customers better and capture their needs. In some Japanese stores, an interactive computer can advise on precise colourings of lipstick and make-up for the individual's skin. When a user of Hewlett Packard equipment calls the help desk (on a local call), the adviser at the Response Center in Palo Alto can call up on screen, in seconds, full details of the actual product and suggested responses built up from similar enquiries. Hotel chains, such as Four Seasons, today can cut out check-in formalities by calling up all the details from the guest's last stay (in any part of the chain) including any preferences such as newspapers, non-allergic pillows, etc. All of these not only provide a better service but also a database from which to assess customer trends.

Such data is beginning to change the way a lot of companies do business. This is most evident with supermarket chains and the consumer goods manufacturers who supply them. Data accumulated from every purchase through the check-out scanners is fed back all the way up the supply chain. This is fuelling revolutionary change in the way suppliers and retailers work together, with many mutual benefits. One is restocking from actual purchase as opposed to woolly sales forecasts. Another is the opportunity for fine-tuning from the real-time knowledge of which lines are selling and which are not. Yet another is the potential for interpreting future consumer needs from the purchase trends. Computer models are helping to assimilate trends and predict emerging tastes and preferences.

Managing expectations

Customer satisfaction can never be a static achievement. It is very tempting once an agreement is concluded with the customer to turn towards other demands and be less attentive. But the agreement is only a guide – an indication of the customer's expectation but one which cannot follow the influences which will shape the customer's needs from then on. Customer satisfaction must be managed. Not by a 'manager' or specialist but by the person doing the job – any job, any level. Going further, one could argue it is not a part of the job – it is the job.

But how can one manage something as variable as a customer's expectations? Certainly, it would be presumptuous to try and control our customers' expectations; these flow from the customer's own environment over which we have, at best, a modest influence. Anticipate, yes; control, unlikely. Therefore our ability to manage expectations is restricted to predicting emerging needs and being ready to meet them. But we should be able to manage our own output and what we say we will do. A component of the customer's expectation is our promise. It is universally true that people underestimate and overpromise.

A Danish supplier was keen to be distinctive in his market and decided to upgrade the service level he was providing above the accepted norm of three days. In a bold move, he told his customers that in future he would always deliver within 24 hours. The company made a big effort and after a period of adjustment maintained a consistent service level considerably improved over the original. But it was actually closer to 48 hours than 24 and the customers, conditioned to expect 24, were disappointed. The company's image suffered totally unnecessarily from the rash promises. Far better to gradually work the improvements up to a higher level of proven consistency, keeping customers informed in a low-key way and seeking their views (remembering they may or may not want this particular improvement). Then a marketing decision can be made as to whether to capitalise on the differentiation by promoting it. If it is of value, the customers will know already.

Managing expectations is one of the hardest practices to achieve, mainly because the customer after all is human and humans are unpredictable. A few years ago, Aer Lingus received a written complaint from an American visitor to Ireland, travelling on their Irish Airlines promotion. In essence she said: 'It's rained for a fortnight and I will never fly Irish Airlines again!' Aer Lingus had their own Quality process by this time and took all complaints seriously, although there was an inclination to put this in the 'fringe' category. However, they thought further and went back to Irish Airlines brochures. Sure enough, pictures throughout were of blue skies and rolling green hills. No mention of how the hills became so green! Aer Lingus changed the style of the brochure the following year.

Recovery

The inverse of customers being hard to satisfy is that we will regularly disappoint them. Managing for customer satisfaction means being attuned to hearing about their problems and doing something about them, rather than praying that the customer has a short memory. Customers always have long memories. But they are still people and people know that perfection is not reasonably attainable in an ever-changing situation. What they want is for you to fix the problem fast and learn from it, so it doesn't happen again. Surveys show that a high percentage of people will rebuy if a problem is fixed quickly and well. And here lies another opportunity for the customer-sensitive supplier. The customer is alerted by the problem; he has noticed us, when often our supply is taken for granted. We now have an opportunity to show what we can do and what we are like to deal with. A good recovery can leave a positive impression on the customer, especially if he is involved in the solution and he can feel it is his idea.

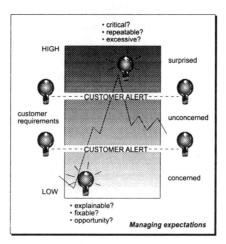

A Plessey company in the UK had been supplying Boeing with components for some time but had not really penetrated the massive supply base feeding Seattle. One day one of their components began to cause a problem in the Boeing assembly process, threatening a delay to some major deliveries. Boeing suddenly took notice of this foreign supplier and was not pleased. Instead of panicking, the Plessey MD gathered his key people and immediately flew to Seattle and worked alongside Boeing designers and production people until the complex problem was unravelled and eradicated. Boeing were not only impressed with this dedication, they had got to know the supplier's management team well. The Plessey company went on to win a Boeing 'supplier of the year' award that year, the first non-American company to do so.

Customer loyalty is a complex thing, with physical and emotional needs wrapped up together inside the customer's head. A problem resolved well generates higher loyalty than when the customer is content and chooses not to complain about anything. Yet another reason for making it easy for customers to complain to us.

Delighting the customer

Of course, we should not be waiting for our problems to trigger our ability to impress the customer. If we are really managing our customer, we are watching for his problems and using our talents to help. This brings us into that rarefied area of customer delight: doing something that feels special to the customer – exceeding his expectations. Not necessarily surprising the customer, this can backfire; not going over the top, this may be impossible to repeat, but simply doing that little bit better.

Richard Branson's dream was not really to run a world-beating record business, that was merely something he was good at; his real ambition was to run an airline. Before starting Virgin Atlantic, he knew he would have to do that little bit better. He knew all about Laker and People's Express, independent players who were unable to withstand the muscle of the airline giants. His first service across the Atlantic was indeed very similar to Laker, offering cut-price tickets which the majors followed. Gradually, Branson worked out a different strategy, adding entertainment (imported from his record business) for his young adult customer base. This led him to his major breakthrough, a superior service for business travellers. Business trade is the lucrative end of airline revenue because of the high and non-discounted ticket prices. Branson talked and listened to business travellers (literally, by regularly travelling himself and getting to know his fellow passengers) and built up a picture of the regular businessman's likes and dislikes about air travel. From this picture, he created Virgin Upper Class.

Upper Class was the first with individual video players, something all the major airlines are copying – slowly because of the huge installation task for the big fleets. He set a style of service which was personal, empowering cabin crew to care for passengers in their own way, rather than to over-standardised patterns, again an advantage of being smaller and focused. He added neck massages and aromatherapy kits because his passengers were concerned about the effect of air travel on their bodies. He looked after his passengers way beyond the terminal, sending limousines to collect and deliver door to door. Richard Branson introduced all these features ahead of his big established competitors; indeed he did the whole thing a little better. As a result, he delighted his customers. They told others and Virgin Atlantic's success was assured. In the early nineties, Upper Class is the service the other North Atlantic carriers are striving to better.

Customer delight is a wonderful thing to achieve. The customer does the reverse of spreading the bad news and tells his friends of his good judgement in finding this special service (as we've seen he won't tell quite as many; good news doesn't travel as far as bad but the good feeling may last). The supplier and his team feel good about their work being valued. But it is a very delicate emotion. He cannot be thrilled every time, but he will miss it if we revert to ordinary service. We have raised his expectation and we have no choice but to set our sights higher and do something better. This is the true power of customer-orientation: to please the customer, continuous improvement is mandatory.

A delighted customer

Victor Rice is Chairman and CEO of Varity Corporation which has its world headquarters at Buffalo, New York. Victor heard about the Toyota Lexus not from an advert or a dealer but from a friend in California who had told him about the Lexus recall. Victor heard that shortly after Toyota launched the Lexus they discovered a potential fault with a very low probability of it causing any problems. Faced with this, they did not do what most companies would do and forget about it: they announced it on television and recalled all the cars. This would have been considered disastrous news for any other car company but Toyota thought differently. They did not want even the remote chance of their customers having a problem. All owners were contacted and their cars collected from their drives at their convenience and returned with the potential fault eradicated. Far from being alarmed, customers were impressed with Toyota's care and the way the whole issue was handled. Victor's Californian colleague was so impressed, he convinced Victor to buy one. Victor was so delighted, many of his staff now also have Lexus cars.

Voice of the customer

Way back in the fifties, a handful of Japanese companies developed a technique which is still quite novel in the West. At Kobi Steel, for example, engineers were trying to achieve a consistent focus on their customer's requirements across all their operations. They already knew the value of fully understanding the customer and painstakingly plotted all the actual and potential requirements they could find from extensive observations, surveys and trials with customers. Their problem was to keep all the functions of their business focused on those customer factors which really mattered and to avoid everyone having their own (different) ideas of what was important or necessary. At the same time, they were looking for the maximum involvement and sharing of ideas across the functions. Their solution is characteristically Japanese but is proving powerful in any environment.

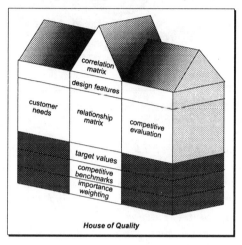

House of Quality

A 'House of Quality' is built up from data gathered both inside and outside of the company. The aim is to match the two dimensions of customer needs and company capability in a visual comprehensive format. The technique is deceptively powerful. The process of systematically testing the leverage of every internal parameter (delivery times, product strength, accuracy...) against customer needs clearly determines the areas of potential distinction. Even more significantly, the process of involving all functions in this evaluation leads to a strong consensus around the findings. Everyone has the same picture and the same knowledge. The technique spread quickly across Japanese industries but took decades before being adopted in the West. The early pioneers possibly helped this delay by devising charts so meticulous and detailed that they seemed as inscrutable as *kanji* characters. Perhaps to protect their invention further, they called their invention by the uninspiring title: Quality Function Deployment. Today, the more repetitive manufacturers (the electronics, computer and car industries in particular) are demonstrating a more methodical approach to precisely meeting customer needs, as a result of applying QFD.

Whether a precise discipline like QFD is needed or not, listening to the voice of the customer will always prove to be one of the most valuable drivers for improvement a leader can have.

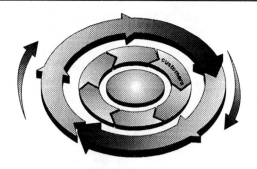

SUMMARY

Think customer; act customer

1. **Who is your customer?** *Identify your markets and focus on the people you deliver to, both inside and outside of your organisation. Aim to concentrate on one person – the customer – at a time. Cut down a mass market into segments and use one customer as a model for that market category.*
2. **Have you allocated time for your customer?** *Believe that your customers are your business and therefore divide your week up so that you see them.*
3. **Do you understand their needs?** *Observe and listen. Immerse yourself in their environment. Watch their customers.*
4. **Have you pinned down their immediate requirements and agreed them?** *Don't make assumptions, test that your interpretation is correct by asking them to confirm.*
5. **Have you built feedback mechanisms?** *Enable the customer to tell you easily how you are doing. Run surveys, open and blind, to check the accuracy of this channel.*
6. **Are you smoothing the interface?** *Continually make it easy for the customer to do business with you. Look at the customer's experience of dealing with you as a whole, from initial enquiry through development to billing; identify and remove any barriers, even if this makes life harder inside the organisation.*
7. **Have you built-in flexibility?** *Expect the customer to have needs way outside of the agreed parameters and be prepared to help by having the capacity to adjust.*
8. **Are you serving, not selling?** *Be attentive and courteous; indifference or arrogance is heavily penalised. He is your partner; don't short-change him.*
9. **Are you looking for trends and anticipating emerging needs?** *Accumulate data on the customer and look for patterns. Look*

around all the influences on the customer – competitors (yours and his), regulatory bodies, community, consumer taste – and imagine how any potential changes would affect the customer and his needs. Be just ahead of the game; don't raise expectations you cannot sustain.

10. **Can you do something special?** Periodically, go out of your way to do something extra for your customer. A delighted customer is your best salesman.

6

Business Needs Lean Processes

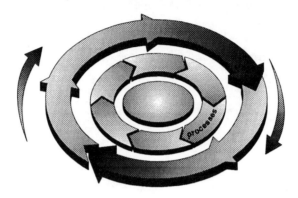

Without processes our business could not function and yet many companies do not explicitly manage their key business processes. Accelerated business improvement simply cannot be attained without the understanding, control and redesign of business processes. The big gains in a Quality revolution can come from re-engineered and transformed business processes.

'Lean production is the second great industrial revolution.' Louis Hughes, President, GM Europe

'Sell one, make one.' Nissan

Business simplified

Business should be simple. We identify a customer's need, devise an attractive service, create the service through a flow of activities which add progressive value to the purchased raw materials, serve the customer and receive payment. That business for most managers is nothing like this is because we try to do so much of it. Our businesses have grown to an extent that many managers may have little to do with the primary purpose. Complexity is rarely an asset. The Quality leader should seek to emphasise the core elements of the business and question anything that is remote from this core. Why do we do this? Why this way? These are questions which lead to a simplified business. A simplified business is an improved one. But a simplified business does not mean one without change. To accelerate this re-creation of the core unencumbered business, the Quality leader has a powerful driver to help: process management.

The 'lean' revolution

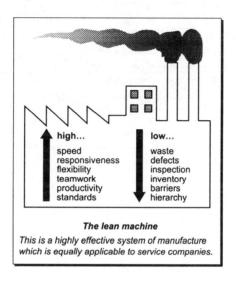

high...
speed
responsiveness
flexibility
teamwork
productivity
standards

low...
waste
defects
inspection
inventory
barriers
hierarchy

The lean machine
This is a highly effective system of manufacture which is equally applicable to service companies.

The motor industry today epitomises the revolutionary changes that arise from process thinking applied in a Quality environment. 'Lean' manufacturing was termed by a study team at Massachusetts Institute of Technology to cover JIT, SE, rapid response, high productivity, low inspection, low hierarchy and all the other attributes of Quality manufacturers in Japan. Now all auto manufacturers, East or West, have adopted the lean manufacturing approach, some more successfully than others.

The pace of change is hot. Peugeot has improved its output per man by 50 per cent in five years; Renault has reduced its workforce by 25 per cent over a similar period. Mercedes-Benz, criticised not for the final product standard of the cars but for the high proportion of inspection in the manufacturing process (inspection time in German car making was calculated at one time to be higher than Japanese total manufacturing time), has built a new lean plant with no assembly line and self-managed teams. But the Japanese continue to press home their longer experience. Nissan in Sunderland brought its production of new Micra cars up to full schedule of 130,000 units a year only 14 weeks after launch in 1992, at a time when Ford was making repeated lay-offs in a depressed market. Ian Gibson, Nissan UK's managing director, claims 12.5 hours per car for the Primera family car compared to about 20 for the 'best of the Europeans'. Alarmingly, he believes that Nissan UK's product quality is on a par with any plant in Japan but on productivity there is a lot more to come: 'We are only in the middle of the Japanese league table.'[9]

Nissan's suppliers in the UK have learned the revolutionary approach from Nissan and fit into 'synchronous supply' – carpet, for example, is delivered from Sommer Allibert (a French supplier with a factory next door at Washington) direct to the line with each set of carpet pieces being made especially for one car; 42 minutes are allowed for the carpet to be ordered, delivered and fitted to the car. Only 10 minutes buffer stock is built in and the average inventory level is 1.6 days, compared to an industry average of 20 days. In all its key markets around the world, Nissan takes just 48 hours from order receipt to delivery of the car to the dealer. No car is assembled until it is ordered; every car is a special with all the variations the customer wants. Sell one, make one.

GM's new plant in Eisenach shows that the changes have gone full circle. Once this site built antiquated East German Wartburgs. Now it is a green field example of lean manufacture. Louis Hughes says: 'The mass production of Henry Ford has no future. Lean production is the second great industrial revolution, after the invention of the assembly line.'[10] Lean processes are not the preserve of the motor industry, nor even of manufacturing. The same radical practice applied to reservations in a hotel chain or the distribution of electricity or lending in a bank can have equally revolutionary impact. Indeed many parts of the service sector in the 1990s offer the same opportunity for revolutionary change as the motor industry has experienced in the 1980s.

Strategic process management

Process management is perhaps the most powerful management discipline in Quality today. Process awareness, process control and process improvement are techniques which every person in an organisation can learn and use. We should all take responsibility for managing the processes which we are involved in. At senior levels, process management can have profound strategic value. The ability to provide a service faster, earlier, more flexibly, more reliably and at less cost can be directly addressed by strategic process management. Innovation is one strategic process to which process management can be applied with advantage. Sony puts 1,000 new products onto the market each year through managing this process explicitly. The development time for each product is brought down with each launch. Competitive advantage for Sony is bringing a new but well-researched, well-engineered, well-designed, well-packaged concept to the market before anyone else. Once the product takes hold, derivatives offering more features, added value or lower price are ready to tempt the market further. It's all part of the process: the explicitly-managed new product development process.

Manufacturing and distribution, the supply chain, make up another strategic process – one that stretches from the product in the customer's hands right back to raw material supplier. Unilever Personal Products is learning how to manage huge chains which they call the extended supply chain. This travels literally from the consumer buying a deodorant back through the retailer via distribution to the Unilever sales department; from here into manufacturing and back to sourcing of materials. Unilever has identified six major sub-processes, crossing several distinct departments, to permit the consumer to be able to select the deodorant she wants, when she wants. It is not only manufacturing companies who have supply chain processes to manage. Insurance companies talk of the 'factory' – the paper-moving process which delivers policies to customers. The advanced insurance societies are using process re-engineering techniques borrowed from manufacturing to revolutionise these conventional factories.

Another key business process is invoicing, or, more broadly, money collection. This can be a much neglected process, crying out for process management attention. Reuters North America, before the introduction of their Quality process, took a typical attitude towards invoicing – it was a low priority and not a real business issue in comparison to, say, managing new technology. Their Quality survey told them otherwise; not only did the minor errors irritate customers and take some of the shine off their excellent image, but the delay in payment whilst the invoices were corrected was costing some $6 million. Massey Ferguson found that, in one division where a lot of customised work was done, invoices were being submitted ten times before final payment was received; the changes in the work being done outdated each invoice before the billing process could catch up.

In other companies, analysis has revealed up to 30 per cent of invoices contain some error or other; indeed, unless the billing process has been assessed, it should be assumed that a substantial proportion will be wrong. A 3σ billing process can be very costly.

Advertising is another business process which is woefully under-managed as a process and yet can have an enormous impact on the performance of some companies. Advertising executive Tony Brignall gives an example: 'Two years ago, the president of Kraft, Mike Mile, toured his kingdom. It is very big realm indeed. Kraft's turnover worldwide was then $23 billion. They spent $1.2 billion on advertising. He visited his agencies (causing, I imagine, Richter scale size spasms), saw all their work, studied all their figures. To his consternation, and no doubt that of the agencies, he found no correlation between sales and ad spend. In some areas he doubled the budget. No difference. In others he halved the budget. No difference. In yet other areas he stopped advertising. No difference.'[11]

Every marketing manager is certain his latest ad is going to be 'the big hit'. Not many are, but a company might still spend up to 30 per cent of turnover on advertising. As Lord Leverhume is reported to have said '50 per cent of all advertising is rubbish; the problem is which 50 per cent.' Applying process management disciplines to strategic processes such as advertising can help identify the good half and eliminate the bad.

For a growing number of organisations a key business process is environmental management. Procter & Gamble are typical of those Quality companies who are being proactive about minimising environmental impact of their operations, seeing sound business advantage in so doing. P & G uses process management to ensure that its plants, products and packages fulfil the strict criteria of its Environmental Quality Policy. In one practical example, a Pennsylvania pulp mill developed a process which reduced the amount of solid waste going to the land-fill by 75 per cent, through converting unused fibres into boiler fuel. With packaging, P & G brought in new packaging technology to eliminate the outer cartons on deodorants, cutting out 80 million cartons, or 3.4 million pounds of waste, annually. In another illustration, they redesigned the Crisco Oil bottle to use 28 per cent less plastic. At P & G, process management is good for the company and good for the community.

Defining business processes

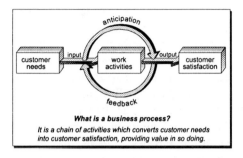

What is a business process?

It is a chain of activities which converts customer needs into customer satisfaction, providing value in so doing.

Business processes in most companies are not at first easy to define. A manufacturing process, or operations in a service business, is obvious enough. New business development, however, can often be ambiguous and fragmented, as is the billing and collection process. What about business planning in a multinational or people development in a retail chain or the continual updating of customer addresses in a bank? In some companies these processes can be quite invisible or very ad hoc. Others, such as environmental or community impact, perhaps, may be woolly and lacking in accountability.

A further problem in pinning down processes is agreeing which are the major ones and which are supporting or subsidiary ones. A compelling argument can be put forward that business is really only two processes – the delivery supply chain and the money collection process (or three if new business is separated out – or even just one if the whole of business is seen as one value-adding supply chain). Equally, arguments can be put forward for 20 or 30 distinct processes which are key to business prosperity. This debate is a not an academic one, for the effectiveness of much subsequent improvement activity is influenced by it. Most senior teams feel most comfortable with about eight or nine strategic processes. This gives enough scale to span functional boundaries (with the improvement gold which lies within), whilst allocating weight to critical processes which would be lost if fewer were chosen. With eight or nine, it sometimes falls neatly that executive team members can champion one process each; but this is a rather secondary consideration. As few as six key processes is workable and as many as 12 or 13, but outside of these ranges, the management team may be making life harder for themselves later on.

Some of the processes selected for strategic attention will actually be support processes, i.e. they are not directly serving the customer. For instance, people development or human resources is a key strategic requirement in many businesses and therefore we should seek to manage it more effectively as a process. Information Technology is another intriguing example. Information is the fuel for improvement; the technology makes it accessible – for management, for workteams, for customers. Information supply is needed for every process. Creating that supply effectively is a major process in its own right. Quality too raises a similar question. Clearly needed in every process and an integral part of all business activities, should it be treated as a separate process? The answer for most companies is a definitive yes. Whilst no one should seek to overlay a permanent Quality apparatus on the business, Quality has its own energy needs, without which it withers and dies.

Foundation processes
- people development
- information development
- TQ development

Business process
- business planning
- business development
- supply chain
- product development
- billing and collection
- managing the environment

Some key business processes

Robust processes

Often the first task with process management is to make the process work. Rather more commonly than we may appreciate, processes do not consistently do what they are supposed to do – they are not under control. Processes are full of variables, some known, some hidden. These are what cause the inconsistency of output; only by managing the inputs can the output be brought under control. Some of these variables can be eliminated through simplification. Others can be controlled once their effect is understood, after they have been isolated and monitored. Yet other hidden ones need to be revealed. A popular analogy is the large lake of water covering rocks; all looks smooth and calm until the water is lowered and the rocks appear. The 'lowering the water' concept is frequently used in inventory reduction, where the inventory is seen to be acting as the water covering all the problems. As the inventory is reduced, so the variables of poor forecasting, machine breakdown and defective materials show themselves and can be dealt with. The analogy works for administrative processes just as well. As the water level is lowered, the sloppy procedures, the unnecessary paperwork, the communication gaps and the long approval times show up.

Taguchi describes variability around the target as the loss to the user.
This should be minimised by continually reducing the variability.

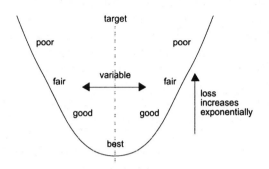

Source of the river

*A truly robust process, one which always does what it is supposed
to do, can only be achieved at the design stage. For this reason,
Japanese companies have always focused much of their
improvement attention on both product and process design. They
call it 'source of the river' - any defects at the design stage will flow
downstream and could become unmanageable later in production.
Twenty years ago, Genichi Taguchi reversed conventional thinking
in design for manufacture by showing the leading Japanese
companies that designing around tolerance limits was a flawed
concept. Instead, his argument was to aim directly for the target -
the centre line of the dimension, e.g. a component size. In this way,
by systematically isolating variables and tightening their deviation
from the target, the process could be made more robust. Using
these techniques, Motorola plan to build on their '6σ' success and
push on for 'one defect per billion' by 2001.*

*Taguchi's approach is complex in practice and is a technique for
design engineers rather than general managers. The concept,
however, of always aiming for the target and not accepting random
variation is applicable everywhere.*

Removing waste

The first step to a leaner process is to tackle the inherent waste. If the
refuse collectors stopped calling regularly, our homes would soon clog
up with waste. Processes do the same but it is often a little bit at a time
and we don't notice it. More like arteries furring up with cholesterol:
once the effect becomes obvious, it may be too late. Waste removal
should be as continuous as delivering the service. One of the first
comments Western visitors used to make on seeing Japanese plants
was 'the floor is spotless'. Years ago, Western manufacturers could not
see why anyone would spend time keeping a factory floor looking so
immaculate. Today, with much more precision demanded, it is obvious

that anything out of place or dirty could cause an error. It is also psychological, echoing the concern of the air traveller: 'If they don't wipe the coffee stains off the tables, what state are the engines in?'

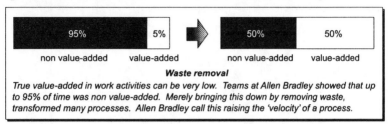

95%	5%		50%	50%
non value-added	value-added		non value-added	value-added

Waste removal

True value-added in work activities can be very low. Teams at Allen Bradley showed that up to 95% of time was non value-added. Merely bringing this down by removing waste, transformed many processes. Allen Bradley call this raising the 'velocity' of a process.

But waste, as we have discussed already, is much more than housekeeping. Waste is anything that is not needed to provide the service. When a company first starts moving with a Quality process, the accumulated pile of waste provides an easy target to try out improvement disciplines. Process improvement teams will reveal wasteful activities and wasteful decisions. As well as the obvious – scrapped materials or faulty equipment, for example – there will be a vast amount that is under the surface: memos written and distributed for form's sake not for information; 100-page reports, when three pages would be more communicable; advertising and marketing campaigns which are authorised but are never likely to run. Much of this seems to be legitimate work until challenged.

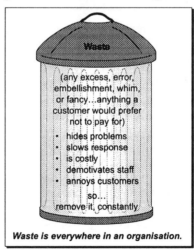

Waste

(any excess, error, embellishment, whim, or fancy...anything a customer would prefer not to pay for)

• hides problems
• slows response
• is costly
• demotivates staff
• annoys customers

so...
remove it, constantly

Waste is everywhere in an organisation.

In many cases, company procedures and standards may legitimise waste. Standard costing is a classic example. Historical budgets are another. Ilford, the black-and-white film manufacturer, provide a typical example from the process flow industry where historical standards often limit improvement. Yields from the production of film were measured against a standard of around 65 per cent – that is, 35 per cent of material was expected to be lost in the delicate manufacturing process. This was even termed *planned* waste. During the early days of their Quality process, the management team, visiting Konica as a result of a joint venture, learned to their astonishment that the Japanese company's equivalent standard was 99 per cent. Released from this artificial barrier, process improvement teams took film yield through 70 per cent to 80 per cent to 90 per cent in a few months of intensive action and subsequently matched the Japanese company. Similar standards used to be accepted on inventory until recessionary pressure forced most companies to challenge their logic of holding stock. In all such situations, the only standard to measure against is 100 per cent, i.e. no scrapped material, no defects, no stocks, no work in progress.

Waste costs big money. One estimate is that the UK manufacturing industry is losing £6 billion per year on material waste alone. A French estimate of the cost of errors and defects in French production lines is FFr2,000 per worker per month or FFr300 billion annually.[12] Another survey looked at the costs of 'poor quality' software, estimated as costing British industry £1 billion a year, more than half the total annual spend on software. These assessments almost certainly underestimate the true impact. Processes which are clogged with waste cause knock-on effects which go way beyond the direct cost. Waste means less space and less capacity. Waste means higher consumption and greater environmental damage. Waste means lost opportunities and lost customers.

Kaizen vs breakthrough

Engineers in Japanese companies are never satisfied with a product or a process. They are looking for small improvements on a continuous basis. They will take out a worker on a line, move a conveyor or sometimes slow a machine down. This is not blind tinkering, but controlled experimentation with the variables in a process to seek out what may be a minute improvement in flow or efficiency. Such small step improvements, or *kaizen*, are a key ingredient in the superiority of Japanese reliability, both of the end products and the processes which produced them. Small steps taken in a planned way don't destabilise the process and they don't take it out of control. In fact, they enable the variables to be tightened that little bit more.

In the seventies, this approach began to show through and a cultural difference was noted. In general, the Western tendency was to leave things alone for as long as possible and then make great leaps forward – big new technology, whole systems replaced (often with non-compatible software), next generation solutions. Big bang...with years of fun trying to master the disruption. General Motors' crash course in automation is probably the ultimate example. Threatened in its homeland both from imports and leaner domestic rivals, GM hit the spend button. During the 1980s, GM spent $77 billion on new equipment and plant. To put this in context, $77 billion is much more than twice the worldwide 1992 sales of Honda, one of the companies causing GM such problems. Even GM could not handle that order of spending and many of the robots remain unused. This technological solution simply could not work without the training, the organisation, the philosophy to support it. GM in North America ended the decade still lagging Ford by a reputed 40 per cent in basic productivity comparisons. GM finds it has no choice but to adjust to a lower competitive base, with plans developed to cut 20 or more plants through the nineties.

During the eighties, it became more and more apparent to the West that Japanese automation hadn't mysteriously appeared overnight but had evolved over many years of continuous improvement. Far from putting in robots wherever they could be fitted, Japanese engineers often prefer low technology, installing hand rollers rather than power conveyors for example, looking for flexibility rather than speed. Far from trying to rid the operation of people altogether, as GM had seemed determined to do, Japanese engineers used technology to complement and support the skills and versatility of their workers. Ironically, GM Europe, one of the West's most improved car manu-facturers in recent years, learned this lesson earlier than most and has pursued a totally different path from its parent. Former president Louis Hughes was in no doubt that what they are involved in is a revolution. He drew together a team who had direct experience of joint venture working with Japanese practice such as at NUMMI or CAMI (GM and Suzuki) or with Toyota in the US. 'We call them advisers but, in another sense, they are more like missionaries – and we are in need of conversion. It is close to religion, it is a life philoso-phy, it is that different.'[13] Coming from the most successful part of the world's largest industrial company, this was revolutionary talk indeed.

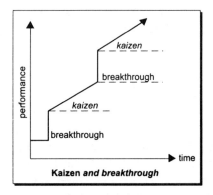

Kaizen *and breakthrough*

Today, as Western and Eastern disciplines are blending together with world best practice, both *kaizen* and breakthrough are sought by Japanese, European and US companies. The rate of change in the market demands it. But the part which remains hardest for Western minds is the step-by-step. It is particularly hard for managers, especially well-educated ones, who are seeking more complex issues than this methodical approach offers. There is a widespread feeling that the simple tools and procedures of *kaizen* are for the workforce. They are, but they are for managers too. Such managers may not be aware that Japanese engineers and managers account for the vast majority of improvements made each year – not the millions of Quality Circles and employee suggestions, important though these also are.

Discrete improvement

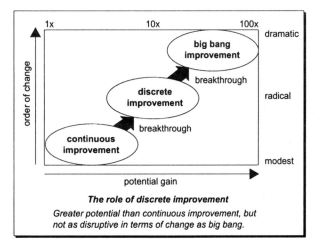

The role of discrete improvement
Greater potential than continuous improvement, but not as disruptive in terms of change as big bang.

Process improvement is a relatively new and exciting business discipline. The practice is often labelled business process re-engineering (BPR), which is examined in the next sections. Before we look at this in detail, it is worth exploring another concept – *discrete* improvement. Discrete improvement can be used to describe the blend of East and West experience which is resulting in major improvement successes. The idea is this: *kaizen* is too slow and unambitious, big bang is too risky and disruptive; why not go for the best features of the two extremes, whilst avoiding the problems? The middle ground offers radical gains made in a controlled methodical way, which can be implemented relatively quickly. This is in effect discontinuous improvement – using breakthrough concepts with systematic techniques.

Discrete improvement is planned to exploit the area between *kaizen* and big bang, as the diagram above illustrates. It will not provide the solution for every process problem or opportunity, but it offers an alternative which may well be the sound route in many competitive situations. Discrete improvement is particularly well suited to an organisation which already has a well-established Quality environment. People are familiar with improvement practices and will relate to the stretch goals which have been set. They will be used to working in teams and be more relaxed about crossing functional boundaries. In a Quality environment, process teams can be quickly set up to tackle strategic goals and their energy and enthusiasm will contribute to the success.

Legal & General illustrated this when they published their service standards to their customers after two years of creating a Quality ethos inside the business (reported in Chapters 2 and 4). One critical standard referred to the turnaround time for new business. This was originally ten days; through systematic improvement using process teams this time was brought down to one day. A radical improvement which couldn't have been achieved without breakthrough thinking, but neither was it a completely new process requiring external expertise to design and commission. A number of such discrete improvements, reinforced by *kaizen* from a large proportion of the 5,000 staff, enabled L&G to capitalise on their Quality environment and achieve competitive advantage.

Re-engineering the process

Discrete improvement is aimed at distinct sizable gains to an existing process; big bang improvement is about completely novel solutions to what the process does. Both are radical, both require breakthrough: one to bring new ideas to restructure a process, the other to replace it, or a major part of it, entirely. Business process re-engineering (BPR) is a term loosely used to describe both of these approaches, but the words are a better fit with discrete than big bang improvement. Certainly, the use of BPR in a Quality company could mostly be described as discrete improvement, with fewer Western companies now trusting to fortune with big bang or playing safe with continuous improvement alone. Jose Lopez, production director at Volkswagen sums it up: '*Kaizen* is yesterday's text, today it is the message of "quantum leap" improvements to generate value for customers. Improvements of 5, 6 or 7 per cent are not enough, it is 30 to 40 to 50 per cent improvements that must be made."[14]

Don't be put off by the label of BPR; it is not at all confined to engineering businesses nor does it need engineers to use it. If the label is a barrier, call it business process *re-design* or *re-structure*, or more prosaically, business process *improvement* (BPI), as many do. BPR follows a systematic improvement methodology (described in 'process of process improvement' on page 205), often combined with technological inputs to 'engineer' a major gain. A typical example is at Western Provident Association where processing of applications for health insurance took 28 days and occupied seven staff before BPR. After systematic re-engineering, applications are turned round in four days by one person, who reviews the medical history, sets up the policy and triggers the payment from the customer's bank account. This amounts to 45 minutes' work on each file; for the rest of the previous 28 days the file was in transit. The technological input was to capture document images on computer and to route these automatically through the computer network to the next user as each operation is complete. Rank Xerox have used a similar approach to produce specialised contracts in two days instead of 100 originally.

Other BPRs exploit modular components to achieve flexibility and speed. Bridgeport Machines brought out a new machine tool range aimed at giving discernible value for money ('Bridgeport quality at Taiwanese prices') using standardised control cabinets and modular components such as spindles mixed and matched to give a range of features. Using a computer-aided design system, their BPR brought the time from concept to launch down to six months, compared to an industry average of 18 months to two years. In the same vein, one of the contributors to Benetton's phenomenal growth in the late 1980s was a re-engineering of their supply chain to enable them to add colour very late in the process. Stocks of grey sweaters turned into

Benetton's 'world of colors' just before they were shipped to the shops, providing Benetton with the Quality edge of running with the fashion as it developed rather than having to predict and commit to colours at the beginning of the season.

Re-engineering processes can cut costs too. Aetna Life & Casualty, a US insurance company under pressure from weak investments, is using the combination of simplifying process flows plus selective input of new technology to take $100 million annually out of costs. One example is for stolen cars claims: it used to take five days to set up a representative visit to the person making the claim and provide a rental car; now it takes one telephone call. The customer is happier and the claims department is reduced by two thirds.

Time to market

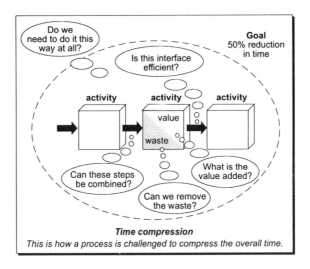

Time compression
This is how a process is challenged to compress the overall time.

What are the main aims of process re-engineering? One is to save time. Processes eat time and time today is competitive advantage. Sharp turns out 100 new products every week. These products used to take years to bring to market; now time to market is measured in months. Honda routinely bring out a new model in 36 months, as opposed to the convention of five to seven years in the Western motor industry. A British designer who had moved to Minolta was delighted to see his own designs coming off the production line; in his previous jobs, the gap between design and build was so long he never saw the end result. The reason that these Japanese companies can achieve this obvious advantage is their painstaking application of Quality to the product development cycle. As a result of this, they have been able to compress the time taken from concept to production without compromising reliability or the value offered to the customer.

The leading Japanese companies first became aware of the competitive power of time in the seventies. By then, they had perfected the disciplines of building precisely what the customer wanted without error and with minimal waste. They then simply transferred these techniques to product development. Process steps were clarified and streamlined. Responsibilities were defined. Very importantly, regular reviews were built in, with strict decision rules. All involved parties were brought together at each key step and unambiguous agreement reached on the achievement so far and the next step. Without agreement, no further step would be made and more research would be called for. Crucially, this ensured that each step could build on the previous one with no time-devouring backtracking. It also permitted simultaneous steps to be taken, without the fear of diverging paths emerging – the reviews brought everybody back in line.

Another key discipline is to limit the amount of innovation to that discussed, planned and agreed. Once agreed, no further change is permitted until the next review and then only when the new idea had been thoroughly tested. Such rigour enables Japanese companies today still to take competitive advantage away from Western businesses with superior innovation skills. Kao, for example, is a successful consumer goods manufacturer in the East but has not matched the likes of Unilever, L'Oreal or Procter & Gamble in original concepts. But when it comes to turning a good idea into a worldwide brand, Kao has shown it can copy the marketing concept, possibly adding an improvement or two, and then distribute the whole package of advertising copy, package design, product formulation around the world faster than the originator. One key factor in this is their standardised development process which is simpler, faster and does not allow anyone to tinker with the agreed specification.

In the West, many companies today have similar ambitions to extract time from their processes. There have been a number of radical experiments which show the potential. Xerox, facing the onslaught of new printers from Ricoh, Minolta and Canon, set up a 'skunkworks' completely unfettered by the then-stodgy Xerox organisation. This team, devoid of hierarchy and job descriptions, turned out a radically-advanced printer in nine months, halving the previous best.

Chrysler have a similar example. The 1992 Dodge Viper was brought from conception to production in three years, again half the going rate. L'Oreal, through concentrated attention on standardised elements and pre-testing, can put a new brand on the supermarket shelves in 16 weeks if the market demands it, compared to the 18 months it normally takes.

But these and many other fine examples merely show the potential: it can be done if we really make a special effort. Today we should be seeking to realise this potential every time, in our mainstream processes, not through off-line experiments. Ford are one of the Quality companies that are doing this. After many years of a Quality process, their environment is such that a concentrated effort to compress time in the major processes is a natural extension of the need for accelerated change. Thus a major process team working on the whole 'concept to production' process has the crucial support of people working in related areas. The whole process was systematically challenged using a Japanese-like seven-step discipline which ensured that once an improvement had been made it would stay improved. The result after about two years of *kaizen*-style continuous improvement was a consistent development process taking 43 months instead of seven years.

Simultaneous engineering

One consequence of the pressure on time to market has been the discovery of simultaneous or concurrent engineering. The concept is blindingly simple – instead of doing steps sequentially, why can't we overlap and have parallel activities? A brilliant idea which collapses the overall time but which demands complete integrity of each step and complete understanding between the whole team involved. The net effect is the enforced breakdown of organisational boxes; designers, planners, production engineers have to work together seamlessly. The ultimate outcome is that they become simply one multi-disciplinary project team working together throughout the lifetime of the development project. The intensely competitive Japanese domestic market has spurred the extension of simultaneous engineering. Today, the main Japanese car producers can all turn a new model out in 30 to 36 months, or less if they are really under pressure. Nissan's 89 Maxima was a completely new concept which was in the

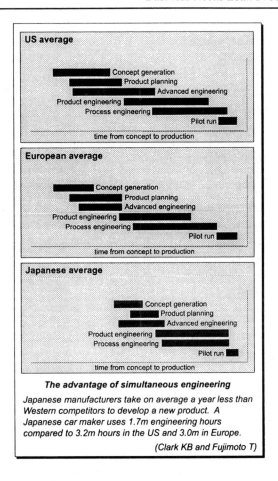

The advantage of simultaneous engineering

Japanese manufacturers take on average a year less than Western competitors to develop a new product. A Japanese car maker uses 1.7m engineering hours compared to 3.2m hours in the US and 3.0m in Europe.

(Clark KB and Fujimoto T)

market in 30 months and went on to top the rankings as the most trouble-free car of 1989 in America. Nissan's first minicar, the Be-1, was produced in 16 months with a big impact on the domestic scene. Honda now take less than 24 months from the first hand-built proto-type to full production. To do this, even suppliers are working on a simultaneous timetable, with Yamashita Rubber Co., for example, working on engine mountings much earlier to allow Honda engineers to build them straight into the engine design.

Again the engineering part of SE is nothing more than a label, showing its origins not its application. SE can be, and is, applied to any development process – for example, a brochure describing a new savings product – and indeed any other business process where the overlapping of steps can secure competitive advantage. Because of its radical nature, SE (and other forms of process re-engineering) can have an irreversible impact on the way people work, which in turn fuels further revolution in the organisation. Deere & Co, the American agricultural vehicle manufacturer, started worrying about its new product process, which was relatively slow and expensive. Many experiments later, the company had simultaneous engineering of a kind: 'parallel tracks which hardly ever met because of the lack of real integration and communication', according to John Gault, director of engineering services.[15] It took recession and a business crisis to force some real change. In the Dubuque factory, which makes backhoe diggers, manufacturing engineers, product engineers and designers were brought out of their separate head office boxes and physically relocated as one unit to create new backhoe models. SE teams (for simultaneous engineering) pulled together other specialists from welding, purchasing, tooling, etc., and stayed in these teams until their product was fully in production. The results were notable: the 310D new model took only 18 months to develop, less than half the previous model; production takes only 10 hours per unit instead of five days, in turn saving $1 million a year inventory costs; product cost is 3.5 per cent less than the previous model despite a host of new features. But the changes are delivering even more benefits. Strategies and business information are now shared with all the people in the plant; decisions are decentralised and appraisals are being shifted to reward team performance and service to internal customers. Process re-engineering has helped fuel revolutionary change in Deere.

Time in the supply chain

Another typical process goal is to cut time in the supply and delivery process. The Japanese distribution system is almost unfathomably complicated to Western minds. Yet as one bottle of Timotei shampoo crosses the scanners at a Daiei supermarket, so another raw bottle is ordered from the plastic moulders. Sell one, make one. Such is the reliability of data in the system and such is the efficiency of the whole supply chain process that this is possible despite the complexities involved. Key to it is the ruthless purging of unnecessary time. Not only is time to market a key factor in capturing customers, time of delivery is a key factor in keeping them and persuading them to buy more.

However distinctive the new product or service, it is not going to win many new customers if it is not readily available to them. The days of customers patiently waiting for a service are gone. When American Express recently took their core business, the charge card, to Japan, where such a payment method was relatively unknown, they found Japanese consumers to be unimpressed with Amex's processes. It took 27 days to produce a new card. To the affluent Tokyo businessman who could order a car to his specification in his own home and have it delivered four days later, this was simply archaic. Amex had no choice but to match the standards expected. Through rigorous application of process improvement techniques, they eventually hit two days. Now this is their benchmark for new card processing worldwide, although replicating the new process is a big challenge. There is a strong incentive for doing so, however, which even the least customer-orientated manager can understand. Simply, that revenue from the new card now flows 25 days earlier. This wonderful route to extra income is being discovered by companies all around the world. Insurance companies can see that turning a new policy round in days rather than months not only impresses the customer but brings in his payments too. AT&T used to take four years to install big new switch gear – no one in the past expected otherwise. Today, they take six months and gain three-and-a-half years of additional income for each installation.

Once a process team has such a goal, as long as they are set up and supported properly, there is every likelihood that they will meet it. The reason for this is that the actual value-added time in a real process is very small. A process improvement team at Perkins Engines has calculated that the actual time spent building a large diesel engine is around four days in total. Lead times quoted to customers were previously as high as 14 weeks. The difference is all the transfer time, the buffer stocks, the multiple handling that is inherent to a large production facility. The process team very quickly brought quotable lead times down to four weeks and ensured consistent delivery to this standard. Their target is two weeks and they know how to get there. They will move to this level, however, only in conjunction with their key customers who also have to manage their supply chain more effectively to take advantage of the improvements. In a similar way, the AT&T process teams who compressed the switchgear installation time reckon they could go down to days rather than months but prefer to move collectively with customers and in line with other processes in the organisation.

This alignment of process capability is another means of using process improvement for overall competitive advantage. Unilever Personal Products looked at all the processes in their European businesses which combined ultimately to provide the customer with a product. They found, as is often the case, that the peripheral processes were the big time-eaters. The cartons for toothpaste, for example, went through many steps and involved many suppliers. To smooth out the flow, the teams ignored all barriers, such as functions or country boundaries. Instead, they optimised the critical flow, eliminating sub-optimal local supply loops. For example, one major supplier was chosen for the bulk of the cartons and a continuous feeder service provided from his locations to the Unilever plants around Europe. Instead of locally-optimising carton supply with full truck loads, the trucks now ran with exactly what had been called off for immediate production, even if the truck was three-quarters empty, thus guaranteeing certainty of supply.

Another ingredient was to harmonise design criteria, again to avoid sub-optimisation. Traditionally, local country marketeers designed the packs for their market. The result when seen as a whole process was a proliferation of minor design changes to basically the same product. Fourteen different colours of red were used on one brand of toothpaste. The customer had no interest in these marginal differences; they were simply local internal preferences. Out they went, reducing ultimately to two standard reds, considerably simplifying the supply lines and inventory. Put together, these process improvements brought the overall supply line down from 17 weeks to seven. The means of going down to two weeks are well understood and planned. Just-in-time supply on a pan-European basis could follow – if the competitive advantage merits it.

Just-In-Time

'Sell one, make one' (SOMO) is Nissan's worldwide manufacturing theme but it was rival Toyota who originated the idea of only making what you can sell and no more. Taiichi Ohno, chief engineer, and Eiji Toyoda, President of Toyota, wanted to rebuild their business in 1950 and start producing cars. They studied the world's best – the Rouge Ford plant in the USA – and concluded that they could not afford the vast investment in plant to stamp out large numbers of body panels to be stockpiled for later assembly. They could only afford to produce what they could sell – thus the revolutionary concept was born. Ohno ingeniously devised ways of making small lots efficiently – interchangeable dies that could be switched in minutes rather than days, for example. The thinking was revolutionary but the practice was painstaking step-by-step experimentation, using the brains of the workforce as well as their hands.

Along the way, Ohno created the *kanban*, which was to become the heart of a completely different way of production planning. In the 1950s and 1960s, Western engineers developed elaborate models to balance assembly lines, juggling sales forecasts, supplier delivery and actual production, with little success. The result was an unhappy compromise with a fixed line speed and parts being fitted if they were there or left to the rectification crew at the end if they were not. Ohno's way was to have a simple card – the *kanban* – which said what parts were to go on a particular car. This card drove the whole process, only the exact parts required for that unique car being available at each assembly point and the car not moving until they were perfectly fitted. The parts were supplied to order; *kanban* squares painted on the floor showed when a new supply was needed. As the square was emptied, another pallet could replace it; there was simply no space made for any surplus or excess parts. This simple discipline revolutionised production and was soon adopted by other Japanese manufacturers. In the seventies, the West saw it as part of the emerging magic of Japanese practice and some companies attempted to transplant the system directly into a Western approach. The resulting havoc put off many companies until the late eighties when a wider understanding and acceptance of all the other aspects of a Quality organisation allowed companies to successfully supply Just-In-Time. JIT simply does not work without a Quality environment; it is in fact better viewed as a *result* of a Quality revolution, an advanced and enhanced management of the whole supply chain.

Flexibility

Just as critical as speed today is flexibility. *Fortune* magazine ran a review in late 1992 of 'Japan's hot new strategy', stating: 'After a mighty effort, top US companies are closing the quality gap but their toughest rivals have moved on to flexibility. It's catch up time again.' Although this implies that Japanese companies flit from technique to technique (missing the big point that the Quality process in Japan is targeted on current competitive distinction, which might be cost reduction, time compression, reliability or flexibility), nevertheless the 1990s target is flexibility. This is partly because there is less perceived differentiation left in product quality or price and more

---

FMS: the ultimate flexibility

Many manufacturers have gone to the ultimate in flexibility - they will produce a batch of one, however small or low in value that unit is. Komatsu is typical of many Japanese manufacturers today in having a number of Flexible Manufacturing Systems (FMS) as islands linked into their large-scale production lines. Often an FMS is unmanned and capable of running 'lights out', i.e. it will run through the night shift with no people in attendance. Komatsu, for example, have totally automated transfer lines for machining engines, with a typical island consisting of 32 automatic cutting machines feeding engines to each other with just two engineers attending to maintenance and set-ups for changeover to another engine size.

Allen-Bradley set up a complete CIM (computer-integrated manufacturing or management) factory many years ago using the FMS concept. The rationale was a strategic necessity: to protect their core North American business in small contactors, they had to counter European imports by being the lowest-cost producer of the unit built to a set international standard. The $15m investment was built without any advance orders. At first, just one or two units went through the multi-station fully-automatic unit. Today, hundreds of different varieties from several thousand to just one (which happens several times every day) are manufactured, assembled and packed entirely automatically. Orders are taken up to 1.30 am and all are despatched the next day. No order has been missed in seven years and the reject rate is an impressive 18 ppm. Despite this near perfection, manager John Rothwell still looks for continual improvement. As he points out, although there is no direct labour, people are still vital - to design, maintain and improve. John sets a challenge to his team every day: 'Are we better today than yesterday?'

---

scope in added features and variety, and partly because that is what the customer wants. Whatever the customer wants, we have to learn how to supply it, quickly and accurately, even if it is only one. This is the challenge which many Japanese manufacturers have set themselves. It is the highest order of process mastery, requiring all the other process aims – reliability, JIT, compressed time – coupled with innovation. 'Customers wanted choices,' explains Toshiba President Fumio Sato about his company's thrust for flexibility. 'They wanted a washing machine or TV set that was precisely right for their needs. We needed variety, not mass production.'[16]

A prerequisite of flexibility is information. If we do not know what people want, we cannot specify what to make. Thus Quality companies spend a lot of effort building a real-time information system which transfers actual needs (what is selling, what people are requesting, what they prefer) into production specifications. At its ultimate, this completely eliminates sales forecasting, which is notoriously unreliable. Instead of a forecast, there is a precise order. But this requires a very slick, fully integrated information system. Kao in Japan supply 280,000 shops with soap and cosmetics, with precise orders delivered within 24 hours. The average order of the relatively low value products is just seven items. To do this, they have an information system holding ten gigabytes of real-time data (128,000 pages of text at any one time). The system is there only to support the philosophy. 'The purpose is to maximise the flexibility of the whole company's response to demand,' according to the systems development manager. At Kao, brand managers can call up daily sales figures and see how their brand is performing against competitors. When a new product is launched, their 'Echo System' integrates point of sale data from 216 stores with focus group analysis and consumer comments from calls and letters. As *Fortune* magazine quotes: 'Kao can know if a product will be successful within two weeks of launch. They know who's buying it, whether the packaging works, whether to change anything.'

A process goal of total flexibility can have far-reaching effects on the organisation of a business. If we are in the computer business, for example, we know our clients want full solutions – not hardware alone. Do we therefore empower our client-focused teams to sell equipment other than our own, perhaps instead of our own? Should we even be in manufacturing at all? These are the tough but exciting challenges posed by process management. The general answer is that, provided we don't jeopardise other imperatives such as reliability and speed, then our process redesign should be built around customer needs, not organisational convenience or history. Thus, process management can be truly revolutionary.

Five generic process goals

- *Reliability: products and services fitting the customer's needs and not failing in production or use; this means no errors whether it is a car door alignment or accuracy of a bank statement.*

- *Waste: continuous waste reduction, whether it is to allow a price reduction to dominate a local building supplies market or to free up more branch staff time to work with customers.*

- *Delivery time: consistently fast supply, whether it's delivery of ice cream to a local retailer or acceptance of an insurance policy.*

- *Time to market: an enhanced rate of innovation through speed, whether it's being first in the market with a new formulation or rapidly following a new software concept.*

- *Flexibility: responsiveness to customers' changing needs, whether it is for a unique computer application or for a unique vacation.*

Consider using these five goals as a start in defining your process goals, then restate them in your own business terms.

Championing process improvement

The Quality leader will want to have revolutionary impact on business processes. But which ones, and how does he start? He can start by identifying and then biasing attention towards the strategic business processes – the ones that will make a difference. The bias is to ensure that these processes are optimised in performance, rather than functions and departments. Some companies, IBM for example, assign senior executives to key processes as 'process owners', in addition to functional responsibility. Over the years since IBM have been doing this, the process-owner accountability has come uppermost, with the high-performing VP biasing his attention that way.

The concept of senior executives as process owners has much merit and, in an autocratic organisation, creates a big shift of emphasis. But it is open to misinterpretation: the Quality leader is not just looking for one manager to own the process exclusively but for everyone in that process to feel responsible as well; too much responsibility can easily focus onto the one executive. Instead, he or she should be the leader of accelerated improvement across the whole process, orchestrating improvement activity, facilitating and stimulating action wherever it is needed. 'Process leader' or 'process champion' are more apt titles – especially 'champion', which can be transferred down the line as each champion coaches those below, who in turn have their own processes to improve.

Building an improvement hierarchy

Big business processes are made up of smaller ones joined together. These sub-processes may also be critical to business success and demand similar attention. In practice, sub-processes often interact with each other and weave a complex web through the organisation. If major processes are chains, at sub-process level they are more like chain-mail. This provides one of the few arguments for a hierarchy (albeit a limited one) in a Quality organisation: that is to stay above a process in order to see the scope for big improvements and also the complexity of unravelling some of the tortuous intermingling of activities that goes on in everyday business. Edwards Deming has always said that a worker cannot be blamed for the results of his process because he is trapped in it and cannot improve it himself. Certainly, it is rare for people to focus their attention much further than the next internal customer. If this is so, then whilst a workteam is concentrating on satisfying their immediate customers, someone – their department manager, perhaps – should be verifying that the transaction between the team and the customer is one which is effective and most directly adds value. This applies all the way back up to the strategic processes for the business.

An improvement hierarchy can be built up around the sub-processes. This not a directive bureaucratic hierarchy but one based on team spirit. The senior executive who is the process champion, for, say, the product development process, brings together the key managers in his process and involves them in a coordinated thrust for improvement. The whole process is mapped and defined and a continuous effort of analysis and challenge is set up. The overall aim is to find a better way and key areas of attack will be identified in order to make the overall process better. These will be focused quite tightly in order to have impact and could well lie inside a sub-process, e.g. product design. This is a natural opportunity for the process champion to empower another level by passing on the disciplines of process improvement and the improvement passion which goes with them. In turn, the new process champion gathers his own team and so it goes on until everyone is involved. This is not a structural change (although some companies have gone that far) and people maintain their normal reporting lines. Indeed, many people will belong to a number of process improvement initiatives as the process populations inevitably overlap. This is all to the good, for one thing that process improvement encourages is pulling people out of their boxes.

Rank Xerox, in June 1993, dramatically stepped up their business process focus for this reason. Seven core business processes were identified and overlaid across all functional departments in Europe. Each top executive became a 'sponsor' for one of the processes and a 'business process board' monitors progress. Below this level, process managers in each unit drive process improvement across boundaries. In conjunction with this, systematic analysis of every activity is being carried out to test for value added. Activities which survive the test are allocated into one of the core business processes. As John Drinkwater, director of business processes, says: 'Now we're re-engineering not just a few processes, but the whole company.'[17]

Mapping a process

Mapping should not be the first step the process champion makes with his team (as we shall see shortly), but it is very significant one.

Mapping their process is a revealing and exhilarating activity for the process team. They will find duplications, redundant steps, long delays, nonsenses...and parts of the process where no one really knows what happens. Try it, it is salutary. The experience of the marketing team at Van den Bergh Foods and is typical. This team has a world-class track record, with successes such as the 1992 launch of 'I can't believe it's not butter' into the UK, and yet astonished them-selves by being unable to pin down how they made key marketing decisions.

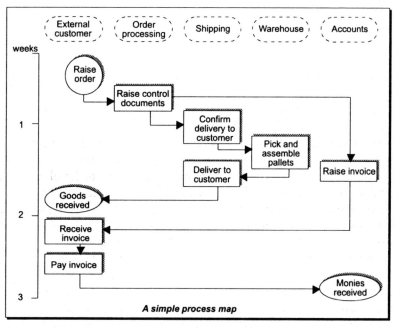

A simple process map

Process mapping is based around flow charting. But it is really much more than that. Handled well, it is explorative, creative and collective. The team are discovering the process and its strengths and limitations in a team environment which will enable them rapidly and purposefully to make subsequent improvements. Mapping should be practical, not theoretical. The team should not make assumptions about what happens but go out there and see for themselves. Walking the process is a good start – following the product or data around the business, noting what happens.

Process maps can be straightforward flow charts. A flow chart is, however, boring and appears opaque to any one not involved in its creation. Far better to make the process map like a geographic map – full of features and illustrations of the terrain. A process map can be a wonderful means of self-expression for an improvement team, recording stages of the exploration. The team should be encouraged to colour in their maps with questions, comments, challenges, numbers. The best expression of all is to put the map and supporting information on a wall as a display for anyone to see. This not only extends the involvement and interaction (and the feedback for the team) but allows them to show the whole process story from what it is now, with all its idiosyncrasies, to what it might be. As improvements are made these are shown too. The process story wall reflects real-time improvement action.

The process of process improvement

A process improvement team needs energy and determination. It also needs discipline. Major processes are not to be idly tinkered with; the disruptive effects can be far-reaching. Most processes are fairly stable, even if low performing; uninformed changes can easily destabilise the process, which, if it leads to upset customers, defeats the object. The improvement team need to proceed in a systematic and rigorous manner and this is one of the first things they should learn. The process of process improvement is the sequence of investigative and executive steps which an improvement team should follow. The first steps are about definition and are the most important. What is the process we are going to improve? What does it do? Where does it start and finish? Early on, the team will need to start thinking hard to really pin down this process. Can we define a mission for it? Can we set some stretching goals to stimulate our improvement ambition? The team may well need to return to these crucial aspects, as they go out and collect data on the process overall.

As for improvement of the business as a whole, improvement of a process can be greatly accelerated through the pull of well-crafted mission and goals. Also, early in the definition stage, the team should have clarity of customer needs, without which the mission and goal statements will be wishful thinking. It is likely that only vague data is readily available, so this is an early information gathering task.

Whilst the team are refining their process definitions, they can also be mapping the existing process. They may well have already put together a high-level map of what they think happens. Now they should go out there and find out what is really done. This trail-finding can take many weeks of intensive digging, following products, documents and

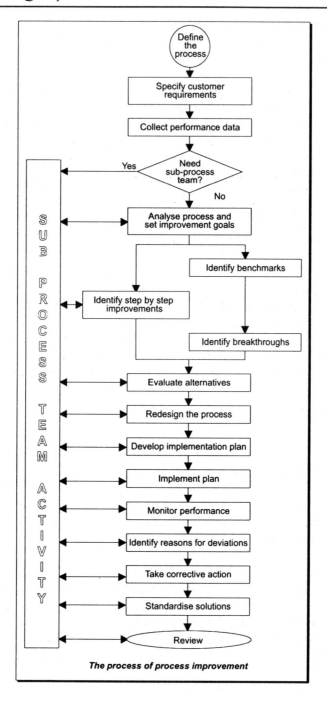

The process of process improvement

information transfers and questioning those directly involved. This can be a highly interactive task, involving the whole population affected by the process. The result should be a map in reasonable detail, but not showing every variation or every task. These should be recorded but only the significant activities and the major flows need be illustrated on the process map.

Once captured, the existing process now becomes the butt of merciless interrogation and challenge. Who is responsible at this point? Where are the measuring points? Why does it take so long here? Why is this done twice? Why are some handled this way and others this way? The process is dismembered and scrutinised. It is at this point that the process champion can begin to empower other teams. Critical areas may require detailed analysis. Sub-processes may now need mapping in order to reveal more detail. Whilst most of the work so far would have been carried out by management, a controlled cascade of process analysis right down to the people operating the process day to day is quite feasible, even in a large organisation. Some caution is needed, however, because it is all too easy to create a proliferation of process maps and cause a severe case of analysis paralysis. When IBM UK first took up business process management, defining their processes became the end rather than the means and 14,000 process maps were beautifully prepared using IBM technology. Needless to say, the vast majority were never looked at again and the whole initiative developed a bad name for a year or two until one or two major process improvements brought in big results.

The analysis is primarily to identify the best opportunities for improvement and should be directly linked to improvement action. Indeed, the process champion may well constrain process analysis to senior levels for a while to avoid proliferation and excessive overlap of effort. One way of doing this, whilst still involving people in improvement, is by setting up a limited number of projects with set objectives. Indeed, this is one of the next steps in the process of process improvement and it is vital that these are chosen with care. Teams can be assigned to the projects on a cross-functional basis (provided they are drawn from the process population – in other words, they have a direct interest). So the process improvement teams may need a spell of managed humility before they will adapt the disciplines necessary for them to achieve durable improvements.

Today or tomorrow?

Do we map the process as it is or as it should be?...A common question for a new process improvement team. Both, is the short answer. We need to capture the existing process with all its foibles as the base for systematic improvement. But there is often a strong argument to say that if we want to get to the position set by our goals, we wouldn't start from here. So we also need to design what the process might be if we *hadn't* started from here. An effective step is to set up teams to map both the *'as is'* and the *'could be'* – separately and in parallel. These can then be compared and debated and an improvement programme created which integrates the two. How much of the existing is retained (but improved) and how much is brand new should be carefully evaluated and planned. Clearly this depends a lot on the effectiveness of the systems and technology in the process.

Many banks, for example, have moved from a heavy reliance on work being done in the high-street branches to centralised transactions for volume work, leaving the branches with less routine services for customers. In this scenario, there is limited value in detailed mapping of the existing process (although still value in recording the problem points to be avoided in future) but an urgent need to pin down the new process so that improvement can start even before it is running. For many processes, though, such revolutionary changes (from market or technological causes) are not anticipated. In this situation, the process champion needs to debate with the team whether they need to create revolutionary change anyway. In other words, is incremental improvement going to be enough to maintain satisfied customers in the future? The answer may well be no, in which case breakthrough disciplines need to be introduced and woven in with the *kaizen* work to maintain accelerated (but controlled) improvement.

Multiplying value

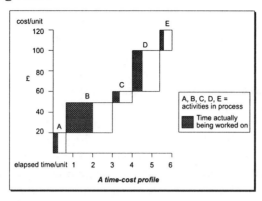

A time-cost profile

The ultimate aim of process improvement is to *multiply* value. That is by removing waste, by compressing time, by simplifying, by assigning clear responsibilities, by focusing on customer needs, our process is sufficiently superior to give us a Quality edge. If the process we are working on is more flexible, responsive and efficient, and we use this distinctively, the resulting competitive advantage is greater than the sum of the value added.

Westinghouse learned the significance of process improvement many years ago. Today the challenge to halve the time in a process is routine. They use time as the main driver but their ultimate goal is value. By challenging process teams to reduce time by 50 per cent, they force radical and innovative thinking. They claim their teams never fail to achieve the goal, on average hitting 60 per cent. With time collapsed, costs go too – typically 20 per cent less. Product quality, consistency and reliability go up dramatically because it is impossible to reach the 50 per cent goal with errors in the system. It all multiplies up to value.

Before Westinghouse Nuclear Fuels won the 1988 Baldrige Award they attacked 56 sub-processes with their 'half' target. Down came the overall time to reload from 36 months to 18. Down too came the cost. The tighter processes enabled them to run with 20 per cent less staff. The engineering department, the critical group, produced 40 per cent more work, as the number of design change notices halved. A small revolution in one part of a $13 billion corporation. Today, Westinghouse has literally hundreds of major process improvements underway and as one 50 per cent challenge is achieved, it is reset again. Carl Arendt, VP for Quality, reckons in administrative areas alone this has been worth $3 billion in savings made. The value in competitive advantage is worth much more.

Reinventing the business

How far do you go? There are no limits to invention in changing business processes. Think about telephone banking, home shopping, instantaneous credit approvals...think how different these processes have to be to the conventional services even though still competing in the same markets. Think about motor industry suppliers building their own dedicated supply units around, or even inside, their customer's plants; or computer businesses, such as Digital, permanently placing staff on customer sites. Or the reverse, all routine data processing – payroll, order entry, invoicing – being out-sourced totally to specialists. Or volume printing being done overnight in South East Asia for use next day in California. Or local calls to a help desk being answered by a customer response centre 6,000 miles away on another continent. In process management, anything is possible if it is the optimal solution to meet customer needs. The net result of continuous process improvement could well be the reinvention of the business. Richard Pascale states: 'Reinvention is not what is, but creating what isn't.'[18]

Process thinking is a foundation for reinvention by challenging the accepted and inviting new solutions. It focuses attention right onto customer's needs for today and tomorrow and disregards historical precedent. It helps bring customers and suppliers into dialogue and encourages cooperation – all the way along the value chain. It highlights value and reveals waste. Above all, it changes behaviour. A radically improved process shifts people into a different work style. The people managing lean processes are not constrained by boundaries or bogged down by irrelevant tasks. They take responsibility, using their skills and their brains to manage their processes effectively. Process management plays a crucial role in the Quality revolution.

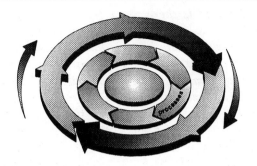

SUMMARY

Think process

Process improvement starts from a mentality of accepting that every-thing is part of a process. Thinking in process terms is part of the revolution which starts with the leader. What are the processes I am involved in? Are they effective? How can they be made better? Think through the following steps to form an idea of the impact of process improvement.

1. **What is my process?** *Choose a small process of some significance as an example, e.g. order entry, message taking, authorising expenditure, organising a meeting.*
2. **Where does it start and end?** *Put some limits around it with inputs and outputs.*
3. **Who is the customer?** *State the person who will judge the value of the output.*
4. **What are the requirements?** *Specify the outputs in the customer's terms.*
5. **How well are they met?** *Does the process do what it is supposed?...in time?...efficiently?...consistently?*
6. **Set the improvement goals?** *State what would give substantially greater value to the customer and the business.*
7. **What are the activities and the flow?** *List the steps the process goes through and show how they are linked.*
8. **Do they all add value?** *Are some steps unnecessary, excessive, duplicated?*
9. **Can they be done quicker?** *Can some steps be combined, linked more directly, by-passed or done simultaneously?*
10. **Is there a radical alternative?** *Forget today's process – could it be done some other way entirely?*

What have I learned? Is there scope for multiplying value by re-engineering this process or is there gain from simply sharpening it up or slimming it down? If the scope is there for this small example, imagine the impact on a critical business process. Imagine too the impact on the whole business and the contribution process improvement can make to business success.

7

People Make Quality

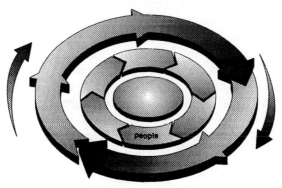

Unless the Quality leader is a one-man band, he is going to have to rely on others. The leader sets the direction, the vision and the example, but someone else still does it on his behalf. No management disciplines or improvement methodologies, still less new technology, can replace the ingenuity of the person doing the work. In a Quality revolution, this latent talent is released, freeing up vast improvement energy. People make Quality; the leader enables them to do it.

'We only use 10-15 per cent of our people's skills and knowledge.' Roger Hartel, VP, Allen-Bradley

'We have learned that nothing is impossible with an inventive mind, an invincible attitude to the goal, self-confidence and belief.' Top Quality Circle at Fuji Xerox

Treat people as people

'People are our greatest asset' is a well-worn cliché. 'You are only as good as your weakest link' is another. 'Your staff are your best representatives' is one more. Clichés, yes; still true, yes. When it comes down to it, products, services, brands, image, facilities, technologies cannot improve themselves...only people can do that. That people of all nationalities and educational level can and will make remarkable improvements, if asked, is proven day after day. The challenge for most leaders is cutting through procedures and management practices which assume that, on being employed, a person's thinking capability is reduced to near-zero. Empowerment is about removing the barriers in organisations which constrain performance and limit potential. It is not easily achieved. People still need guidance, direction and support, but given these they can take full responsibility for satisfying their immediate customers and make a strong contribution to the performance of the whole business.

Empowerment encourages people to become the managers of their work activities – they make the work decisions day to day, activity to activity. But it is not democracy or even consensus; leadership is a vital component. Machines are considered to be more reliable and predictable than people and yet any engineer knows that a neglected machine quickly becomes inefficient and eventually will cease to perform. People need more attention than machines but their potential and versatility are infinitely greater. So the Quality leader allocates time and thought for his team because he knows they will repay him in performance.

In any event, the Quality leader does not have much choice. Professor Dean Berry says: 'Companies may not start out with empowerment as a goal. But when they strip levels out, try to compress time to market and redesign other processes, they end up with it. Even with advanced information technology, you can't really run a de-layered organisation by "command and control" methods. The people route is more timely, simpler, more cost effective and less risky.'[19]

What do you call them?

Employees, personnel, workers, staff, blue collar, white collar, hourly... these generic labels give no feeling of identity and hardly make people feel they are important. A good first step to showing respect for your people is to find a name which is positive. Most Quality companies coin a term which gives a special identity and at the same time minimises divisions between levels and functions. At Milliken, everyone (including management) is a Milliken 'associate'; this has been widely copied by many other companies. At John Lewis, everyone is a 'partner' - literally in this case as John Lewis Partnership is owned by a trust on behalf of all staff. Again this is becoming a popular term. Others build around the big team concept - Team Xerox, for example.

A first step is to respect people as individuals: respect for people is one of the cornerstones of Quality. Motorola sums this up in a recent full-page advert headed 'To get people to care about quality, you have to care about them.' Motorola's key beliefs, which are unequivocally stated on cards carried by all staff, starts with 'constant respect for people'. They back this up with full commitment to training and personal development. Despite being a hard-driven, fast-moving company, Motorola strives to keep up with its statement: 'There is only one way to care about people and that's one at a time.' All the leading companies in the world would echo these sentiments and strive hard in practice to live up to them.

To empower people without abdicating, the Quality leader builds on respect, ultimately reaching every individual, however big the business. The leader has many approaches he can use to build on the receptive base of respect in order to harness and channel work behaviour and grow the enthusiasm for improvement.

Making empowerment work at Jefferson City

The Jefferson City plant of Chesebrough-Pond's was acclaimed in 1992 as one of the top ten factories in the USA. Plant manager Joe Roy runs the plant with a Quality philosophy and has applied many of the practices described here. The plant's success is tangible – 99 per cent of products right first time, $10 million taken out of manufacturing costs and 20 per cent improvement in productivity over a five-year period. Empowerment is a core feature in this success. People working on the production lines are called 'associates'; supervisors are 'coaches'. Responsibility for problem-solving and local innovation is at associate level, with an expectation that associates will improve their work. Joe believes control has been replaced by communication, with the aim of keeping everyone fully informed and pulling together. The transition to empowerment has been carefully managed. It is popular with the associates, even though the demand on them is greater. One associate's view: 'This has really broadened my outlook on life. It has given me self-esteem. I realise, if I can solve problems here, I can solve them elsewhere. That's pretty powerful stuff.'

Ten principles for empowering people at Jefferson City:

- Tell people what their responsibilities are.
- Give them authority equal to the responsibilities assigned to them.
- Set standards of excellence.
- Provide them with training that will enable them to meet the standards.
- Give them knowledge and information.
- Provide them with feedback on their performance.
- Provide them with feedback on their achievements.
- Trust them.
- Allow them to fail.
- Treat them with dignity and respect.

(Source: Chesebrough-Pond's USA, Quality News, September 1993.)

Daily practice

Business is done moment by moment – the thousand moments of truth described by Jan Carlzon, president of SAS. He was referring to the customer/employee contact points when, at that moment, the whole service is down to how that one representative behaves. The same moments of truth apply generally to all business situations, not just at the customer interface but at the back end of the organisation too. These business moments are controlled entirely by people – the real people who make and sell things. But people are variable and we don't want variability, we want consistency. How do we control that variability? Conventionally, we contain it with a system, such as a production line or administrative procedure, and then we divide the tasks into very small elements which are repeated continuously. Responsibility for the correct functioning of this system is placed on managers who adjust and correct the system continually to make it deliver what is required. People are required to do what they have been instructed to do and not use their initiative. What do we achieve this way?...mediocre performance again.

If we have this type of operation (and most processes are set up this way), then completely new thinking is needed to break through this performance barrier. The process in which people are working is almost certainly the biggest barrier to breaking out of this trap. Far from controlling variability, the process has inherent variability of its own. Containing this variability through systematic process improvement has been discussed in Chapter 6 from a top-down management perspective and major strategic improvement of the process should remain the responsibility of senior management. But there is a whole additional area of potential improvement coming from a bottom-up perspective: the day-to-day running of the process can only truly be mastered by those who do the work. The day-to-day improvement should be in their hands too.

There are many influences on people at work. The Quality leader seeks to manage these influences for the benefit of the business. He wants these influences to stimulate and support consistently high standards of daily work...and the search for improvement too. That people are capable of handling the more responsible role of managing their part of the process should not be doubted. Most people today manage complex processes in their private lives and only suspend this capability at the door of the business because that has been expected. But they will need training, support, information, freedom to act and guidance. Given these enabling factors an individual workteam can achieve phenomenal performances. As many Quality leaders have discovered: 'for every pair of hands we are getting a free brain.'

An example of what is possible is the speciality chemicals team of Milliken. Milliken set up a new plant to supply chemicals at a green-field location a few miles from their Spartanburg headquarters. Once the facility was built, the operating teams of three shifts took over completely. Management were back at head office and didn't need to visit often. The shift team did everything from taking the orders, planning the workload, managing the flow through to delivery and checking that the customer was satisfied. The whole team of 24 has run for two and a half years without a complaint, without any rework, without any off-standard work and without any mistakes. Zero defects in practice. As Tom Malone, Milliken's president says: 'When a team believes they can do it, anything is possible.'

Teams work

A motivated team is a powerful force in an organisation. This force may not always be used for the benefit of the company, so the Quality leader must be vigilant in turning natural teams into strong workteams for improving the business. There are many kinds of teams and the Quality leader should encourage a variety of forms. Teams can be focused on processes or projects; on problems or opportunities. They can be permanent or live only as long as the problem exists. They can be formed locally or draw people in from outside – including customers and suppliers. They can be focused on breakthrough or continuous small-step improvements. They can be peer groups or totally mixed levels. They can be voluntary or mandatory. Such options provide the Quality leader with many ways of engaging and nurturing the latent talent lying in the organisation.

Teams do not work well naturally. Discipline and energy are always needed to achieve high performance and the leader's main role is to feed these on a continuous basis. Clear purpose is also vital: any team without a defined mission which clearly benefits the business should be dissolved and reformed around an issue of substance. Committees or meetings of representatives tend to be low in energy and should be used sparingly. To be very effective, teams need to be trained in how to work well as a group and in the improvement disciplines which are most relevant to them. They may also be more effective if they are facilitated, although both training and facilitation should be on a practical basis, providing the team with better means of achieving their goals.

Project teams

Project teams are the most common way of converting Quality thinking into practice. Projects are built around well-defined issues (either a problem or an opportunity) and most practitioners prefer a project team to have a prescribed life – usually the complete resolution of the problem or the realisation of the opportunity. In practice this means a judgement should be made as to when an issue is handed over to someone else. This is because every problem should be 100 per cent resolved, but that cannot be proven without doubt for some time. Also an opportunity might develop into something bigger than the original project scope.

Successful projects require a mandate and a structure. A project leader must be appointed and often a sponsor – a senior-level mentor – to help the project team through any road blocks. The project leader and the sponsor, helped by the facilitator, choose the team. They should choose only those people who they think can materially influence the issue and should aim to keep the team small. Location and position should be of small importance in team selection. Once chosen, the Quality leader needs to ensure that the team is not going to be constrained. Only important subjects should be chosen for project treatment and, therefore, because it is important, significant time should be made available to work on the project. Full-time input isn't usually necessary (there are occasions when it is justified) but the project teams need to reach a critical mass of input or the result will be a certain disappointment: 15-20 per cent is probably about the right minimum time spent on a big project. This in itself forces two more disciplines: projects should be short and sharp – six months maximum – and any one individual should be involved with only one (or sometimes two) projects at a time. This still leaves scope for enough projects to clog up a business – a very common problem in the early years of a Quality process. A further discipline will help with this: keep to less than five major projects per managerial level at any one time. This permits time for the line to absorb new methods and behaviours from the project findings.

Lead teams

A good way of ensuring project disciplines are adhered to by teams is to set up another team to do the overseeing. This should not become a bureaucratic layer second-guessing the project teams, but a group which guides and influences the project teams with the benefit of an overview of all the improvement that is happening. The lead team determines (in a rigorous way) which project ideas are of most benefit to the business. It helps identify which projects are ready for implementation and alerts other teams of the plans. It seeks out projects which are trailing and gives facilitating help to bring them back on schedule. It ensures every improvement is recognised and where appropriate publicised. This means the lead team tends to have a wider brief than supporting the project teams and may well be given supervising responsibility for the day-to-day mechanics of the Quality process in an area.

How does this fit in with the line structure? The lead team could well be the section management team, in which case there is no conflict. Many companies start out this way; it is clear, it reinforces and emphasises management's role and avoids any temptation for parallel structures to grow. On the other hand, the Quality leader may be seeking to push towards the collapsing of layers and boundaries. Adding people from different levels and other sections to a core management group helps this and brings in fresh perspective and challenge.

Organising project teams

The Quality leader should think through how project teams are to be used. They can be highly exciting experiences or they can be damp squibs. Like the Quality mushroom effect of upset customers, a bad project will sour the environment and deflate energy. Much of the outcome of a project can be predetermined. Success of a project is a significant improvement which has material (and demonstrated) benefit for the business. Generally speaking, such success is far more likely if the project has been set top-down, if it links to strategy (for example, if the project is aligned to a major process for which improvement goals have been set) and if it receives senior level attention. There are always exceptions and, in a highly-energised environment, mavericks will appear who will make a success of something which no one else would back. Such initiative should be encouraged, publicised and learned from but, for hard results, 80 per cent of successful projects will probably come from top-down directed initiatives and 20 per cent, at best, from locally inspired ideas.

The other common determinant of success is the 'grounding' of the project – keeping it down to earth with scope in proportion to ownership. Thus, multidisciplinary task forces are most appropriate for breakthrough solutions and should report to the highest lead team, which includes the chief executive. As mentioned earlier, there should be very few of these anyway and they should be of the highest significance – the ones that will lead ultimately to a Quality edge. Even so, 'elephant' projects should be avoided as a basic and inviolate discipline: if it is too big, break it up and make two or more projects. Other projects can be grounded at department level where the emphasis will be on small breakthroughs and continuous improvement. Here the departmental lead team will assign the project leader but team members may be drawn from inside or outside of the department.

Milliken improvement teams

There is no doubt that Milliken believe in the power of improvement teams. In 1989, Milliken had 8,769 corrective action teams, 2,722 customer action teams, 779 supplier action teams and 8,039 process improvement teams: 20,309 teams in all. The number of employees in 1989 to fill these teams?... just 27,000.

Local improvement teams

When many people think about small improvement teams, they think about Japan and Quality Circles. So far, we have looked at management-led teams, involving managers primarily but not exclusively. There is no reason at all why the same directed approach to project-based improvement should not go all the way down the line and involve the whole workforce. Indeed this is desirable and the most certain and direct way of ensuring improvement gains are made. However, the Quality Circle approach, or small improvement teams at local workteam level, has considerable merit too. Both approaches should be used for maximum improvement activity and they are entirely compatible, if handled well.

Contrary to common belief, Circles in Japan are not think-tanks and not alternatives to line management. They are disciplined local groups trained to apply improvement methodologies. As a result, they will meet formally once a week for probably an hour to review progress briskly and probably undertake some more training. Their improvement activity takes place during and around work to disciplined steps (based on PDCA, or Plan-Do-Check-Act, introduced to Japan by Deming), often taking six months to complete. Circles are built around natural work teams and tend to be around eight in number. They are voluntary...but few in Japan decline to join.

The extent of Circles in Japan illustrates how far one can go in harnessing teams for improvement. Many Japanese companies have 100 per cent participation; that is, in Komatsu or YKK, management belong to Circles as well as all of the workforce. Circles have grown phenomenally in Japan, officially involving two and a half million people, but unofficially involving an estimated 10 per cent of the population. As a result of this vast uptake, the Circles movement in Japan has evolved to fulfil many needs. Not only does it provide training and improvement discipline for staff, it gives them a sense of purpose and belonging, together with the satisfaction of contributing in a way over and above the basic job. Significantly, the local, regional and national structure set up originally by the Japanese Union of Scientists and Engineers (JUSE), but often paralleled by big corporations, provides a natural and complementary form of recognition. All teams have a turn in reporting their QCC (Quality Control Circles, as they are still called in Japan) story locally. The best receive awards and are invited to tell their story at regional level and so on. To a Japanese workteam, an invitation to a QCC convention is a high honour and the recognition goes right back to the local section and plant. The *Journal of QC Circles*, which is a fairly technical tome produced by JUSE, is bought by 200,000 workers per month. Joining a QCC in Japan is not merely joining an improvement group – it is joining a club.

The symbolic value of Circles

In Japan, symbols are important and QCCs are symbolic of the contribution and willingness of the Japanese worker. There is a famous example dating back to 1970 when one of the first Circles in a large bank proposed that the 'door close' button on lifts be removed. Their logic was that the electricity cost wasted was Y20 per button. The bank had 240 offices with many elevators, thus the team calculated a theoretical saving of Y100 million. The bank's president ordered the recommendation to be implemented and duly all the close buttons on lifts were blanked off. Such an action would have been dismissed as trivial by any manager in the West, but the impact was profound. The president had not only shown respect for his people by adopting their suggestion but the blanked-off panel was a symbol which everyone saw every day, reminding them of his interest in his people. Within months, Circles had spread through the bank, ultimately growing to tens of thousands. Up to this point, QCCs were felt to be for factories. This example helped spread the movement into financial institutions, restaurants, trading houses, hotels, taxi services, leading up to the next famous example: Bunny Girls of the Tokyo Playboy Club, who entertained other winners at a QCC convention by presenting their QCC story in their working costumes!

Although still wearing their original training label, QC Circles, local improvement teams in Japan work on whatever type of improvements are the most important, albeit on a small and controlled scale. In normal times, most Circles will address housekeeping issues, looking to make the local workplace more efficient. But companies with a strong Circles culture find they can use this to align the business to a shift of priorities. During the oil crisis, energy reduction was the favoured Circles topic; during the high yen period, cost reduction. Thus Japanese companies can effect a clear linkage between major improvement goals set for the company or plant (*hoshins*) and local small team activity.

For instance, Fuji Xerox, with 100 per cent QCC participation, set goals during the high yen period of 1986 which filtered down to section level as 'challenge 20' – a 20 per cent productivity gain. For the next year, virtually all the 400 plus QCC teams directed their efforts to this goal, ensuring the overall target was easily met. One example came from the 'Yamato & Star Part II Circle', whose chosen approach to meet the target was to go directly for labour hours. Their chosen method was to pair people off to work alongside each other and exchange skills. This cut out a third of the man-hours and raised the skill level. Not content with that, the team widened its membership and became the 'Yamato & Star Part III Circle' and went for the bigger target of the 60 per cent of all man-hours which went into moving materials around the factory. Having decided that agv's (automatic guided vehicles) offered more efficiency, they evaluated various products. Not sufficiently impressed with what was on offer, they decided to build their own. Working in the paired format they had perfected earlier, and learning about the technology as they went along, they constructed a new process. Using their own version of PDCA, study-think-try-adjust, they brought the process into full operation at a fifth of the cost anticipated. This Circle brings in six project implementations per year (the Japan norm is two) and not surprisingly is felt to be one of the best in Fuji Xerox. As the Circle members themselves say: 'We have learned that nothing is impossible with an inventive mind, an invincible attitude to the goal, self-confidence and belief.'

Western application of Circles has been at best mediocre. Enthusiasm for this latest Japanese 'miracle' was very high in the late seventies and application spread rapidly in Europe and the USA. Few managed to sustain the early promise, for reasons which are obvious now: the managerial environment has to be wholly supportive for the Circles to flourish. In most Western organisations in the early eighties, it wasn't. Circles became 'something the top wanted the bottom to do' without any corresponding initiatives at senior level (signalling 'we are all right, we want you to do better') and, crucially, by-passing the middle levels entirely. Thus, senior management would at first listen spellbound as nervous shop-floor workers related their common-sense improvements. Local managers saw it differently – it was *their* job to report to management and often didn't help the implementation. Soon senior management became too busy again to keep listening to all of these teams – and, lacking any other support, the Circles faded away.

Some companies who believed passionately in the idea of small teams, such as Florida Power & Light, learned how to set up structures of support teams to keep the local teams going. By 1988, FPL had around 1,400 improvement teams, most of them small local work teams. Others such as Hewlett Packard found, like everyone else, that their promising Quality Circles initiative was fading in the early eighties. However, as one of the early pioneers of Total Quality thinking, HP was already initiating top-down improvement drives by around 1983. The result was an unexpected resurgence of Circles activity: it now had a conducive environment in which to grow.

3M had a parallel experience: 30 circles in 1979, 700 in 1982 but slackening off thereafter as 'the low-hanging fruit had been picked'. With a new management-led Quality process having an effect in the mid-1980s, the improvement teams flourished again rising to 1,400. At 3M though they have a slightly different slant. 3M is rated as a world-class benchmark on innovation and this is very important to them. So the Circles, now called Quality Action Teams, are biased towards innovation and over two thirds of their recommendations are about new approaches, either as new product ideas or as process innovations (such as one team who carved the time taken to submit a quote from two weeks down to one and a half days).

Natural workteams

If small local improvement teams are a good thing and fit well with a Quality process, should we therefore follow the Japanese model and encourage everyone into Quality Circles? In a sense, yes, because, as the Japanese companies say, this helps create a responsive and adaptable workforce in tune with the need for continuous improvement. The qualification is that not every improvement or every person needs to be incorporated into a formal improvement team. Improvement needs discipline but not just the one form of it. In reality, Western businesses who are well into their Quality process find their improvements fall into a pattern. Typically it may be that 20 per cent of the benefit comes from the small number of large impact cross-functional projects. Maybe another 40 per cent will come from departmental projects. The remaining 40 per cent come from managerial and workforce improvements, not through formal teams but from adopting new Quality disciplines, such as understanding the customer better. The best home for such improvements might be a Quality Circle, if a detailed search for root causes and alternative solutions is required. Equally the Circle discipline might prove cumbersome and unnecessary in many cases.

FPL Quality structure
To link together management action, team action and improvement in daily work.

This is where empowerment of the local natural team comes into play. If a small problem is found or an opportunity surfaces, sometimes the need is to deal with it quickly. However, some discipline is needed to ensure we are not tinkering with the process, with the risk of causing more problems. The natural team, with the support of their leader acting as a coach, should learn to deal quickly and effectively with these day-to-day issues. One or two people may be assigned to investigate further; engineers or maintenance or suppliers may be called in – but it doesn't merit the full improvement team methodology. FPL recognises this in its Quality framework as a key leg of their improvement structure – Quality in Daily Work – which is distinct from another leg – Improvement Teams. The third leg, Policy Deployment, completes the frame and complements both.

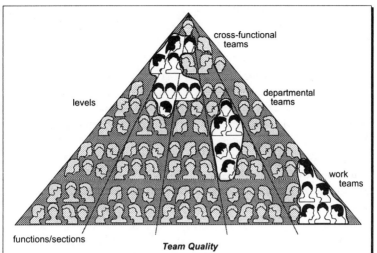

levels

cross-functional
teams

departmental
teams

work
teams

functions/sections

Team Quality

Quality companies use many forms of teams and can have hundreds in action at any time. Here are some typical examples:

Cross-functional teams*... An illustrative cross-functional project might be at Ilford where the best technical brains, including external professors, had failed over many years to eradicate a very occasional 'spotting' on high-speed black and white film, which caused some concern with professional photographers. A cross-functional team was set up with the authority of the Board and systematically followed the process through from raw material to exposed film. Key variables were isolated and brought into a tighter control band. The spots disappeared and to ensure they did not return, operators continued close monitoring through control charts. A project team working in parallel tightened the variables on another film product to such an extent that customers and competitors thought it was a completely new product.*

Departmental teams*... Florida Power & Light,with hundreds of projects per year, provides many examples, such as Jim Metz's team, who are field service installers and repairers. Jim's view is that as a team of engineers they felt 'we are great guys, we can fix anything'.When they formally asked customers what they thought about them they found a big perception gap... us: 'We got the lights back on in a fast time,' and them: 'Why did they let the lights go off at all.' Suitably humbled, Jim's team focused on key areas of discontent such as connecting a meter at the time requested, pinning down four or five key metrics and plotting each engineers performance against them. One by one the gaps between target performance and actual moved to zero.*

Work teams*... A team of fitters at Perkins Engines became fed up with a part of the engine-making process which required a salt bath to remove burrs caused when conrods were drilled. The problem was corrosion in the bath leading to breakdowns in the flow, requiring a buffer stock in turn. The shop floor team studied the process and determined that an extra machining operation, a countersinking drill, would do the job equally well if not better. The result is no stocks, no stoppages and the company £1.5 million better off.*

Empowering individuals

Not everyone wants to be a team player; many in fact would prefer not to have the pressures and responsibilities of collective work. The benefits of teamwork are so great, however, that we should encourage team identity wherever it makes sense. Nevertheless, there will be numerous occasions when an individual is working relatively autonomously and some people who will always be more comfortable in this role. A Quality process should not leave these people out – the need for improvement is just the same and the capacity for higher individual contribution can be enormous. If the formal small team improvement activities are voluntary, then the less gregarious person can stay out of the meetings but still play a significant role in local improvement. Local improvement goals, clear customer requirements and local process data enable an individual to take informed corrective actions and spot opportunities.

Other mechanisms may help stimulate further contribution. Measurements which track and display local parameters can quickly become a source of pride and healthy competition. But they must be chosen well; if they do not relate well to local effort or expertise, then they are soon ignored. The best way of ensuring this does not happen is to let people devise the measures locally. 'People defend what they have helped create' is a factor here, as is the common finding that people will set tougher standards and less woolly measures themselves than their manager would set for them. Repeated over and over around the world, is the example of Lipton's manufacturing plant in Independence, USA, where the newly-empowered workteams challenged the target set by management to raise production to 450 units per day. In the past, they would have argued for 250 to 300; this time they said 'We want to do 600.' Because it was their target, 600 was what they achieved consistently and to higher standards than previously.

Capturing ideas

The key to empowering individuals is to involve them and for those who are shy of joining improvement teams other channels of involvement should be available. Any workforce is a vast sink of ideas waiting to be tapped. Sadly most businesses simple don't bother. Even small businesses where the owner/manager ought to be closer to his people tend to miss this source of improvement despite evidence that most product or business ideas come from inside rather than direct from the market. In a recent survey, only 16 per cent of companies picked up ideas from competitors in the market place against nearly 50 per cent coming from staff and management. Less than one in 12 had a formal suggestion scheme.

Quality companies, on the other hand, have no doubt that this is one of the key pieces in the jigsaw for accelerated improvement. Tom Malone, president of Milliken, used to say that his OFI system (Opportunities for Improvement) was the fuel of involvement. OFIs at Milliken started life as the more downbeat Corrective Action Requests – a form which a Milliken associate could complete to request assistance when a problem was spotted or suspected. This was fine for a while and moderately used, but Tom knew there was more to come. Tom's inspiration was to flip the concept over to Opportunities for Improvement; this instantly made the whole thing more positive and appealing. Now, associates could suggest improvements and make constructive comments, as well as still highlighting problems. The number of OFIs rose considerably, then plateaued. The blockage this time was the age-old difficulty of providing feedback – giving the associate a response. If the person's pet idea goes into a black hole and it doesn't re-emerge or it seems to be taking for ever, that person is disappointed, feels offended and thinks 'forget that'.

Instead of accepting the inevitable (which has beset many a suggestion programme before), the Milliken team devised a new process to handle OFIs. A management rule was established which put teeth into the process – the 24/72 rule guaranteed an acknowledgement in 24 hours and a considered response, indicating the action to be taken, in 72. This, coupled with lots of recognition (discussed below), was the accelerator for the improvement fuel: the number of OFIs shot up the chart to over 200,000 per year by 1990. Of course, this did not satisfy Mr Milliken, who is always looking for more ideas. He took to asking his visitors for their ideas and this quickly caught on. Now every one of 20,000 visitors to Milliken in South Carolina is asked to complete an OFI – it used to be one per visit, now it is two.

The OFI concept has been well-copied in the Western world and translates without difficulty to all cultures. Many people doubted that the Wigan plant of Milliken would be able to sustain such American-style initiatives. No problem at all; Wigan quickly moved from an average of 1.4 OFIs per associate to 52 by 1992. But not many other companies are approaching Milliken-scale returns yet. The reason?

Other management teams have conveniently dropped the 24/72 discipline, the accelerator, allowing replies to take two weeks to three months. The big lesson here is: if accelerated improvement is wanted, then major effort is needed. If it is important, make serious time for it; if not, don't do it at all.

Even Milliken's figures look pathetic against the typical Japanese company's. Many achieve averages of 100 ideas per person per year; some as high as 200. Toyota has two million every year; mid-sized Mazda has over one million. Ricoh has one employee who submitted 11,000 documented suggestions in 1991 – 30 per working day. He *does* do a job as well. Canon has one employee who has reached 6,000 in a year and one lady who manages 150 per month on average, as well as being a working mother with two children (very unusual in Japan). All of these people, and the many who manage 100 per year, are *thinking* while they work. How can we do this better? What if we tried this? The super-scorers come in early and try things out. They make notes as they work and they write their suggestions up at home that night.

Big numbers, but how many of these suggestions are used? Typically in Japanese manufacturing companies, 95-97 per cent of proposals, as they are called, are implemented. This is a statistic which is monitored and published and rarely varies. The Japanese service sector, such as banking, lags behind at 80 per cent, but they started 20 years after the leading manufacturers. How are these thousands of ideas implemented? In the simplest possible way. The local team discuss them in informal meetings, often for just ten minutes, before or after work. The supervisor checks out any implications, they are authorised and in they go – almost always implemented by the local team in their own area.

Storyboards

To many companies, a notice board is a place for formal information – i.e. notices. To the Quality leader, it is a focal point of enormous potential.

A display can become the place where people record and debate problems and opportunities; where teams share their improvement progress; where managers and other teams come to learn what is happening; where the leader comes to talk and listen about Quality; where people can compete, show off a little, take pride. A good

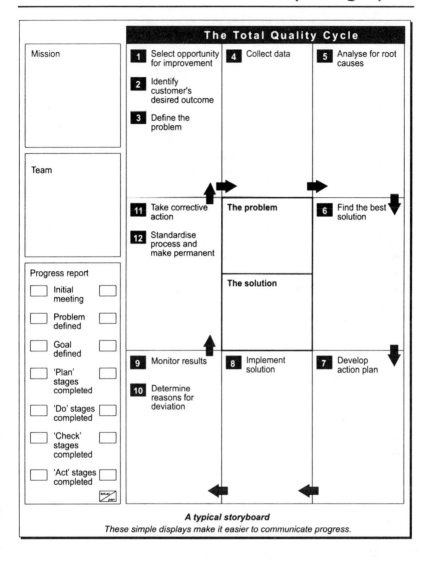

The Total Quality Cycle

Mission

1	Select opportunity for improvement
2	Identify customer's desired outcome
3	Define the problem

| 4 | Collect data |

| 5 | Analyse for root causes |

Team

| 11 | Take corrective action |
| 12 | Standardise process and make permanent |

The problem

| 6 | Find the best solution |

The solution

Progress report
- Initial meeting
- Problem defined
- Goal defined
- 'Plan' stages completed
- 'Do' stages completed
- 'Check' stages completed
- 'Act' stages completed

| 9 | Monitor results |
| 10 | Determine reasons for deviation |

| 8 | Implement solution |

| 7 | Develop action plan |

A typical storyboard
These simple displays make it easier to communicate progress.

Quality display – perhaps a whole Quality wall, perhaps a small enclave at corridor crossroads – not only informs, it helps educate, guide and stimulate people. It can be fun; it does not have to be dry numbers and technical statements. However, some discipline is useful. Indeed, storyboards are a good example of reinforcing disciplines through a visual medium. Storyboards are special versions of Quality displays which feature the story of an improvement team, illustrating the main steps they go through from project inception to the successful incorporation of the improvement into the business. The

230 The Quality Revolution

Japanese invented the storyboard for Quality Circles, but it is Western companies who have shown the fuller value which storyboarding can bring.

Peer pressure

Peer pressure is enormously powerful. Teams who take over the responsibility for running their own show are much stricter on standards and performance than the supervisor ever was. Underperformers feel the disapproval keenly. This can lead to difficulties if allowed to go too far, with individuals being thrown out of teams and elite groups barring new members. But well-coached and facilitated, the need 'not to let the side down' can be highly motivational. The Japanese companies make use of this in their visibility walls. These are not just for recognition of improvement teams and communications about the improvement activities going on; there is also an individual section, which commonly is a league table or bar chart comparing proposals (suggestions) submitted. Typically a line is drawn across the bars with a target – say 80 per person this year. Those individuals below the average and away from the target are reminded of it every time they pass.

Milliken unashamedly use similarly pressure. Charts (on display in every corridor, every corner and on every filing cabinet) are used to display a whole array of Quality data. It is not all positive data. In some areas, alongside the pictures of OFI submitters, are the names of *potential* OFI submitters. Not very subtle but it works for them. Perhaps the most direct example is Milliken's exposure of its suppliers. Like many companies, Milliken has a top ten suppliers' list – prominently displayed in the main foyer. Equally prominent is the *worst* ten suppliers' list. Apparently, no one who has seen themselves on this list (and the list often contains big multinationals) allows their name to stay on for long.

Partnering

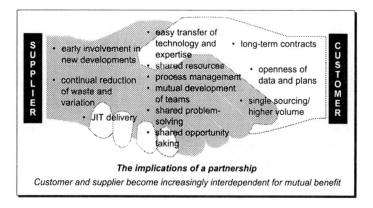

The implications of a partnership
Customer and supplier become increasingly interdependent for mutual benefit

A powerful Quality concept is the idea of partnership. The whole population involved with an organisation can learn to think of others who they are interdependent with as partners. Management, workforce, customers, suppliers, dealers, distributors, agents, departments, teams...all can be partners in action and prosperity. Indeed, Lipton in the US is one company where this has such a high profile that the whole Quality process is entitled 'Partners in Quality'. For many, however, partnering plays the strongest role at the interfaces – supplier to customer, customer to supplier, both inside and outside of the organisation. Partnering can be a powerful extension of empowerment, as a partnership arrangement aims to bring out the best of both parties for mutual benefit. This means treating external suppliers as valuable contributors towards competitive advantage and involving their people much more fully as a result.

As with empowerment inside the organisation, the partnership style of supplier management may turn on its head traditional ways of managing suppliers, which probably rely on divide and rule coupled with an adversarial style. The opposite attitude is simply to think of the supplier as an integral part of the organisation – given the same information, monitored and stimulated, educated and developed, supported and demanded in exactly the same way. Perhaps the only conceptual difference is we don't pay their salaries directly. The same goes for agents and dealers and others in the forward supply chain – anyone whose performance impacts on our service and our reputation.

Empower your suppliers

Just as empowered workteams may amaze you, so can empowered suppliers. Attitudes to suppliers have been established over decades of mass-production thinking and most suppliers expect to be treated discourteously, to have vital information withheld, to undertake development work for a customer with no guarantee of obtaining the business, to be allowed only to deal with the purchasing department, to have the business taken away from them on a whim, to be only given part of a contract, to win or lose the business ultimately on the price tag. Today, most Quality companies have reversed this stance. Companies like Ford, who had a reputation as one of the toughest managers of suppliers, reversed their policy in the mid-eighties from 'divide and conquer' to partnership relations.

It is no less tough. Indeed, suppliers who found it easy to play the old game of obtaining a contract with the purchasing department, now found they had to demonstrate consistency and improvement. They had to win contracts on guaranteed service with no defects at a *total* cost to the customer – not the misleading entry gate price. They also had to show they were better suppliers than any others...for the simple reason that companies like Ford were saying: we cannot develop partnership relations with very many suppliers, so we only want one clutch manufacturer, one electrical harness maker, etc. The shock this caused led to the transformations which started many companies on their Quality revolutions. Further shocks came when the Japanese manufacturers set up in Europe and the USA. Even higher standards of product, delivery and continuous improvement were (and in many cases still are) demanded.

But those who survived by raising their game dramatically have found a whole new environment. They are respected and involved fully in all aspects of the customer's business. Their new-found efficiencies have made them highly competitive and able to obtain new and different business. Suppliers to the Jefferson City plant of Chesebrough-Pond's found the drive for a smoother and faster flow through the plant was very demanding on them. But those that stuck with it now have greater certainty of orders and better utilised plant, freeing up huge amounts of machine time for other business. Win-win for customer and supplier.

Ownership

Ownership is a strong concept in achieving empowerment. A large retailer became aware that the tractors hauling the delivery containers were not as spotlessly clean as they would like in image terms: 'If they are dirty outside, what condition is the food like inside?' There were ample facilities for washing and plenty of time to do it. The problem turned out to be ownership. For efficiency, a pool system had been introduced, maximising the use of the tractor units. But this meant no one felt ownership of any tractor and no one felt it was his responsibility to clean it. On reintroducing one-man, one-tractor, the problem disappeared overnight, as the drivers re-established pride in their own vehicles.

Kyocera illustrates another dimension to giving ownership. Kyocera's fine technical ceramics business grew from zero to the 24th largest company in the world in 28 years by always doing it better than anyone else. To maintain this edge, they have always given their people a lot of freedom. For instance, no budgets are used, because this might constrain ingenuity. If someone has proved his competence, then he can ask for anything he wants. As a result, 30-year-old engineers have been known to spend up to Y3 billion or 5 per cent of revenue, without any controls. All senior management would check is whether it is being spent in the most vital part of the business and whether it enables them to create or maintain a niche. After that, the person is backed totally. Kyocera talk about the equation: achievement = ability × attitude × zeal. Of these three personal components, ability is reckoned to be commonplace, attitude is critical and zeal is something which the organisation can enhance and encourage.

Stop the process

For years, Japanese factories have had overhead cords above each workstation. These are for the operator, any operator, to pull if he or she finds a problem or even suspects one. The effect can be dramatic: the line stops, red lights flash, a display board signals which workstation has the problem and teams of engineers descend on the operator. Meanwhile everyone else on the line, which may stretch for hundreds of metres, is idle. One might think that under such attention and pressure the operator would be inclined to let the issue pass. Far from it, the operator is the hero of the moment for finding another jewel – a possible defect. On the other hand much shame would fall on him if the problem had been missed and been found downstream where it is harder to rectify.

'Help cords' are only just coming into Western production processes as we begin to see that such deliberate disruption to the process, in order to learn about the problem and effect a permanent solution, is nothing compared to the continuous disruption of trying to build complex products with faulty inputs. Western car producers, for example, could never raise production above a certain hourly level, even with shortages or mistakes being left to be put right off-line at the end. Toyota, meanwhile, needed to stop the process less and less as manufacturing problems were eradicated, effortlessly surpassing Western production records – with the bonus of perfect products at the end of the line, ready for shipping.

Stopping the process has much wider application than car or hi-fi assembly lines. Think, for example, of advertising copy which may be very expensively produced under outrageous time pressure with rarely a question asked until the client, at the end of the line, says 'No, I don't like it.' Would the creative designer point out that the brief is too flimsy or could the copywriter admit that the core message has been lost? Yes, if they feld empowered to stop the process. Or the researchers, designers and marketeers who designed, produced and distributed across thousands of UK stores a child's drinking beaker with a closing lid that no mother had the strength to turn? Would it not have saved weeks of lost production, not to mention reputation, if someone had stopped the process early on and said 'We need to test this again'? Or the printer who produced a batch of stapled books with brittle paper which pulled through the staples allowing the pages to fall out? Might it not have saved that printer's reputation if the machine minder or the packer had ignored the deadline pressure and stopped after the first book? Such incidents are happening every minute in every organisation. The person who sees something is not right may well not have the solution or even understand what the problem is...but knows that the first action is to stop the process. In a fully empowered organisation, every person not only has the opportunity to stop the process but the responsibility not to let the process run unless it is totally right.

Prevention mentality

Empowering people to solve and fix problems is the first step to something even more competitive: preventing such problems occurring at all. People can work in a preventive way or in a reactive fix-it-when-it-breaks way. The Quality leader wants an environment in which the bias is strongly for prevention. Prevention is about planning, preparing, rehearsing and testing before the activity is started. It is about thinking what could possibly go wrong...before it does. It is about understanding and learning from past errors and problems, looking for patterns, trends, irregularities, in order to predict weaknesses. It is about looking after the next user of the service, the immediate customer, not passing on suspect product or data but providing a robust service to help that customer succeed with his task. It is about working with the supplier to achieve continually more precise and reliable inputs. In other words, it is about managing the process in its fullest sense, from upstream through the value-adding activity to downstream.

As such, prevention applies to whole organisations as well as workteams and individuals. There are many prevention disciplines and techniques which can be applied, but ultimately it comes down to individual action at a point in time. A primary task of the Quality leader should be to encourage preventive thinking – to create a prevention mentality in the organisation.

Prevention should thus be one of the behaviours which are stressed and exemplified from the top down. The Quality framework should reflect a preventive viewpoint through the company values or mission. Leaders should demonstrate prevention through their decision-taking and communicate the reasoning behind their actions. Workteams should be empowered to spend time on prevention and to shout when potential problems are discovered. Appraisals, feedback and recognition should be biased to reinforce preventive activity. This is particularly important as prevention work is hard to spot and often not as exciting and dynamic as problem-solving. Problems attract attention naturally – from people and their managers; prevention has less natural attraction and thus continuous reinforcement is needed, especially in the early years of a Quality transition.

As the Japanese manufacturers have demonstrated, a point is reached when the occurrence of problems is quite low and more time is available for planning to make the process even more robust, as well as faster and more efficient. By this point, the prevention mentality is well-engrained and people feel very uncomfortable if any compromise is suggested. Indeed, it has been noted that the Japanese workforce and engineers are pretty poor in a real crisis; they have never learned how to behave in such a situation. They also have little interest in acquiring such skills: they prefer to concentrate on making sure the crisis never happens.

Preventing disasters

Most company disasters come down to what is often called human error. Perrier is estimated to have lost at least $200 million by allowing minute traces of benzene to bleed into the production process through inadequate filtering. Such situations cannot be made 100 per cent foolproof; in Perrier's case, the design and even the procedures were to a high standard. What was lacking was the empowerment of the individual to stop the process before a malfunction built up into a major problem. This is the case with many company disasters. Million-to-one chances happen quite regularly in any volume process. The only safeguard between these problems and the community is the line workforce. The same applies to all the minor problems which occur day-to-day which can become relative disasters if they go through to the customer.

Speak out

'I don't care what your engineering background is, no one knows the job better than the grunt on the line,' says Rick Holdsworth, operator at NUMMI, the Californian joint venture between Toyota and GM. The Quality leader is not just encouraging people to think, he will want that person to share his thoughts, as they do at NUMMI. It is very common to hear in all sectors of business that a section has got into a mess because so-and-so left and 'she was the only one who knew how it was done properly'. Or, 'we can't pin down that process, it is a black art, only the people who have been there twenty years can do it.' Such comments reflect on the leadership of the companies involved. Everything that is important about a job or process should not remain in a few people's heads but should be shared, dissected, challenged, standardised and improved – continually. This should be a requirement for every workteam. If the process is too complicated to describe then it is ripe for simplification.

It remains, however, that 'the grunt on the line' does know that job better than anyone else. So we should also tap into his ability to spot variations and potential deviations away from the norm. Ricoh has a 'something strange' mechanism: operators who may have nothing more than a suspicion that something is not quite right are encouraged to call an engineer or simply pass on a small pink 'something strange' form to record the potential deviation from the norm. All too often in the West, it is management who cause the deviation, usually without explanation and consultation. Even in a strong Quality environment, managers can cause variation for legitimate reasons and not be aware of the subsequent effect. Again, if the operator who sees the consequence of the change is not empowered to act, then we may have triggered a costly problem. If, on the other hand, the operator alerts us, we can catch and remedy the problem before it develops.

One simple behavioural mechanism is to encourage people simply to speak out when anything of concern arises. This might be a standard which has been missed or a procedure which has not been followed. In such a case, it is an issue for the local team to discuss and resolve, probably team member to team member. If it is a management-inspired issue, then the individual should alert his manager who should take responsibility for it. For the sensitive issues – it may be the person's own supervisor who is pressing for a compromise on standards – then another broader speak-out channel should be established. Many Quality leaders publicise an open-door or telephone hotline route for people to come direct to them with such issues. If the leader means it, i.e. if he is going to act on the information received, then this can be a powerful way of establishing a new mentality.

For example, it is reputed that the transformation at Harley Davidson got off the ground because one lady brought an example of management compromising standards to the president. He backed her and the story spread through the organisation that he was serious about changing the way things were done. The Quality leader who adopts an open-door policy can expect surprises. Brian Willmott, managing director of the Perkins Engines business in Shrewsbury, found an irate mechanic banging his desk one day over a document for design changes which had collected fifteen signatures before he could do what he wanted to do. Brian had no idea that the well-meaning change notice procedure had become a bureaucratic burden.

Incidentally, the need to encourage speak-out should not be thought of as being targeted at shop floor or office people. Management can be surprisingly inhibited in their roles, right up to senior level. There are many factors contributing to this, often strongly influenced by the culture of the organisation. Political game-playing can lead to a reluctance to put a contentious point forward. Any tendency to 'shoot the messenger' will also keep heads down. The personality, or merely the success, of powerful leaders also tends to be intimidating to some. An open speak-out channel, as part of a thorough empowerment process, will help to spring information out of reluctant managers.

Sharing and using ideas

Many solutions to problems can be used elsewhere in addition to
where the solution was developed. Conversely, many problems and
opportunities will have been encountered before. This represents a
huge potential for multiplying improvement value in large organisations. One way to realise this potential is to replicate project
successes. A successful improvement project in a retail store or a
branch of a bank may well be directly applicable in all the other stores
or branches. However, anyone familiar with the way large organisations work knows that this is unlikely to happen naturally. There are
many impediments. One is the parochial mentality of many local
managers – they are simply too busy to look at what their colleagues
are doing. Another is the related but tougher barrier of NIH – 'Not
Invented Here'. A further one is the information channelling which
feeds the project upwards into regional and central management
where it may well disappear.

As always, overcoming these barriers requires an integrated
approach using new mechanisms but most of all a new mentality. The
mentality is one of using and adapting other people's
ideas...creatively. The implementation of the improvement idea is
owned by the local team and probably requires as much imagination
and expertise to apply successfully to match with the local situation as
the original. The mechanism is the lateral transfer of information, i.e.
directly from one team to a similar one. Unilever Personal Products
have created a worldwide project database to address this opportunity:
all improvement projects are logged into the system, not for management to review – that is handled with another process – but for all
improvement teams in France, in Canada, in Australia, in Turkey to
see for themselves what their distant colleagues are doing. All
projects are categorised under key business process headings and
enough information is displayed for a local team to spot anything
relevant to their work. As the data builds up, scanning the database
becomes a standard early step in the project story.

Lateral transfer of information need not be confined to projects.
Information is the fuel of improvement and many forms of data may
be useful. Best practice with respect to procedures, standards and
methodologies may be sent from unit to unit, section to section.
Customer data, visit reports, external benchmarks, competitor
activity...all can usefully be shared. This requires appropriate media
and some coaching to ensure good data is offered but, with the right
mentality established, appetite for such data can be enormous.

Today, technology offers wonderful opportunities in this area. Digital have for many years used their own systems to create information channels which give easy access to everyone regardless of location. A particularly impressive use of this network is through their 'Notes'. This system allows anyone of any level to raise a question or make a suggestion or offer an idea – and anyone else can not only read it and use it but add their own comments. Thus someone in Boston could report reading about, say, an approach to tracking customers' needs and, by the following morning, could have ten more ideas or comments on that subject from Tokyo, Basingstoke, Geneva and Sydney. Meanwhile, hundreds more will be reading the correspondence as the interchange between two or three of the interested parties develops. For many organisations, a fully-interactive real-time information exchange is not practical. Instead, much simpler paper-based systems can be used, the main objective being an easy lateral flow of data and knowledge.

Knowing the neighbours

Another barrier to easy communications and ready transfer of information is that people do not know each other very well. This may be surprising when some staff have been in the organisation for years, but the way work has traditionally been divided means we do not have the opportunity to find out much about what others do, even though we may be very dependent on them for our own work. When Blaine Hess, president of Lipton, started mixing people on Quality training sessions by function and level, he and his senior colleagues were amazed to hear how valuable this was; prior to this, people did not know what Finance did or what happened in Marketing. He pushed it further and set up events for people to share their work with others, rather like open days. The biggest was a full day for the head office site at Trumbell, Connecticut, where their 'Resource Expo' opened up every section for people to wander around and visit, with a big meeting area containing stands for each section to display and demonstrate what they do. The positive results of this have led Lipton to look for regular opportunities to bring down the walls between departments and introduce people to each other. As Blaine Hess says: 'People simply do not know what others do, even when they work close by.'

British Airways took the concept of knowing colleagues better a step further, with a major programme designed to introduce all 50,000 plus staff to each other. It took two years to achieve, built around a one-day event – 'Day in the Life' – where 170 BA staff at a time, from all levels, locations and regions, learned what other sections did. The highly interactive and stimulating environment for this event helped staff to take the most out of the day and make as many contacts as possible for later networking.

Such events are mechanisms for stimulating contact and interchange. Ultimately, however, it should develop beyond a periodic event and become regular practice. When a workteam or an improvement team wants to know more about another area, they should arrange to visit. As good neighbours and partners, the receiving team should be ready to welcome the visitors and demonstrate their work and improvement needs. As the Quality process takes hold, such visits become a regular part of the improvement scene, with teams visiting suppliers, customers, other plants, head office, agents and dealers and so on.

Recognition

Recognition closes a loop. When someone does a good job, the feedback from the customer should provide the confirmation that the person's work is valuable. But it doesn't always happen like that and, anyway, people need far more reassurance, support and encouragement than the customer has time for. Recognition is the leader's way of bridging that shortfall and adding reinforcement of his own. This way of thinking about recognition is important; it is very easy to confuse people with imprecise recognition and very easy to send mixed or wrong messages. Adding to these caveats, recognition is one of the hardest things to get right, as most experienced Quality leaders will confirm. It is easy to demotivate nine people by rewarding just one or offend one team through praise for another. Equally difficult is the judgement of cultural sensibilities: what is fun in Georgia can, at first, be embarrassing and even distressing in Munich. That being said, recognition is a vital ingredient in a Quality process and one that helps sustain improvement over the long term. It is worth persisting with until the most appropriate mix is found (although, like most things in Quality, recognition is very much a dynamic and the right mix will change with Quality maturity).

The range of recognition methods used by Quality companies around the world is seemingly infinite; this is one area where innovation is rife. The Japanese are quite formal with their recognition, relying mostly on the presidential review process to highlight teams who have good stories (both in terms of process and results) and present them to others. Japanese teams soon learn to cover all the key steps in five minutes and still make their presentation original and sometimes amusing. The president's review builds up through the year with departments, then units, then locations, each reviewing a large batch of improvement stories. Finally, the best teams are invited to present their stories to a major gathering presided over by top executives, including the company president. Attendance is a great honour and the teams prepare with much excitement and some trepidation.

Similar sessions have been adopted in the West with equivalent effects; people like their work to be shown off, especially in teams. At Milliken, an acknowledged benchmark company for recognition, every opportunity is taken to put 'the fans in the stands' as Tom Malone describes it. Milliken has 'sharing rallies', big jamborees loosely built around the Japanese concept but with every opportunity taken to put an ordinary associate on a platform for Roger Milliken and his executives to applaud. Improvement teams go up there, OFI proposers have their turn, exceptional performers take a bow – anyone who has earned a little bit of attention gets a lot of it for a short while. The effect is electric and the glow lasts for a long time.

This isn't all the recognition that goes on at Milliken. Training is important to Milliken and to recognise it, every one who goes on any training course receives a certificate signed by Roger Milliken. Certificates fill the tops of filing cabinets and anywhere else where there is space. There is a Hall of Fame for patent holders and pictures of award-winning teams alongside their projects in every corridor. Awards are big news at Milliken, as at many top corporations. Indeed, it would be tempting to be cynical of companies awarding 'supplier of the year' and 'best vendor' awards to each other, if it were not for the fact that the majority of companies receive no awards at all – the best are recognising the best. To win these external awards, whole business units have pulled together to make a special effort to please their customer. In return, companies like Milliken have numerous internal awards ranging from 'Quality project of the period' to 'Associate of the month' (who also benefits from his own parking bay). They may sound shallow and gimmicky but they are only if the attitude behind them is shallow and gimmicky. In other words, if the leader believes in such means of recognition and gives his time to it, then the workforce will value it too.

Of course, what goes down well in the non-union extended-family atmosphere in the 'bible belt' of South Carolina may not work so well in a militant industrial town like Wigan. Or does it? To everyone's surprise, Clive Jeanes, chief executive of Milliken Europe, has transferred all aspects of Milliken's Quality process to Europe and found

---

Twenty ways to recognise

1. Send letters to improvement team members when they establish a team, thanking them for their involvement; send another one at the end of their project or key action, thanking them for their contribution.

2. Develop a 'behind the scenes' award specifically for those whose actions aren't usually in the limelight; make sure such awards are in the limelight.

3. Create a 'Best ideas of the year' booklet and include everyone's picture, name and description of their best ideas.

4. Feature a Quality team of the month and put their picture in a prominent place.

5. Honour peers who have helped you by recognising them at your (or their) staff meetings.

6. Let people attend meetings, committees, etc., in your place when you're not available.

7. Involve teams with external customers and suppliers, sending them on appropriate visits to solve problems and look for opportunities.

8. Invite a team for coffee or lunch at any time, not necessarily when you need them for something.

9. Create a visibility wall to display information, posters, pictures, thanking individual employees and their teams, and describing their contributions.

10. When you are discussing an individual's or group's ideas with other people, peers, or higher management, make sure that you give them credit.

11. Mention someone's outstanding work or ideas during your own meetings and at meetings with your peers and management.

12. Take an interest in someone's development and set up appropriate training and experience to build on their initiatives.

13. Get your teams' pictures in the company newspaper.

14. Write a 'letter of praise' to people to recognise their specific contributions and accomplishments; send a copy to your boss.

15. Ask people to help you with a project you consider to be especially difficult but which provides real challenge.

16. Send a team to special seminars, workshops or meetings outside that cover topics they are especially interested in.

17. Ask your boss to send a letter of acknowledgement and thanks to individuals or groups that are making significant contributions.

18. Honour outstanding contributors with awards which are formally presented and publicised.

19. Have a stock of small gifts to give to people on the spot whom you 'catch doing things right'.

20. Promote, or nominate for promotion, those people who contribute most to improvement over a period of time.

---

strong acceptance in all locations including a big plant at Wigan. When it all fits together, it does not seem so alien and people are always prepared to adapt when things make sense. Clive Jeanes has created a unique culture in the Wigan plant that is largely independent of any national or regional culture. Recognition has played a key role in this.

Richer recognition

Richer Sounds plc is a working example of focusing on people. The company has achieved a unique record - the highest sales per square foot in the world. With 14 stores emulating the flagship at London Bridge Walk, which generates £17,340 per square foot selling hi-fi separates, founder and chairman Julian Richer clearly knows how to attract customers. Central to this is the Richer Way of doing things aimed to 'provide second-to-none service and value-for-money for our customers'. Staff receive a lot of training in the subtleties of serving customers. For instance, Richer staff learn not to be pushy to close today's sale, with the risk of losing future sales, because the customer may take away a feeling that the buying decision was not entirely his or hers. Another example is for staff to learn to be attentive right until the customer leaves the shop. 'The last minute with a customer is dead serious,' says Julian. 'Having spent their savings on something with you, they are feeling vulnerable and if you are moving on to another customer as they are saying goodbye, you have messed it up.'

To achieve this level of personal customer attention, Julian takes a lot of care of his people. They are not only well trained but well paid, with good perks and a profit share three times a year for everyone. A high value is placed on loyalty and integrity. New recruits are told they can make a hundred mistakes as long as they admit to them and learn from them. But covering up or lying is a serious issue. Promotions are on ability and accountability is tight. 'The fact that, say, a manager has been promoted to regional director means that his own shop must be running well in the first place. He can't expect to keep his position if his own shop is not performing.'

Feedback at Richer is continuous – from customers, from peers and from Julian himself, who spends most of his time visiting stores and talking with staff and customers. With every receipt, customers are given a simple eight-question report card which is sent freepost direct to Julian. If poor service is reported, not only the store manager but also the salesperson will write to the customer with an explanation. A grading of excellence for any item puts £2 extra in the salesperson's pay packet; a customer letter of praise a further £4. Extra-special service is recognised by awarding gold-plated aeroplane badges for high-flyers.

Julian encourages staff to come forward with ideas, with over 2,000 suggested by 90 staff in 1991. He believes in rewarding these on a little and often basis, giving everyone between £5 and £25, together with additional recognition such as trips on the Orient Express for the best ideas each quarter. Once a month, Julian gives a branch or depart-ment team £5 each to go off and have a drink and an informal brainstorm. The result is good team fun and sometimes 20 or more suggestions.

Fun is one of the key elements in keeping staff motivated at 'the world's busiest retailer'. Each month, the top performing shop is given the use of a Rolls-Royce Silver Spirit (licence plate: LUNIE). Most training is done at Julian's country house at York, where informal dinners are regularly hosted for staff, with new recruits sitting by him. The fun theme extends to communications, where weekly review meetings at branch level are supplemented every two weeks with a 20-minute video, incorporating a question and answer quiz with staff shouting out the answers as Julian pulls a face on the video. This may make Julian look stupid but the results he gets suggest otherwise. Julian's staff are in tune with his business objectives and delivering what he wants. His belief is that continued success comes from showing people they are appreciated and making them accountable for performance. (Adapted from M. Williams)[20]

What about money: where does that fit with recognition? Opinion divides on the efficacy of bonus or extra payments or performance-related pay when it comes to recognising improvement. Many Quality companies are moving towards quite large performance-related elements of pay, related to contribution at unit level and sometimes workteam level. But the emphasis here is reward for achievement; in other words, when we have had a good year, we all share in the benefit. This is not the same as incentive payments or recognition awards. In practice, the majority of experienced Quality leaders today will counsel against using money as a recognition device. Yes, the Japanese do pay for suggestions, but it is a token 300 Yen and of symbolic value only (unless, like the man at Ricoh, you make 11,000 proposals!). Big money for improvements can be very divisive (it is rare for any individual to make a breakthrough improvement alone so who do you include or, more to the point, who do you leave out?). In fact, people invariably say they don't want money for improvement; they value more highly the acknowledgement of their contribution.

Many companies prefer awards to be in kind – tickets to a show, vouchers for a restaurant meal for two, even a free meal in the canteen. But the Quality leader will quickly learn one thing. When it comes to recognition, what people value most is your time and attention. As Laurie Stark, TQM manager at BP Chemicals, advises general managers at his plants around the world, 'Don't send them gifts through the post, go and see them.' That's recognition in practice.

Developing people

The Quality leader develops people because they will become more valuable to the business as a result. Some may be concerned that a higher value person will want to leave or will be poached, but, on the contrary, in a Quality environment people tend to stay. Not all companies want to keep their staff turnover low – some preferring a regular injection of new blood – but most do, especially after investing in training and job knowledge. One result of a good Quality process is a significant drop in people leaving, partly because they feel good about being part of a winning team and partly because, in a Quality company, they are well looked after. Image helps attract people (British Airways and Disney, for instance, are inundated with unsolicited applications), but Quality helps keep them. Disney has to work hard to keep its star-struck youngsters, who often apply on the spot as they visit the Magic Kingdom. The induction process is a tight loop of selection, placement, training, supervision and evaluation, all against rigorous criteria. But Disney skilfully weaves the feeling of magic and show business through it all, with clips of Walt Disney outlining his founding vision, which still fits well today. The operational areas are all underground and Disney staff 'go on stage' by going above ground to meet the public, always in uniform and only after training and regular pep talks. That the sweeper-up who follows the horses at parade time feels important is obvious to any Disneyland visitor. Walt Disney has passed down two key beliefs which are well applied in the huge Disney group: 'Quality will out – and will endure long after I go' and 'Take care of the cast, so they take care of the guests.'

Compaq also take care to look after its people. Once the world's fastest growing company (from start-up to a billion-dollar company in five years), founder Rod Canion instilled a profound belief in Quality from inception. Like every other phenomenal business, Compaq hit a difficult patch in the early 1990s as prices plummeted. Rod Canion did not survive but the company has, recovering and repositioning well in a cut-throat marketplace. The earlier attention to people helped this transition. Compaq's staff are all minor shareholders and are treated as such. The factory at Houston is more like a high-tech office, spotlessly clean with open spaces, plants, atriums and leisure areas. Work is very flexible with people prepared to be trained for any role. Flip charts are placed on corridor corners for people to make improvement suggestions on the spot; engineers go there first when entering an area. Everyone feels a sense of purpose: a cleaner sees his job not merely as keeping areas clean but as 'raising morale'. The feeling of caring spreads outside the organisation to dealers and suppliers. Compaq have always tried to make dealers feel part of their plans, even when they are selling IBM and Apple products as well. Suppliers are rarely taken off the list, Compaq preferring to keep developing the relationship as a long-term investment.

Training is clearly a central component towards making people feel valued and developing their contribution to the business. Many Western companies, especially through the tough recent years, believe they can get by with little or no training for staff. In contrast, Quality companies, such as Motorola, Corning and Xerox, have no doubts at all that they will not survive without it, setting goals in the order of five days training per person per year. Impressive though these goals are, they fall somewhat short of Toyota's norm of 20 days per year. Training is very much a regular part of the job at Toyota with small areas set aside near the production areas or in the offices so that no time is wasted. At Toyota, the oft-quoted Ishikawa phrase is put into practice: 'Quality starts with education and ends with education.'

Some corporations, such as IBM and Unilever Personal Products, intend to move towards Toyota levels and have set current goals of ten days per year. Ten days training each year takes some organising and many companies are highly innovative and flexible about how to achieve more. The Quality solution is to empower the individual and make him responsible for his own personal development, guided and assisted by the line manager. There is no lack of content today which can be made accessible to the individual or team, not only in direct job skills but in Quality skills and competencies – from how to answer the phone well to how to assess customer's real needs. Management is certainly no exception. There is a vast array of essential management competencies which are inconsistently applied in most organisations. Running meetings, communicating, giving feedback, monitoring products: there are 30 or more basic building blocks of Quality management in which we all need regularly refreshing. Who needs it most? It is often a fact that the people at the top have received the least training. When John Hudiberg, past-president of Florida Power & Light, was becoming really serious about Quality around 1984, he was persuaded to undergo 11 weeks of training. How many CEO's spend even a few days training in year? Hudiberg's example showed commitment and humility, something FPL found they needed much more of, in their subsequent preparation for the Deming Prize.

Hearts and minds

A strong Quality environment reaches everyone in the organisation and touches each one in some way. If I am a worker on a warehouse floor or at a laboratory bench or behind a VDU screen, I may or may not be active in team improvements or putting forward ideas, let alone taking part in events like sharing rallies. But if the Quality process is a sound one, I will still be putting Quality into the business. I will do this because I feel part of a worthwhile concern; I have respect for my fellow workers, including the management; I know what is expected of me and I know how to do it well. If something needs putting right or needs doing, I will take the responsibility for doing it.

Such an attitude is the net result of a mature Quality environment. Quite a number of companies are sensing this more and more as their Quality processes become stronger. When the hearts and minds are behind the company, people do not have to be persuaded to take responsibility, they do it naturally with no fuss. Toshiba in Plymouth is well known for negotiating the first single union, 'no-strike' agreement in 1981. It ought to be better known for the positive attitude which pervades the company. Before becoming a Toshiba television assembly plant, it used to be a Rank one. Manager Mike Jago graphi-cally describes the difference that a decade of good management led by an Englishman, Des Thomson, has achieved: 'Everybody is responsible for what they do. We don't get any of the evil things that happened in the old days, such as empty fag packets shoved into TV sets or the production line wired up to live electricity.' Toshiba Plymouth, with 900 staff, has been consistently achieving Japanese-level performance figures for years.

Another example is Unipart, once seemingly terminally riddled with restrictive practices going back to BMC days. A few years ago, Unipart had the good fortune to be considered by Honda for the supply of exhausts in the UK. Many companies got no further than the first eval-uations. But John Neill, the chief executive, was already into a radical improvement programme after taking Unipart out of the then Austin-Rover Group to survive on its own. Today, Unipart's 4,000 workers are all non-union 'staff status'. At their Premier Exhaust Systems plant in Coventry (once a run-down unit refurbishing engines and now Unipart's show piece), everyone has the same status illustrated by uniforms, no privileged parking and one dining room. The 175 workers have no supervisors but work in small flexible teams with one worker acting as team leader in each. Premier Exhausts has just ten managers under MD Frank Burns and no further layers – just the workforce. Pay is graded by mastery of tasks and standards consistently achieved, with a star rating system extending up to five stars as the person acquires experience across a wide range of equipment and responsibility. Small improvement teams, called contribution circles, have already created £1.8 million of savings in around nine months at Unipart.

Such concepts would have been unthinkable in the UK motor components industry of old. That it could be achieved relatively quickly by John Neill and his team is down to hearts and minds. John reached every person in the group and explained what and why. He didn't fudge and he didn't equivocate. He asked people to support him and they did. As the new style, backed by performance, spreads through Unipart, Honda have sourced more and more components to them, as have other Japanese and European companies who have noted the major changes. Attitude has been critical – right from obtaining the first contract with Honda. As so often, the Unipart atti-tude flows right from the top. John Neill is clear: 'You have to be personally offended by producing a product which is not perfect. Japanese people get emotionally upset; so far, the Brits don't.'[21] John has changed that attitude at Unipart. In his goal of making Unipart a world-class supplier, he has his people solidly behind him.

Quality is personal

Finally on people, when we say people make Quality, this means *everybody*...including you and me. Quality can easily become something that everyone else should be doing. Quality ultimately is a personal thing; what am I doing to improve? We all must accept this responsibility for the organisation to succeed. So for every task, every role, every day, people should challenge themselves: how good is *my* Quality? How much have *I* improved? As with everything else, the Quality leader must set the example and show that he is applying the thinking and practice, which he expects everyone else to do, to his daily work. This is in addition to the projects, the training, the recognition events and all the leader's inputs into the Quality process. This is a personal challenge: how am I doing my day-to-day job better?

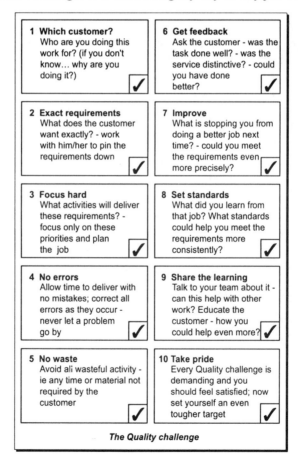

The Quality challenge

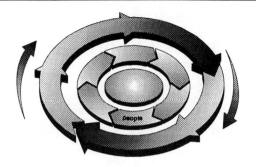

SUMMARY

Make the most of Quality people

1. **Do you respect people as individuals?** *Respect people as individuals: each one has the potential to contribute more and will respond to being treated as a thinking person.*
2. **Do you use teams – lots of them?** *Teams stimulate and encourage people beyond their individual talents; but teams only work well with good team disciplines.*
3. **Are you capturing people's ideas?** *Expect people to give you improvement ideas – and then use them.*
4. **Do you display performance and progress?** *Visibility encourages an environment of challenge and healthy competition and also makes it easier to spread ideas and to recognise contribution.*
5. **Do you encourage sharing?** *Help people to help each other improve.*
6. **Are you developing partners?** *Partnerships extend the teamwork well beyond organisational boundaries.*
7. **Do you give time for prevention?** *Time to think and plan generates much more time later.*
8. **Are you recognising?** *Catch people doing good things and show them that you are interested and value what they are doing.*
9. **Are you making people more valuable?** *Make people more valuable, encourage people to take responsibility, to challenge, to add skills, to learn new methods, to develop their own ideas.*
10. **Are you doing it too!** *Quality is not a way of life in your company unless you are doing it as well.*

8

Disciplined Improvement

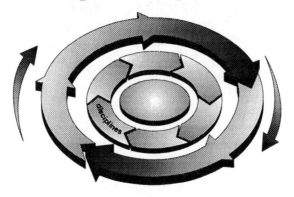

Without discipline, a revolution can dissolve into anarchy or oblivion. Disciplines are necessary in a Quality process to help stimulate and organise accelerated improvement and to prevent any gains being lost. Numerous Quality disciplines are now available to assist the improvement process and the Quality leader should make good use of them.

'Many understand Quality but don't deliver it.' John Kelsch, corporate Quality director, Xerox

'A team without a scoreboard is only practising.' Clive Jeanes, CEO, Milliken Europe

Thriving on discipline

Tom Peter's best-seller *Thriving on Chaos* brilliantly conveys the sense of disorder and flux which marks the business world today. Tom's hypothesis is that chaos and uncertainty are the reality of the environment around us today. But to achieve the revolution that Tom calls for in his book and take advantage from it, we need discipline inside the organisation. Not command discipline, not bureaucratic control, but disciplines which take us further than our natural instincts and ambitions.

Disciplines alone cannot create the belief in Quality nor the drive and enthusiasm for improvement; that is why they are discussed last of all the Quality drivers. Early Quality programmes built around tools and techniques gradually faded away through lack of that magic ingredient, energy, and insufficient support from the other drivers, such as leadership. But energy and leadership need reinforcement and this is where disciplines come in. Laurie Stark of BP Chemicals uses a good analogy. He likens the Quality process in an organisation to pushing a heavy wheel uphill. Much energy is needed to move the wheel and as the slope steepens (no one has yet described implementing Quality as rolling downhill), progress inevitably slows. Lawrie suggests a wedge of systems upgrading is needed at this point to stop it rolling all the way back again; in other words, changing procedures and norms to the new position to hold it in place.

This is one crucial role of Quality disciplines: holding the gains made through enthusiasm and determination. But disciplines also have a role in pushing the wheel further up the hill, especially at the steeper end, when energy and goodwill alone may not be enough. The organisation has to learn to thrive on discipline.

Dealing with anti-discipline

Disciplines are not popular with some categories of worker and even some nationalities. At the risk of stereotyping, Japanese, German, Swiss and Scandinavian managers seem more comfortable with disciplines (and uncomfortable without). British, American and southern European managers tend to like disciplines less. Researchers, creative people, craftsmen also tend to be suspicious of disciplines, especially if they come from outside their domain ('Won't this constrain my creativity/independence/flexibility/intelligence?'). Whether it is a whole unit or an individual that is anti-discipline, the problem is one mostly of fear of the unfamiliar. Once used in a proper context, many people find their creativity/independence/flexibility/intelligence is enhanced by an appropriate discipline. Get them to try one that is relevant to their work . Give them plenty of choice, it matters less which tool is used. Allow the really stubborn ones time to see their peers applying new techniques. Show the results and give plenty of recognition. Show that you are using the tools yourself. If people are still not interested, they are telling you that they do not like the way things are going. Time for straight talking.

Multi-level improvement

A good Quality process achieves improvement on a number of levels. This is one of the big differences between Total Quality and single-dimension solutions, which have limited impact. Within the organisation, Quality should be active and thriving on a business process level; similarly on a project by project level; yet again at a workteam level and finally at an individual level – whether a manager or a worker.

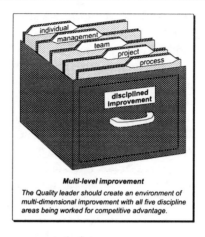

Multi-level improvement

The Quality leader should create an environment of multi-dimensional improvement with all five discipline areas being worked for competitive advantage.

Thus a Quality company, at any one time, should have business process improvement underway, ideally on the two or three processes which can make a big difference to competitive advantage. It will also have a number of improvement projects, ranging from cross-functional task forces (linked to the process thrust) to joint action across two departments. It will also have many improvement activities within departments and within workteams, striving to raise their service to others and put their own houses in order. Finally, individual managers will be making small improvements in their areas and individual workers will be correcting problems and identifying opportunities as they go about their daily work. At all these levels, there are Quality disciplines to help people make improvements effectively. Some disciplines are techniques, such as project management or Cost of Quality, which can be used across all these levels; others are particular to process improvement for instance, or are more relevant as tools for small team or individual use.

There is a vast array of methodologies, tools and techniques available to channel more discipline into improvement and the choice is growing. The Quality leader should ensure that his Quality process makes the best of these accessible to people across the business. Some of the more useful are discussed in this chapter, not to explain how they work (there are many books on Quality techniques) but to illustrate the role and effect they can have. Of the many to choose from, the disciplines which are discussed here are those which can be readily used by any and every manager and likewise any and every worker. In other words, the tools which require more specialist knowledge and expertise, such as design of experiments (DOE) or failure mode effects analysis (FMEA), are left out. Some might argue that these are quite widely used in some organisations but most managers in most organisations are more likely to find the disciplines selected below to have more direct utility.

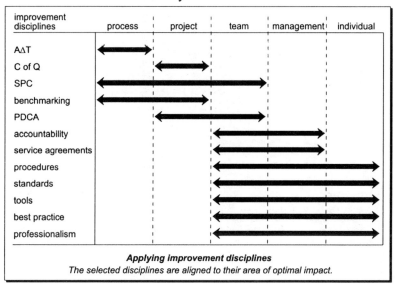

improvement disciplines	process	project	team	management	individual
AΔT	⬌				
C of Q		⬅			
SPC	⬅		➡		
benchmarking	⬅		➡		
PDCA		⬅	➡		
accountability			⬅	➡	
service agreements			⬅	➡	
procedures			⬅		➡
standards			⬅		➡
tools			⬅		➡
best practice			⬅		➡
professionalism			⬅		➡

Applying improvement disciplines
The selected disciplines are aligned to their area of optimal impact.

Process disciplines

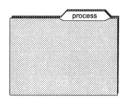

A few of the significant techniques for aiding business process management were introduced in Chapter 6 on processes. These included process mapping, one of the most powerful of all Quality techniques. Process mapping can range in technology from sticking 'Post-it's on flip charts to software-generated flows printed out on large-scale printers. They also range in complexity from critical path calculations to simple flows in and out of departments. The more sophisticated approaches are not necessarily the best: physical systems, such as magnetic pieces on white boards, have much more team appeal than computer screens.

Mapping is one discipline; analysis is another. One of the key technique areas is to identify value and, conversely, waste. Westinghouse have developed a value vs. time profile which builds up a picture of the value creation along a process change. Shop floor teams at AMP Inc. found that the true value-adding time in many processes was often as little as 5 per cent. All the rest was handling or waiting time.

Digital have created an approach, called A delta T, which compares the actual process against the theoretical best – using time as the universal measure.

A delta T

A= Actual: *what is; the way things are*
T=Theoretical: *the best possible (given what we know today)*
Δ=Delta: *the difference between Actual and Theoretical*

AΔT is the way to get from A to T, i.e. from reality today to the very best, by eliminating the current deltas and preventing new ones arising. By applying a standard methodology, teams at Digital have found 'deltas' of 50 per cent or more in processes and have gone on to cut them down drastically. One example is a financial administration process known as the Red book. The AΔT team plotted the actual process for this, logging a time of 27.4 person hours per month. Then each step was challenged as to its theoretical necessity, paring the process down to its core. This came to 11.1, leaving deltas of 16.3. Each delta was then investigated, looking for root causes and brainstorming solutions to these. Quite quickly, the team eliminated 12.3 hours of deltas, bringing the Actual to Theoretical ratio down from 2.5 to 1.36. Naturally, they continue not only to challenge the remaining deltas but also the theoretical too, now the process is better understood. The team's review of their progress underlines the merit of a disciplined approach: 'We found that once steps were highlighted as deltas, the solutions were easily identified and implemented. The AΔT analysis had changed our perspective on the process. We had moved from seeing the process steps as "standard operating procedure" – with all the checks, fixes and special handling – to viewing these process steps as "Band-Aids" and waste. Once we had grasped this new vision of the deltas, it was astonishingly quick and easy to eliminate them.'

Cost of Quality

Time-based disciplines such as AΔT are useful for attacking the historical waste in processes. Cost-based disciplines are also helpful, although usually less dramatic in impact. Activities can be categorised as adding value or waste. In practice, many activities may fall into a 'not sure' category of not directly adding value for the customer but not clearly being waste. A Cost of Quality (CoQ) analysis is helpful to determine the worth of these activities. Basically, the Cost of Quality is defined as the cost of those activities which an organisation or process has over and above the minimum required to do the job well. Thus any costs associated with correcting failure or clear-cut waste go into the Cost of Quality, as do any assurance or appraisal activities built in to cushion customers from the effects of such failures. A further set of activities are those in which we attempt to prevent such failures occurring at all, such as through effective design, market research or training.

Cost of Quality statements, built up by analysing activities section by section and allocating the costs of each activity into one of the main categories, can offer a new insight to managers. First of all, the accumulated figure for Cost of Quality can be as high as 50 per cent of turnover, with 25 per cent to 30 per cent being common. All of these, remember, are costs over and above the pure cost of doing business. Of this figure, probably half will be failure costs – graphically showing the scope for improvement. A further quarter may be appraisal costs, extra inspection and checking, which, with more Quality installed, might also become unnecessary. The remaining prevention costs, however, may well be insufficient and most companies see a swing towards more prevention and less appraisal and failure through the implementation of a Quality process. Renault is a good illustration of how CoQ can reveal and focus this need. Their early Quality process had reduced the 'Non-Quality Index' from 100 at the time of the Super 5 introduction down to 32 when the Clio was launched. But the success of the Clio brought other effects. The Cost of Quality, which by then had been calculated, rose by 6.6 per cent as Renault responded to demand. This represented FF12 billion or 25 per cent of the cost base at that time. Of this, 58 per cent was failure cost of one form or another. Renault, having benchmarked their Japanese competitors, aimed to shift this equation to show over 70 per cent of CoQ to be prevention activities. This helped focus a further successful drive for accelerated improvement, which in turn brought the CoQ down significantly.

Cost of Quality statements reveal many other clues to improvement scope. For instance, a high cost of one element across many departments gives an immediate pointer to early gains for Quality projects. In addition, CoQ analyses can be extended to cover the total cost of products and processes, i.e. the whole associated cost, including knock-on effects. A high maintenance figure or a failure in use are examples of extending the cost beyond the company walls. On some occasions an external cost is reflected back inside, such as in warranty costs and field service resources, but others are left for the customer to worry about. A total cost statement enables the responsibility for these costs to be assigned back inside. Lost opportunity costings are also of value: the revenue we could have had if we had been more reliable/faster/attentive. Obviously these have to have high face validity to be acceptable and can be usefully built around actual examples.

Cost of Quality analyses generally need some care in creation and some caution in use. They are not usually accurate to more than ±20 per cent on individual items and the time and disruption involved in making them more precise is of questionable value. However, if constructed well, the overall figures will be quite sound; to be useful, they have to stand up to the scrutiny of most accountants, as well as having good face validity. The primary role of a Cost of Quality analysis is to give early indication of the scope of improvement around and pointers towards the areas of most potential. A danger is that some managements, seeing big numbers, believe they can remove these costs directly, without using the disciplines of Quality improvement. Unfortunately, if that were so, they would have been taken out already. Cost of Quality can, therefore, be used as a rather basic educational tool, explaining the role of a planned improvement process as distinct to arbitrary cost reduction.

Another frequent mistake is to establish a continuous CoQ monitoring system to provide an alternative MIS. There is nothing wrong with this in theory, it just takes too much time to keep allocating activities. Ciba-Geigy USA was typical of many organisations in the early eighties in spending the best part of two years struggling to do this, with committees tied up for months on end to little benefit. CoQ figures are not really comparable between businesses as the methodology and allocation varies so much. However, it is of some interest to know your CoQ is 35 per cent of turnover when your foreign competitor is around 5 per cent.

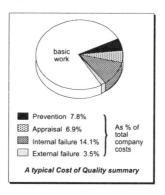

A typical Cost of Quality summary

By far the best use of all of CoQ is as one of the quantifications of improvement projects. Improvement teams can be challenged by asking how their work will affect the CoQ and then they can be requested to show a CoQ improvement in their results. It should not be the only measure of success or even the most important (that should be customer satisfaction), but it does help to give a comprehensive picture. These project-by-project CoQ improvements can then be tracked and accumulated to give an indication of progress. Allen-Bradley collected $129 million of savings in this way, with a 60 per cent reduction in CoQ over eight years of Quality improvement.

SPC

Perspectives on Statistical Process Control (SPC) vary widely. It can be viewed as a major discipline with revolutionary potential or as a set of basic tools (the same can also be said for JIT, BPR and some other major disciplines). Quite where you position it in this wide spectrum is a matter of preference. Disciples of Dr Deming are of the persuasion that SPC can be the driving force for real change in the organisation. In their perspective, appropriate statistics are indispensable in the continuous search for 'profound knowledge', as Dr Deming graphically defines core facts. Ford provides a classic example of a Quality process heavily dependent on SPC, at least in the early years. SPC was used not only for internal improvement throughout the whole corporation worldwide but pressed, rather forcibly, onto suppliers as well. There can be no doubt that this approach made a valuable contribution to Ford's turnaround in the early part of the 1980s. But large-scale SPC has its problems and limitations. One is the general point that no single discipline, however broadly based, can achieve the transformations needed in a full Quality process (as Ford discovered by the late 1980s). A related one is that the statistical route to profound knowledge tends to disregard the irrational, but very real, nature of organisations and the need to manage change. A third is that people do not like statistics very much: their effect in practice can sometimes be the antithesis of high-energy, dynamic improvement.

That said, SPC is an amazingly powerful discipline. BP Chemicals trained all their staff in simple SPC many years ago. Process charting is done routinely by operators to maintain the production processes in control. These and other SPC tools are also used to challenge and improve processes of all kinds from effluent waste to sales forecasting. Every three months BP Chemicals arrange a SPC forum where people gather to share and exchange their SPC stories. A typical example is shown in the box.

British Steel is another avid user of SPC in recent years. In Teesside Works, some 150 SPC projects are producing a regular £1 million of savings every year and another 150 SPC teams are coming out of training to extend this. Many are quite small applications, but some

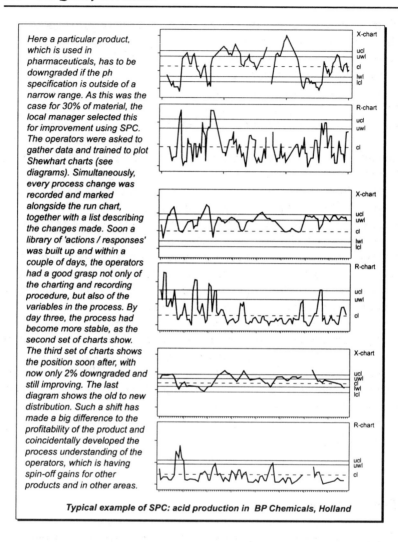

Here a particular product, which is used in pharmaceuticals, has to be downgraded if the ph specification is outside of a narrow range. As this was the case for 30% of material, the local manager selected this for improvement using SPC. The operators were asked to gather data and trained to plot Shewhart charts (see diagrams). Simultaneously, every process change was recorded and marked alongside the run chart, together with a list describing the changes made. Soon a library of 'actions / responses' was built up and within a couple of days, the operators had a good grasp not only of the charting and recording procedure, but also of the variables in the process. By day three, the process had become more stable, as the second set of charts show. The third set of charts shows the position soon after, with now only 2% downgraded and still improving. The last diagram shows the old to new distribution. Such a shift has made a big difference to the profitability of the product and coincidentally developed the process understanding of the operators, which is having spin-off gains for other products and in other areas.

Typical example of SPC: acid production in BP Chemicals, Holland

have major consequences. One example alone has added another £1.5 million to these savings at Teesside. Known as the 'return fines' project, this started life as a workteam brainstorm which identified scope for improvement in the yield of a process which screens raw material going into a furnace. Basically the screen should separate out the raw material by size; in operation, undersize material slipped through into the furnace from time to time and oversize material crept into the return fines system, where it was wasted. A team of operators from sections whose work depended on this system formed an improvement team and began charting the process. The SPC charts showed up a number of problems centring around the maintenance of the screen. This was a dirty, cold and heavy job and the screen holes were often damaged because the regular cleaning process was too crude. One by one, new procedures were trialed and introduced, ultimately changing the tools used, the screen material and the monitoring and trigger points for action. Some of the changes were obvious, like replacing heavy crowbars with pneumatic picks to clear the holes and using rubber hammers for refitting the screen without damage. But the obvious had never been highlighted before. Indeed, the operator sitting in the control room had been receiving and logging three sets of control data on the process for ten years. In his words: 'I did nothing with it and management never asked for it.' The simple disciplines of putting control charts in the hands of an empowered team brought the yield up to 95 per cent, with dramatic benefits for the rest of the process. Having fixed the recurring problems and built preventive steps into the process, the team are now planning to go one step further and tightening the input variables so that the screen can be eliminated altogether.

Such SPC examples, big and small, are quite commonplace in many organisations, particularly process-type businesses, such as chemicals and repetitive manufacturing like motor industry components. But their use in other sectors is very patchy. The processes in financial services have similarities to a chemical flow process, except the flow is paper or information or money. But only a few insurance companies are experimenting with SPC with any enthusiasm; others are entirely ignorant of the possibilities.

Benchmarking

With benchmarking you find out that somebody is doing it twice as well as you are. Then you learn how. Ford US discovered that their Japanese partner, Mazda, handled the accounts payable with just ten people; Ford had 500. Having seen the impossible, Ford learned how – picking up new methods and practices, such as an invoiceless system which eliminates reams of paper by using the receipt as the payment trigger. After carefully adapting the Mazda ideas to suit their own business, Ford were able to reduce their accounts payable staff to 200. That's benchmarking: finding a horizon-lifting number and using it to stimulate major improvement. There is still a big gap between Ford's 200 and Mazda's ten, giving lots more scope for Ford, but nevertheless Ford's process itself has now become a benchmark target, with over 50 companies a year having a look at their new accounts payable process.

Xerox discovered benchmarking in the early 1980s as part of their Quality process and used it to speed the transformation of their business. At the time, the prevailing attitude was that Xerox reigned supreme: 'We knew what people wanted, a Xerox machine.' But their world was changing fast: suddenly, a hundred companies were making copiers. Despite this, the attitude at Xerox was that customers would always buy Xerox. Xerox copiers would not copy blue ink; the word was tell the customers only to use black. Xerox copiers would not copy oversize paper; the paper stockists said only 2 per cent of paper used was oversized, so tell the customers only to use standard size. The trouble was 95 per cent of customers wanted to use oversize paper some of the time and some of the time they wanted to copy blue ink. So they began to switch to the Japanese machines which could do these things.

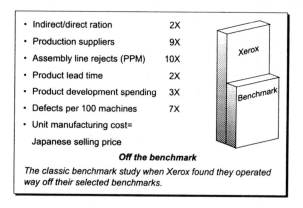

- Indirect/direct ration   2X
- Production suppliers   9X
- Assembly line rejects (PPM)   10X
- Product lead time   2X
- Product development spending   3X
- Defects per 100 machines   7X
- Unit manufacturing cost=
  Japanese selling price

Off the benchmark

The classic benchmark study when Xerox found they operated way off their selected benchmarks.

Meanwhile, David Kearns had made many trips to Japan and knew there was a different mentality. He sent a technical team with the specific task of working through their joint venture subsidiary, Fuji Xerox, to find out the differences. The resulting 'off the benchmark' numbers shocked Xerox into action. They found that Canon was selling a copier for $9,600 when the Xerox manufacturing costs were $13,000. More data collection visits followed by Xerox line managers. The big breakthrough came when the data teams started comparing processes. They would ask customers and suppliers 'Who does this best?' and then find out how. They found LL Bean, for example, was three and a half times more effective than they were at picking and packing. They found their invoicing process had a 6.5 per cent error rate; their benchmark American Express had just 1.7 per cent. The process was subsequently re-engineered around the acquired knowledge of what drives an accurate invoice, eventually beating the benchmark with 1.3 per cent of errors. This allowed a measured $139 million to flow to the bottom line. Thus benchmarking quickly became an important discipline at Xerox.

Despite these examples, benchmarking is a discipline which is probably more talked about than done. This is partly because it is easy to put the grand label, benchmarking, on any inter-company dialogue or comparison and partly because the reality of benchmarking is hard, disciplined work and many give in at the superficial level. Benchmarking as a discipline should be positioned beyond the useful management actions of networking, competitive analysis and even corporate learning initiatives such as study tours, travel missions and listening posts. All of these have a supportive role in benchmarking (and have valuable contributions to a Quality process in their own right) but strict benchmarking is the acquisition of hard data from the best practitioners on specific topics. The hard data means both numbers (the actual benchmark) and information on how those numbers were achieved.

Quality companies today are attracted to benchmarking because it can stimulate and challenge the improvement processes. The fact that it is a required and important ingredient of the European Quality Award and the Baldrige Award has also concentrated a lot of attention on benchmarking. By far the most fruitful application is to focus on process benchmarking and to make the comparisons as specific as possible.

Unilever is one company that is becoming a benchmarking devotee; their application also shows the practical differences between approaches which are often loosely branded as benchmarking. Unilever have for decades taken their competition seriously and regularly compile competitor analyses, primarily for market intelligence – how competitors are responding to trends and how they are trying to satisfy customers. In addition, internal data is collected and compared on how relatively similar operations perform. For instance, the Foods group collates comparative data on best manufacturing practice in the operating companies, so Brooke Bond and Van den Berghs can compare stock turns and process yields or Birds Eye Walls managers in the UK can see how the yield on their ice cream process and changeover times compares to Algida in Italy or Spain. Similarly, the big laboratories have best laboratory practice which informs Port Sunlight researchers in Liverpool how their standards relate to those of Edgewater in New Jersey. But for Quality-minded managers, which all of these management groups have become, neither the internal data nor the competitor information is stretching enough. Benchmarks should help take one beyond the current achievements and set new targets.

With this aim in mind, Unilever has organised a number of benchmarking initiatives in strategically important areas, such as innovation, the supply chain and marketing practice. The supply chain benchmarking illustrates the scale and organisation needed to make benchmarking worthwhile. This was led by Tony Burgmans as chairman of the Personal Products group. Tony's aim was to push forward the Unilever frontiers on supply chain thinking and practice. Over an intense period of about a year, Tony, supported by John Rothenberg and Tony Walker, responsible for logistics and manufacturing respectively for the whole group, created a renewed concentration on the supply chain through four integrated steps.

The first step was to open the minds of the top management in the group to the significance of managing the total process – from raw input through to the consumer. A key element of this education was a week-long study tour to Japan for the 30 top executives from around the group to see very different supply chains in action. People came back from the tour ready to look afresh at their own supply process. At this point, step two came into play – the benchmarking proper. A benchmarking planning team, with members drawn from the companies, first learned the discipline of benchmarking, then set about the first steps. Having mapped six sub-processes in detail and obtained the internal standards which would be used for comparison, some 20 benchmark companies were identified for direct contact. The planning team produced a detailed questionnaire of information required and discussed this with the target companies. For some of these companies, benchmarking was an established discipline and they were able to respond readily with detailed written answers. Crucially, Unilever included their own data and answers with the questionnaire; there are few companies around who are prepared to enter a one-way information flow – they want *your* benchmark information in return for their effort. The whole exchange was covered by confidentiality, important to many companies who need to keep an edge over their competition, but are happy to share data with non-competitors.

Having analysed and absorbed this data, benchmarking visits to the companies were set up. To mark the significance of the visits and to encourage direct involvement, directors from the operating companies led the visits, supported by members of the planning team. The net result was a very detailed benchmark handbook, listing hard data from the best examples with explanations of how and why it was done. This data is now being used to spur significant improvements in the supply chain sub-processes. Step three comes in at this stage – process improvement training – followed closely by step four – accelerated improvement of the processes. Throughout this intensive focus on improvement, regular contact has been kept with many of the benchmarked companies. Benchmarking is not a one-off exercise but a continuous learning opportunity for many different levels in an organisation.

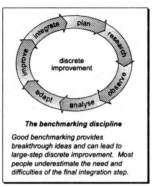

The benchmarking discipline

Good benchmarking provides breakthrough ideas and can lead to large-step discrete improvement. Most people underestimate the need and difficulties of the final integration step.

With practice, benchmarking becomes yet another Quality discipline which is a way of life. Many companies appoint a benchmarking manager, but this has mixed advantages, just as there are pros and cons for a Quality manager. Although it may make sense to have a coordinating role to channel initial contacts and information exchange, benchmarking should very much be a line role, practised in a disciplined way by most managers. Some of the most experienced companies in benchmarking, such as Xerox and Alcoa, find that the best benchmarking is at a local level, directly integrated into a process improvement methodology and carried out by the people charged with the improvement. Centralised benchmarking runs the risk of perpetual data collection and little implementation. This problem often comes up anyway, because companies underestimate the transition needed to adapt the new practice, especially the psychological barriers at senior levels. Fred Bowers of Digital sums up the typical executive reaction as 'We want improvement but not *that* much!'

Robert Camp of Xerox cites another typical problem with benchmarking: over-elaboration. Xerox decided to investigate whether its order processing was too heavy for some of the low-priced items it was now selling through retailers. It duly set up a team working to the very high standards which Xerox had learned for benchmarking. The answer was fairly predictable but still shocking: Xerox was spending $80 to $95 processing each order, compared to benchmarks of $25 to $35, a difference potentially worth millions of dollars. However, the whole cycle of research and adaptation of these benchmarks took over two years, partly because of the rigidity of the approach and partly because of management's reluctance to drop some procedures. Meanwhile both the market and Xerox' strategy had moved on, making many of the recommendations redundant. Time to market in benchmarking is as important as in any other process and thus quick, sharply focused studies have much to commend them. Westinghouse achieves this by applying benchmarking mostly at a sub-process level (that is focusing on, say, order picking or tool changes), spending only five to six weeks on a full study.

One of the beauties of benchmarking studies is the discovery of something quite routine in other companies or other industries which is revolutionary back home. *Fortune* magazine quotes the Mellon Bank in Pittsburgh, which had a problem with credit card billing and the way disputes were handled. A team of eight people from different departments, mostly middle-ranking, benchmarked seven companies, some in the industry, some outside. They quickly discovered that complaint and enquiry handling in high volumes was a sophisticated process and one which had received a lot of attention elsewhere. For instance, software was available to bring all the documentation for an enquiry together and companies used help desks with dedicated terminals to solve customer problems directly rather than passing from department to department. Armed with such evidence, the benchmarking team persuaded top management and changes were quickly made. Complaints came down rapidly from 5,200 a month to 2,200 and the time to resolve them from 45 to 25 days. There is plenty more improvement to come, but the benchmarks clearly gave the impetus and direction for significant improvement.

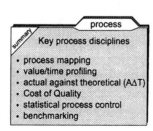

process

summary

Key process disciplines

- process mapping
- value/time profiling
- actual against theoretical (A∆T)
- Cost of Quality
- statistical process control
- benchmarking

Project disciplines

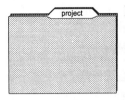 Project work is the backbone of improvement and most Quality companies have hundreds of projects on the go, of all shapes and colours. The variety and use of projects was discussed in Chapter 7, so will not be repeated here. But many companies find that their projects are quite ill-disciplined in practice. Indeed, the most common training need in a company which is past the first flush of a Quality process, is for project management training. Surprisingly, this applies even to those organisations whose main business is project-based, such as applied research or consultancy. Quality brings a new dimension to the professionalism of such work. Moreover, even in well-organised operations, project disciplines bring out a new order of performance and satisfaction.

Effective projects

A project will be more effective when:

- *It is linked to a key process*
- *It is aimed towards meeting an explicit company improvement goal*
- *It is measured and monitored*
- *Its final outcome is explicitly stated*
- *It does not take more than six months*
- *It is important but not too large*
- *A project leader is appointed*
- *A project sponsor is nominated*
- *The team members are chosen for their contribution*
- *The team is small - around five members*
- *Regular reviews and presentations are made*
- *It is visible (open project office, publication of progress)*
- *A project methodology is maintained*
- *The team is trained as a team in group dynamics.*

Quality projects are teams formed for and directed at a specific improvement opportunity. As such they are dependent on team dynamics, the strategic suitability and clarity of the project task and the effectiveness of its execution. All of these are susceptible to disciplines. The way the team works, for example, can be effectively moulded through team disciplines and these will be discussed shortly. Project choice is bound up with the deployment of policy, as discussed in Chapter 3. The clearer the strategic picture for the business and the tighter the improvement goals, the easier it is to choose the right project. Many companies create their own selection technique with a short criteria list which can be ranked and weighted.

Typical criteria for choosing a project might include: fit with improvement goals, impact on a key process, impact on customer satisfaction or dissatisfaction, reduction in Cost of Quality, scale of project. The first two criteria here are often tightly specified in practice, because the project selection process has been cascaded down as a coordinated plan. Thus the improvement goal and the process has been pre-determined (e.g. 50 per cent compression in time of the new product development process); the project selection then focuses on the most rewarding target areas in that process. The customer satisfaction criterion is an essential test to bring people back from the detail and avoid the trap of wonderful internal improvements which the customer hates. A target Cost of Quality figure is another test to make sure such a project makes money in one way or another. The final criterion, project scope, is in many ways the most important of all. Almost all project teams, especially in the early days of improvement, go for something too big and too difficult. This criterion forces them to think through what they are taking on and what they promise to achieve.

Elida Gibbs UK now has a thriving project input to their Quality process which is making a big contribution to the business. But when they first started in 1987, four or five big project teams were set up to tackle the major issues which had come out of their Quality survey. One of the project teams, on innovation, was still struggling to make any headway at all two years later. There was no question that the rate of innovation was critically important; the problem was that it was far too big for any project team to have influence over. This pattern of trying to eat the whole elephant in one go is repeated time and time again by new project teams when there is no discipline to counter it. This problem is by now a well-known one; received wisdom is that only small easy projects should be tackled first – the tip of the elephant's tail for instance. The argument is that the team will learn from this how to tackle the whole tail and move on to the body bit by bit. In practice, this loses both time and the vitality which comes from doing something important. Small starts tend to stay small and then fade away. Far better to go for a strategically important target, the poor elephant's eye or trunk, and do a quick and effective job. Thus guidelines should be established for project selection and adhered to firmly. Democratic and emotional choice have little contribution to effective projects.

The other key project discipline is the methodology with which the team works. This is absolutely vital: people, unfettered by method, make judgements without examining evidence (or even collecting it), jump straight to solutions without evaluating alternatives and generally work on gut-feel assumptions, not data. Couple this with the politics and emotions of team dynamics and the outcome can be bizarre. The natural inclination is not to bother with a logical or step-by-step approach (especially in the West and especially managers), so people have to be taught to be systematic and logical. Most improvement methodologies have PDCA (Plan Do Check Act – in daily use by thousands of people all around the world and perhaps Edwards Deming's greatest contribution to the Quality movement) at the core, although they may use different words to make the steps more precise. This concept is simply to counter our natural tendency to jump straight in with action, action being easier than thinking. 'A bias for action' was one of the characteristics highlighted in *In Search of Excellence* in 1982 by Peters and Waterman. It is interesting to note the shift in our understanding in the decade to follow. During that period, Milliken has changed only one of its core beliefs: from 'a bias for action' to 'a bias for *planned* action'. Action is as important as ever; PDCA makes sure the action is the right action.

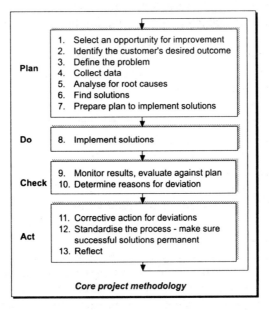

Core project methodology

Most project teams today use extended versions of PDCA to achieve a balanced and controlled methodology that allows them to make progress efficiently through the duration of the project – usually through six to eight steps which can be published on a progress display board or reported on a pro-forma sheet. The diagram shown here extends this to 13 steps, which may seem complicated, but which is readily learned and applied by project teams.

A further discipline is the monitoring, reporting and transfer of projects. Projects should never work in isolation. Sending a team away with an instruction to report their findings in three months is not the Quality way of doing it. Progress should be monitored, reviewed and debated, with amendments made accordingly. This is needed for the guidance and feedback of the project itself (a necessary loop to feed the vitality and energy of the team) but, possibly even more importantly, for the effect of the project on others. For instance, a project may be one of a number set up to hit a major process. If the implications of these projects are not thought through and their effects integrated, then not only will subsequent implementation be a shambles, but the net impact may well be disappointing. The only sensible way to manage this is dynamically as the projects progress. This applies to small local projects too, for nothing works in isolation and the disruptive effect of a project's implementation can outweigh the benefit if others are not brought into the planning early on. This whole area of integrating improvement efforts is dealt with more thoroughly in the next chapter.

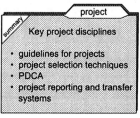

project

Summary

Key project disciplines

- guidelines for projects
- project selection techniques
- PDCA
- project reporting and transfer systems

Team disciplines

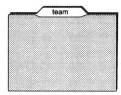

team

Teams are fragile entities; cohesion and energy can dissolve very quickly, leaving only fragmented effort and dispirited individuals. Teamwork is at the heart of any organisation and the Quality leader must build strong teams if the business is to improve and prosper. Good teamwork is needed for projects to be successful; good teamwork is needed for workgroups to deliver good output to customers. Team disciplines play a vital role in raising the performance of both of these essential activities – day-to-day, minute-to-minute service plus ongoing improvement.

Research shows that the most common cause of an ineffective team is confusion over goals and roles. In a Quality environment, a guiding framework should exist to provide the team goals, as discussed in Chapter 3. The Quality leader should test whether this has been translated into clear objectives for each team as a primary discipline. Equally, he should test whether the roles of team members are clear and in accordance with the new practice he is striving to create. Confusion today is as likely to be over responsibility as over who does which task. Multiskilling allows flexibility of role but flexibility demands a higher responsibility. Accepting more responsibility at team level is one of the major aims of empowerment and better clarity of what this means is an important contributor to better team performance. Examples are taking responsibility for work planning, for recording data, for analysing process variations, for making process adjustments, for checking work output, for communicating with internal customers and suppliers and many more. One discipline is to document these responsibilities and other key information as a role description, or better a role agreement, which the team promises to fulfil.

Followership

Jack Schweizer is the country manager for Digital in the Czech Republic. During a debate on leadership with some peers from other Digital units, Jack exclaimed: 'We not only want clear leadership, we want better followership too.' Jack had put his finger on a problem which is rife in the upper levels of many large organisations – people not following a course of action agreed upon, but doing their own thing instead. Team disciplines help to keep people together and follow an agreed plan. Good followership is necessary for good results.

Team accountability

Hand in hand with responsibility comes accountability, a key discipline for cutting out ambiguity and confusion at team level. Alcatel Electronica Industrial, based in Spain, shows one illustration of the key use of accountability in teamwork. As part of their Quality process, Alcatel have encouraged many types of teams from workforce development teams to management project teams. The project teams are used to break down some of the functional barriers. One example of the improvement to an existing product, a d.c. converter, shows how. The team was drawn from six separate departments who had involvement in designing and producing the product. Their first task was to write a mission for the project and specifications which defined the improved product features, target cost and time to market.

These had to be reasonably stretching targets with the aim of gaining renewed competitive advantage; the team specified a halving of the cost and a time to market of one third of the original. Next they gave their commitment to do it. No leader had been preassigned; the team was allowed to decide who would represent them, and the natural leader was put forward. The crucial element was that no single department could claim command of the task and even more importantly no one department could opt out of the collective responsibility. All team members were equally accountable for meeting the commitment, regardless of functional allegiance.

Project monitoring focused on progress towards the committed specification. If the time schedule was two days out or the cost projection varied by 2 per cent, somebody shouted. An agreed change through altered circumstances was allowable, otherwise the commitment had to be met. The general manager empowered the team to do whatever was necessary to meet the targets and concentrated his monitoring on their achievement. To smooth the path of this and similar projects, he held a weekly meeting of functional heads to make sure the demands of the project teams could be met. The result was a redesigned product on the market in eight months (from a previous norm of 18), costing 16,000 pesetas instead of the original 27,000 and having a much enhanced technical specification. But the big result was the change of attitude of managers involved. Working together was the only way to achieve what they were now accountable for.

Service agreements

Another area where team disciplines can have a significant effect is at the interface between supplier and customer. Many problems between customers and suppliers come down to misunderstanding: a mismatch between what the customer really wanted and what the supplier thought was wanted. Both sides have a responsibility and incentive to reduce this misunderstanding, but undoubtedly the supplier is going to be most motivated to do something. The supplier's objective should be to pin down the customer's needs sufficiently tightly to offer a specification to match up against it. If the supplier knows the customer really well and has regular contact, he has a chance of doing this; if he is not close to the customer, then he will always be operating on a hit-or-miss basis. But if he is in contact, then the match of specification to requirements can be brought closer and closer to a point when an agreement can be reached. It is very much in the

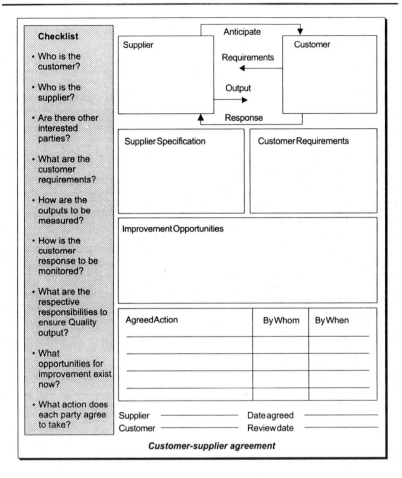

Checklist

- Who is the customer?
- Who is the supplier?
- Are there other interested parties?
- What are the customer requirements?
- How are the outputs to be measured?
- How is the customer response to be monitored?
- What are the respective responsibilities to ensure Quality output?
- What opportunities for improvement exist now?
- What action does each party agree to take?

Anticipate

Supplier   Customer

Requirements

Output

Response

Supplier Specification   Customer Requirements

Improvement Opportunities

Agreed Action	By Whom	By When

Supplier ———————— Date agreed ————————
Customer ———————— Review date ————————

Customer-supplier agreement

supplier's interests to make this agreement as explicit as possible – for both internal and external customers. Obviously, if the supplier is working directly with a mass market, then the actual agreement has to be notional, but everything else is the same, with defined requirements for the market segment and specified outputs to meet them. For many internal and external situations, a person can be identified who represents the customer. This person should formally agree that the supplier's specification is what he wants.

Service level agreements, or customer/supplier agreements (CSAs), are of obvious value between businesses and even greater potential inside an organisation where service ambiguity is rife. So CSAs can be created along supply chains to smooth the overall process, and between support functions and user departments. When Kodak first woke up to the competitive danger of Fuji, they found

Providing what the company wants		Providing what coordination wants	
Company		Coordination member	
Coordination (supplier) specification A	Company (customer) requirements B	Company (supplier) specifications B	Coordination (customer) requirements A
Improvement opportunities		Improvement opportunities	

Agreed action	By whom	When	Agreed action	By whom	When

The ABBA agreement

Often, it is difficult to pin down a one-way flow to establish who is the customer and who is the supplier. For example, Unilever Personal Products found that the complex relationship between operating companies and the central group didn't fit the conventional customer / supplier model. Sometimes the executive at the centre is the customer (eg for financial returns) and sometimes the company executive is at the receiving end (eg for technical advice). The problem is that this is often a simultaneous need, as the exchanges happen when the two executives meet or talk on the telephone. At the Selsdon Park conference, this was one of the issues put to the whole group of executives, who came from both sides. The outcome was a new format of customer / supplier, supplier / customer, or ABBAs, as they became known. At the conference, each central executive met with his opposite number from each of the companies and each of these teams constructed an embryo ABBA. Over subsequent months, these documents were refined down to efficient working agreements stating the expectations of both sides. The reduction in lost energy and miscommunication was tangible.

themselves heavily burdened with overheads which had grown in easier years. All service sections (those not in a direct supply process to the customer) were challenged to prove that they were supplying a competitive service in comparison to outside providers. Without such evidence, the departments would be closed to save cost and any service needed would be sourced outside on an as-needed basis.

After a flurry of activity, Kodak settled on customer/supplier agreements as the means of defining and proving the service achievement. Very quickly, departments such as personnel, legal and data processing, which traditionally worked on a product-out basis, with little responsibility for the use of the service, became very interested in who was using their output and how it was used. Survival was at stake. Within a few months, these departments had identified their customers, trimmed their service to what they required and reached agreements. The CSA format became second nature. Vague promises were no longer accepted. If someone working in one of these sections was stopped in a corridor and asked for a service, then a contract would be quickly agreed stating the requirement, the deadline, the determinant of success and the resources to be used. Ultimately, very little was contracted out. Instead, Kodak created a more efficient support resource with, to the surprise of all involved, highly motivated teams. Unlike the bland anonymous situation before, these people were now providing services which were valued.

Team procedures and standards

One of the outcomes of a Quality process is a new common practice: operations performed at a consistently high standard. Discipline is needed for this too and standardised procedures are one way of providing direction and guidelines for a work team – not the type of procedures that go into thick manuals and stay there, but active visible ones.

Japanese factories have methods boards showing, very simply, the standard method to be adopted. It is surprisingly important for consistency to stick to one method; when a better way is found this is then adopted as the new method, but formally, with the changes completely clear to everyone. The team should be given the responsibility of adhering to this discipline, as it is often impossible for anyone else to know what they have done. This is the main advantage of procedures. A procedure tells a member of the workteam what the optimum sequence is and the checks that are necessary to ensure high performance. There will always still be variability around these steps and the team member will often need to use discretion and initiative. This is where guidance on behaviours becomes important. Equally, a step can often be foolproofed at a critical point to prevent error. Improvement of these procedures can be from engineer's suggestions or from the team themselves. A workteam will move more readily to commonality of practice through adopting procedures which they have helped create. At Canon, workteams regularly use stopwatches or video cameras to obtain data on what they are doing, so that they can investigate further improvement.

This type of investigation leads to measures and standards. Measurement criteria at workteam level should ultimately be defined by the team themselves, in order to assure themselves that their performance is good and getting better. Standards become especially useful at this stage because they give quick and immediate comparisons. A standard is the minimum performance level acceptable and the team should always perform above their standards. Standards might be hard numbers or soft. As the performance above standard stabilises at a higher level, so the standard can be raised.

As has been mentioned earlier, British Airways achieved a Quality revolution in the early eighties. Always a big airline, they had not been regarded highly by travellers, especially business passengers, when state-owned. The then chairman Lord King first cut out all the old game playing, whether by management, pilots, baggage handlers or reservations staff. Most jobs were changed, especially at senior levels. Sir Colin Marshall was then brought in as chief executive from Avis to raise the level of service – the big bugbear.

The transformation was a complex one (as they all are), addressing all levels. The new vision was no longer to be the biggest but to be the airline of choice. At senior levels, Sir Colin made it clear that service improvement was the number one priority. He biased all decisions that way. He rejected all requisitions not related to service improvement. Managers soon understood the new rules; soon all submissions for the chief's attention were presented from a customer service angle. But the biggest change was at the customer contact point. For some time BA had been listening to the customers through a variety of market research methods. When BA listened properly, they found the customers saying some surprising things. Yes, they wanted reliability and safety, but they took the latter for granted and accepted that delays were for a variety of reasons, not just down to the airline. However, they mostly wanted to be treated as people – shown warmth, courtesy and personal attention. They wanted information – business travellers wanted to know about delays: tourists or family travellers wanted to know what happened next. BA built up a segmented picture of different types of travellers and began to address their needs directly.

A new frame was built to guide the customer contact staff. Pilots were required to keep passengers informed – even if the information was not flattering to themselves or BA. Hard standards were created for staff to work to – queue lengths for boarding or cabin cleanliness, for instance. But BA had still not addressed the factors that would provide distinction: the Quality edge in their business. These were the soft areas of courtesy, contact and warmth. They had nothing remotely like a standard for this. Nevertheless, they persevered and did what many determined teams do when they cannot find a quantifiable measure to define what they want. They described it in qualified terms and built behavioural examples around typical scenarios. Cabin and ground staff were trained against these, which, with development, became very precise.

BA had established new practices and successfully built a framework around them for staff to perform consistently. The difference began to show. Within two or three years, BA moved from being the airline everyone complained about to the one people talked about – favourably. Business customers who had said they would never again fly BA heard about it and tried again. BA had become transformed and went on to become the world's most profitable airline.

Team improvement tools

Quality tools suitable for non-specialist use

- *Action plan*
- *Asking why*
- *Benchmarking*
- *Brainstorming*
- *Cause and effect analysis*
- *Check sheets*
- *Consensus reaching*
- *Control charts*
- *Cost benefit analysis*
- *Customer-supplier, or service level, agreements*
- *Data display*
- *Decision charts*
- *Force field analysis*
- *Gantt charts*
- *Affinity diagrams*
- *Paired comparisons*
- *Pareto analysis*
- *Performance expectation grid*
- *Process mapping*
- *Relations diagrams*
- *SWOT analysis*
- *Time/value analysis*

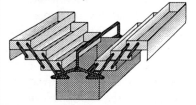

The basic improvement tools of brainstorming, cause and effect diagrams, pareto charts, run charts are so synonymous with Quality programmes, they have almost become a parody. And yet we have discussed already that most managers in the West do not use them, whereas most workers in Japan do. It is a fact that the seven Quality tools are taught in the school in Japan and fishbone diagrams (cause and effect) are even featured in the shinto bible which can be found in every hotel room. So why don't *we* use them? Probably because we do not work in the disciplined environment which would encourage us to do so more naturally and habitually. So building these tools into team improvement disciplines is quite important – a team can sustain the discipline longer than an individual might. And they do make a difference.

Today, a manager in a Quality company should be able to choose from a comprehensive Quality toolkit which would probably have 20 or so useful tools, ranging perhaps from cost/benefit analysis to relationship matrices. Part of the Quality training process should ensure that the manager is familiar with most of these and thus feels comfortable in making his own choice. There is absolutely no reason why non-managers should not have access to such a wide range of tools and indeed, through repetition, people of all levels can become skilled with sophisticated tools.

Management disciplines

We discussed leadership in Chapter 4 and noted that the leader has a strong role-model influence on people around him. It follows that if the way the leader manages is ill-disciplined, then so too will many others in the organisation. In a leader's case, it is not only the reflected style which is a problem. The knock-on effect of careless managing can multiply the damage. Take the everyday situation of the boss being late for a meeting: ten others sit there totally unproductively while he finishes a phone call. Or perhaps his slapdash running of the meeting means that too little time was given to the most important decision, with expensive consequences. For these reasons and the many similar occurrences every day, management must have its share of discipline. The quality of management is central to the Quality of the business.

The most fruitful area of attack on management ill-discipline is on the basics of managing, which every manager is supposed to know but few practise well. Such skills as running meetings, delegating a task, briefing a team ought to be second nature, but it might have been 20 years since the manager received any training in how to do it well. He probably thinks he does make an adequate job of it but people at the receiving end can become very frustrated by the lack of care and thought that goes into these fundamental interactions. There is no doubt that refresher training in core management competencies can have a lifting effect on the way things are done. If this is coupled with a role model assessment, especially one with subordinate input such as used by Xerox, then discipline in the essentials of management becomes important.

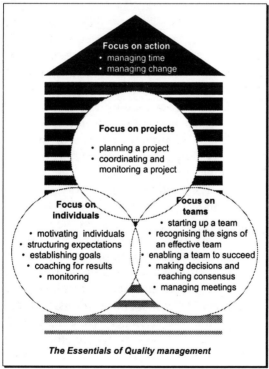

Focus on action
• managing time
• managing change

Focus on projects
• planning a project
• coordinating and monitoring a project

Focus on individuals
• motivating individuals
• structuring expectations
• establishing goals
• coaching for results
• monitoring

Focus on teams
• starting up a team
• recognising the signs of an effective team
• enabling a team to succeed
• making decisions and reaching consensus
• managing meetings

The Essentials of Quality management

In fact, a good Quality process always puts pressure on managers to upgrade their act. When training in management essentials is made accessible to managers during the implementation of a Quality process, there is a big uptake. Managers sense their own incompetence (possibly for the first time) because of the new focus on improvement and do something about it quickly. Those that do not become the odd ones out and invite closer attention.

Another form of attack uses examples of best management practice, which can be specific to the industry (such as best laboratory practice or best retail or best banking), or even specific to the company. Best practice defines the preferred way of handling common scenarios. It can be captured as a set of mini-procedures which managers are encouraged to adopt.

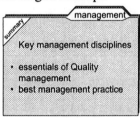

Individual disciplines

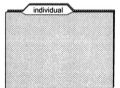 In a Quality environment, most people will be caught up in one or other of these discipline areas. They may well be involved in the maintenance and improvement of a process, whether it is a manufacturing line or an administrative system. They may have been co-opted onto a dedicated improvement project, perhaps inside their department, perhaps well outside. They will certainly be part of a workteam; even if they are in an isolated part of the business and have irregular contact with others, within a Quality process they should be encouraged to play a team role together with the people they interact with. So all should be exposed to disciplines of one form or another, especially the team ones of sharing responsibility, adhering to procedures, informing others of actions taken. Nevertheless, it still remains that a lot of the time an individual will continue to make his own decisions, working to his own frame of reference. They may be small things, whether to answer someone else's phone, whether to pick up some litter on the factory floor – or potentially large, such as whether to take on an unhappy customer's complaint and resolve it for him, or whether to shut down a machine because something is not quite right. Encouraging that decision to be one which helps the business is what a Quality environment is all about and it takes all of the elements we

have explored – leadership, empowerment, team building, recognition, peer support – to achieve it. Are there any other disciplines which can help?

One area worth exploring is around that loose group of behaviours known as 'professionalism'. This term means all sorts of things in different contexts but is quite often used to describe a disciplined pattern of behaviour. For example, a secretary who always writes out the name, company, number and subject of each telephone message she takes is perceived as professional. A sales assistant who draws on a knowledge of the product range and can explain technical issues simply and clearly is being professional. So is the salesman who demurs from knocking the competition. So too is the car park attendant who is never seen in public without a uniform and a smart appearance. These are learned behaviours but in most cases are acquired from long experience. A Quality company short-circuits this learning by defining role professionalism and providing every assistance and encouragement for people to adopt the desired behaviours. They do not have to be universal across the business; indeed they should not be, because they should relate directly to the local situation. Professional behaviours are ones where a person takes initiatives which help the business. It can be as much about style as content – how something is done as well as what is done.

The discipline of extending such professionalism through a business has to be flexible. Best practice in different situations has to be described, probably through the example of an experienced person in the role. This may be captured onto video or illustrated in books, but the personal example will always be the most direct way of learning. The leader has a crucial role here too. Spotting the little details which make up professionalism or lack of it and feeding back in a positive way, showing that they are important. However, this area is not very receptive to a top-down imposition of standards. The leader is there to reinforce what the individual is striving to achieve. This is a personal challenge and one which leads directly to pride in work. The leader's role is to spread that pride across the workteam and across the business. When a business supports professionalism in its staff, it shows.

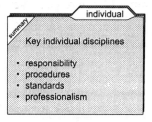

summary

individual

Key individual disciplines

- responsibility
- procedures
- standards
- professionalism

Orchestrating the disciplines

Discipline is only one of the Quality drivers and it should not be the foremost, otherwise we would be using the wedge to push the wheel uphill – an exhausting effort. Discipline is something that the experienced Quality leader brings into play in support of the main energy drive, underpinning the gains. To switch to another analogy, the leader is like the conductor of a large orchestra, organising individual and small team efforts into a well-planned movement, creating harmony and rhythm from their separate contributions, guiding specialists into working together to the one chosen score.

In business, the Quality leader must patiently build the linkages between process, project and team improvements, insisting on approved disciplines to smooth the blending, using best management practice and professionalism to bind the whole together. On top of this, he can tease out the virtuoso performance, the individual and small team excellence, adding the delightful extra to the solid performance.

Quality procedures

Achieving that orchestrated disciplined background, the day-to-day repeatability of high-standard service, has long been recognised as a business challenge. ISO 9000 has been evolved over many decades of experimentation as a universal approach to disciplined procedure in business. Originating in Europe in the late eighties, it has received considerable attention in North America, Australasia and the East in recent years. Many companies who strive for ISO 9000 accreditation seek only the ticket to do business with those European organisations who insist on it. This is the minimum reward for those who have sweated for a couple of years to pass the assessment. In practice the entry ticket means little more than admission to the game; competition for business is as discriminating as ever, with no further value attached to the ISO label. Customers require standards which are higher and much more specific to them than ISO 9000 can ever assure.

However, there are a growing number of companies who see ISO 9000 as a core part of their Total Quality endeavour - a solid wedge to ensure that disciplines are well documented and well practised. Companies embarking on a full Quality process find ISO 9000 a natural and very acceptable step to take along the way. Providing the evidence of assured procedures which ISO 9000 demands is not easy, even for a Quality company and especially for a service business. So aiming for ISO 9000 accreditation two or three years into a large change process is a good test of progress and a good wedge to underpin further progress. Companies who go for ISO 9000 before implementing a Quality process often experience an uphill struggle against the natural processes of the business. Their heroic effort may achieve the registration but leave them too exhausted to continue to make lasting change in the way the business runs.

Thus ISO 9000 is a good indicator of how well the disciplines for day-to-day business and improvement have been integrated and as such has great utility inside a well-planned long-term Quality process. But it will not change the business in its own right and it is not revolutionary. In short, it is not an alternative to a Quality process but a significant contributor to one.

Integrated improvement

Orchestra conductors are revered for their skill; the Quality leader's role is no less demanding and there are similarly only a handful of stars who are truly outstanding. Indeed, the Quality leader has an additional dimension to accommodate – the wholesale change of the business as well as the orchestration. The next two chapters look at the biggest challenge of all for a Quality leader: how to integrate all these elements in a dynamic way, changing and integrating at the same time.

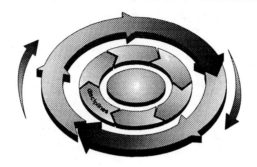

SUMMARY

How disciplined is your organisation?

1. **Are processes managed as well as functions?** *Process management can have more impact on business than functional excellence.*
2. **Are projects directed and reviewed against laid-down criteria?** *Projects should achieve results – results which should benefit the consumer.*
3. **Is teamwork developed and exploited?** *People will try harder and achieve more in teams, many business needs are better addressed by teams.*
4. **Are benchmarks used?** *Benchmarks reveal the gaps and the potential; use them to stir up dissatisfction with current performance.*
5. **Do departments agree explicit service contracts with each other?** *Without specific agreements, people will make assumptions, losing clarity and energy.*
6. **Are procedures written down and published?** *When someone has found the better way, make sure it is documented and used; don't leave it in that person's head.*
7. **Is the management process defined and are managers assessed against it?** *Don't tolerate management muddle; require your managers to be skilled and practised.*
8. **Is 'followership' practised?** *Only one leader per team is needed; others should follow agreed methods and plans.*
9. **Do people know what being professional means?** *Define the standards you expect from people representing the business.*
10. **Is all improvement activity integrated together?** *Orchestrate the improvement disciplines for maximum impact.*

9

Putting Quality Together

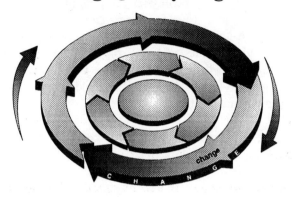

Installing Quality into an organisation successfully is a major challenge requiring good planning as well as energy. Many companies have made big mistakes with their implementation which others can avoid. Choosing the right elements is important; putting them together under an implementation strategy is more so. The Quality leader must manage the dynamics of change throughout the organisation.

'I thought Total Quality was a religion; now I know it is a fundamental business practice.' Giorgio Maschietto, chairman, Lever Chile

'Quality is not a natural thing which people will just pick up.' Don Davies, CEO, Allen-Bradley

A competitive Quality process

The way we implement and use Quality is itself a competitive weapon. In other words, if we apply Quality better than our competitors, then we stand to gain competitive advantage. We can expect to meet our customers' needs more closely than the competition and we should be more efficient and flexible in how we do that – and, crucially, we must achieve this earlier than our competitors. It follows that our process of installing and applying Quality has to be the most efficient and robust. There is a bit of 'catch-22' here: we need Quality principles and practice in our Quality implementation process *before* we have gained any experience with them. This dilemma is echoed by the most effective users of a Quality process tending to be those companies who are already good at what they do. They already have some of the Quality thinking and practice in place and their implementation process consolidates these strengths, whilst adding new dimensions to their drive for improvement. On the other hand, some squander these advantages by adopting a conservative approach to change, allowing others to leap-frog them with a high-energy process that transforms their business. This is the ultimate competitive opportunity available to anyone – but it demands the highest standard of Quality implementation to do it.

Putting Quality into Quality

It is not difficult to spot the Quality leaders who will succeed. Belief, involvement, focus, energy...all those vital elements will be evident. But there is another crucial factor which can make the difference between an exciting transformation and a long and painful battle. This is planning. Planning should be the first Quality input into the transformation process. It makes the difference between an ordered transition, with events and activities complementing and supporting each other, or a seemingly uncoordinated series of actions which may lead nowhere. It is, for instance, quite commonplace for people to turn up for training sessions with no idea of why they are there, or to leave such sessions with still no idea how what they have learned fits into their work – or for major projects to start without a clear understanding of the objective. Such actions are obviously inefficient but are bound to happen without good planning. They invite the cynical reaction 'and this is the Quality programme?' or 'call this Quality?' and the loss of enthusiasm that goes with it. With planning these scenarios are thought through in advance and a programme designed which cuts out such reactions and, instead, impresses people whenever they are involved with the implementation process.

Design for the long term

A Quality process is a change process. Successful Quality leaders manage the change in their businesses and design the change process to go the way they want. The commonest implementation error is to

---

On religion, gurus and hype

Quality is about the practice of improvement. Put as baldly as that, it is not very appealing and can seem mundane. Certainly this sounds a long way from being revolutionary and misses the critical ingredient of energy. So the Quality leader who is looking for the optimal implementation strategy needs to weigh carefully the balance of inspiration and pragmatism. Religion offers many parallels. There is certainly a role for missionary zeal and evangelical passion. Belief in Quality is the core around which the improvement practice is built. But here lies the first big dilemma with an evangelical approach to Quality. As Mike Perry, chairman of Unilever plc, observes: 'We may all have the same belief, but we don't all subscribe to the same church.'

Many companies have followed the teachings of the gurus who pioneered Quality in the West and built their implementations around their principles, especially in the eighties. Tom Peters used to say (in the days before he became a guru himself), "It doesn't matter which Quality guru you chose to follow as long as you chose only one". Many early practitioners found the guru teaching light on the process of change and thus difficult to follow in practice. As a result, they created their own implementation process building around the principles learned from the guru. Sometimes these principles too become inhibiting, as people worked out their own better ways to guide practice. This suggests that a more efficient process today would anticipate this and not promote external dogma which are seldom owned internally. Far better to use the power of the missionary to unite ... but around the organisation's own beliefs and culture. This can be personified through the leader in words and deeds.

Even this needs much care in finding the right pitch. Over-promotion of one set of principles will offend those who have already developed their own, or are in process of developing their own, or even would like the opportunity of developing their own. The fact that people often come round to similar ideals eventually, does not lessen the opposition which may be generated at the time. This applies to all aspects of internal marketing of the Quality process. Merchandising through slogans, pens, mugs and banners is often perceived as trivialising serious work, whilst branding puts a label ('someone else's label') on activities which are best owned locally. Mike Perry works continuously to draw together the improvement 'churches' around the giant Unilever corporation. Although a master of global marketing, he has studiously played down the branding and the religion. No one, however, has any doubts about his belief or his determination: he lives it, minute to minute.

plunge right in because the concept is so compelling and then become disheartened because it is not taken up fast enough. Virtually all companies who have installed a Quality process successfully say it took them a lot longer than they expected. So we should learn from their experience and set our own expectations accordingly – with one proviso: those companies which went into Quality early in the West were pioneers; with the experience available today, we should be aiming to do better and achieve a much more efficient implementation.

Who should do the planning? This is a job for the Quality leader. The Quality plan must be his plan or it is doomed from the start. But the leader will need advice and able assistance, for this is an area in which he most probably has limited direct experience. A small planning team might be set up to think through the transformation in depth and determine the key steps, building them into an outline of a Quality plan. The leader and his advisers have some major decisions

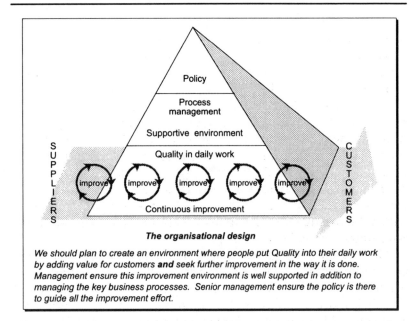

The organisational design

*We should plan to create an environment where people put Quality into their daily work by adding value for customers **and** seek further improvement in the way it is done. Management ensure this improvement environment is well supported in addition to managing the key business processes. Senior management ensure the policy is there to guide all the improvement effort.*

to make. They will need to shape a basic strategy and, within this, define the core activities around which the Quality process will be built. They will be very wise to research what others have done before committing to a plan. Their research findings might well generate more confusion than clarity, as a rich variety of implementation practice is displayed today and only the beginnings of accepted best practice are evident. This, in itself, provides an exciting prospect right from the start for the ambitious Quality leader, for the better choice and construction of these implementation activities may directly impact competitive advantage later.

Learning from others

Before South West Electricity began a major Quality process across the whole of their organisation, they spent eight months acquiring data on what others had done. A group, drawn from different levels and functions, was formed and became known as the acquisition team, as outside knowledge was accumulated. The team collected published reports and, from these and contacts they had made, drew up a short list of companies to visit and understand in more depth. The team of about 15 people split into groups of three and four to visit these other Quality implementors and report back to the full team. Over the eight-month period, the team, whose members ranged from the secretary in the finance department to the corporate development director, submitted the data they had acquired and debated its merits. They learned what had gone well for other companies and where mistakes had been made. Gradually they evolved the elements of their own implementation plan, learning from others but relating the knowledge to their own company's needs. The result was a report for the board which was rich in practical illustrations and directly relevant in its recommendation. It gave the board confidence in making a decision to proceed with their own Quality process and, at the same time, provided the board with a knowledgeable, committed team of champions from the acquisition team to help install it.

Many leading companies today will be very willing to share their Quality knowledge and experience with others. Not only do they remember when they too were looking for similar information to start their process, but as Quality companies they will be persuaded of the mutual benefits of exchanging information. In addition, being known as a leader in Quality has never done any one any harm. Some, such as the Baldrige winners, have been inundated with visit requests and organise special open days for people to learn about their Quality work. The EFQM has a regular round of open days for its members to learn from each other, with a host company opening its doors for the day to share their experience in Quality. Such open days are beneficial in feedback for the host company as well as for the visitors. British Airways is one company which sees the value of sharing its experience and receiving comment, inviting outsiders to take part in the Quality events, such as 'The Day in the Life'. Every visitor is a potential customer and the exposure helps reinforce the image.

For the Quality learner, visiting a company further ahead has immense benefits. Not only can lessons be learned the easy way and confidence gained through hearing what the other company has achieved, but seeing that someone else is actually doing it is a great persuader. One of the most successful initiatives at the launch stage of Unilever Personal Products' Quality process was the study tours for the operating company chairmen to learn about best practice first hand. Hearing other chief executives talk with passion and conviction about what they had done and seeing the evidence of their changed organisations was more compelling than any lecture or report.

Learning from the best

In two years, Unilever Personal Products took over 250 senior executives from around the world to learn from the best. In groups of around thirty, the executives spent a week visiting the very best practitioners. The first four tours were all in the USA and were designed to allow the company leaders to develop their own motivation for a Quality process. Each tour represented the beginning of a wave of implementation starting every six months. The tour group stayed together for the whole week travelling by chartered jet, with debate and reflection on the experience encouraged throughout. The tours themselves were designed as high-energy experiences and a full debrief at the end of each tour brought the learning experience to a head. Almost all the executives went home with a positive attitude to implementing Quality. Comments such as 'the best week of my twenty-year career' were not uncommon. Personal Products have continued this format for learning from others well after the need to persuade has gone, often on focused topic areas such as supply chain or innovation. Two or three tours are run each year in Japan and Europe as well as the US. For each tour, a lively report is produced and sometimes a video but the most enduring effect is the story-telling and enthusiasm of the participants themselves, which goes deep into the organisation.

Quality companies are not too proud to learn from each other. Digital had been one of the host companies which Unilever Personal Products visited. Two years later they decided on something similar to fuel the changes needed in their European operations. All through September and October 1992, the top 200 executives in Digital Europe assembled in groups of 12 to spend two and a half days visiting three other top companies in Europe. Eighteen groups in all visited over forty companies. The experience was phenomenal. The mixed groups (from different locations and functions) debated issues with the host companies and the discussion, often heated, continued on the chartered planes and well into the night at the hotels. A feeling for change built up tour by tour. The last tour consisted of the European Management Board. They had already heard the findings and feelings of the previous tours and, building on the energy developed, went immediately on from their tour to plot the priorities for change. A major improvement process resulted and was cascaded through the whole organisation in 1993. The inspiration of learning from others made this possible.

Implementation strategies

The many elements of a Quality process need to be woven together into an implementation strategy. Those acquiring knowledge from other Quality implementors will be struck by the absence of such a strategy in many applications. Action is seductive and most leaders charge down the most obvious path, confident in their belief that they can wing it as they go along. It works for some; it fails for many, who often have to have a second or a third start. The striking aspect for an observer of Quality implementations is that those that do have prede-termined strategies may vary widely in nature. Some are top-down; quite a lot are bottom-up; a few are middle-out. Other implementors prefer to infuse a philosophy equally through all levels; yet others recommend lighting fires at key points around the organisation. One or two advise guerrilla warfare.

Over the years, the leader who is serious about Quality and in it for the long term, may well apply a blend of all of these. To determine the most effective strategy, the leader first needs to have a clear view of what he wants out of it. Hence he will need a sharp focus on his vision and the culture he is striving for and the behavioural changes he is seeking over the long term, as discussed in Chapter 3. He will also need an equally sharp focus on the immediate steps, the current base and the first 18 months of activity, because he can only improve from where he is now. In between, he needs a general picture of the strategic aims, but can, and should, leave tactical details for later planning as the process unfolds.

Top-down

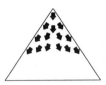 If the company is at an early stage of Quality practice a top-down process focuses attention on management's needs to change, before involving the rest of the workforce. Perkins Engines is an example of this approach. Before anything was said to the workforce as a whole, management had spent 18 months in creating a strong understanding of Quality practice throughout management. By the time that non-managers were trained in Quality, management were able to display not only a more consistent message but some very visible improvements too. One of the strongest arguments for top-down is that the greatest scope for improvement in an organisation is usually buried within management. The management muddle which is endemic in many organisations, coupled with the territorial defences which are often equally rife, provides plenty of improvement potential...without disrupting the people doing the work.

Another good reason for a top-down strategy is to bind in senior management participation from the start. There is no stronger way of demonstrating management involvement than having senior managers lead workshops and training sessions, i.e. becoming trainers themselves. Many companies have had great success through each level leading the next one down into Quality: a 'cascade' or 'waterfall' approach of each level learning from the one above. A cascade also ensures that no one is left out. A disadvantage is that this takes time for a large organisation. Xerox trained all 100,000 of their staff in this way in their 'Leadership Through Quality' process when they began their Quality revolution in 1984. It was a strong process, led directly by David Kearns as CEO, but it took nearly five years and much of the material was out of date towards the end. Nevertheless, this was still a great success and provided the foundation for Xerox to go on to a broad array of Quality initiatives in subsequent years. IBM have adopted a similar training cascade for their latest infusion into the organisation, 'market driven Quality', with most of their US staff going through this cascade in less than a year. Ian Raisbeck at the Post Office is also a strong believer in the disciplined cascade, not only for the introductory TQ training, but for later more advanced training such as for business process improvement.

Bottom-up

 'The direction comes from our chairman down; the change comes from the bottom up.' Thus does Steve Schwartz, corporate Quality director, describe what is intended at IBM: even in a strong top-down process, there is a role for bottom-up improvement action. Some companies are impatient with working the old hierarchy and prefer to stir up action where the real work is done. Ragu Foods in the US are creating great energy by going straight to the workteams early on in the process. They are working through the company, plant by plant, with an intensive concentration on each plant for about a year. Key to the action is the mapping of local processes by the people who work them. Every individual in the plant has a one-on-one discussion with a consultant to map the person's main process and surface opportunities for improvement. The resulting improvement energy is harnessed by local improvement teams into coordinated action.

Ragu is a rare example of a managed bottom-up process, with the leadership team being ready to guide and direct the improvement energy when it is released. On the other hand, there are countless examples over the years of bottom-up initiatives generating tremendous enthusiasm in the short term, for it all to fizzle out months later. Quality Circles programmes; idea-generating campaigns; cost containment drives...they have all been and gone in many companies, but the aftermath lingers. People who have had their enthusiasm squandered in an ill-supported campaign do not show it so readily a second time and maybe not at all a third time.

 Bottom-up really has its place *inside* a top-down process, rather than an alternative approach. Bottom-up puts pressure on managers in a different way to top-down. Managers are well-practised in covering themselves from above but can be very exposed from below. Empowerment is not just about allowing people to do their jobs better but also to allow them to challenge anything they feel is preventing them doing so. So a manager who tries to ship a suspect order may find the displeasure of his team much harder to ignore. Or the manager who continually tries to score political points over his peers may find he is no longer supported in this by his staff.

Some companies deliberately provoke this pressure by mixing levels in Quality events such as training or workshops and encouraging people to speak out. National Starch, for example, engineered a full mix on their training events from operators to directors. Lipton, as another example, aimed for totally random mixing by choosing the participants for each of their head office training sessions simply by working through the internal telephone book. These examples notwithstanding, revolutions in business simply do not happen from the bottom up. At all times and with all successful examples, the inspiration and leadership comes from the top of the organisation.

Middle-out

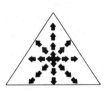 For larger companies, the Quality leader may seek to stimulate and provoke the organisation with a middle-out approach. This is akin to bottom-up in a smaller company in that the aim is to break out of a rigid hierarchy and challenge upwards. The difference is the target population is not the workforce as a whole but middle management and managers at interrelated organisations, such as suppliers. Marks & Spencer illustrated this approach when they introduced their 'making it better' programme in 1986. M & S has always had a deep Quality ethos from inception, but concern was growing that the size of the business by the mid-eighties could stilt the inherent responsibility for high standards and improvement. The 'making it better' programme was designed for 'the people who operate the business' i.e. store managers and supervisors, departmental heads, merchandisers, technologists. These people went away for a week at a time in small groups with a brief to discover what was

limiting improvement. Mixed in with the M & S managers were managers from the major outside suppliers, so that the population was a true horizontal representation, middle-out. Towards the end of the week, key underlying issues were revealed, invariably processes not adequately under control, specifications which were too vague and high wastage of time and energy sorting out mistakes. At the end of the week, teams were formed across organisational boundaries (internal and external) to take the investigations further and, in addition, each manager was asked to write in to say what they were going to do personally to strive for improvement. The result was a considerable increase in improvement energy.

Mobilising for action

 We have seen that top-down and bottom-up implementation strategies are not alternatives but two interlinking dynamics. One does not work well without the other. Broad bottom-up initiatives alone dissolve in unsympathetic environments; narrow top-down initiatives run out of steam when the last cascade is done. So the Quality leader who has studied other implementations may well seek to balance the discipline and effectiveness of top-down with the challenge and energy of bottom-up. The resulting integrated strategy is usually built around a top-down installation with the leader setting the example and providing the direction and inspiration for improvement, but with an additional aim of bringing lower levels into the process quite quickly. This can be readily achieved in a small unit where it is practical to hold whole-unit events for impact and where mixed-level training can be done without big time delays between the first and last trained people being brought into the process. In large units, the leader may look to middle-out activities to accelerate the process and mobilise action across an organisation. For example, a large retail bank will have certain central processing functions and numerous branches. An orderly top-down approach could take four or five years to reach the cashier at the counter who actually meets the customer day to day. To accelerate this and achieve an improvement which shows through to the customer, an implementation design is needed which simultaneously works both along processes from backroom to the branches and laterally across the branches. The action must still start at head office to ensure direction and commitment, but can target branch managers and assistant managers early in order to mobilise their energies.

Implementation focus

The implementation design also needs to consider broad content.' ᴅ we focus on the tools and techniques of improvement, for example, or 'the hearts and minds'? Again this is a matter of timing and depends on the maturity of the company in Quality terms. In general, however, most Quality leaders will be seeking to change everyday practice in the organisation, supported and guided by Quality principles. This means changing behaviours at all levels and this should be the primary focus. An early aim is to create an environment where behaviours are better understood (what we *really* do) and more consistently managed. This means an individual's behaviour with respect to his customers, his colleagues, his team, his suppliers and his leader. With this grounding, the manager is better equipped to transfer the Quality message through his actions as well as his words.

But he does need more. He needs to know the most effective way of making improvements. He needs to learn the broad disciplines of Quality, ranging from process management to customer listening – and he needs to learn them through lots of hands-on practice. What he needs *least*, at the early stage, is detailed knowledge of the tools. In fact, like any good craftsman, the skilled improver can do a good job with any set of tools; it is his understanding and approach that matters most. Nevertheless, improvement will be more efficient with good tools and these should be introduced to managers, so that they can select and apply them as they feel appropriate. In other words, tools and techniques, from fishbone diagrams to CoO statements, should not be seen as the drivers of improvement activity.

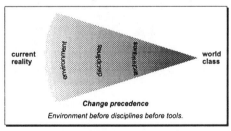

Change precedence
Environment before disciplines before tools.

The same applies at non-management levels. Behaviours, from speaking out, to checking the process variables, to taking notice of the customer, are the most significant changes to be required. With a well-constructed implementation process, the behavioural changes expected will be supported and reinforced by the managerial environment already established.

Sustaining the energy

The most common effect of improvement programmes with little strategic underpinning is a yo-yo of effort and enthusiasm. Thus a campaign on 'make a difference' or 'buck a day' will receive intensive attention for a few razzmatazz months, raising involvement (and expectation) to new heights, only to be followed by a period of deafening silence and inactivity, whilst management work out what to do with 5,000 suggestions. Or, even more commonly, management teams are sent away to be indoctrinated with the Quality message and return, all fired up, to the wet blanket of business as usual. Such occurrences are more than frustrating: they dissipate energy which is needed for change and improvement. When the leader hears about these problems or learns that an initiative is fading, the temptation is to devise hastily another quick stimulant; the process of yo-yo energising repeats itself.

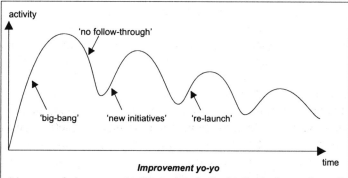

Improvement yo-yo

It is common for improvement activity to start off with a lot of enthusiasm and one-off communications, raising expectations sky-high. Without a planned follow-through, energy plummets and activity trails off, until management come in with a second hit - continuing the yo-yo effect. The net result is an overall decline in involvement and action as people become disillusioned. A steady, planned build-up of activity is much to be preferred, giving the feeling of purposeful, irrevocable progress.

Large-scale yo-yos are simply down to lack of strategic thought and planning. They consume tremendous energy and can be terminal.

But even in well-planned implementations, smaller-scale ones can occur through the dynamics of change. For instance, as improvement energy builds up and a positive environment takes hold, improvement teams may begin to form spontaneously. Often though, this spontaneous feeling applies to everybody at the same time: everybody wants to be involved *now*. Providing the support, guidance and encouragement for these enthusiasts may exhaust the capacity of both line management and facilitators at this point. A vacuum results for those not already receiving immediate attention, with inevitable backlash as frustration builds up. The best way of minimising the occurrence and effect of these dynamics is to design an implementation process which has a steady build-up of involvement and activity. For this, the bigger energy hikes must be predicted and relatively controlled. For example, as people come out of Quality training, they are immediately brought into a disciplined programme of local projects and actions, or as people submit their ideas for improvement a mechanism is ready to inform them quickly of progress. To manage the smaller less predictable peaks, the facilitators and local champions must be ready to help.

The energising cycle

A very pragmatic way of planning and managing Quality improvement locally is to build around the generation of improvement energy. In simple terms, people need to be persuaded of the need for improvement (communications) first. Then they will be ready to learn about how to make improvement (training). They will then want to apply what they have learned (action) and through this experience may well want to know more about it, thus completing the cycle. This simple concept works for small teams and for whole organisations; the tighter the cycle, the greater the energy generated and the better the result will be. This cycle appears obvious: would anyone train people before they know what it is about?...or let them loose on improvement activities without training? The answer is yes, all too often.

Creating an ordered schedule of activity across a complex organisation is quite a challenge and many fail it. Thus it is common for attendees at Quality training sessions not to be briefed, other than being told to turn up on Monday. Equally common, people come out of a high energy event straight into the brick wall of business as usual, hitting a line management unimpressed with their new-found enthusiasm for improvement. The result is squandered improvement energy or, worse, no energy at all, with the organisation continuing merrily on in its mediocre way.

To counter this, the cycle of communications, training and action needs to be planned as tightly and seamlessly as possible, so that each person goes through the sequence naturally and easily.

Communicating the need

The first things any sensible person will want to know about the Quality process are what and why – specifically, what does it mean to me and why should I bother? The Quality leader should have the answers to both well prepared, if he wants people to follow him down the Quality path. He will already have taken stock of the current position with respect to Quality in the organisation and now is the time to share his findings. People will want to know how customers perceive their service and how it compares to the competition. They will be interested in what competitive businesses are doing to raise their performance. They will readily absorb the rationale for accelerated improvement and the need for management to lead it. But most of all, they want to know what's in it for them – both the upside and downside. This includes the action required – what they have to do – and the outcome – the likely effects and results. The more specific and personally relevant this is, the better people will respond. So, the leader must have his points well prepared, based on facts, and he should be ready to explain these points many times over, in many different ways. It is impossible to overcommunicate, but easy to bore.

The best way of communicating Quality is face to face. The Quality leader should use this to the full, both directly (i.e. talking to groups of people himself) or through a cascading mechanism such as team briefing. The leader can supplement this with other media, provided the temptation to substitute is resisted. Many companies, for example, use videos featuring the CEO talking about Quality. Not only is this hard to do without resorting to exhortation or appearing patronising: it inevitably invokes the cynical response 'If it's that important, why isn't he here himself?' Videos are very good, however, for conveying best practice and for publicising what people have achieved later on in the improvement process.

The written word doesn't have great utility at this stage. Posters and banners with neat phrases seem to have little impact and go unnoticed and unremarked. After all, in terms of practical improvement, our target audience is a sophisticated one, with little respect for rejoinders to 'do it right first time' or 'Quality saves jobs'. However, an imaginative display of performance measures, successful improvements and process of involvement will be worthwhile at a later stage in the improvement cycle. Similarly, internal newsletter reports or memos from the CEO can achieve only a limited impact at this introductory stage and perhaps should be restricted to confirming what the leader has said verbally and illustrating the forward plan (i.e. when does it affect me?).

Training in practice

 Training is not the most descriptive word to convey the ideal experience for people being brought into Quality. Because the main aim is to influence behaviour and to generate the energy for doing that, classroom teaching is not always the most appropriate vehicle. Indeed, the transfer of knowledge that most training courses aim for is probably the lowest need in Quality. Quality *practice* is more apposite than Quality training. Practising the right way of doing things and debating the options with colleagues until the best practices become clear, is far more effective than listening to theory or principle. Practice is not only more active and stimulating, it feels much closer to the real world outside.

Quality training in practice is served better with facilitated workshops and events than by courses run by experts. The most effective style is one of self-learning and discovery, drawn together by the facilitator, who will be more concerned with keeping the energy high than feeding in knowledge. Some knowledge input is needed to stimulate thinking and discussion, although, with Quality, much of the content is already there in the group, especially if the group is drawn from different functions. One readily acceptable form of input is what other companies have done in a particular Quality area, especially from a sector the group can relate to. If the learning point is, say, awareness of the internal customer, examples of practice from other companies can bring the concept to life, leading to discussion on the benefits, the problems and the practicalities of applying the ideas locally.

Events

In 1987, National Westminster Bank embarked on a very un-bank like initiative. Some 60,000 staff, ranging from clerks to regional directors, went through a unique one-day experience called the 'Quality Awareness Day'. What was unique were the venues - six purpose-designed structures, like rigid marquees, located at stately homes around the UK. Inside the environment was physically matched to the content, with themes, displays and videos supporting the Quality messages. 150 people at a time went through the event, mixed together from different locations and ranks. The day's experience consisted of examples of Quality scenarios played out by theatre or video with syndicate debate. The whole effect was highly memorable and motivating.

British Airways is another strong advocate of events. Their latest is a 120-staff-per-day session called 'Focus on Customer Retention'. Groups are completely mixed by role, level, function and culture (overseas staff are flown in) over the 400 events, which started in April 1992 and continue for two years. The event is structured into five themed workstations equipped with interactive and linear video and a facilitator. Groups of around 25 spend 40 minutes at each station working with the data, finishing each session with a quiz on the particular topic. Topics are: what is important to customers; the internal service chain; service recovery; understanding why customers might leave us; what will make loyal customers. For the plenary sessions real customers drawn from corporate clients and travel agents join in a debate on customer retention. As with all BA's previous events, Sir Colin Marshall attends the vast majority, mingling with the participants and giving his views.

Philips is another company which has experienced the value of major events. Looking for a way to mark the massive changes in attitude and performance needed across the whole organisation, CEO Jan Timmer hit upon the idea of a 'customer day'. This was no ordinary customer day and no ordinary event. On 7 January 1992, some 125,000 Philips employees across Europe were linked together in simultaneous activity focused on the theme of 'our customers'. Some 100,000 people in 18 countries kicked off the day by hearing Jan Timmer live through satellite broadcast. Local company workshops followed in 1,000 units, each one concentrating on local customer issues, but all using the same structured analysis applied in small teams facilitated by some 250 pre-trained managers. This process generated some 22,000 ideas, questions and suggestions. 1,000 questions were fed by fax or E-mail to Mr Timmer, who conducted another live broadcast with answers and debate to kick off the afternoon session. The event was a great success and rated highly by all participants. The extra energy created was a useful boost to the more conventional Quality activities taking place throughout Philips.

Discussion, however, is not practice and the skilled facilitator will have a structured experience ready to take the group through some parallels with real-life internal customer situations. Such sessions are more rewarding than conventional training but riskier too. Emotions are stirred, many questions are raised and the atmosphere can become hot. This is a wonderful opportunity for the Quality leader; he should be ready, with his senior colleagues, to come in and provide the direction and guidance that many people will seek at this stage. This leadership role in Quality training can be maintained by the CEO (many top leaders attend a part of these Quality events throughout the company on the grounds that they are unique opportunities to demonstrate their belief and commitment) or carefully passed down to local leaders. In many cases, both the local manager *and* the CEO can demonstrate leadership roles, taking on the real issues that are raised. Much preparation will have been done between the leader(s) and the facilitators to ensure that the group perceive firm direction, a clear framework and much support, but that the responsibility for improvement is theirs.

Picking up the action

To move fluidly from training into improvement action, some companies design the last period of a Quality training workshop around small projects which take people through all the key improvement disciplines compressed into one day rather than spread out over six months, as will be so when practised for real later. Other companies use the end of training as the beginning of action. As people finish their training, they are asked to choose one issue which they will tackle back at base. This 'post-grad' assignment can be any improvement opportunity in the person's place of work and applies to both managers and non-managers. All are encouraged to approach the issue in a disciplined way and to form an improvement team, if the issue warrants it. After three months, the training group typically meets again for a day and the 'post-grad' improvements are reviewed and debated by the group. Some are well underway; some are struggling to start. But by the end of the next three months most have gained valuable individual learning from tackling an improvement opportunity of their own.

Whatever link is used, the most important requirement is for people to *do* something when they come out of training. Local management need to be well-prepared for this and may already have a disciplined improvement process in place to select improvement issues and allocate people to them. Additionally, the individual, or a team which formed on the training, may be keen to pursue an own line of improvement. This should be endorsed if it is small and local; if the issue is bigger or complicated it should be brought into the project selection process, keeping the individual or team involved throughout. Either way, the local manager should be building up a mix of improvement activity which he can bring people into as they come out of their initial training. To guide him, he will have, or be creating, mechanisms for setting up better links with his customers and suppliers; for regularly reviewing output performance against customer needs; for monitoring the key local processes. From this data, his team will be making adjustments day to day, minute to minute, looking for immediate small gains. As well, they will be making proposals and submitting OFIs to be reviewed for longer term improvement work. Some of these will become small improvement tasks with one or two people assigned to investigate, report and implement. Others will require the discipline of a full project, probably involving other departments, with selected team members. Still more, the manager may be involved in providing input for a major process improvement, utilising yet more of the talents of his people.

The local leader's task, with the aid of his facilitator, is to harmonise all these dimensions of improvement into a coherent positive force, in which everyone has a fulfilling contributory role. At the same time, he has today's operations to perform to the highest standards and today's customer's orders to meet without error. It's not surprising that the local leader's role quickly becomes full in a Quality process. As he was probably already over-busy, the leader more than anyone needs to apply Quality disciplines to his decisions and actions if he is not going to sink under the new load. Quality soon spotlights the outstanding leaders and reveals the mediocre ones as the improvement cycle is really under the local leader's control. If he turns it up too high, he will swamp his section with projects and improvement ideas, lose coordination and produce modest results. If he plays safe and keeps it low-key, he will stay under the energy threshold and be mediocre. The adoption of a top-down strategy to guide and prepare local management to handle this leadership test minimises the disruption from local managers getting it badly wrong.

Communicating the action

 Once improvement action is under way, the Quality leader keeps the cycle going with more communication, or, more accurately, further extension of it, as the communications should never stop. At this stage, the emphasis is on what is happening and the progress being made. Improvement teams will want to know what other teams are doing and how they are doing it. When people implement local improvements or submit proposals for improvement, others want to know about it. The people involved want others to know about it too. Recognition through publicity is stimulating.

This is where all the media can be brought in to good effect. Local displays featuring people and their achievements; newspapers and newsheets; videos, even television; not forgetting the most effective medium inside an organisation, word of mouth. Some companies put a great deal of effort into communicating what is going on and what people have achieved and they find that it is valued by many. Lipton, for example, have gradually moved away from the glossy quarterly newsletter to frequent newsheets produced locally and full of factual information about what people have done. Some of the Lipton plants are down to *weekly* publishing schedules, such is the volume of good data to communicate. The big quarterly journal is still produced and contains Quality articles, but the regular communication line is the weekly flier.

Quite a few large companies have internal television systems. Federal Express and Monsanto, for example, produce regular television bulletins featuring daily performance figures and improvement achievements, with interviews from the people who have made the improvements. Many others, who can't run to their own television studio, will commission videos to capture what teams have done and convey it to others. Well-produced video can capture, better than any other medium, that magic ingredient: energy.

But communication doesn't have to be high tech and certainly should not be dependent on it. Flip charts placed in strategic positions can have just as much impact.

Follow-on training

Quality improvement never ends and neither should Quality training. Almost immediately after the initial training, people who are being brought into the Quality process should have access to more learning experiences. This might be a deeper understanding of the concepts now that they are more involved, or introduction to additional disciplines and useful tools and techniques. For instance, in virtually any company of whatever nature and capability, sooner or later in the Quality process someone will request more training in project management disciplines. The reason is simply that many more people are using projects for real now and can see the obvious value in doing it properly.

Other common needs are for leadership and deployment skills (again because such skills are now being demanded in a serious way) and for tools such as customer/supplier agreements. Once tasted, the appetite for more Quality training of this kind can be hard to contain. The right type of training, presented in the right way, can be very popular indeed. There are, however, many ways to meet this demand efficiently. The primary aim is to keep the emphasis on the practice, allowing people to 'pull in' new input as they appreciate the need. Local training input can be built into regular team meetings, or half-days provided, running from late afternoon into the evening. This type of input is down to the local manager and his facilitator to organise efficiently, but someone has to design and produce the offering first.

Some companies prepare modular training sessions to cover the key Quality disciplines and popular tools and run them regularly, allowing managers to book people at the most appropriate time. Others recognise that training is going to be a permanent feature of the internal environment and provide facilities to suit. Elida Gibbs built a purpose-designed Learning Centre in their main factory at Leeds, mainly to accommodate the vast amount of training for all levels anticipated as a result of their Quality drive, but also to make learning accessible to everyone over a variety of topics. Distance-learning modules, interactive video and all types of self-start learning aids can be brought in as extra support. What starts as Quality training can evolve ultimately into a learning environment, where Quality is the core philosophy providing the stimulus for people to improve themselves through learning. The person benefits not only from the skill and knowledge acquired but also the self-value of acquiring it. The company gains from the added capability and the greater self-esteem of the person. Win-win again from Quality.

The sheer volume of training is another dimension which needs to be addressed and managed. Legal & General invested 10,000 hours of training in their first Quality year; Texas Instruments 16,000; Fiat 20,000. This level may not be necessary in subsequent years but the demand will remain high and a healthy Quality process feeds on training. Van den Bergh Foods started tracking training days as one of their key goals after they had a couple of years' experience with Quality. They had finished their introductory TQ training and yet local plant managers were raising the training level higher still to meet the great demand for skills, knowledge and awareness in the new environment. From a standard of less than one day per person per year before Quality, Van den Bergh Foods in 1992 were *averaging* 9.2 days per person per year. Although this was still below their long-term target of ten days, the average masks an even more striking picture for two new plants had been added to the group that year and were showing very low figures. At the other end of the distribution was one plant with an average of 28 days per person.

Keeping the action going

 Support structures for a Quality process vary widely. AT&T has over 50 people centrally on Quality. Unilever has no one. Both are huge complex multinationals with a predilection for Quality. Which is right? On further analysis, both companies have similar improvement initiatives; the divergence is around ownership or origin of these initiatives and the difference reflects the cultures of the two corporations. AT&T has by background and nature a centralised focus and new initiatives start at the centre or gravitate there for development. Hence the various Quality functions, where courses are designed, trainers trained, techniques developed, benchmarking data collected. All of this is offered to the business units through internal consultancy. This is the AT&T way and people are comfortable with it.

Unilever, in contrast, is built around strong operating businesses, managing brands at country level. The only central roles which are tolerated are those necessary to achieve coordination within business groups. It would thus be unnatural for a central Quality role to be created and, indeed, even the Personal Products group, which has the most advanced Quality process in Unilever, combines the Total Quality coordinator role with an existing senior executive role. But at company level, many Unilever companies have a full time TQ coordinator and Personal Products achieve much of the equivalent of AT&T's central resource by bringing these coordinators together through a Quality Council.

So what is right is what is right for the culture. For most companies, it will be something between these two examples – some central resource to assist with the demand for training and the need for enhanced communications – but not enough to take the ownership and the attention away from line management. The latter point is what should guide the decision on the nature and extent of support for Quality. Everything should be implemented through the line, starting at the top. The question then is what does the line need in addition in order to make this process efficient? Often the answer is no more than a Quality coordinator for each business unit and a Quality facilitator for each big department or section.

In a large organisation, the coordinator may be full-time but the facilitators desirably should be around half-time, permitting them the legitimacy of a line role too. Companies give these roles a variety of names: Quality coordinator, facilitator, counsellor, champion, advisor, consultant; in practice, the role requires something of all of these. BT uses the title 'Implementation Support Manager', or 'ISM' for short; 'Quality Support Manager' or 'Improvement Support Manager' are also quite popular. All such names are suitable; the only ones which allow potential misinterpretation are 'Quality Manager' and 'Quality Director', which not only imply ultimate control of Quality, but may also associate the role too closely with the technical roles of assurance and audit.

Notwithstanding this, many companies, especially in the USA, now do have a Quality director, partly to ensure Quality receives continued board level attention (really the CEO's job) and partly, perhaps, because the Baldrige guidelines encourage a board-level Quality contact. In contrast, Japanese companies do not have designated Quality directors, the highest ranking Quality specialist usually being a TQC programme manager, a middle level role aimed at coordinating Quality training.

Whatever they are called, Quality coordinators and facilitators can play a key role in building up Quality energy. Selected well and developed well, they become early champions, planted around the business to spread the word and infect people with enthusiasm. As improvement action takes off, they are there to provide help and encouragement, reinforcing the local management and adding expertise where it is needed. A large unit might have 50 to 100 facilitators and not find the investment in them to be excessive. They are often middle and junior managers by origin, but could be drawn from any level and any role. Perkins has two machine operators in a group of around 40 facilitators; although drawn straight from the shop floor, they took to their new roles, which included training managers, as well as anyone, despite the huge shift in attitude and background entailed.

Organising for Quality

Some companies create a steering group for Quality, usually the top executive group, and have separate meetings to focus on Quality. Others prefer to maintain the same meeting format but provide the time and attention for Quality by putting it first on the agenda. In practice, there is little to choose between these two approaches. The steering group tends to provide more time and concentration, simply by being separated from regular business matters, but, conversely, weakens the message that Quality is all about business. A few companies overcome this paradox by alternating between the two: i.e. on a two-week meeting cycle, the first meeting will be a normal business meeting with Quality first; the second is a longer dedicated session on Quality implementation.

Below the executive level, most companies prefer to keep Quality directly linked into line meetings, although larger and more fragmented businesses have additional steering groups at separate sites. Most companies do have some overlay, however, usually formed around the facilitators or implementation support people. A forum for sharing information and experience for people in these roles can be very productive and many companies establish a Quality Council, or equivalent, to spread Quality expertise. Some deliberately seek to reduce the hierarchical barriers through their design of organising bodies and selection of people for them. South West Electricity, for example, has formed a Council which consists of both Directors and selected managers from two or three levels down. In their case, the Council is the steering group for Quality implementation, and, although 18 strong, this composition does bring a rich perspective into the meetings. Large steering groups will most likely require a smaller team to feed information and planning inputs and at South West Electricity this is achieved by a Quality planning team with a three-person core, to which others are seconded according to need.

Reporting Quality

Reporting Quality improvement should be a normal line responsibility and should be aligned with regular performance reporting. Line management accountability is a crucial factor in continuity of improvement and it obviously makes little sense in a system which creates a lot of fanfare around Quality initiatives but ignores them

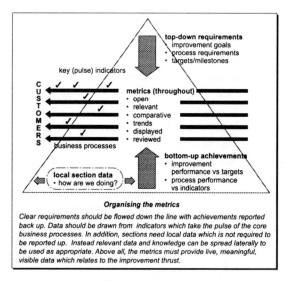

Organising the metrics

Clear requirements should be flowed down the line with achievements reported back up. Data should be drawn from indicators which take the pulse of the core business processes. In addition, sections need local data which is not required to be reported up. Instead relevant data and knowledge can be spread laterally to be used as appropriate. Above all, the metrics must provide live, meaningful, visible data which relates to the improvement thrust.

when reporting results. Indeed, one of the most telling initiatives a manager can make early on is to improve the Quality of his weekly meeting, starting with the data collected from the Quality survey. With encouragement and practice, people quickly learn to report new data, such as customer feedback or process variation, and interpret trends. Van den Bergh Foods' UK operation, for example, now reports an array of Quality measures through the line: customer complaints, production to plan, operational efficiency, product quality, internal service achievements, material wastage, rate of innovation, invoicing performance and others.

As well as the hard data, the Quality leader will want to encourage reporting on the process of Quality; how teams are doing, what disciplines are being used, which tools are popular, what kind of ideas are being submitted and implemented, how behaviours are changing. Interest in such matters must be started at the top and encouraged all through the line. Van den Bergh Foods first reported measures are involvement, which is a combined index of improvement team participation and idea generation, and training. Chairman Guy Walker is the sponsor for these metrics and has the responsibility to the board for promoting and championing their use. With this level of attention, such new measures eventually are reported naturally and regularly.

This often changes the nature of weekly management meetings as the Quality process cannot be conveyed adequately in numbers alone. It requires interaction and feeling to sense what is going on. The number of teams active and the number of OFIs implemented tell us only a little about how people's attitudes and behaviours are changing. To bring more feeling for this into management meetings, many leaders invite people, usually in teams, to present what they are doing. As was discussed in Chapter 7, short team presentations and subsequent debate are not only rich in information, they are highly motivational for the team members. With practice and discipline, ten minutes – five for presentation, five for discussion – is enough for a team of any level to convey their progress, findings and status and receive feedback from the management group. An hour of a meeting spent in this way can be very effective.

Overall, the Quality leader needs upward reporting for two main purposes. One is to be able to tap into the implementation process at different levels. The other is to assess progress against the Quality framework set for the organisation and to seek to mould improvement activity around the key elements. Van den Bergh Foods' reporting measures, for instance, tie up directly with the company's improvement goals. They are set top-down but are collated (and have been modified to make them more effective) bottom-up.

Spreading it around

There is another need for reporting on progress and results. That is the need for other sections, departments and units to learn from each other. The most relevant illustration of the validity of an improvement activity (other than learning it for yourself through doing it) is seeing a colleague do it successfully. Thus transfer of experience laterally across an organisation can be valuable. This applies to improvement disciplines, to techniques, to training, to communication, to projects and to the implementation plan as a whole. It is not a straightforward channel to construct, as 'not invented here' and internal competition blocks the learning from next door. But one of the leader's objectives will be to eliminate this in the new culture – thus building a successful transfer route has double advantage.

Mindful of this, Unilever Personal Products has developed a framework for exchange and transfer of experience which is sensitive to local ownership needs but provides interchange at a number of levels. First of all, a Steering Group was established to oversee the continued development of the Quality process. This body is made up of senior executives from the operating companies. The Steering Group does not interfere with implementation at company level but looks ahead, aiming to anticipate the companies' needs and initiate planning accordingly. Any development initiative, for example a benchmarking study or advanced training, is achieved by drawing people from the operating companies into working parties. Marketing and technological developments are handled the same way. Great care is taken over choosing the participants and one factor always taken into account is the mix of companies with respect to dissemination of knowledge gained and transfer of experience. Thus, usually represented are: large companies and small companies (not always the same ones); European, American or Far Eastern (if it is a global initiative); technical, commercial or marketing functions (if, as is usually the case, the topic crosses conventional boundaries). Finally a check is made to ensure that the resulting mix is practical on geographical lines; the group doesn't have to work side by side but they do have to meet from time to time.

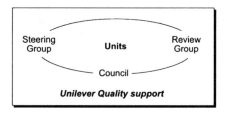

Personal Products has two other corporate bodies to support the Quality process. One is the Quality Council, mentioned already, which consists of 20 or so Quality coordinators, meeting for two days every three months to exchange information and swap experiences. After three years of meeting, this Council has evolved into a strong body of Quality knowledge into which new people are brought in and others take their knowledge back into the line as the job of company Quality coordinator is changed every two years or so. To keep the meetings lively and challenging, round-the-table progress reports have been replaced by storyboard displays where everyone wanders around engaging their colleagues in debate with the aid of a display from each company. There is usually a theme; at one meeting, for example, each coordinator was asked to bring two display posters, one illustrating a major success with the Quality process and one a failure.

The other Quality body is the Review Group. The Review Group is, in fact, all the directors of the Personal Products businesses – some 150 in all. The primary aim was to help keep the energy for Quality flowing after the initial implementation period, through a series of progress reviews where each company in turn is visited by others and their experiences with Quality shared. All 150 directors do not go to each review, of course, but six at a time are drawn from across the companies to attend a particular review, which lasts for an evening and a day. Over a two-year period, with a review every six weeks or so, most directors have attended at least one review in addition to his own.

The impact has been considerable. Not only does Quality activity increase significantly in the company in the period before the review, but sharpness of understanding and explanation of what is happening also goes up considerably. Such peer reviews are important affairs, even though the style might be informal. The benefits are also long-lasting. The whole company is aware that their Quality process is being reviewed and some of the teams will have had the direct experience of presenting their work to the visitors. The recognition and motivational value of this is high. The host company receives benign criticism of its Quality process and suggestions arise both in the formal discussion and in the informal meetings over dinner and coffee breaks. As well as this, the reviewing team members go home to their own company with new ideas and renewed energy for their own process. The whole activity is well reported in a meaty journal, called the *Quality Digest*, which is distributed throughout the group. The Review Group is a very popular complement to the Quality organising bodies in Personal Products.

There is still more though to the Personal Products' mechanisms for experience transfer. After a couple of years of Quality implementations, many hundreds of improvement projects had been established. Some were great successes, some much less so; but most had some practical lessons which might be of use in a similar application elsewhere. In other words, the team who had spent six months methodically eradicating labels being stuck on slightly out of true had something of potential use to every other factory sticking on labels. Of similar wider use was the discovery by an improvement team that the basic card used for building sales promotion displays was a frequent bottleneck in achieving slick coordinated promotions. The card was ordered and stored as a routine purchase with the result that one day there was far too much, the next not enough. Looking at it again as a process ensured a consistent supply and eliminated months of stock. Such improvements could be replicated in every sales office around the world. The problem was that these local initiatives were not being exploited elsewhere, simply because others did not know about them. The solution was to create a database which all the companies could tap into, showing current and past projects with their most relevant details.

In Personal Products, all of the mechanisms for transfer of experience are enhanced by the most important route of them all: networking. Personal Products' managers from around the world have been on study tours together; they have trained together; they attend conferences together, like the one at Selsdon Park. They may well sit 5,000 miles apart but two managers will know each other well enough to help each other out. Networking has always been an important way of life in Unilever; in Personal Products, the language of Quality takes networking to another level.

The power of the informal network has combined with the Quality movement in Unilever to trigger some far-reaching changes. In New York in 1991, the key marketing people of the US and European businesses came together with their counterparts in the advertising world to talk about one of the most important issues in fast moving consumer goods: the Quality of advertising. This was not exactly a new subject; separating Lord Leverhume's 50 per cent good advertising from 50 per cent bad had taxed the creative minds of generations of marketing people. This conference was a little different though. First, it was interactive group work, based on a similar design to Mike Perry's successful Selsdon Park conference. Secondly, it used some of the Quality terminology and concepts to try and put a new angle to an old issue.

The reaction was strong: many marketeers felt concepts such as the process of advertising and its creative essence did not mix at all. Much heat was thus generated but over the three days, the structure of the workshop enabled a few key areas to be pinned down and the group agreed to further work being undertaken. As the heat died down after the event, it became clear that these were big items. One was quite straightforward but had never been accomplished previously: a Unilever award for advertising. The advertising industry has many awards of its own and this is an important part of the culture, but not one from the customer. The working party played the network to find a way through all the political difficulties, leading to a recommendation for an award which would show that advertising had a crucial role to Unilever's prosperity. In October 1992, Mike Perry, as chairman of Unilever plc, awarded the first Unilever Great Advertising Award to Lever US, to considerable internal and external impact.

Another outcome of the workshop has much greater ramifications. For decades, advertising agencies have been paid 15 per cent of the spend on the advert, a simple formula but one which both sides felt gave little incentive for performance. A bad advert earned the same as a good one. Poor service was paid the same as outstanding service. Neither the Unilever companies buying the services, nor the better agency people who wanted their contribution valued more directly, liked this system, but it had always been just too big, too complex and too dangerous to tinker with in the web of interactions between 600 companies and their local agencies. Enough ground was broken at the workshop for one of the companies, Chesebrough-Pond's US, to take the issue further. Peter England, their marketing director, had already successfully implemented a Total Quality process at the smaller company at Chesebrough-Pond's Canada, so he knew the Quality way of approaching this. He set up a multi-unit team and followed Quality disciplines to establish a blueprint for a different system. A year later, that model for performance-based fees has been adopted by all Unilever companies worldwide and enthusiastically supported by all the agencies involved. The Quality philosophy and practice is thus providing new solutions to old issues in Unilever.

Remember the revolution

A planned ordered change process will bring much more success to the Quality leader than a reactive ad hoc approach. But the plan itself doesn't create the changes; neither will it give all the answers to the issues which arise. Remember that change demands a continual supply of energy, as we discussed in Chapter 2. Energy feeds change and the planned change process requires continual management of improvement energy too.

Thus the leader has to remember his revolutionary role, especially when the programme of training and project-setting has rolled out. They must be ready to stir things up again, stoking up dissatisfaction with the status quo. They should always be looking out for the opportunity to inspire and challenge their fellow revolutionaries, who may just be falling back into the ever-open jaws of business as usual. Large scale improvement is never achieved through the delivery of a mechanical programme. Quality must always embrace planned change *and* improvement energy. Successful Quality is revolutionary in design and practice.

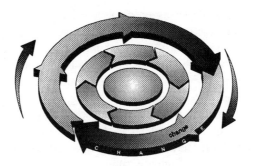

SUMMARY

Have you designed a sound change process?

1. **Have you studied others and learned what works well and what works poorly?** *Avoid the mistakes of others and apply the best experience directly to your needs by researching, visiting and absorbing good Quality applications from a variety of sectors.*

2. **Have you planned ahead in some detail, especially the first year?** *Take plenty of time for the initial planning and build in a data collection and preparation phase to allow the plan to be tested and tuned; resist the temptation to go straight into improvement action.*

3. **Have you constructed an implementation strategy that suits your organisation and current position?** *Your strategy should be unique, albeit drawing on others' experiences; use this strategy with the implementation plan to sustain a proactive stance to change.*

4. **Are you completely ready to drive it yourself?** *Know where you want to point the Quality process and know what you have to do, as leader, to keep it on track and at speed; be prepared to take personal initiatives to keep the energy and the action flowing.*

5. **Do you have a robust communications process?** *Be sparing with theory and hype; emphasise facts and practice.*

6. **Do you have a robust training process?** *Use training to practise improvement before doing it.*

7. **Do you have a robust improvement action process?** *Create disciplined coordinated directed action where practical; recorded action where not.*

8. **Are you ready to support the line?** *Quality implementation puts more pressure on your managers; make sure there is enough support to help them through it...and help them change.*

9. ***Are you set up to keep taking the pulse?*** *Prepare some key indicators and establish a regular monitoring system.*
10. ***Do you recognise your fellow revolutionaries?*** *Inspire, encourage and support those who are with you...and keep things stirred up. Quality without energy will not bring change.*

10
Making Quality Pay

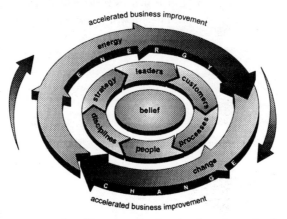

accelerated business improvement

A Quality process should repay the leader handsomely for the extra-ordinary efforts he or she will have made to make it work. Today there is much experience to draw on around the world, for the leader to develop a faster and more enduring implementation and obtain his return much earlier than the pioneers.

'Total Quality is a management model for creating value.' Carl Arendt, Westinghouse

'By the end of the nineties, the only successful companies will be those who have successfully implemented Quality processes.' Digital Equipment Corporation

Expect multiple benefits

Where should the leader set his own expectations with Quality? He should aim high. Revolutionary change. Transformed practice. Anything less could mean his organisation will hardly change at all, the forces for inertia are so strong. If he does not expect great things, he is certain not to achieve them. The world is full of mediocre achievement and an ordinary expectation guarantees repeat member-ship of this club. In contrast, a Quality revolution can bring multiple benefits. The breakthrough into a higher performing world brings big rewards.

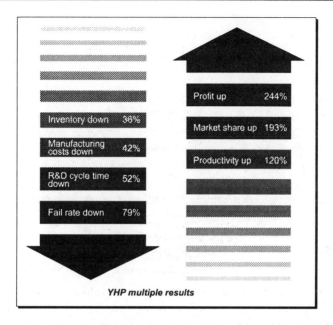

Inventory down 36%

Manufacturing costs down 42%

R&D cycle time down 52%

Fail rate down 79%

Profit up 244%

Market share up 193%

Productivity up 120%

YHP multiple results

Yokogawa Hewlett Packard (YHP) are a classic example. In the sixties, as HP's wholly owned subsidiary in Japan, they were rather looked down on by the rest of the hugely successful HP operation. President Kenso Sasaoka, decided to do something about it. Over a relatively short period, he started up a process of improvement of everything that was done in the company. By 1970, the transformation was such that he applied for the Deming Prize for YHP, achieving it in 1972. From being a good average company, YHP had joined the elite of Japanese businesses. Through determination, discipline and a planned change process, YHP was transformed from the part of HP that no one was interested in to the one everyone wanted to learn from.

HP people saw the multiple results YHP achieved and were amazed. Profits and market share up – dramatically. Cost and time down. HP has a strong culture and one of its most enviable traits is its capacity to learn. The story of the YHP transformation coincided with John Young's famous tenfold improvement goal. The Quality revolution spread across HP. Over the next few years, unit after unit turned in multiple benefits. The HP revolution continues today, more than a decade after it was first taken seriously as a business issue. The rewards for HP have been great. In 1991, HP was the only major computer manufacturer to post good profits. In 1992, HP was able to respond quickly when the whole hardware market plunged into a price-cutting war, again outstripping its main competitors by offering advanced products at prices comparable to the clones flooding the market from the far east. Within HP, there are no doubts that Quality has enabled them to achieve their enviable position in a desperate market.

In a totally different sector, Dun & Bradstreet offers another example. Unlike HP, Dun & Bradstreet do not have a long experience of Quality (as we saw in Chapter 4, it was only recently that Richard Archer realised that what he was doing was implementing a Quality process), but like HP, they have very determined leaders. John Young set a challenge for HP and Richard Archer set a challenge for Dun & Bradstreet Europe. Both made it clear that outstanding results were not only possible but expected. Carlos Vasconsellos had just become the general manager for Dun & Bradstreet Portugal when Richard began to articulate the way forward for Dun & Bradstreet Europe. Dun & Bradstreet Portugal was an ordinary business of 160 people, possibly even a little complacent, with over 50 per cent market share. Carlos set about changing this position with gusto. As Richard had done for the management of the whole European group, Carlos brought his team together to discuss the issues – but not just the management, he brought the whole company together in groups built around the strategic processes. A Quality policy was thrashed out and ten commandments set in stone, covering minimum standards on everything that was important, from answering the telephone to the turnaround of a report (the policy is set in stone, but the standards are reviewed and often upgraded every quarter).

Everybody was to be trained in Quality. This was not to everyone's liking; some said: 'I don't want to waste time in a classroom, I want to get on and do it.' Carlos did let the noisiest get on and do it; most of them found it harder and harder, in contrast to those who had been trained. Within a short time, the mavericks also put themselves through the training process. Carlos cut the structure down from five levels to two, explaining that what was required in the new way of managing was thinking not controlling. Cost of Quality was measured and used to indicate areas of wasted effort. A 'you and your customer' programme was launched to put more people out there with customers (with contact hours logged and a minimum amount required each month, 'like a pilot's log, if you don't do enough hours you shouldn't be flying'). The 'three-point promise' was introduced and the key processes set up to achieve the standards promised.

The net result of this intensive change of approach was a substantial shift in the way the business performed. Before, the company had

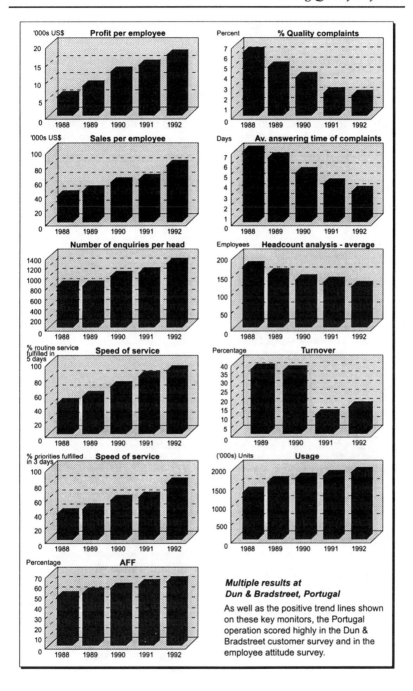

**Multiple results at
Dun & Bradstreet, Portugal**

As well as the positive trend lines shown
on these key monitors, the Portugal
operation scored highly in the Dun &
Bradstreet customer survey and in the
employee attitude survey.

launched about 10 new products in as many years; in 1991/2, some 35 new products came out. All the measurements against the Quality standards showed positive trends, such as time to answer a customer enquiry down by a third. Staff levels had been reduced by 40 without any disruption and staff turnover had settled down from a previous 34 per cent to less than 10 per cent. But best of all, in a recessionary climate, the business had put 20 per cent growth on the top line for each year since Carlos had taken over. Carlos' view on his three years as a Quality leader is: 'We've changed the way we run the business. Much of it was uncomfortable but most people have come with us. We are in a strong position to compete.' Richard and Carlos both expected high results and then made sure they got them.

Multiple change

Benefits of a Quality process can be much more than the hard numbers show. The shift in the way an organisation acts brings multiple benefits of another kind. A research team surveyed a group of major US corporations with mature Quality processes (such as Baldridge Award winners) and compared them to industry in general. Their research conclusions are that Quality:

- *flattens organisations*
- *increases the span of control*
- *fosters changed incentive systems*
- *restructures inputs to strategic planning*
- *expands organisational boundaries and renders them more permeable*
- *reduces waste and increases productivity*

The Quality companies also showed double the growth rate of US companies – 8.3 per cent per year revenue growth on average, compared to 4.2 per cent per year for average US manufacturing company revenues. However, they also reduced their staffing levels by 6.5 per cent over the seven year period studied, while the average companies increased theirs by 8.8 per cent. Greater revenues from fewer people – a good indication of the changes that these companies have achieved.[22]

A royal road to results

The Quality process *has* to be unique to the organisation. If it is not aligned behind business goals, if it is not directed towards actual customers, if it is not built up from the current reality of the business performance...then it will undoubtedly fail. These demands force the Quality leader to devise his own unique approach. But over the last decade a core approach has evolved which incorporates the major ingredients of success and prevents the gross pitfalls in implementation which many companies still experience. This is not a prescription – more a royal road, which provides the most direct route to success.

Divergence too far from this road may raise the risk of being bogged down or caught in blind alleys or just plain lost.

The royal road starts with the need to plan or map the early stages. Quality is a never-ending journey but the first steps, the installation and embedding of a Quality culture, can be carefully mapped out. Many of the companies who have implemented a Quality process successfully map out four or five phases of action, which incorporate the key activities needed into a programme. Some may scorn the concept of a programme, saying, rightly, that Quality is a process, with no start and end point. Pragmatists, however, can retort that such a pure approach may quickly have an end point: the failure of the Quality process. A planned and structured programme is needed to ensure the Quality process stands a chance against the resistance and in-built rejection system of the organisation.

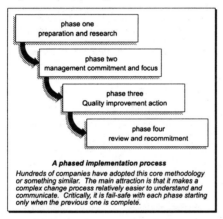

A phased implementation process
Hundreds of companies have adopted this core methodology or something similar. The main attraction is that it makes a complex change process relatively easier to understand and communicate. Critically, it is fail-safe with each phase starting only when the previous one is complete.

The key phases which can be structured are:

one: design and preparation – preparing not only in planning terms but psychologically conditioning senior management for the Quality process and their crucial role.

two: management commitment and focus – converting belief and conviction into hard practice and committing to it.

three: involvement and improvement – the action phase when people are brought into the improvement process in a disciplined and coordinated way.

four: review and recommitment – building on achievements and committing to another push forwards.

Such phases are readily understood by all levels and are thus easy to communicate. People, from the CEO down, are brought into the process in a planned way and this can be clearly explained to them.

These phases are superficially simple; under the surface, they incorporate some fail-safe mechanisms. For instance, if the necessary preparation has not been done in phase one, then senior management will not have the data to commit to action in phase two. Equally, if management cannot commit to collective action (perhaps some Board members are not convinced), then the move into phase three, which would involve more and more of the organisation, should not yet take place. Instead more phase one work should be done to clarify the issues and make the compelling case for Quality.

This does not mean the implementation process should stop dead because one or two people remain agnostic. Far from it, as discussed earlier, the Quality leader is seeking to build up energy in a controlled but unstoppable way; the royal road is his guide to that. As leader, he still has to make the judgements as to when is the optimal time to move to the next phase.

Proof of the pudding

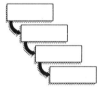 Of the companies who have learned from other's experiences and succeeded with this disciplined approach, many are quite ordinary companies from all walks of business. They are not giants like IBM or BP, nor are they facing disaster like Xerox was in 1984. Neither do they have miraculous product opportunities like Microsoft or Glaxo. Simply, they compete for customers as does everyone else. The only common distinguishing feature is that they have leaders who have determined they are going to improve – and do it well. As a consequence they have achieved enviable results. Here are some snap shots of their implementation experiences. None found it easy but all view the experience to be very positive.

Legal & General

Legal & General are a textbook example of installing a disciplined planned Quality process. One of the biggest names in UK insurance, the management of the 4,000-person Life and Pensions division first began to explore Quality in 1990. The motivation for Quality at L&G lay in the recent history of the UK insurance industry, which had become very sales-led, with volume growth of 20 per cent per year being common in the leading companies. This drive for new sales had led to a poor industry reputation for service and the rapid growth had outstripped the systems which supported the sales. When recession hit the industry, many companies were left with little differentiation outside and weak processes inside. The leading companies, L&G amongst them, began a 'flight to Quality' to address these serious Quality gaps.

L&G's strategy was simultaneously to create more robust administrative processes (especially for the processing of policies and correspondence with customers – the 'paper factory') and enhance the service through their main distribution channels (independent financial agents, tied agents such as building societies, and the direct salesforce). Once they had stronger control of their 'factory' and distribution processes, they could differentiate their services in a crowded and stagnant market. Quality was their vehicle for implementing this strategic aim. After attending a variety of workshops and conferences, key members of the Board were clear about the initiative they wanted to take. Robin Phipps, director of Customer Services (and responsible for half the staff) sought a tailored approach, with an early focus on the intermediaries (the independent agents for example) as customers of the internal factory. The bias was away from hype and more towards practical data-driven improvement. Tony Hornby, ex-sales manager who was appointed as the first Quality development manager, observed it thus: 'You will not see a "Quality starts here" mat; we don't spread the word Quality about the place and our long-term goal is to integrate it into the business.'

Nevertheless, Quality was very much the driver of change in the organisation. L&G followed a classic four-phase implementation, with a comprehensive survey up-front to find the base to build on. Notwithstanding the very high reputation which L&G held with policy holders and agents, plenty of Quality gaps in the service were unearthed. Waste in the system, as detected through a CoQ and key process analysis, was much higher than management had expected. All the data, which had been fed back to the many managers, agents and staff who had contributed, was pulled together and used by the Board at a workshop to commit to the Quality implementation plan. The focus had now moved to management and the leadership of the business. By now, the original managing director had left, leaving John Craddock to take up the strategic reins and lead the Quality process. As we saw in Chapter 4 on leadership, John became converted to Quality and became a champion for the changes needed.

He and his colleagues devised a new vision, articulated as the L&G mission and values, and allowed these statements to be debated and tested long before they were made public.

The primary vehicle for introducing people to the new mission and values was the Quality training process. This had been in preparation for many months in advance to be ready for the roll-out of planned involvement which followed the board workshop. Everyone was to undertake the Quality training: not merely a logistical exercise in a large organisation but a cultural one. Traditionally all training at L&G was product training; this was more about attitudes and behaviours. Peter McGinn, who managed the training process, recalls the tremendous effect of the training, which absorbed some 10,000 training days in the first year. In particular he notes the remarkable impact on sceptics – winning over the managing director amongst many!

A key discipline was established early on: every manager and supervisor was expected to complete an improvement project on return from training. Each project had to conform with certain conditions: it had to lead to reduced waste or an improved work process (through simplification or compression of cycle time) or increased customer satisfaction – and be capable of successful completion in six months. The Board attended training on an individual basis, mixing with managers of other levels and committing to personal projects too. The project activity gave momentum to the Quality process and the improvement energy expanded quickly. Many projects would seem quite ordinary, almost mundane in description – but this view belied the rigour with which they had been assessed. For instance, one project was aimed at reducing the amount of misdirected internal mail – a seemingly trivial objective, until it was calculated to waste £100,000 a year. The project team quickly achieved £20,000 worth of savings. Within six months of management training, some 380 projects had started up, with little overlap or confusion because of the discipline applied to the project selection and the clear priority areas highlighted by the survey.

Meanwhile John Craddock and his Quality Council (the Board plus the Quality development manager) were taking action to ensure that the energy did not fade. They established key monitors, covering measurements like response times for customer contacts, rework levels, accuracy of information and grouped them into two themes – the 'voice of the customer' and the 'voice of the process'. Under the voice of the customer, regular customer surveys were established. Any responses in the *poor* category were followed up by a call directly to the respondent, in order to unearth any underlying problem. A complaints monitoring system was also set up, with the computerised CARE (complaints, advice and remedy) system used to identify improvement opportunities from complaints. Robin Phipps talks about *increasing* complaints to maximise this opportunity. On the voice of the process, management looked into cross-functional activity using team purpose analysis (TPA) to identify gaps and overlaps in internal supply chains. The big business processes were carefully analysed and cross-functional projects targeted for greatest impact. One typical project was aimed at more effective new business administration, significantly reducing complaints and allowing 50 people to be redeployed to more productive work.

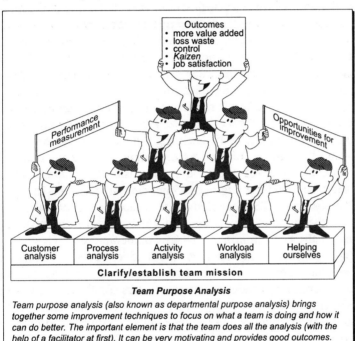

Team Purpose Analysis

Team purpose analysis (also known as departmental purpose analysis) brings together some improvement techniques to focus on what a team is doing and how it can do better. The important element is that the team does all the analysis (with the help of a facilitator at first). It can be very motivating and provides good outcomes.

The Quality Council also set out to make Quality both serious and fun, obtaining the optimum energy this way. Much work was done on changing management behaviours to support and encourage Quality. Recognition systems were introduced, using a variety of ways of showing management's interest and gratitude for good work and improvement effort. One such was an internal competition to improve the standard of letters (a survey had revealed wide inconsistency); prizes included cash donations to charity or a meal with the customer service director, quickly dubbed 'talking turkey with Robin'! As management began their improvement activities and the new environment was beginning to take hold, the training was rolled out to non-management. This was delivered by managers – 'local, credible people' according to training manager, Peter McGinn. As well as the opportunity to become involved in an improvement project, people coming out of training were introduced to the OFI (Opportunity For Improvement) system. The target is one OFI per person per year and, within a few months, some 2,897 had been submitted from an enthusiastic workforce. Of these, 2,319 or 80 per cent had been implemented, an important statistic not only for the improvement activity but also for sustaining a high energy level.

At their first formal review after a year, John Craddock and his Board were rather astonished at the progress they had made. All 4,000 staff had been trained and many were already involved in some kind of improvement activity. The attitude was tangibly more positive, despite a continued difficult trading period. Project activity continued to grow in the second year, reaching over 800 after about eighteen months. This was worth over a £1m per year in cost savings. But the bigger benefit was in the marketplace. By now, customer surveys were being used in a precise way, focusing on the payments process, for example. The survey results were showing a marked shift in the perception of policyholders, the ultimate customers, with many of the service parameters showing over 95 per cent of customers rating very good/fairly good. This enabled L&G to go for their Quality edge. After much testing to ensure they could live up to their promise, L&G published their 'Commitment to Customer Service'. This sets out standards of performance for those areas of service which L&G know the customer is interested in and says what L&G will achieve. The acclaim from independent financial advisers for this move has reinforced the confidence of the improvement teams inside L&G. The infectious enthusiasm which has become apparent at head office and the processing centres is keeping the Quality energy high. John Craddock and his management team are now in a position to exploit this to competitive advantage in a marketplace which is increasingly seeking out Quality.

Colworth Laboratory

Unilever

Unilever has two huge laboratories in the UK, one at Port Sunlight and one at Colworth in Bedfordshire, both serving Unilever businesses worldwide. Each laboratory has enthusiastically embraced

Total Quality, but independently and not without struggle. Colworth was the first. The idea of a Quality process had been talked about for years at Colworth – and that in itself was one of the problems, plenty of talk but little action, or so it was perceived by people outside. Dr Tom Little was a Colworth scientist who had left the laboratory for a variety of technical roles in Unilever companies, culminating in technical director at Birds Eye Walls. At Birds Eye, Tom oversaw a production revolution in the 1980s as automatic processing brought the need for plants and staff down exponentially. The inevitable rationalisation was painful but smooth, with operators adopting a new 'work style', itself a minor revolution. So when he was appointed back to Colworth, Tom had no hesitation in stating immediately that the laboratory would go through a Quality process.

The phase one survey was revealing. The customers, who were exclusively Unilever companies, had a view of 'Colworth Man' which was not flattering. No one questioned the standard of science, which was fully accepted as world-class, but few were content with the service. At the extreme, Colworth Man was seen as insular, detached, impossible to communicate with and uninterested in business. Inside, inter-section rivalry inhibited cooperation and staff dissatisfaction was high, leading to pockets of militancy. Underlying the discontent was an unanswered question of Colworth's future: what role does the laboratory have in the evolving Unilever structure?

Tom's view was unequivocal. Colworth had to make its own future by becoming a better supplier. The Quality process was central to this. After digesting, with much discomfort, the findings of the phase one survey, the management committee sat down to the phase two task of committing to an improvement process. Two breakthroughs in thinking emerged from the dynamics of the workshop: the scientific process itself could be pinned down and improved; and the functional structure of the laboratory was cutting across key delivery processes to customers. The implementation process was thus designed to be cross-laboratory and built around the scientists themselves.

Scientists are by training, if not by nature, sceptical and questioning and can be dismissive of anything that cannot be rationally defined. Thus Colworth Man was not enthused about Total Quality. This huge psychological barrier was broken by gentle involvement. Quality was not talked about much; instead improving the laboratory in the areas that mattered to people was. The implementation programme became 'Excel', which fitted well with scientists' motivation. The training content was heavily biased towards researchers' needs, with the management committee piloting it to ensure that it was scientist-friendly. Tom briefed everybody in the laboratory about Excel in a series of informal presentations. Gradually people began to feel that perhaps this might not inhibit their science too much and went in for training. Everybody in the laboratory from professors to lab assistants went through exactly the same training. The trainers were selected from various levels in the laboratory and trained as facilitators. The training was a resounding success with virtually every individual saying that it was of use to them. Improvement projects were set up, some driven across the laboratory, others left to local sections to start up and manage. The whole phase three programme of communications, training and start-up action was completed for 1,100 researchers in about six months.

Twelve months after starting, a formal review was carried out. The feeling was positive. People liked the process, they felt Colworth was doing something together at last, it had been managed well and the whole effect was exciting. Hundreds of improvement projects were up and running and most of the laboratory was actively involved. Most of the vociferous early critics had become quietly supportive or active missionaries. But there were some concerns. The customer hadn't noticed much change, but to some extent that was expected at this stage. A bigger issue was that the projects had tended to gravitate around peripheral issues and not dig into the core science as was hoped.

A new plan was put together for another year of improvement, building on the base achieved. Customer involvement became a priority. Process improvement projects were set up working on and around the grey interface between Colworth and the client. Managers and engineers from the client companies joined the project teams and even the training in process management, which was offered throughout the laboratory. Training remained at an intensive level, with QFD, project management and benchmarking being injected into the laboratory. In fact, training became such a feature of the improvement culture that a new learning centre was set up to accommodate it and make it accessible to all. In parallel, a more rigorous reporting mechanism was established and the new practice was steered strongly towards the core business – the output of usable scientific information.

At the time of the second review a year later, customer perceptions were markedly different. In the words of one major customer, Guy Walker, chairman of Van den Berghs, 'Colworth is a completely different place.' Visitors remarked that the laboratory was markedly more customer-oriented, as well as being much more focused and effective in their contributions to their customers. One old Colworth hand, Dr Graham Lawson, technical director of Borax, revisited Colworth after an absence of six years. Graham found his old training ground to be virtually unrecognisable. In particular, he was struck by the prevalence of measurement. In his day, measurement was confined to experiments; now it seemed every significant activity was measured and displayed.

Such is the change in a period of three years, that many other research laboratories have been to visit Colworth to see how they have achieved it when their own Quality processes have had much less impact over a longer period. The biggest change is undoubtedly in the attitude of staff. New Colworth Man is much more attuned to clients' needs and to clients in general – in other words, they acknowledge their primary service role. There is also demonstrably a much more positive atmosphere with good team spirit. Most of all, the output is enhanced. Customers are receiving more precise, directly usable injections into their businesses enabling them to gain competitive advantage, either as new products, such as Elizabeth Arden time capsules, or Sky chocolate ice-cream bars, or process improvements enabling some factories to achieve over 90 per cent overall yields despite frequent changeovers.

The Co-operative Bank

Banking is not an industry in which change is accepted as a way of life; indeed much of the regulations and traditions of banking favour those who adopt a status quo approach. So the shocks of recession, bad debts, unpopularity with consumers, new competition from insurance companies, building societies and an opening Europe have traumatised some senior bankers. Terry Thomas at the Co-operative Bank saw it as an opportunity. Taking over as managing director in 1989, Terry was faced with threat on all sides. The Co-operative Bank could never become a major clearing bank but it was nevertheless competing head to head with them. On the other hand, with 5,000 staff spread across the country, it did not have the flexibility of a regional building society or insurance company. We have seen earlier in Chapter 2 how Terry has turned this problem around by seeking out the niches and becoming excellent in servicing them. The Total Quality process played a vital role in this. Terry took the Bank through the formal four phase process to create an internal Quality environment which allows the Bank to respond quickly and surely to market opportunities.

The phase one survey was predictable in many ways: the Bank was perceived as very conservative internally, with plenty of wasteful inspection activity and robust but cumbersome processes. Unlike other banks at the time, customers were quite satisfied with the personal and friendly service but occasionally driven to distraction when things went wrong and it took forever to sort them out. Overall a fairly bland picture: not bad, not outstanding. This in itself gave a pointer to future direction: how could the Bank develop a sharper image? Part of the answer lay right back in the roots of the Bank as part of the unique Co-operative movement. Although at that time the Co-operative movement had an image of being in decline and out of its time (much less so today with many changes in the huge retail side), the original 'Principles of Co-operation' laid down in 1844 held much relevance and merit in providing value today. Terry started a process of pinning down values which were consistent with the original beliefs and fitted where the Bank wanted to be today. The resulting mission statement proved to be core to the Quality process as it later rolled out across the Bank.

Despite this, the early phases of Total Quality implementation seemed to be slow and difficult. A group of managers had been selected from around the group and trained as facilitators. They were raring to go, but were being stonewalled by their senior line managers. After building it to a head, the conflicts came out at a senior management forum of about 25 people. The problem was largely one of mixed and complex demands on senior managers who were driving key projects for the new design of the Bank and they saw Total Quality (and the mission statement) as an additional drain on their time and resources. At that stage, they did not perceive Quality as the vehicle for delivering the change nor did they see that the major projects could come under the Quality umbrella to mutual benefit. The breakthrough came when the senior management turned the planned Quality roll-out on its head: going from head office outwards instead of branch (and customer) inwards. The logic was sound (the big projects were all about changing the back-office areas, not the customer-contact points) but more importantly the senior management group now owned the implementation programme. It was no longer the consultant's, the facilitator's or Terry Thomas' plan...it was *theirs*.

By 1991, all 5,000 staff had been trained. As manager Chris Smith says: 'The training was the jewel in our TQM crown.'[23] Managers received five days of workshop training; non-managers two days. The bulk of the training was led by managers themselves – 'giving us a wealth of skilled trainers for future developments which we have used many times', according to Chris. Training and subsequent improvement action was structured into waves, which basically progressed along the key business processes, bringing people into the programme in a logical and meaningful way. Process improvement charting using simple SPC control charts is a popular outcome of the training, as are local service level agreements.

Overall, The Co-operative Bank has achieved multiple benefits from implementing the Quality process. Hard results are quantified as reduced customer turnover, fewer 'dormant' accounts, lower cost of account per person, perceived customer service improvement by 20 per cent and savings made by small improvement teams totalling £1 million a year. During the period, staff levels have been reduced by 20 per cent and new flexible working methods have been introduced, leading to higher productivity. Softer measures of success which are acknowledged by people inside and outside of the Bank include a more open style of management, a common language throughout the group, allowing faster resolution of problems, better teamwork between departments and a strong feeling of confidence. Above all, though, is what the Bank has been able to do with it. As well as being first to market with a number of initiatives as reported earlier (Chapter 2), The Co-operative Bank has achieved a major coup by being the first bank to publish ethical principles. This stance, which has received much publicity and support in an environmentally-conscious population, gives the Bank a unique platform, linking its cooperative roots to modern issues. In 1992 more than 50 per cent of new accounts mentioned the attractiveness of this position.

Perkins Engines Group

Perkins Engines was transformed in two years from a good engineering company to a flexible and responsive service provider under the leadership of Tony Gilroy. The installation of the Total Quality process was described in Chapter 2 as an illustration of the crucial need to manage the improvement energy in the business. Tony adhered to the four-phase disciplined approach to implementation despite pressure from the parent company for shorter-term gains. Tony's resolute support for a long-term change, despite the immediate and severe effects of worldwide recession in the company's markets, was a key determinant of later success. This is not to say that Perkins' managers loftily ignored the world around them; they made major adjustments to market conditions, but never allowed this to divert them from the task of changing the company for the future.

Two years after starting with a comprehensive survey, Perkins went through their phase-four review. Results were impressive in all four business units: much faster and precise deliveries to customers, better relationships with customers, fewer defects and errors, substantial cost savings, higher morale across the workforce, coherent motivated management teams. By far the most significant achievement though was universally felt to be the 'hearts and minds buy-in' from people in a previously traditional and hierarchical engineering culture. Key to this change was the transition in management attitudes ('recognising that people had a contribution to make') and behaviours ('from controller to coach').

But what to do next to keep the momentum and enthusiasm going? Each business unit held a re-commitment workshop. This had similarities to the ones held in phase two to design the implementation programme and commit to it, but with a big difference. This time the management teams were not looking back at their problems and working out an improvement process to address them; these workshops addressed how they would become world-class. Preparation for the workshops included detailed research on what were the world-class standards for their precise market needs and how other companies had achieved them. During each workshop this research was used to pin down three overriding goals by which the business would obtain further distinction in the marketplace, measured against the world-class standards.

Once the goals were in place, the management team then focused on the processes which affected them, drawing up a matrix of goals against processes. Once clarified and agreed, this matrix was then used by management to construct a radical improvement process over and above current improvements. This is what Perkins' teams are now doing, re-engineering the targeted processes to have direct effect on the set goals. Each business unit is also well aware of the need to keep the improvement energy flowing, especially after the first big wave of workshops and training has passed. In fact, training continues at a high rate to fill the Quality gaps which are still being unearthed at both management and workforce level. Some 73 facilitators support this training and the local improvement effort, spending around 40 per cent of their time this way (Perkins management originally thought they would have dispensed with the need for facilitators by now, but, like others, they have found the need increases as more improvement activity is unleashed). Improvement teams continue to expand and embrace more members, with teams on alternate shifts organising themselves to work together to improve their mutual processes. A typical example of the empowerment being achieved every day is the machine operator in a team which won a Michelin award for shop floor involvement: 'I've operated this machine for ten years but I had not realised I could improve the process until I went on the TQ training.' With an internal environment prepared and equipped for change in this way, and customers and suppliers well in tune, Perkins has every intention of extracting even greater business benefits from Quality than have been obtained so far.

Unilever New Zealand

Unilever

Ron Walledge was on his last Unilever 'posting' when he took over as chairman of Unilever New Zealand after previous positions around the world. One might have expected his last three years before retirement, in the pleasant environs of Wellington and Auckland, to be relatively uncontroversial. Not a bit of it. Ron found his participation on one of the Personal Products study tours to the best US companies to be highly stimulating and a good opportunity to reflect on all he had learned in 40 years in industry. With his new company, he had the chance to put it all into practice. On the video of the tour, Ron sums up his viewpoint: 'I now know what Total Quality is all about; I now need to go home and do it.' He did just that.

Unilever New Zealand was not an homogeneous company in 1989 – it had been put together by recent acquisitions to cover the broad range of Unilever services in foods, detergents and personal products, but from half a dozen distinct companies. These parts had their own company cultures, complicated further by having two main centres 600 km apart. Three years later, despite the worst recession in New Zealand's history, the business was very strong and Total Quality well established. Ron's view of the role of Quality is that it united the independent businesses, replacing 'internecine sniping' with a common language and common goals. It put NZ$3 million on the bottom line (an additional 15 per cent per year) through the combination of effective strategic management coupled with the enabling effect of Quality and the direct gains from the improvement projects. And, very significantly for the future, it has engaged the minds of the Pacific Islanders who make up 90 per cent of the workforce. Before, the Islander culture was very much the opposite of being company-oriented, with the company perceived as a necessary place to go to earn a living. Now, many Islanders are working enthusiastically within improvement teams and hundreds of OFI ideas are being submitted.

Ron took the company through the classic four phases, starting in early 1990 with a full survey and building up to a top team workshop which thrashed out the design of the Quality process and the significant changes that would be required. Before this critical event, Ron took his senior management away into the New Zealand hills to learn about Total Quality and its implications. Concentrating on creating the managerial environment first, a launch seminar was held for all managers after the workshop, followed by Quality training. All 205 managers went through four days of practical workshops, supported by facilitators drawn from line management, who had been extensively trained for this role. As they came out of training, managers either set up, or joined, a Quality improvement team. By the end of 1990, most managers felt they were sufficiently comfortable with the Quality process to involve their staff. So 1991 started with a coordinated programme to bring 700 more people into the process through training (50 courses held in six locations) and communications. The communications explained the new mission statement and the roll-out of the Quality process. Again staff were invited to join an improvement team as they came out of training and, simultaneously with the training programme, an OFI system was established. Thus everyone who wanted to could find a relatively easy way to participate.

By the end of 1991, 150 teams were running, involving 46 per cent of the workforce. Some 20 teams had already completed their projects, posting benefits calculated at $650,000; 451 OFIs had been submitted, of which 235 had been implemented to benefits worth $200,000. All of this was well publicised in a monthly highly professional staff journal concentrating on Quality news and reinforced with a new recognition system. This has no additional financial reward but empowers project sponsors and the lead teams (who monitor and encourage teams in their location) to fund a wide variety of spontaneous and planned recognition activities.

Everyone was pleased to have this obvious short-term success from the Quality implementation in 1991, but there was a lot more going on behind the scenes. New procedures were being put in place at managerial level to ensure that standards were irreversibly raised. Drawing on real data from the Quality survey, special task forces built a new customer listening system (intelligence gathering and feedback system from retailers and non-retailers), a staff listening system (regular survey plus a listening framework), a supplier management process and an array of new metrics. The 'business performance measurement pack' is a comprehensive document for all managers, covering metrics and supporting information which includes financial health, consumer satisfaction, trade satisfaction, operational efficiency, people health, Total Quality health and opportunities/threats.

Not content with all this, Quality management behaviour was taken head-on through a workshop which identified and confronted constructive and non-constructive behaviours and then captured them in a 'standards for a public role model manager'. The appraisal system was realigned to suit, with subordinate input against the role model standards. These key infrastructure improvements (plus many more such as customer/supplier agreements and a computerised project/OFI tracking system) were not created in reactive mode but carefully planned and accomplished in a disciplined and purposeful way.

At the end of 1991, Ron felt that the managerial environment was much more cohesive and that the Quality process was well installed. He was ready for his next big step, which was to tackle the major business processes. The supply chain was the most crucial and this was systematically mapped and analysed; projects were set up to meet the stretching goals set with the aid of benchmarks from other businesses. One of many examples of improvement achieved relatively quickly with this focus was the reduction in credit notes to the trade from 100 per month to 10 and still shrinking. This represents big savings but even bigger gains, through removing potential irritations with customers. Early in 1992, Ron commissioned a Quality Maturity Review to reveal the strengths and weaknesses of the Quality implementation and keep the energy high. Armed with this a new year of improvement targets were set and another wave of improvement began.

Overall, Unilever New Zealand spent around two years installing Quality and were achieving quantified gains from around the 12-month mark which made the implementation process self-financing thereafter. Subsequent gains have been running at around six to one. The current expenditure on the Quality process is low but the return is still increasing. Quantification aside, those involved are convinced that the biggest gain by far is on the people side, both management and the whole workforce. The view of the consultant team who were involved throughout was that the unwavering commitment of the board had made it a smooth transition. Ron Walledge had no doubts about where he was heading and the results confirmed his confidence.

The payback

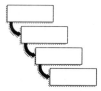 The above examples have been selected because they represent diverse activities from service and manufacturing. All achieved a strong shift in behaviour and practice within two to three years by applying their own version of a core implementation discipline. Many others have similarly benefited; other examples cover the whole spectrum of business, such as Avon Rubber, Philippine Refining Company, AMP Insurance Group, Lever Chile, BSS (UK), South West Electricity, Clerical Medical Insurance Society, WRc (a research laboratory in the UK), CSA (a computer services company in Australia), Atlas Copco Mining (USA) and the company featured in Chapter 1, L&K: Rexona.

All of these companies and the five illustrated above invested in a data collection and preparation phase before taking improvement action. Time spent this way ranged from three months to a year; all insist that this is an essential prerequisite to later results. Phase two, management commitment and focus, was typically quick, three to five months, because of this preparation, and phase three, intensive action, was similarly fast. Most of these companies trained all their managers in the first year and the whole company within two years, some within one. All had projects up and running immediately after the management commitment phase, mostly management-led projects, some focused on early wins and some focused on longer-term needs. These projects alone generated good payback for the companies – many exceeding £1 million a year for a one-off investment of between a quarter and a half of that. Project payback, i.e. return from the project over spend on the project, averages between 5:1 and over 10:1. The biggest impact, though, has been in the way these companies now do business. The way they lead their people; the way their people behave; the way they respond to their customers; their passion for improvement; the buzz around the place...this is the revolutionary change which these 'ordinary' companies have achieved. None would say they could have done it without Quality and none would say they would have got so far without a disciplined managed implementation process.

Complex applications

Although the principles of implementation are similar, multi-site, multi-country companies present additional challenges. Conversely, the scope is usually enormous because the most ineffective part of a large corporation is often the inter-unit activity, especially where it has been assembled through acquisition. Some corporations, whilst acknowledging the potential benefits, find the prospect of a whole company-wide improvement process to be daunting to the level of paralysis. Most who do attempt it approach it sub-optimally, leaving units to run with their own separate Quality processes. This is good for local ownership but weak when it comes to knitting together the benefits of programmes which can often be virtually incompatible. The considerable benefits of a common improvement (or management) language for a large corporation, with easy transfer of techniques and applications, are often lost to such companies at this point. Indeed, it may well be counter to the corporation's business direction to reinforce local autonomy, as more regional or global strategies are sought.

Others choose to ignore the complexity for a while and concentrate on the home country first, or on one product group. When this application is running well, the approach, together with all the developed technology, is rolled out around the world or across the other groups. Unfortunately, many find the rolling-out unexpectedly rough, with the recipients proving rather ungrateful. By the time everything is smoothed out, many years may have passed, with not too much to show for the energy and momentum expended.

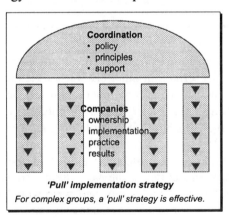

'Pull' implementation strategy

For complex groups, a 'pull' strategy is effective.

The way through these problems for major corporations is really as for single business units: the approach should start with planning and with research, if the organisation is complex there will simply need to be more of it. Unilever's Personal Products invested six months in preparing the ground for their complex application and no one, at any time since, has felt this time was wasteful. For many organisations, the optimal implementation design may well be found in exactly the same way as for a single business unit: focus on both the forward strategy (the business aims) and the current reality. Certainly, this was the case for Personal Products. Whilst it was clear that future distinction would be in international brands and pan-regional supply chains, the current reality was strong country operations, with powerful and talented chairmen leading them. The implementation strategy therefore had a long-term goal of leading towards major process improvement in brand development and product supply across the current company boundaries but, crucially, started with the short-term objective of turning the local company chairmen into Quality leaders.

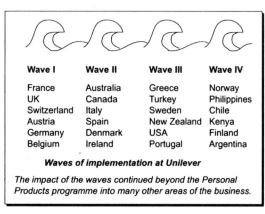

Wave I	Wave II	Wave III	Wave IV
France	Australia	Greece	Norway
UK	Canada	Turkey	Philippines
Switzerland	Italy	Sweden	Chile
Austria	Spain	New Zealand	Kenya
Germany	Denmark	USA	Finland
Belgium	Ireland	Portugal	Argentina

Waves of implementation at Unilever

The impact of the waves continued beyond the Personal Products programme into many other areas of the business.

This was achieved effectively with a combination of workshops and study tours (described in other chapters) which made the case for Quality and related it to the chairmen's business needs. The implementation strategy then concentrated on encouraging ownership at company chairman level, whilst maintaining consistency across and between them. It was made clear that it was up to each chairman whether he wanted to pursue a Quality process or not but that if he did it should be done properly. At the same time, a major development effort was made to create collectively the support materials and mechanisms a chairman would need (training materials, survey methodology, etc.) and to make these readily available for when he would need them. The result was that most of the Personal Products companies opted to use the centrally produced material and the process designed for them. This has subsequently provided the common language and ease of transfer of experience sought, without any need to force an approach on anyone. Waves of implementation were formed to encourage this exchange, which continues today across other Unilever groups around the world.

Unilever Personal Products are now moving on to advanced Quality applications with the advantage of a sound common base. It has taken three years to achieve this, with the companies providing direct bottom-line return along the way. The corporate benefits of a managerial philosophy which links sixty plus companies around the world, common stretch goals, accelerated transfer of best practice, breakdown of barriers and not-invented-here...are now available to exploit for competitive advantage. Tony Burgmans is determined to do just that. Current initiatives focus hard on substantial improvements to the whole supply chain from point of sale back to raw material supplier. Organisational barriers are not acknowledged in this chain. Similarly, innovation centres are being established to pump more new ideas into the system. The location of these centres is where the best talent is; organisational ownership is no longer a driving issue.

Complex businesses like Unilever Personal Products have more to gain from a Quality process than single units. Through Quality, they can add an ingredient often missing on this scale: a managerial philosophy. Quality can give a unique expression to large groups. The managerial philosophy, the language, the style, the practice can be recognised wherever in the world the company operates. Large businesses like Ciba and Unilever know that this global consistency can mean competitive advantage. Ciba Geigy has steadily created a corporate Quality philosophy under president, Heini Lippuner. Before the process started in the Dyestuffs Division with Heini, who then led that part of the group, group synergy was limited. Indeed, there was a discernible line between the old Ciba and Geigy even though they had merged ten years earlier. The Quality process has helped sweep this away and provided many other benefits too. Today, the group is known just as Ciba – unthinkable a few years ago.

Success or failure?

When it comes down to it, what makes the difference between fighting a tough battle but coming through with satisfying results and fighting a tough battle with nothing to show at the end of it? The main points have been made already but are worthy of summary again here. The first and foremost factor is leadership. Without a leader who is prepared to pick up the Quality mantle and hold on to it, the Quality revolution won't even manage a few sparks. Equally, the leader who showers the organisation with enthusiasm needs the skills and experience to convert other leaders to make the revolution ignite. Surveys usually put this factor down to management commitment, but leadership provides commitment, not necessarily the other way round. A related issue is perceived ownership, i.e. does the CEO and the board own the Quality process or does the quality director or the manufacturing director? If there is any doubt whatsoever, this weakens commitment.

The second crucial factor is one that does not show up explicitly in surveys but is there under the surface. That is sensitivity to culture. In other words, if the Quality process builds on and out from the current culture, then it has a chance of building up a strong movement. If it is too counter-culture, then the culture simply rejects it. Obvious examples of insensitivity to organisational culture are training packages not tailored for local relevance, such as using terminology and examples which jar, or attempts to move directly from an autocratic regime to empowered teams without creating a supporting environment.

A third general determinant of success is what this chapter is mostly about: planning, and the resource allocation to do it. Few companies see this till afterwards, yet many seriously underestimate, underplan and underresource their Quality implementation. A small number, usually large corporations, overplan and overstaff their Quality process and squeeze the energy out of it. But most companies remain a long way from overdoing it.

The fourth major factor is again hard to distil from surveys. It is discipline. Many leaders shy away from discipline in the Quality process, sensing conflict with the objectives of empowerment and removing bureaucracy. There is no conflict if sensibly applied; discipline enhances the realisation of these aims by providing guidelines to behaviour during the flux of change. Discipline is needed in the scheduling of events and activities; in the practice of improvement; in the measurement and reporting of progress. Discipline, coupled with planning and leadership, delivers results.

Yet more results

Companies throughout Europe are achieving the scale of results usually associated with Japan or the USA. Today, these results are being achieved much more quickly. Here are some examples of multiple improvement achieved in less than five years.

Philips, Eindhoven
Service call rate	11%	➡ 3.4%
Outgoing problems	4%	➡ 0.3%
Fall-off rate	45%	➡ 11%
Product defect rates	2,000ppm	➡ 20ppm

Italtel, Milan
Materials order process time	25 days	➡ 2 days
Product development process time	54 weeks	➡ 16 weeks
Component authorisation process time	19 week	➡ 3 weeks
Wrong invoices	13%	➡ 8%
Incorrectly processed invoices	32%	➡ 7%
Missing orders	57%	➡ 15%
Credit notes	7%	➡ 3%
Totalling period for personnel time recording	30 days	➡ 1 day

Girobank, Liverpool
Reconciliation costs to process settlements	£3m	➡ £1.8m
Reconciliation time	28	➡ 13
Reconciliation income up	£1m per annum	
Error rates at counters	26.3 per 1,000	➡ 5.1 per 1,000
Productivity increase	42%	
WIP time	7.75 hours	➡ 1.25 hours

Renault Parts
Fill rate	91.3%	➡ 98.0%
Deliveries	72 hours	➡ next day
Stock order lead times	22 day	➡ 7 days
Stock rotation	3.81x	➡ 4.53x
Distribution costs/turnover	13.7%	➡ 7.4%

ABB, Västeras
On-time delivery increased	22%	➡ 95%
Delivery times reduced	15 days	➡ 5 days
Absentee levels	19.8%	➡ 5%
Staff turnover reduced	39%	➡ 5%
Productivity increase	25%	
Average cycle times reduced	20%	
Inventory reduction	35%	

Planning the return

When do the benefits come through? It all depends on the Quality of the improvement process. With a sound implementation plan, high-standard events, good planning and determination, benefits will accrue from early on in the process. In the first 12 months of his Quality process, Mike Nash at L&K: Rexona had greater internal efficiency and a more cohesive management team working towards common goals. Customer irritation points such as out-of-stocks were significantly reduced. Additionally, they had saved A$ 2 million from improvement projects. This was no accident or mere good fortune. All the benefits were planned.

The savings were needed to fund the continued investment in the process and they had been targeted and planned for, along with the customer value improvements. Some companies may not wish to focus hard on an early return via cost savings, but they can be the first outcome of disciplined improvement, as teams remove the waste that has accumulated over the years. Removing local waste is a safe way for people to practise improvement and to learn to make it a way of life. Once started, waste reduction, and consequential savings, can be expected on a continuous basis, especially if stimulated by a company-wide goal and reinforced with local measurement. Indeed, a good Quality process will generate a steadily increasing volume of savings as more people are brought into the process. In large organisations, it can take three years to surround everyone with the kind of environment which encourages local improvement activity.

However, local improvements do not have the big impact which many companies need, not only to raise their performance but to raise the energy level too. Strategic process improvements and big projects do this. Effective part-time project teams will be able to implement permanent improvements after three to six months of investigation and results from process improvement will usually start to flow after around six months. But effective process work rarely starts until senior management have thrashed out the vision and the goals for the company and until management as a whole has been trained in Quality. So the big benefits, the ones that the customer would notice, are unlikely to occur before 12 or 18 months have passed. These are the ones that cut the cycle times and provide the distinctive service that our customers will value.

Not all the benefits we seek are conventionally quantifiable. Behaviour is one. We want significant changes in managerial behaviour first, followed by shifts in workforce behaviour as a whole. Management should be behaving differently by the end of the first year, or we run the risk of going too slow. By 12 months, Quality management behaviour should be observable, albeit not yet consistently across the company. Managers should be well into establishing Quality as the priority, demonstrating this by their decisions, biasing their interactions with people to talking about customers and standards and explaining what needs to be done. They should be setting their Quality objectives and the measures to go with them. They should be involved in project teams, as sponsors, leaders and members. All of these actions are observable. So is their use of their own time – more with customers, more on working with their teams, less on paper shuffling, less on politics. They may be growing confident in showing the Quality example – the Quality way – and beginning to coach and empower. The shift in managerial behaviour can be plotted against checklists showing Quality role model behaviour. Additionally, the workforce can be asked; they will certainly know if there has been any change.

What about workforce behaviour in general: people in the office, in the field and in operations. There is unlikely to be much shift in their general behaviour until the managerial environment has changed. However, this can and will change faster in some parts of the organisation than others, as some managers enthusiastically embrace the new way of managing. Response from the enthusiastic manager's team will follow quite quickly, with attitudinal and behavioural changes becoming evident. This workforce transition begins to show after about 18 months but can take years to spread across a large business. This is not through workforce reluctance; it just takes time for the environment to change. The wise leader learns to cultivate another attribute through this – patience. If everything is in place and the right things are being done to stimulate and reinforce change, then the transition will come through.

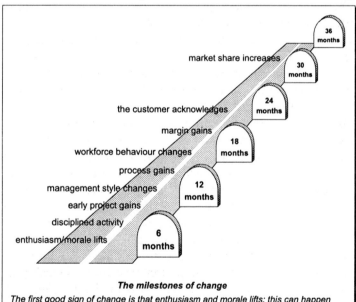

The milestones of change

The first good sign of change is that enthusiasm and morale lifts; this can happen very quickly with a good process, as disciplined activity gets underway. Early results from waste removal can be achieved from six months on, but management style is unlikely to become consistent before twelve months. Workforce behavioural change will follow management and major process gains can flow from twelve to eighteen months. Margin gains through more effective processes may be seen soon afterwards but the customer is unlikely to be impressed until progress is proven and, the big test, earned market share may not come through for three years or more. All of these milestones are fast track; most companies do not achieve them.

Finally the most telling factor of all: has the customer noticed? Disappointingly for most Quality leaders, the customer takes a long time to acknowledge any change. First of all, it really is very hard to make a new impact on the customer and to make it stick. It takes all the energy, discipline and planning we've talked about to do this and it rarely drops out easily. We may be making tremendous improvements internally but stringing it together to make that distinctive mark on the customer seems to take years rather than months. And then, the customer is not likely to jump up and down saying how great we are. He is going to bide his time to see whether it lasts and whether this is really a permanent change that will make for better services in the long term. So impact on market share from a Quality transformation is not likely to be realised for many years.

This longer-term return from a Quality process is frustrating for many leaders. It is even more so for the 'bankers': the head offices, holding companies and external institutions who find it difficult to focus on longer-term improvement. The Quality leader should not waver for a moment. It may be taking time to attract more customers but without an overall improvement process today, shrinkage of the customer base tomorrow is pretty well guaranteed. Survival is a real issue for any size of organisation, as those like Xerox and Kodak, and now IBM, will testify. *Earning* market share through being a better supplier is the only solution.

However, the Quality leader who focuses only on the long-term goal is also making a mistake. Short-term benefits are a vital part of the improvement process and, skilfully managed, can assuage the demands of external bodies. For growth is only one of the two big improvement focuses; the other is margin and this can be addressed more directly and much earlier than market share. A well-planned and managed Quality process can deliver continuous return from six months onwards, steadily growing as waste is removed and improvement disciplines take hold. More value added and less waste in the internal processes starts to make the place feel better. Things get done more quickly, more easily, with less fuss. More is possible; enthusiasm rises; energy builds. The shared feelings of pride and prosperity spread through the organisation. It is at this point that others notice – suppliers, agents, friends of the staff, the local community, the industry. The place is different, transformed. This is the end result of a Quality revolution. For most, it will take at least five years...and then it is just the beginning of another era. But the rewards, short-term and long-term, can be great. These results, together with the challenge of always trying to do better, keep Quality leaders pressing on year after year. In the words of Don Davies at Allen-Bradley: 'You hear about Quality being free; I tell you, it's a lot better than free!'

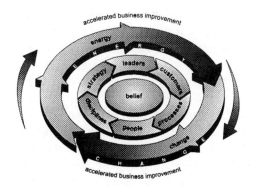

SUMMARY

Is your Quality process going to pay you back?

1. **Have you planned for a return?** *Think through your strategy again and set yourself some targets consistent with your long-term aims which you could stretch to achieve in 18 months, quantifying the potential benefits; test your implementation plans to see if they are capable of delivering these results in that time.*
2. **Are you expecting multiple results?** *Set up the metrics to monitor those key results, making sure they cover the critical areas which will make a difference and review all improvement activities against these factors.*
3. **Have you designed a comprehensive implementation process and communicated it to all those who are to be involved?** *Design the plan to deliver what the business needs and to engage all the people in the organisation in working to achieve those needs.*
4. **Is your plan based on best practice today and drawn from experience of successful change processes?** *Study the practice of the best companies and relate their successes to your organisation and situation; aim to manage change explicitly.*
5. **Have you invested enough...in terms of resource, advice, support?** *Quality will cost time, effort and money; aim for returns and set up a good level of support to achieve them, recognising that change will be harder, more complicated and slower than you thought.*
6. **Have you prepared enough?** *Think through all the elements of the implementation plan again; leave nothing to chance and have everything ready when it will be needed.*
7. **Have you thought through what you are going to stop doing in order to make space for Quality?** *You already have too much to*

344 The Quality Revolution

do, so be ruthless about cutting unimportant activities before the
additional load of a change process is felt.

8. **Are you ready to push and pull to keep people fired up?** *Improvement energy can be generated and sustained through leadership; flagging energy can be revived by timely actions from the leader.*

9. **Are you ready for the unexpected?** *The plan can only prepare you to a point, the rest is dynamic and change takes you further into the unknown; belief, clarity and determination help sustain the pace.*

10. **Can you be patient?** *Organisational change cannot be forced but can be influenced; the Quality leader tips the balance of change his way, but knows when to ride the ebbs and flows to stay in for the long term.*

11
Becoming World-Class

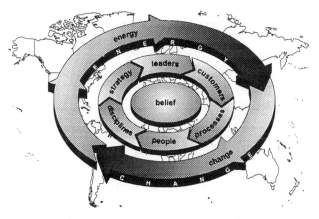

Successful revolutions deliver a new order. With Quality, a company aspires to a new order of higher performance which ultimately must be world-class in standard. World-class performance comes from world-class practice which is in turn created by world-class management. It is a rare achievement: perhaps 50 organisations worldwide earn the world-class label. But many more are using Quality in a determined campaign to join them.

'We are no longer the company we were; we are not yet the company we want to be.' David Kearns, past CEO, Xerox Corp.

'Perfect service is an unclaimed crown. Quality gives a common language to help achieve it.' Bernard Fournier, MD, Rank Xerox Ltd

Beyond Quality

Revolutionary fervour does fade. So does the uniting value of Quality which provides the inspiration. But the need for improvement and the energy behind it will always be needed, so the leader has to find ways of continuing the stimulus and excitement of improvement, year on year, decade on decade. Quality itself may no longer be the focus. Quality becomes the foundation, the base from which new initiatives are spawned. Quality, by this stage, is well embedded in the way things are done. No longer is it viewed as an act of faith but as a direct contributor to business results. People know what the Quality way is and would not think of compromising the standards established. In this scenario, the leader needs to put the focus on new initiatives which maintain the energy level. In going beyond Quality, the focus should provide new stimulation, new challenges and new targets but at the same time reinforce what has been achieved already.

It is difficult to generalise on what these initiatives for the advanced company should be: they are invariably specific to the company and its environment. But most of the world's leading companies are tending towards similar practices as they continue their relentless drive for improvement. Thus, one company may have a two-year major push on time-based competitiveness; another may introduce the concept of total productive maintenance; yet another might fashion an improvement focus around a service charter. The initiative might be unique, it might be borrowed from someone else; it might be pioneering or catching up on what others have done. That is not important. What is important is that the improvement energy built up with the Quality process is kept high and that the initiatives are chosen to continue the process of business improvement.

Dropping the Q-word

Do world-class companies still talk about Quality? Yes ... but they don't labour it. Day to day they use precise terms to describe customer needs and internal improvement opportunities and avoid using the word in the general sense. Strategically, they will apply major improvement disciplines and label them appropriately - policy deployment, business process re-engineering and so. The overall Quality process will have a lower profile and the emphasis on the Quality word is less apparent. But it would be an inaccurate observation to assume there is no longer an overall process for integrating and stimulating improvement in the organisation. Continuous change is needed at least as much in world-class organisations as elsewhere. Staying at the top is probably more demanding than getting there. All world-class companies have a process that keeps management and workforce attention on accelerated improvement. The Quality revolution continues with or without the Quality word.

Quality maturity

At what point does Quality mature in an organisation? At what stage do companies need to go beyond Quality into other concepts to keep the acceleration high? Looking at the leading practitioners, there is a very wide spectrum of experience between the 40-year experience of the early Japanese companies and those in the West who have employed a Quality process in the last decade. The Japanese companies have kept the profile on Quality very high throughout and their new initiatives still have a Quality focus. Many of them have retained the formal Quality process to hold it all together – TQC – but, in reality, this merely describes the procedures. The custodian of Quality in Japanese companies is management practice, which is highly consistent today. In the best Japanese companies, Quality and management are synonymous. The Western companies who are leading the Quality revolution have not achieved this degree of consistency (indeed some might argue against it).

As companies install Quality processes and go on to achieve and maintain accelerated improvement, they go through patterns of common experience which can be generally translated into phases of maturity. *Level zero* is when the management of the business has decided they do not need Quality. They are ignoring the movement, content with their firefighting and fixing, relying on intuition and luck. Such a blinkered, insular existence is hard to comprehend and yet does still exist. *Level one* is when a company begins to explore the field of Quality, often through the necessity to conform to standards such as ISO 9000. Outputs and inputs receive more attention. Product assurance is strengthened and suppliers controlled more. Management start to learn about Quality and talk about it. Awareness sessions are often set up. The phase is a very frustrating one because the real underlying issues are not being tackled and indeed there probably is no common understanding of how to approach them. Managers and staff who see the reality of the business day to day are very sceptical of the new emphasis on Quality. They do not believe it is for real.

Level two is when it begins to be seen as a reality. An installation process is devised and many people are trained, supported with much communication about Quality and what it will do. Cross-functional initiatives are established and champions emerge who push the process hard. At some point, the energy level pushes the feeling from sceptical to enthusiastic.

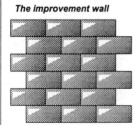

The improvement wall

Many leaders talk about hitting a brick wall at a point in their Quality implementation. Nothing seems to work as well as it did; the excitement wanes and people mutter about whether this is so good after all. The resistance to go forward can become enormous. The leader has no choice but to wind up the energy and power his way through this wall. Quite a few companies have had to relaunch or reinvent their Quality process to do this - their original approach was simply not powerful enough to overcome the blockages.

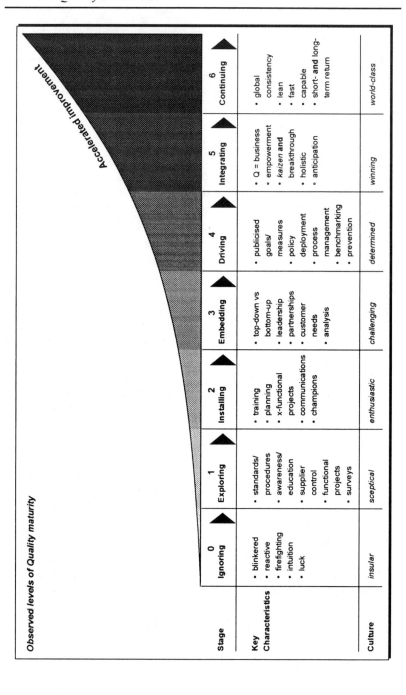

Observed levels of Quality maturity

Stage	0 Ignoring	1 Exploring	2 Installing	3 Embedding	4 Driving	5 Integrating	6 Continuing

Key Characteristics	• blinkered
	• reactive
	• firefighting
	• intuition
	• luck
		• standards/
		  procedures
		• awareness/
		  education
		• supplier
		  control
		• functional
		  projects
		• surveys
			• training
			• planning
			• x-functional
			  projects
			• communications
			• champions
				• top-down vs
				  bottom-up
				• leadership
				• partnerships
				• customer
				  needs
				• analysis
					• publicised
					  goals/
					  measures
					• policy
					  deployment
					• process
					  management
					• benchmarking
					• prevention
						• Q = business
						• empowerment
						• *kaizen and*
						  breakthrough
						• holistic
						• anticipation
							• global
							  consistency
							• lean
							• fast
							• capable
							• short- **and** long-
							  term return

Culture	*insular*	*sceptical*	*enthusiastic*	*challenging*	*determined*	*winning*	*world-class*

Accelerated Improvement

Then most companies have their hardest phase. People have enjoyed their training; they like the ideas and the practice. They want more. Where is it? Those who are well into Quality are becoming frustrated because it is harder than they thought. The projects are taking a long time and there are too many of them; they clash over resources and priorities. Others are getting fed up of the amount of effort and time that has gone into the whole thing – what about the business? This is a test for the leader and the more determined he is, the faster this stage is bridged. *Level three*, embedding the Quality process, means fighting for organisational living space and the fight is a tough one. The challenge is to see it through and achieve that state of inevitability which allows the Quality process to survive. Most often, the leader will firm up on a top-down process at this stage, even when his sympathies may be more for bottom-up.

Level four is reached when the CEO starts to make the Quality process sweat. He wants to use it for business advantage and drives the process accordingly. This is the big differentiator between those who do and those who do not succeed with a Quality process. In driving the process, the leader will set hard goals, install sharp measures, establish benchmarks from external sources and gear every-body up for delivery.

The results of this take the company into the *Level five*, where strong returns and widespread success fuel continued improvement. It is a time of integration of many activities which had not sat comfort-ably together. *Kaizen* and breakthrough; leadership and empower-ment; the Quality process and business objectives. Knitting these together takes leadership skill and time.

By this time, the company is receiving accolades from outside. Suppliers are doubly keen to win the business; customers are more attentive; competitors are watching closely. Visitors want to see what it is that the company has done. Awards are won and more attention is poured on the company. The company has reached the toughest step of all: continuing to improve despite the success. Those that do so, that manage further improvement at this stage, are going beyond Quality. They will not find a methodology which takes them into *Level six*. They have to create it uniquely from the platform they have achieved. They have become lean, fast and capable. They are consis-tent in their approach wherever and in whatever they do. They are an elite group – those companies which are truly close to world-class.

Real maturity

Real life is never the smooth curve as depicted; despite everyone's good efforts inside, the world outside is always trying to throw us off-course. Alcatel's Spanish division offers a good illustration of the sheer determination needed to keep pushing up the curve in the face of adversity. A significant part of the giant Alcatel Alsthom telecoms group, Alcatel Standard Electrica employs around 10,000 people across eight major locations. The Alcatel group, headquartered in France, has a mission to be strong in Europe (reporting from national units is already routinely made in ecu's and Alcatel has applied for a European statute to reflect this emphasis). Number one in Europe in telecoms equipment, in digital switching, in cables and in several other related fields, Alcatel operates a hands-off policy for its national divisions, provided that a major contribution to this overall position is maintained. This has proved challenging to Alcatel Standard Electrica.

Quality first came on the scene as a Quality Circle programme in 1984. This was level one in Quality maturity with all the problems of a well-meaning initiative struggling for life in an indifferent managerial environment. Cristobel Serra, Quality director, fought hard to keep going, switching the emphasis to development circles with the more sustainable aim of developing people rather than problem-solving. Facilitators were trained to work with middle management and a plan for ISO 9001 accreditation was launched; a shaky level two was reached. As Cristobel now says, 'We started bottom-up but I wouldn't recommend it.'

Then came the first reality test from the business. A major restructuring was needed to cope with the technological shift from electro-mechanical gear to electronic. Some operations which used to take 16 people now required 0.5. Through the mid-1990s, an astonishing 50 per cent of jobs were lost. A new agreement between the Spanish government (who was the major customer and user), the unions and the company was thrashed out to make the new operation viable. Crucially, a new company president was brought in. Still in his thirties at the time, the new president reversed the hierarchical management structure, building units with decision-taking closer to the market, cutting across functions and leaving only a tiny head office. But much more than changing the boxes was needed and a Total Quality programme was devised to bring in a different management style. Bottom-up now became top-down – level three on our maturity scale. Product quality was becoming more reliable by now and the 1,100 inspectors were replaced by a 170 off-line auditors. Customer satisfaction became the stated top priority as Total Quality training sessions were rolled out to the units. Some took off fast as the local enthusiasts saw their opportunity and took up the empowerment they were being offered. But others were slow to follow, with only a gradual spread across the units as some of the successes became visible. By 1989, three years of Total Quality had passed and little additional progress was being made, even though all the key elements were there. Alcatel had hit the wall.

A Quality task force was set up to find out why. Other programmes were examined and showed that it wasn't really the content. Perhaps it had just stagnated? A relaunch was devised for the middle of 1989. This time it was left to permeate through naturally; simultaneously, a plan was created and resources built up to power through the blockages. A new Quality Council of all the unit managing directors was established, chaired by the president. Now no one at senior level could opt out; all were held accountable for Quality, whether a champion or sceptic. Each unit set up a steering committee from line management with a trained coordinator in support. The profile for the coordinator was strictly met, with many units having to go outside to meet the requirements. The steering committees appointed improvement teams top-down, made up cross-functionally to address key problems; membership was non-voluntary; 20 hours training in improvement methodology and techniques was given to all team members, reaching some 1,600 people in all. Engineers received additional training in specialist techniques and the whole workforce attended three hours of workshop education on the new approach. To reinforce the whole endeavour, a recognition day was run in December 1990 to review the team achievements and celebrate the successes of some 550 teams – a great success in its own right and repeated each year since.

Such intensity of effort from 1989 to 1991 took Alcatel through the wall into level four. Management was determined and visibly so. Then came big reality test number two. From the 1986 restructuring onwards, growth of 30 per cent per year had been achieved. This came abruptly to an end when the main customer, the Spanish government, brought the investment in telecoms infrastructure to a premature finish. Suddenly Alcatel's market was dissolving. A new strategy was quickly devised. Manufacturing was revived after a progressive move towards subcontracting. The world was scoured for export markets. Soon destinations in China and North America were being posted on the electronic information board detailing the big systems being built.

But still at the cost of more jobs. This had a double blow effect on the Quality process. Morale was low and many people who were strong participants in the teams were leaving.

The leaders did not give up. Rather they redoubled their efforts. People issues came into even sharper focus. Eduardo Montez, one of the managing directors and long committed to the Quality process, had been spending 20 per cent of his time on Quality in one form or another. Now he doubled it. His description of the development teams, which had flourished since the relaunched programme, was 'like mushrooms in England in the autumn – suddenly they are everywhere, then just as quickly they've gone.' He deliberately and visibly invested in more training to show commitment. He rapidly introduced cross-training for people to learn additional skills and soon 60 per cent of the workforce had certified skills in two tasks and 15 per cent in four tasks. He personally inspired a 'Pride of Team Spirit' campaign and backed it with tangible changes. He introduced music on the factory floor, uniforms, a no smoking rule (very bold in heavy-smoking Madrid) and an open space concept (even trickier: no private offices were allowed in the company at any level). His open-door policy meant he was inundated with visits, mostly to complain about the changes. But the majority stuck with him and the feeling of a new factory began to emerge. The pride returned. Improvement activity started to rise again.

Meanwhile at the centre, Cristobel Serra had his best idea yet. The rather ad hoc measures that had been in use in the group were superseded by a carefully thought through and well-tested series of metrics. These enable local development teams to link their contribution right back to group strategy. The metrics have been evolved to 23 sharp indicators ranging from competitors' market share to percentage of products delivered without objections. Today, Eduardo discusses his strategic plan, defined by these indicators, with his whole team in one big meeting before presenting them to his president. The president, in turn, is more interested in the indicators than the profit and loss account which is submitted with them. He looks particularly at the metrics describing progress on inventory, on people and on customers; he knows these will effect the *next* profit and loss account.

All in all, Alcatel Standard Electrica has had a good return from its Quality process. The process has reached level five in some units such as Eduardo's. One observer, a supplier, expresses amazement that Quality still survives, despite restructuring, down-sizing and a culture change. Eduardo and Cristobel would say it is only because of the Quality process that these huge changes have been possible. To go further, and this is central to Alcatel's strategy, the business has to look outward. Benchmarking is being established. Assessments to external standards, such as the European Quality Award criteria, are being introduced. Alcatel is one of the growing number of companies which have clearly set their ambitions to achieve world-class standards and this is where it is headed, despite the tests set by reality.

Assessing maturity

As companies come through the brick wall and drive for world class, leaders begin to ask how they compare with others. 'We've worked hard to build up to 38 per cent of the workforce in improvement teams but it's stuck there. Is this as far as you get or are others doing better?'; or 'We're achieving a four to one average return on our improvement projects. Is this a good standard?'; or 'We've taken 30 per cent of time out of this key process. Is this all we can expect?' Many similar questions arise as companies begin to have a clearer picture about their own achievements. There is a thirst for comparison, both inside, between units, and outside with other improving organisations. This is a healthy sign of developing maturity with Quality and the leader should be prepared to respond. An objective assessment is an opportunity for focused learning and re-energising.

Some large companies create their own assessment criteria and develop a process which provides local units with an assessment for their own improvement plans plus data to integrate into an overall assessment of company progress. Hewlett Packard, for example, have for some years evaluated units against a simple star framework with five main elements. For each of the five elements – customer focus, improvement goals, process management, the planning process and total participation – a score of one to five is given to each of over a hundred business units. A central Quality team does the assessment interactively with the local management team. HP's main aim is consistency across the group and they have set a target of an overall score of 3.5 for 80 per cent of units by 1994.

Some groups in Unilever have a similar approach, but using outside consultants to conduct a maturity review directly with the local business unit. The consultants develop the evaluation to a maturity model customised for Unilever. The aim here is direct assistance to the local unit by drawing out implementation strengths and weaknesses. To this end, the local facilitators and workforce groups contribute to the evaluation as well as management. The data is not collected centrally and it is up to the local unit whether they share the information with anyone else.

Westinghouse have designed their own Quality Fitness Review, which they have been using since 1981 to assess their business units. Units do self-assessments against 12 criteria areas, supported by a week-long input of structured interviews by people from outside the unit. The unit receives a strengths and weaknesses assessment, recommendations against the 12 points and a score. The score is important and, over the decade or so of use, continuous progress has been tracked. In fact, Westinghouse has sufficient data over the years to make some fascinating correlations. Graphs plotting three key indices at Westinghouse – profit/sales ratio, a composite of financial objectives known as 'the green tag' and a composite of reliability and failure costs – show very strong relationships with the fitness score (correlations of 0.957, 0.992, 0.961 respectively). As a result, managers at Westinghouse have little doubt about the relationship between Quality and business success.

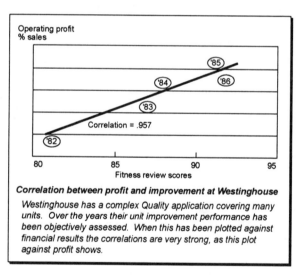

Correlation between profit and improvement at Westinghouse

Westinghouse has a complex Quality application covering many units. Over the years their unit improvement performance has been objectively assessed. When this has been plotted against financial results the correlations are very strong, as this plot against profit shows.

As Quality companies raise themselves higher up the maturity curve, they increasingly want to know how they compare with the world's best. Benchmarking helps them with specifics like time to market or service levels but does not give an overall comparative picture, especially on a global basis. The Malcolm Baldrige Award and The European Quality Award are increasingly used for this purpose. The Malcolm Baldrige National Quality Award (MBNQA) has been around for a few years and is well known by many managers. It has been won by some of America's best companies and has embraced a reasonable range of organisations in its winners: from big manufacturers like Motorola or Westinghouse to small ones like Globe Metallurgical; from high tech such as Zitec to service in Federal Express and Ritz Carlton. As such, it has universal attraction and hundreds of thousands of companies reputedly use MBNQA criteria for self-assessment.

In reality, much fewer of these have a disciplined assessment process. Of those that do, Du Pont is typical. Every division of Du Pont world-wide is required to assess its Quality achievement against MBNQA criteria every year. The assessment is self-administered by the local unit management team, but it must be done to an accepted methodology and help is given if needed. One of the big advantages for Du Pont is that they can allow a lot of freedom of implementation to divisions (and, indeed, each division has its own programme with a different theme and different emphases) but there is an overall comparative guide to progress which can be normed internally and externally. There is nothing like a score to motivate a business unit.

MBNQA scores a theoretical maximum of 1,000, with an Award-winning score being in the region of 700 plus. Once a unit understands the criteria, rapid progress can be made if the management is determined enough. IBM Rochester went from a self-assessed score of 340 in 1987 to win the Award three years later. Some of Du Pont's units have made similar rapid progress once they have understood their position. For instance, one unit went from 280 to 440 in 12 months. Dieter Wullschleger, the Geneva-based TQ manager for the Electronics division, has been coaching units in self-assessment for some time and in many cases he finds an assessment can be now made, without fuss, in one day. From time to time, however, Dieter encourages units to accept an external assessment, which usually rates tighter than the self-assessment – sometimes to the order of 100 points. The difference is often how the management team perceives its own leadership and its own accomplishments in valuing people. Having an externally-benchmarked number has great motivational value.

MBNQA is not a perfect fit for companies working their way up the Quality maturity curve. Indeed, it has been extensively criticised by practitioners for being too focused on the process of improvement and not sufficiently on the results. No business today can afford the luxury of an improvement process that does not directly lead to business results and this factor has to taken into account by anyone using

**THE
EUROPEAN QUALITY
A·W·A·R·D**

The European Quality Award

The European Quality Award model is being used by many companies for self-appraisal of their position against common criteria. Indeed many companies have had key managers trained as assessors so that the self-appraisal can be more consistent and more comparative. Others use outside consultants to be completely objective. There are nine criteria, split into the two groups of enablers and results, as the model shows.

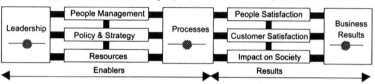

The TEQA criteria

In the enablers group, the first item is leadership. Using TEQA guidelines for self-assessment, an assessor would look for evidence of visible involvement in a Quality process, both inside and outside the organisation. Personal commitment to the process is expected, coupled with recognition of the contribution of teams and individuals. Item two is policy and strategy - the organisation's vision, values and strategic direction and the clarity of them. The assessor will look for how the policies are determined and the mechanisms of their deployment and how tightly Quality fits with business plans and how strategy is communicated and reviewed.

Item three looks at people management: how the organisation releases and harnesses the full potential of its people towards the continuous improvement of the business. As such, the assessor will examine the structures for the development of people, how involvement is effected, how continuous improvement is organised.

The fourth item in the enablers is called resources and can be sub-divided into four: financial resources, information resources, material resources and application of technology. Each one is assessed independently, seeking out the means of managing cash and working capital, for instance, strategies for effective information flow, raw material management and the appropriate use of technology for competitive advantage.

The next criterion links the enablers and the results - processes. This investigates business processes and how they are managed, looking for a systematic approach to the identifying of value-added processes and the measurement and improvement of performance.

The results group is to ensure that the whole Quality endeavour does not or has not become a theoretical or conceptual activity with little return. Big returns are expected and the process should be geared accordingly. An assessor here is looking for hard facts, particularly trends over a period of years. Metrics are mandatory; assumptions and feelings are not counted. An assessor will want to see comparative data: the organisation's targets for each measured result area, the relevance of this result area to the stakeholders, actual performance against the target and a comparison with competitors and/or 'best in class'.

Item six, and the first of the results criteria, is on customer satisfaction. The assessor looks for quantified evidence of customers' requirements being met, together with data on the perceptions of customers about the organisation. Item seven is a similar one on people satisfaction, looking at evidence of what people feel about the organisation and indirect measures such as absenteeism, staff turnover and ease of recruitment. Item eight looks at results of the impact on society: the perception of the community on such areas as the organisation's role and involvement in the community, the effect on the environment and the use of global resources.

The final result criterion is the ultimate long-term test - business results. The assessor here is looking for the achievement of the organisation against its own business plans in absolute terms: how all the financial ratios have been influenced by the Quality process plus appropriate non-financial measures such as market share, new product percentage, cost reduction, inventory turns, cycle time reduction. In a Quality business well on its way to world class, the evidence of TEQA assessment should show a clear thread from strong enablers to sound results.

the MBNQA for self-assessment. The creators of The European Quality Award (TEQA) were fortunate in being able to take this view into account. TEQA was formally announced in 1991 at the London forum of the European Foundation of Quality Management (EFQM), the sponsoring body, and the first award was made at the Madrid forum in October 1992. Prior to this, three years of intensive research and practical development was invested in creating TEQA.

Roy Peacock, who led the programme to develop TEQA for the EFQM, painstakingly reviewed all the Quality awards in the world and the experience of their use, paying especial attention to MBNQA, which is by far the most well-known. In addition, many Total Quality practitioners and EFQM member companies were involved in creating the most expressive form of Quality evaluation which could be devised. The outcome has much in common with MBNQA but with significant differences. The biggest difference is that the results criteria lacking in MBNQA are very well counted in TEQA. TEQA criteria are grouped into two: one to cover the *enablers* – the process of improvement or the how things are being done – and one to cover *results* – what has been achieved as perceived by the stakeholders in the organisation. This split goes all the way through the assessment, with assessors looking at each specific criterion in two parts: first the method chosen for, say, managing processes more effectively, and secondly the deployment of that approach – what has been achieved in practice. This makes for a powerful assessment tool. A company or unit may have a wonderful intention and a compelling theoretical or conceptual description but if it is not getting results it won't score highly.

TEQA criteria are not cast in stone and will inevitably evolve to match a changing environment in the future, but all the signs are that they represent the best comparative assessment which an organisation could choose to evaluate its progress to world-class.

One company's journey to world-class

Rank Xerox would not claim to be world-class. Like all the leading companies in the world, they have a rigorous assessment process which highlights the gaps against other outstanding performers. They know where they are not yet truly world-class, but they also know they are on the right track. That said, the Xerox group have won national Quality awards in Britain, Mexico, France, Canada, Holland and Australia plus lots of specific awards such as 'best factory'. Even more telling, Xerox subsidiaries have won the big ones – Baldrige in the USA, Deming in Japan and, now, TEQA in Europe. Despite this unique achievement, of which they are very proud, Xerox remains humble about its status as a global model. This stance is also revealing: it is a characteristic of the very best to have pride with humility. Xerox has clear intent not just to achieve the spirit of being world-class but to measure performance within the international peer group of Quality-led companies.

Rank Xerox was formed in 1956 as a joint venture between the Rank Organisation and Xerox Corporation to manufacture and market reprographics and other office equipment outside of the Americas. Rank Xerox today has operations in over 80 countries around the world including all of Europe, Africa, the Middle East and India. The story of its journey towards world-class is a tale of a classic Quality revolution. In the 1960s, Rank Xerox had the seemingly wonderful position of a monopoly in reprographics, a booming sector. Nowadays we know that monopoly positions never last and, worse, breed complacent habits, and Rank Xerox was no exception. When the patent protection ended in the 1970s, Rank Xerox was shown up by the youthful Japanese competition as expensive, complex, bureaucratic and slow. The Quality wave that hit the Xerox businesses could not have been bigger.

By the 1980s, survival was a big question. As so often in good Quality stories, the right leaders arrived on the scene at the right time. David Kearns was not interested in past glories and not tainted with any delusion of superiority. He knew the Japanese (Ricoh, Canon, Brother, Minolta) had the better management model. Fortunately, he had his own model within the group: Fuji Xerox, a joint venture between Rank Xerox and Fuji Corporation, had, since the mid-1970s, been seriously applying a Total Quality process to counter the intense local competition. In 1980, they won the Deming Prize in Japan and this triggered a stream of learning between Tokyo and the rest of the group. A corporate-wide process began in 1984, called Leadership Through Quality.

The first years of this process were conventional enough. A formal training programme in Quality was rolled out across all 100,000 people in the group, taking five years to finish. A key ingredient was using managers to front the training, with a strict cascade level by level. Thus managers actually experienced the training twice – as learners with their peers and then as leaders of their family group at the next level down. After training, people went into problem-solving teams and applied the techniques learned. This phase took nearly four years at Rank Xerox before the process was complete and all 28,000 were initiated in Quality. The result was a thorough awareness of

Quality and steady improvement practice. However, when the Rank Xerox management team stood back from it, they knew it was nothing like enough to keep up with the competition.

At this crucial stage another Quality leader emerged. Bernard Fournier, managing director of Rank Xerox, admits he was sceptical when first introduced to the Quality concept. He now says: 'This changed when I discovered that it could help me with my two main issues of the day – moving from management to leadership and encouraging everybody to contribute to the company's goals.' A strategic review told his management team that, on the things that count (customer satisfaction, employee satisfaction, market share and return on assets), the Quality process was not making sufficient impact. They did some benchmarking and prepared to break through the brick wall which was holding them back. A Quality intensification plan followed in 1990.

This plan shifted up a few gears. It was led personally by Bernard, who firmly believes in leading from the front: 'At Rank Xerox, I ensure that Quality is driven from the top. Throughout the organisation, it is managed in the line by the line.' The new plan knitted together some of the separate strands of the Quality process under six key categories: management leadership, human resource management, process management, customer focus, Quality support and tools, and business results. This was not a reshuffle of components. Crucially, for each category a statement was made which defined sharply what the aim was and all six were combined on one page to become the new vision statement. Metrics were set up for each and the measurement mechanisms built. Assessments were made to evaluate progress and overall results on the six categories began to determine promotion prospects. For further reinforcement, Business Excellence Certificates were introduced for all units as a way of emphasising both the business consequences of Quality performance and the means by which results are achieved. The certification process evolved into a road map for success by which units could assess themselves and identify gaps in performance, followed by specific improvement action. Certificates were awarded via a formal examination, carried out by senior Rank Xerox managers, which recognised both progress and approach. This big shift in internal emphasis was reflected back to the marketplace: Rank Xerox was now 'the document company' offering a 'total satisfaction guarantee'. Quality was now driven by customer and business requirements.

This new plan had a big impact and Rank Xerox went on to the next level with Quality. Naturally, no one was satisfied. In particular, there was a feeling that the process of Quality was quite strong, but was it really hardwired to business results? The new emphasis became 'from process to business excellence' and drew heavily on the disciplines of policy deployment and business process re-engineering to link the Quality effort directly to business results. Where once Rank Xerox units had 40 or 50 priorities with never enough budget to go round, now they have three or four 'vital few' with the focused resources to ensure achievement. The whole planning process deploys down from the 'Rank Xerox Vision 2000' to individual objectives at every level, with open measures and visible tracking of performance. To match the vital few at unit or division level, business processes are hit with routine process simplification targets of 100 per cent improvement in three to six months and radical process re-engineering targets of 1000 per cent improvement in two to three years.

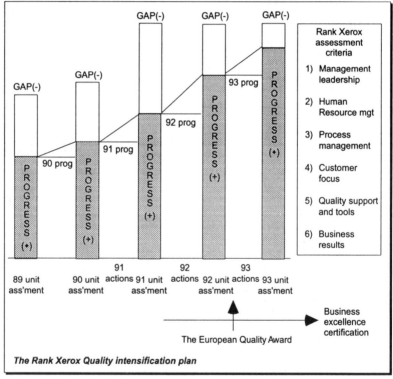

The Rank Xerox Quality intensification plan

Rank Xerox are always seeking to maintain high energy and integrate their improvement activities. A new opportunity for this was presented with the announcement of the European Quality Award in 1991. Xerox had gained enormously from winning the Baldrige Award in the USA, particularly from the challenge of external scrutiny and the enthusiasm generated for the competition in 'Team Xerox'. The Rank Xerox management saw the opportunity for a similarly uplifting experience in Europe and the catalytic benefits at their stage in the Quality journey. This was a chance to add new dimensions to the business excellence certification process by benchmarking against Europe's best and adding the rigour of outside evaluation. The new challenge reinforced much of the planned activity and helped raise the overall consistency, whilst highlighting some areas not previously emphasised. Starting with customer satisfaction, a closed-loop management process had been established for some time across the company. This means: listening to the external or internal customer; understanding his or her requirements; developing and delivering solutions to any problems; measuring and reviewing performance. This closed-loop way of managing overlaid with the radical improvement disciplines enabled further progress to be made. With this improvement activity linked directly into Policy Deployment and the Business Excellence process, Rank Xerox was soon well set to contend for the award. Rank Xerox became the inaugural winners of The European Quality Award in October 1992.

How Rank Xerox won The European Quality Award

Competing for the first European Quality Award was not an end in itself but a means to take Rank Xerox closer to world-class standards. However, once the decision was taken to compete, it was compete to win. Quality director Rafael Florez took it on as one of his 'vital few objectives' and put together a small team to submit an application. This team knew from their own internal assessments that the business units had already accomplished a tremendous amount; the task now was to present the Rank Xerox Quality story in a compelling light.

For 'the document company', here was an opportunity to display some capability and the 75-page submission was a masterpiece of written communication, fully desk-top published with illustrations and examples. The content came from Rank Xerox people themselves with every department in every country telling their Quality stories to the team. The application passed the first hurdle - an assessment by external examiners. Next the assessors requested site visits. Rank Xerox' submission was for the whole company, so the visiting assessors had a right to examine any location. They chose three: International Headquarters at Marlow, Rank Xerox Belgium (a marketing unit), and a manufacturing operation at Venray in Holland.

In the short notice period before the visits, teams at the local units were rehearsed with difficult questions. In the event, it didn't matter, for the assessors went wherever they chose, talking to people around the business, testing the pervasiveness of the approach. The assessors' reports and comments were evaluated rigorously before a jury of eminent European industrialists made their decision. Rank Xerox came out the best.

These are some of the practices and accomplishments which made the Rank Xerox Quality story the best in 1992:

1. Leadership

Rank Xerox leaders do not support Quality – they lead it. Executives are directly involved in improvement projects; for instance, the management team in Germany visited personally 300 customers to understand areas of dissatisfaction in electronic selling price delegation to the local sales team; merit pay increases down to the local manager; implementation responsibility for QITs. The Rank Xerox 'capacity to act' policy, introduced in 1988, has helped to define and clarify empowerment in practice.

4. Resources

Financial resources (cash, revenues, working capital and cost) are well managed at Rank Xerox, being treated again as closed-loop processes. Cost of Quality (CoQ) was used in the early years of Quality implementation, recording some dramatic shifts such as the increase in prevention and appraisal activities from 12 per cent to 45 per cent of the CoQ at the Welwyn manufacturing plant which led to a reduction of CoQ from £32m to £4.5m, or the billing process which over five quarters was raised in accuracy from 95 per cent to 97 per cent whilst cutting $4m off the CoQ.

Information is also treated as a valued resource with an overall aim of all information being up to date and accurate. Billing accuracy is now moving close to 98 per cent in most units. Customer data accuracy at Rank Xerox Portugal is over 99 per cent, an internal benchmark for other units to match. All information systems are being fully integrated with some units reaching a total integration figure of 80 per cent (high compared to external benchmarks) and fast approaching the targets in '93 of over 90 per cent.

Material resources are managed through well-established JIT, which has halved inventory levels. A dedicated team of 414 suppliers (reduced from an original 5000) are linked together through the Continuous Supplier Involvement Process (CSIP). This process ensures that the 80 per cent of production costs which are bought-in are tightly managed with an emphasis on prevention well up the supply chain: 95 per cent of parts are certified and line fall out is down to 125 parts per million.

5. Processes

Rank Xerox have valued process management since the beginning of their Leadership through Quality activities. At first, processes were managed at QIP level as teams learned about improvement in their work systems. Gradually this practice spread cross-functionally and eventually cross-organisation. In 1990, all the experiences with processes was brought together and an integrated process structure devised. Known as the Business Architecture, this knits together all the key business processes and the 76 subprocesses which feed them. The Business Architecture is the Rank Xerox template for future systems and organisation development. All processes have assigned owners who are responsible for setting process standards and meeting performance targets. Feedback is collected routinely from external customers, internal customers, suppliers and comparisons made to internal best practice and external benchmarks. To ensure that processes are improving they are audited and scored each year. But the best assessment of an improved process is how quickly and well it has met with the stretch objectives set through the policy deployment; in other words, how it has impacted overall results.

6. Customer satisfaction

For Rank Xerox, the most important result is customer satisfaction. Millions are spent each year finding out what the result is, through a combination of anonymous and sponsored surveys. The Rank Xerox targets were to be rated number one in customer satisfaction for all reprographic and all printing products and in all countries by the end of 1992 and to make significant progress towards 100 per cent measured satisfaction. In 1989, customers rated Rank Xerox number one vendor in nine out of 75 business sectors. In 1992, Rank Xerox were first in over 60. Three years ago, 71 per cent of customers across Europe said they were satisfied; in 1992, dissatisfaction was down to an average of 3 per cent, with some units maintaining the ultimate goal of 100 per cent satisfaction. The key to the rapid progress has been the closed-loop drive for improvement based on real data, with a focus on the identified dissatisfiers. Consistent with the improved ratings and to maintain a pioneering approach, Rank Xerox launched their Total Customer Satisfaction Guarantee in January 1991. This offers the customer an exchange of any product which is not completely satisfactory for a three-year period. This has been favourably received by customers, with some units reporting 20 per cent citing this as a significant reason for purchasing an Rank Xerox product. Less than 0.5 per cent exercised this option in the first year.

printing (subsequent actions led to this unit moving from number three to number one in customer satisfaction). Every manager is expected to lead by example which means using Quality tools as normal management practice and complying with a strict role model of management behaviour. All managers communicate strategy and improvement goals to all their staff and are accessible in a variety·of ways to people for information and discussion. For instance, Carlos Pascual in France holds monthly meetings with a broad cross-section of staff; Bernard Fournier at international headquarters holds regular breakfast meetings which anyone can attend. Such practices are pervasive across the organisation. Rank Xerox managers are also expected to be Quality champions and promote Quality inside and outside of the company. The once very introspective organisation is now committed to sharing its experience and managers in the units regularly host visitors or make visits to other companies to spread the Quality message.

2 Policy and strategy

Rank Xerox use Quality as the base for policy an strategy. A set of values, known as 'the way we work', underpins all activities. These have been refined over the years with input from staff. The 'vision 2000' positions Rank Xerox now as 'the document company' and defines what this means in strategic terms. Supporting this are four business priorities. At the start of the Quality journey, there were three - return on assets, customer satisfaction and market share in that order. Through the Quality process, customer satisfaction became the first priority, employee motivation and satisfaction was added as the second, followed by market share and return on assets. To impact these four imperatives, Rank Xerox have designed powerful information and measurement systems, feeding current data on performance against each priority.

All of the above gives the essence of the Rank Xerox business. To make it work dynamically, Rank Xerox managers are enthusiastic users of policy deployment. Three- to five-year goals are set for the business based on benchmarking, analysis of the market and Rank Xerox capability. Every business unit and every department within a unit takes these goals and agrees a 'vital few' (four or five) annual improvement objectives which define their contribution to the mid-term goals. Quite often, new strategies and new processes are required to deliver the objectives. The goals and objectives are cascaded down the whole organisation and captured in what is known in the UK as 'The Blue Book' ('le livre bleu' in France and 'das Kursbuch' in Germany). Every Rank Xerox person is involved in the development of the local 'blue book' which is actively used to make local decisions and guides improvement action.

Bernard Fournier points out: 'We use a formal process to cascade the company's policy and strategy throughout the organisation, so that every individual has clear personal direction and targets, can relate his or her activities to those of other people and can understand how to contribute to the success of the company.' The downward cascade of objectives at the beginning of the year is followed by quarterly upward reviews, always bringing the focus back onto the four business priorities. Awareness of these priorities across Rank Xerox units is an astonishing 96 per cent.

3. People management

Rank Xerox manages its management: the recruitment, assessment and development of all managers is managed as a complete process called 'management resource planning' (MRP). Managers are assessed on five criteria: business results, leadership through quality, human resource management, teamwork, corporate values. Note that four of these five are on the 'soft' people-related issues showing how important people management is to Rank Xerox. A closed-loop process is used to ensure that the management of 28,000 people is effective, driven by data from the annual employee satisfaction survey. Issues identified from this survey are tackled by Quality Improvement Teams (QITs), thus involving people in improving their own environment.

Skills development is an important part of the deployment of policy, with needs determined by the strategic goals. As a result, much training is undertaken, varying from cross-functional needs such as effective meetings to specific needs such as service attitude for salespersons. Some 7 per cent of payroll cost (2 per cent of revenue) is spent on training, with a minimum target of 40 hours training per person well exceeded. Rank Xerox people of all ranks are appraised against set objectives and individual development plans agreed. Empowerment is active on many fronts: self-managed teams in service centres;

7. People satisfaction

This second business priority is monitored annually against organisation-wide criteria which include career development, pay, team spirit, training, work environment, communications and overall satisfaction. To meet the benchmark goal targeted for 1995, Rank Xerox are looking for marked improvements in survey scores from their weakest country units. Thus Greece, Finland and Portugal showed big improvements from 1990 to 1991 (92 per cent, 53 per cent and 48 per cent), whilst all but two countries showed improvement above their set percentage target. This means that every unit has a big challenge to improve employee satisfaction score which already go up into the 80s and 90s. The closed loop improvement process means that any gaps found in the employee survey are actioned directly. For example, Bernard Fournier sponsored six QITs to address issues arising from the 1990 headquarters survey. He personally led one of these and assigned the others to board members. These and other QITs resulted in a 35 per cent increase in the overall satisfaction rating.

8. Impact on society

This criterion was not one of Rank Xerox' four business priorities; nevertheless it is a serious issue and Rank Xerox view themselves as being at the forefront of requirements in this area. By way of evidence of this, Rank Xerox can demonstrate performances that beat industry standards and match world benchmarks on a number of parameters. Their safety record beats the acknowledged benchmark - Du Pont's 0.5 incidents per 200,000 working hours; ozone emissions from products are less than half the industry standard and are targeted lower still; dust emissions likewise; noise emissions have been reduced well below competitor standards. Site environmental audits have been running since 1984 and energy conservation, waste reduction and product recycling is measured and systematically improved. Community involvement is actively encouraged, primarily in the areas of charity support, education, sports and arts. To promote the further development of Quality in society, Rank Xerox has undertaken to open its doors to other organisations wishing to learn from its experience.

9. Business results

Market share is the third Rank Xerox business priority. Reprographics is still the big market at 70 per cent of revenue and this has steadily grown from 1986/87 when the Quality process started to bite. Indeed, in all the main segments in which Rank Xerox competes, Rank Xerox has countered the expectation of a Japanese take-over of the market, dominating the high-volume segment at 85 per cent, overtaking the leader, Canon, in mid-volume and forcing new inroads into low-volume copiers. Printers are also faring well, despite intense competition, with the high-volume segment share improved by 25 per cent in four years. Return on assets is the Rank Xerox fourth business priority and the trend shows stability at around 21 per cent in conventional measurement terms, some 50 per cent above Dun & Bradstreet's upper quartile rating for the industry.

A big contributor to this success has been the major upgrade in operational effectiveness. Manufacturing process variability is measured by the Cpk factor which shows the relationship between specification and achievement. The Rank Xerox target is 1.33 (which equates to 99.994 per cent of output within specification) and this has risen from 41 per cent of processes beating this target in 1990 to 70 per cent in 1992. Delivery targets have been raised from 80 per cent achievement of daily commitments to 99 per cent, whilst days of supply (whole manufacturing inventory) had been reduced from 36 to around 20. Cycle times have been compressed throughout: manufacturing lead time has been cut by 46 per cent, warehouse to customer time by 60 per cent and new products are brought to the market much faster. On the service side, outstanding customer queries have been systematically reduced; for instance, queries still outstanding after five days have been brought down at Rank Xerox Netherlands from an average of 340 to 50 in two years.

Finally, all of these improvements have led to a healthy balance sheet. Revenue and profit after tax have risen consistently over the last ten years and were held at a high level in 1990/1 at a time when many high technology companies made losses.

(Adapted from Rank Xerox's submission document for the 1992 Award)

Continuing the journey

Winning this award is a marker along the path to world-class for Rank Xerox. It has enabled them to take stock of their journey and ask the question: has it been worth it? Their answer is a collective yes. In their award submission on business results, they were able to demonstrate that over the ten-year period of a Quality process, they had enjoyed an almost uninterrupted revenue growth and a related profit performance, even in 1991 when many similar high-technology businesses showed losses. Their submission concludes: 'Our performance reflects the success of our commitment to customer satisfaction through our Quality strategy. This, together with our investments in employee satisfaction, market share, new products and improvement programmes, will provide the basis for continued profitable growth.' Bernard Fournier put it another way in his award acceptance speech: 'We started the Quality journey in 1984. Rank Xerox was 28 years old and was rapidly losing market share. We had become complacent and were losing sight of our customers. Now we are one of the few companies that is actually winning market share back from the Japanese – slowly but surely.'

Rank Xerox did not reflect on this success for long. They are proud of what they have achieved and do not shun the advantages of a Quality image but their pride also demands they fill the gaps in their world-class canvas. They have no intention of resting on their laurels; they know there is so much more to do. They also know Quality pays and they are greedy for more of it. Pride and prosperity are powerful motivators. On accepting the award from King Carlos of Spain, Bernard said: 'This is a crucial step on our journey to 100 per cent customer satisfaction. It recognises our achievements and gives us the drive to go further. Make no mistake – encouragement is important. One of the lessons I have learned over the past eight years is that Quality does not come easily. It has to be permanently managed.'

The drive for improvement at Rank Xerox continues to be managed; it is not left to chance. Rafael Florez, as Quality and customer satisfaction director in 1993, had a specific responsibility for coordinating activities for that most important one of the vital few – customer satisfaction. On his wall was a storyboard of the closed-loop process which links corporate values and priorities, customer feedback, analysis, actions and results. Twelve charts depict each stage. There is no exhortation or slogans; each chart is factual, either a statement or data. The last chart in the loop shows Rank Xerox' own data on why customer satisfaction is a business priority: 52 per cent of very satisfied customers state they would definitely repurchase from Rank Xerox and 65 per cent of very satisfied customers would definitely recommend Rank Xerox to others. Any visitor to Rafael's office had little doubt that, European Quality Award or not, the pressure to meet the customer satisfaction goal is unrelenting.

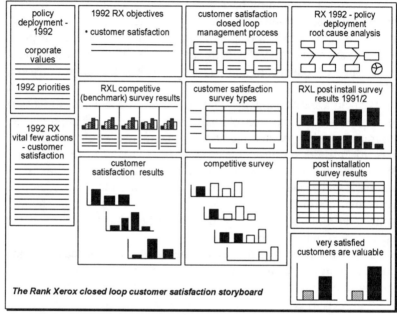

The Rank Xerox closed loop customer satisfaction storyboard

Rank Xerox is clearly well motivated to keep its Quality revolution in motion. As Bernard Fournier concludes: 'Perfect service is an unclaimed crown.' Rank Xerox have their sights set on that crown.

Always learning

At the 1992 European Quality Award presentations, Clive Jeanes was not feeling quite so pleased as Bernard Fournier. Clive, as managing director of Milliken Europe, had been presented with the European Quality Prize as one of the runners-up to Rank Xerox. That evening, as he reflected with his colleagues on how close they had come to the top award, Clive suddenly realised what an opportunity he now had. He had the perfect challenge for his 1,160-person team spread across four countries – they would compete again next year, but this time they were going to win. 'Our corporate culture engenders a dislike of coming second,' he disclosed shortly afterwards.[24]

So he and his colleagues returned to Wigan well motivated for a renewed effort but with a nagging problem. They felt they had already given their best effort – how could they improve further? Applying self-assessments based on the award criteria, Clive quickly had teams at all levels right across the European operation, scrutinising what they were doing and how they were doing it. These teams quickly spotted gaps to work on. Clive himself learned about many ways that he could improve. One was to help establish more of a pan-European feel to Milliken Europe which was previously focused on a country basis. Clive introduced formal European team meetings. 'We built a fantastic team spirit as a result of that.'

The new improvement energy paid off. At the subsequent EFQM Forum in Turin, Clive Jeanes was the proud recipient of the 1993 European Quality Award. Over a few years, Milliken Europe had made a remarkable transformation from being a disparate collection of acquired companies to a world-class unit. Invoice process time was slashed to ten minutes by 1993 from eight hours in 1989. On-time shipment was up to 99 per cent in 1992 from 75 per cent in 1985. Product defects were steadily eradicated – down 49 per cent over the last decade. Better than these point-in-time results, Milliken has created a consistent Quality culture that unites a work team in, say, Milliken Denmark with counterparts in Spartanburg, South Carolina. This culture, together with the leadership passion for Quality, will help Milliken to continue to re-invent itself to compete through the 1990s. As Clive states: 'I would guess that if there is a destination for Total Quality, we are no more than 25 or 30 per cent on the way towards it.'

Continuous revolution

Leaders like Clive Jeanes of Milliken, Bernard Fournier of Rank Xerox, Mike Perry of Unilever, Tony Gilroy of Perkins, Tom Little of Colworth laboratory, John Craddock of Legal & General, Mike Nash of L&K: Rexona and all the others mentioned in this book are permanent revolutionaries. Their styles range across the whole spectrum from flamboyant to restrained and their backgrounds are equally diverse. But they share a belief in Quality and find they have a common language – the language of improvement. Their business practice has many similarities too. They are all striving to do better. They are all using Quality as an accelerated way of improvement.

They all aspire to world-class standards. And they are prepared to change anything and everything to get there. Today there is a growing club of like-minded leaders, as the Quality revolution continues to embrace more and more organisations. Continuous revolution may sound like a contradiction in terms but these Quality leaders are living proof that it exists.

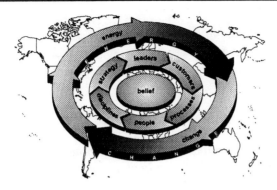

SUMMARY

Will your Quality process take you to world class?

Try these summary questions about your approach to improvement across the business. Be tough on yourself: if your immediate answer is 'not sure' or 'not much' or 'not everywhere', then it's no!

1. Belief: setting the revolutionary mind-set

	Yes	No
• Is your belief in an overall improvement philosophy well understood across the business?	☐	☐
• Are you continually reinventing the business to meet new market challenges and opportunities?	☐	☐
• Have you defined your Quality edge and are you anticipating emerging Quality gaps?	☐	☐
• Are you prepared to change anything and everything in order to maintain accelerated improvement?	☐	☐
• Are you in it for the long term – that is, are you prepared for continuous revolution?	☐	☐

2. Energy: generating improvement vitality to transform the business

• Are you explicitly managing the process of change?	☐	☐
• Are you keeping the energy sources (champions, excitement, events, pace) well stoked up to power through blockages as they occur?	☐	☐
• Are you continually attacking the energy sappers and keeping vigil for new ones?	☐	☐

Yes   No

- *Are you, personally, setting a high-energy example?*   ☐ ☐
- *Have you converted the great unmoved...are they energised for improvement?*   ☐ ☐

3. Strategy : putting Quality behind business

- *Have you communicated the future practice of the organisation – what is valued and the way things should be done?*   ☐ ☐
- *Have you created a clear strategic framework from an overall vision down to day-to-day behaviours?*   ☐ ☐
- *Do you have stretch improvement goals which lead to a Quality edge, with clear metrics to track progress?*   ☐ ☐
- *Is your business plan live, with an active planning process top- down and bottom-up...do people use it to make decisions?*   ☐ ☐
- *Is the Quality process fully intertwined with the business processes?*   ☐ ☐

4. Leadership: showing the Quality example from the top

- *Are you the Quality role model for the business?*   ☐ ☐
- *Are you both visionary and missionary, pointing the way and guiding people to get there?*   ☐ ☐
- *Has your commitment to tomorrow's business stood up to the test of today's?*   ☐ ☐
- *Are you able to let go and empower leaders beneath you?*   ☐ ☐
- *Do you have a personal development plan – that is, are you improving yourself?*   ☐ ☐

5. Customers: aligning the business around customers' needs

- *Is 'customer' the big word in your business – the trigger for action?*   ☐ ☐
- *Does 'customer' mean something important every-where in the business?*   ☐ ☐

Yes   No

- *Are you successfully and consistently managing each customer's expectations and response to your service?* ☐ ☐
- *Are you reading tomorrow's customer needs and preparing for them?* ☐ ☐
- *Do your customers really need you?* ☐ ☐

6. Processes: building the lean route to effectiveness

- *Are processes more important than functions in your business?* ☐ ☐
- *Is it clear what the strategic business processes are and how well they perform?* ☐ ☐
- *Are your key processes being systematically slimmed and/or re- engineered and are your non-key processes being removed?* ☐ ☐
- *Is your process management multiplying (rather than adding) value?* ☐ ☐
- *Overall, is your business lean and responsive?* ☐ ☐

7. People: harnessing talent and pride

- *Is teamwork natural and flexible throughout the organisation?* ☐ ☐
- *Do you have a continuous flow of people ideas and are you using them?* ☐ ☐
- *Is your business one big community where every-body knows what everybody else does and everyone helps out?* ☐ ☐
- *Are your people continually developed for their roles in the business?* ☐ ☐
- *Do they feel valued?* ☐ ☐

8. Disciplines: achieving structured coordinated action

- *Do people know the cost of waste and the value of good work across the business?* ☐ ☐
- *Do people work to agreed procedures and make improvements and changes in a methodical, ordered way?* ☐ ☐

<table>
<tr><td></td><td>Yes</td><td>No</td></tr>
</table>

- *Do people, including managers (that means you too), use improvement tools?* ☐ ☐
- *Do your people work to standards: could they say what being professional in their work means?* ☐ ☐
- *Can you see multi-level improvement disciplines being applied simultaneously in the business and are you orchestrating their combined effect?* ☐ ☐

9. Integration: pulling it all together to accelerate improvement

- *Do you manage the change process through a pro-active implementation strategy, communicated in an explicit Quality plan?* ☐ ☐
- *Have you learned from others' experiences and are these lessons built into the plan?* ☐ ☐
- *Are you using all the key interventions (workshops, surveys, events, training, communications, displays, disciplines, tools, recognition etc) and integrating them into a coherent process?* ☐ ☐
- *Are you managing the dynamics of change through the line?* ☐ ☐
- *Is the rate of improvement increasing?* ☐ ☐

10. Results: making Quality pay

- *Have you set and communicated specific expectations of multiple benefits?* ☐ ☐
- *Are you managing for short-term benefits as well as long-term success?* ☐ ☐
- *Are people outside interested in what you are doing...is it showing?* ☐ ☐
- *Is the improvement process self-financing and handsomely so?* ☐ ☐
- *Is your business demonstrably better than 18 months ago?* ☐ ☐

A positive answer to most of these 50 questions shows you are well on the way to world class: congratulations. By the way, have someone else score it too – you may just be flattering yourself. More than 12 negatives shows there is still a lot to do and these areas need immediate attention. More than 25 negatives and your Quality process probably needs a major overhaul...it is certainly not revolutionary. If you have 35 or more negatives, perhaps you should go back to Chapter 1 and start your Quality revolution right now!

References & Bibliography

References

1. Dickson, M., *Financial Times*, March 24, 1993

2. Mathews, J., *Newsweek*, September 14, 1992

3. Bemowski, K., *Quality Progress*, May 1992

4. Lorenz, C., *Financial Times*, June 29, 1992

5. Kellaway, L., *Financial Times*, February 14, 1992

6. Holberton, S., *Financial Times*, April 12, 1991

7. Holbertson, S., ibid

8. Krantz, K. T., *Harvard Business Review*, September/October 1989

9. Done, K., *Financial Times*, September 24, 1992

10. Done, K., ibid

11. Brignull, T., *The Guardian*, September 21, 1992

12. Miller, P., *Financial Times*, July 9, 1991

13. Done, K., ibid

14. Done, K., *Financial Times*, 9 September, 1993

15. Buchan, J., *Financial Times*

16. *Fortune*, September 21, 1992

17. Lorenz, C., *Financial Times*, June 25, 1993

18. Lorenz, C., *Financial Times*, January 12, 1994

19. Lorenz, C., *Financial Times*, September 18, 1992

20. Williams, M., *Managing Service Quality*, September 1992

21. Griffiths, J., *Financial Times*, March 9, 1992

22. Becker, S. W., Golomski, W. A. and Lory, C. D., *Quality Management Journal*, January 1994

23. Smith, C., Fargus, P. and Smith, S., *Managing Service Quality*, July 1992

24. *Quality Link*, November/December 1993

Other Sources/Recommended Reading

Clark, K. B. and Fujimoto, T., *Product Development Performance*, Harvard Business School, 1991

Nicholson J, *How do you manage?*, BBC

Peters, T. and Waterman, R., *In Search of Excellence*, Harper and Row, 1982

Rank Xerox EQA Submission,1992

Smith, W. S., *The Quest for Quality*, Quest Quality Consulting, 1989

Womack, J. P., Jones, D. T. and Roos, D., *The Machine That Changed The World*, Harper Collins, 1991

Index

The Quality Makers
The Leaders and Shapers of Europe's Quality Revolution
Robert Heller

(HB, £25.00, 272pp, 270mm x 195mm, ISBN: 3-907150-47-3)

Robert Heller charts the development of TQM in Europe with in-depth studies of 20 European organisations that are at the vanguard of the total quality revolution. Companies studied include world-class multi-nationals like Ciba, Rank-Xerox, SGS-Thomson, Groupe Bull, British Telecom, Volkswagen and Societe Generale: divisions or affiliates of leading corporations like Honeywell, British Airways, and American Express; national champions like Italy's Alenia and Britain's Post Office.

ABOUT THE AUTHOR
Robert Heller was the founding editor of *Management Today*, now Britain's leading monthly business magazine. He has written many books, including most recently The Superchiefs (also available from Management Books 2000) and continues to write regularly for a number of leading periodicals.

Global Quality
The New Management Culture
John Macdonald & John Piggott

(HB, £16.95, 228pp, 234mm x 156mm, ISBN: 1-85251-039-0)

Global Quality is an established guide to the principles and practices of quality management.

ABOUT THE AUTHORS

John Macdonald is recognised as a pioneer in bringing the quality revolution to Britain. He is a frequent contributor to the national and business press, TV and radio and is a well-known speaker on quality. Having joined forces with Philip Crosby in 1983, he left Crosby Associates in 1988 to write this book and to develop his concepts with consultants Resource Evaluation Ltd.

John Piggott is a member of the Board of Management of the British Quality Association and a member of the Institution of Production Engineers Quality Management Activity Group. In 1989 he helped form the Total Quality Management group of Resource Evaluation Ltd.

'An easy-to-read introduction to TQM...accessible to the typical British manager in a way that some other summaries of this topic are not' *Financial Times*

'An excellent introduction to the theories and practice of TQM' *Virginia Bottomley*

'For those interested in implementing Global Quality this book provides an excellent background' *Total Quality Management*

But We Are Different!
Quality For the Service Sector
John Macdonald

(HB, £16.95, 224pp, 229mm x 148mm, ISBN: 1-85251-131-1)

A new guide from the authors of *Global Quality*, applying the pioneering principles of TQM to the service sector.

This book highlights the desperate need for quality improvement in a variety of service organisations. Experience and research shows that the waste of resources in the service sector amounts to more than 30% of operating costs. Additionally the customer is not getting the service he demands. However, a major barrier to progress lies in the service perception that the lessons of quality management only have practical application in manufacturing.

But We Are Different (subtitled *Quality Sells Services*) recognises the differences in the service sector and explains them in a wide range of areas. It demonstrates that the principles of TQM are common principles which apply to all organisations. The book describes these principles and then provides a practical guide to their implementation in each area.

ABOUT THE AUTHOR
John Macdonald is recognised as a pioneer in bringing the quality revolution to Britain. He is a frequent contributor to the national and business press, TV and radio and is a well-known speaker on quality. Having joined forces with Philip Crosby in 1983, he left Crosby Associates in 1988 to develop his concepts with consultants Resource Evaluation Limited. He is co-author of *Global Quality*, also available from Management Books 2000.

The Benchmarking Book
Michael J Spendolini, PhD

(HB, £24.95, 224pp, 228mm x 152mm, ISBN: 0-8144-5077-6)
(PB, £15.95, 209pp, 228mm x 152mm, ISBN: 0-8144-5077-6)

Benchmarking – the systematic evaluation of the best of the competition – is the new buzzword in quality/product planning.

The Benchmarking Book is a definitive synthesis of lessons learned from pioneering benchmarking companies.

Drawing on the experiences of such diverse companies as Boeing, Xerox, AT&T, DuPont, DEC, Motorola and IBM, *The Benchmarking Book* provides anyone interested in the process with the steps they need to establish a benchmarking programme – and a basic model to use or adapt.

The author lays out each major stage of a structured benchmarking process:

- determining which products or processes to benchmark
- forming a benchmarking team
- identifying benchmarking partners
- collecting and analysing benchmarking information
- taking action

The Benchmarking Book shows how companies that compare themselves to excellence in others can bring out excellence in themselves.

'I believe our country needs a new law. No one can utter the word "benchmarking" until they have read carefully Mike Spendolini's The Benchmarking Book' *Electronics Publishing*

Guides to W Edwards Deming's Quality Theories

W Edwards Deming was arguably the founder of Total Quality Management. His pioneering approach first came into public acclaim when he was employed by the Japanese to assist in their corporate reconstruction following the Second World War. Honoured by the Japanese for his remarkable success, Deming went on to become the recognised master of Quality.

Management Books 2000 publishes a unique collection of guides to Deming's theories and principles, as set out below.

The Deming Management Method
Mary Walton
(HB, £16.95, PB, £9.99, 256pp, 234mm x 156mm)

The definitive basic guide, reprinted several times since publication in1989. Recommended by the British Deming Association as an introduction to the Deming's theories and principles.

'Lucid, practical and thoroughly convincing' *Business*

Deming Management At Work
Mary Walton
(HB, £16.95, 256pp, 234mm x 156mm)

A companion volume to *The Deming Management Method* this book is a review of Deming's theory *in practice*, taking a detailed look at six successful companies which have followed the Deming methods. It explains both theory and application.

'A useful, easy-to-read guide for employing the master's methods.' *Los Angeles Times*

Guides to
W Edwards Deming's
Quality Theories (contd)

Dr Deming – The Man Who Taught the Japanese About Quality
Rafael Aguayo
(HB, £25.00, 304pp, 234mm x 156mm)

'Dr Deming has become synonymous with quality. But the essence of his masterly teaching, excellently expounded in this book, is that quality is synonymous with everything that makes the difference between bad management and very good'
Robert Heller

The Deming Route To Quality and Productivity
William W Scherkenbach
(HB, £14.95, 176pp, 234mm x 156mm)

In 1982, at the recommendation of Dr Deming, William Scherkenbach joined Ford Motor Company with responsibility for guiding the implementation of Deming's philosophies throughout the company. Based on his success at Ford he is now helping General Motors implement the Deming philosophy.

The Keys To Excellence - The Deming Philosophy
Nancy R Mann
(HB, £12.95, 156pp, 216mm x 138mm)

A concise guide, written by the former Vice President of the American Statistical Association.

'A rattling good read...As clear a message as you're likely to find anywhere' *Executive Development*

World Class Quality
Using Design of Experiments to Make it Happen
Keki R Bhote

(HB, £22.95, 212pp, 228mm x 152mm, ISBN: 0-8144-5053-9)

A ground-breaking look at the ideas of quality guru Dorian Shanin and his powerful techniques termed 'Design of Experiments'.

By using Design of Experiments, readers learn to progress from the usual high defect levels to zero defects and beyond. *World Class Quality* shows them how to:

- eliminate re-work
- reduce superfluous inspections
- improve customer satisfaction
- switch from problem-solving to problem-prevention
- achieve higher productivity, shorter manufacturing cycles, and faster design time

ABOUT THE AUTHOR
Keki R. Bhote is senior corporate consultant on quality and productivity improvement at Motorola. He is the author of *Strategic Supply Management*.

'Reasonable, convincing, and compelling. (Bhote) has made a believer out of me in the power of Design Experiments, and this book shows how to make it happen.' *C. Jackson Grayson, Jr., Chairman, American Productivity & Quality Centre.*

Vital Signs
Using Quality, Time, and Cost Performance Measurements to Chart Your Company's Future
Steven M Hronec

(HB, £24.95, 256pp, 228mm x 152mm, ISBN: 0-8144-5073-3)

Written by Arthur Andersen's worldwide manufacturing industry director, *Vital Signs* reveals the weaknesses of traditional measurements, such as: complex, abstract ratios that have little direct bearing on the work done; measures that just look at results (or effects) instead of processes (or causes); or measures that don't tie in to corporate strategies.

This startling new look at how to find the *facts* about a company's performance, explains every step needed to set up and run highly effective measurement systems.

Vital Signs demonstrates how to make powerful use of often-misused tools and techniques, such as benchmarking, competitor/market analysis, surveys, and focus groups. Examples from Federal Express, Motorola, Milliken, and others illuminate the author's points.

With Action Steps at the end of each chapter, *Vital Signs* shows readers how to install truly efficient performance measures that:

- focus on the customer
- improve processes
- understand and control costs
- encourage and facilitate change

The Quality Roadmap
How to Get Your Company on the Quality Track - and Keep it There
Ray Svenson, Karen Wallace & Guy Wallace

(HB, £22.95, 196pp, 227mm x 152mm, ISBN: 0-8144-5117-9)

Presents readers with a sophisticated, but highly pragmatic model that they can apply to any kind of quality improvement effort. This model has been applied with great success by the Council for Continuous Improvement, a 60-member consortium of high technology companies. It shows readers how to:

- measure improvements in more than just financial terms
- choose the most useful quality 'tools'
- focus on major targets for improvement
- integrate quality efforts with company-wide strategic goals

The authors are all senior executives of US TQM consultancy Svenson and Wallace, whose clients include Dow Chemical, Mobil, Motorola and Kentucky Fried Chicken.

The ISO 9000 Book (2nd ed)
A Global Competitor's Guide to Compliance & Certification
John Rabbit & Peter Bergh

(HB, £24.95, 160pp, 227mm x 152mm, ISBN: 0-8144-5175-6)

Newly updated to reflect 1994 changes to the standards, the authors explain:

- What ISO 9000 is (with details on the 20 different areas in which companies will be judged)
- How to meet the standards for certification
- How to handle the final audit

'If you expect to compete in the global economy, read this book.'
Tom Petillo, President, Qualtec Quality Services

The Essentials of Total Quality Management

Richard L. Williams

(PB, £9.99, 80pp, 225mm x 175mm, 0-8144-7833-6)

A concise guide, in workbook format, showing:

- How the Total Quality movement got started, including Deming's 14 points, Juran's philosophy, and the three elements of TQM.
- How to use accepted quality tools and techniques to implement TQM.
- What all employees can do – from the mailroom to the boardroom – to improve quality in their organisation.

How to Achieve Zero-Defect Marketing

Allan J Magrath

(HB, £19.95, 192pp, 227mm x 153mm, ISBN: 0-8144-5123-3)

'Provides dozens of practical tools and tips, including action checklists, charts and models, and examples from more than 200 companies that have successfully applied quality concepts to marketing challenges' *Quality Progress*

Extraordinary Guarantees

A New Way to Build Quality Throughout Your Company and Ensure Satisfaction

Christopher W L Hart

(HB, £19.95, 176pp, 227mm x 153mm, ISBN: 0-8144-5064-4)

'Shows how guarantees can help energise an organisation and rally all employees around a common goal of customer satisfaction.' *Charles Moritz, Chairman and CEO, Dun & Bradstreet*